The Ethics of Nuclear Energy

Despite the nuclear accident at the Fukushima Daiichi plant in Japan, a growing number of countries are interested in expanding or introducing nuclear energy. However, nuclear energy production and nuclear waste disposal give rise to pressing ethical questions that society needs to face. This book takes up this challenge with essays by an international team of scholars focusing on the key issues of risk, justice, and democracy. The essays consider a range of ethical issues, including radiological protection, the influence of gender in the acceptability of nuclear risk, and environmental, international, and intergenerational justice in the context of nuclear energy. They also address the question of when, and under which conditions, nuclear energy should play a role in the world's future supply of electricity, looking at both developing and industrialized countries. The book will interest readers in ethics and political philosophy, social and political sciences, nuclear engineering, and policy studies.

BEHNAM TAEBI is Assistant Professor of Ethics of Technology in the Philosophy Department of Delft University of Technology and Research Fellow at Harvard Kennedy School's Belfer Center for Science and International Affairs. He is the author of *The Morally Desirable Option for Nuclear Power Production* (2011) and the editor of several volumes, including *The Socio-Technical Challenges of Nuclear Power Production and Waste Management* (2015).

SABINE ROESER is Professor of Ethics in the Philosophy Department of Delft University of Technology, the Netherlands. She is the author of *Moral Emotions and Intuitions* (2011) and the editor of numerous volumes, including *The Ethics of Technological Risk* (2009), *Handbook of Risk Theory* (2012) and *Emotion and Value* (2014).

The Ethics of Nuclear Energy

Risk, Justice, and Democracy in the post-Fukushima Era

Edited by

Behnam Taebi and Sabine Roeser

CAMBRIDGE
UNIVERSITY PRESS

University Printing House, Cambridge CB2 8BS, United Kingdom

One Liberty Plaza, 20th Floor, New York, NY 10006, USA

477 Williamstown Road, Port Melbourne, VIC 3207, Australia

314-321, 3rd Floor, Plot 3, Splendor Forum, Jasola District Centre, New Delhi-110025, India

79 Anson Road, #06-04/06, Singapore 079906

Cambridge University Press is part of the University of Cambridge.

It furthers the University's mission by disseminating knowledge in the pursuit of education, learning and research at the highest international levels of excellence.

www.cambridge.org
Information on this title: www.cambridge.org/9781107674974

© Cambridge University Press 2015

This publication is in copyright. Subject to statutory exception and to the provisions of relevant collective licensing agreements, no reproduction of any part may take place without the written permission of Cambridge University Press.

First published 2015
First paperback edition 2018

A catalogue record for this publication is available from the British Library

Library of Congress Cataloging in Publication data
The ethics of nuclear energy : risk, justice and democracy
in the post-Fukushima era / edited by Behnam Taebi and Sabine Roeser.
  pages cm
Includes bibliographical references and index.
ISBN 978-1-107-05484-4
1. Nuclear accidents – Risk assessment. 2. Nuclear industry – Moral and ethical aspects. 3. Nuclear energy – Moral and ethical aspects. 4. Nuclear engineering – Moral and ethical aspects. 5. Nuclear energy – Government policy. I. Taebi, Behnam. II. Roeser, Sabine.
TK9152.E84 2015
174′.93337924–dc23
                                                 2015008253

ISBN 978-1-107-05484-4 Hardback
ISBN 978-1-107-67497-4 Paperback

Cambridge University Press has no responsibility for the persistence or accuracy of URLs for external or third-party internet websites referred to in this publication, and does not guarantee that any content on such websites is, or will remain, accurate or appropriate.

Contents

List of figures and tables	*page* vii
List of contributors	ix
Acknowledgments	xi
Abbreviations	xii

1 The ethics of nuclear energy: an introduction 1
BEHNAM TAEBI AND SABINE ROESER

Part I   Risk 15

2 Nuclear energy and the ethics of radiation protection 17
SVEN OVE HANSSON

3 The unknowable ceilings of safety: three ways that nuclear accidents escape the calculus of risk assessments 35
JOHN DOWNER

4 Rights to know and the Fukushima, Chernobyl, and Three Mile Island accidents 53
KRISTIN SHRADER-FRECHETTE

5 Gender, ethical voices, and UK nuclear energy policy in the post-Fukushima era 67
KAREN HENWOOD AND NICK PIDGEON

Part II   Justice 85

6 The need for a public "explosion" in the ethics of radiological protection, especially for nuclear power 87
STEPHEN M. GARDINER

7 Distributive versus procedural justice in nuclear waste
   repository siting   119
   PIUS KRÜTLI, KJELL TÖRNBLOM, IVO WALLIMANN-HELMER,
   AND MICHAEL STAUFFACHER

8 Nuclear energy, justice, and power: the case of the Pilgrim
   Nuclear Power Station license renewal   141
   BINDU PANIKKAR AND RONALD SANDLER

9 Non-anthropocentric nuclear energy ethics   157
   JOHN NOLT

Part III Democracy   177

10 Morally experimenting with nuclear energy   179
   IBO VAN DE POEL

11 Global nuclear energy and international security   200
   THOMAS E. DOYLE, II

12 Nuclear energy, the capability approach, and the developing
   world   216
   PAOLO GARDONI AND COLLEEN MURPHY

13 The role of nuclear energy in the future energy landscape:
   energy scenarios, nuclear energy, and sustainability   231
   RAFAELA HILLERBRAND

Bibliography   250
Index   284

Figures and tables

Figures

5.1 British public views on replacement of nuclear power station. 70
7.1 Survey data from the Swiss Canton of Nidwalden in 2006 on respondents' perception of procedural fairness issues in repository siting for nuclear waste. 126
7.2 Survey data from the Swiss Canton of Nidwalden in 2006 on respondents' perception of distributive fairness issues in repository siting for nuclear waste. 127
7.3 Survey data from the Swiss Canton of Nidwalden in 2006. Respondents of Wolfenschiessen's directly adjacent neighboring municipality Dallenwil feel less fairly treated and less well involved in the process. 128
7.4 Repository siting areas with favorable geological conditions under consideration (current state, 2014). 130
7.5 Survey study of 2011 on the perception of nuclear waste and hazardous waste issues. Importance of procedural fairness aspects (political process, planning process, etc.) is shown. 133

Tables

2.1 Factors that may have a legitimate impact on the choice between the two major methods to ensure protection of groups that are sensitive to some detrimental environmental impact, such as the carcinogenic effects of ionizing radiation. 25
7.1 General perception of procedural vs distributive fairness (in the frame of nuclear waste). 128
7.2 Example of a vignette representing an unfair procedure (procedural justice, −PF), an mid-fair distribution (distributive injustice, +/−DF), and a negative outcome valence (−OV). 131

7.3 Major results of vignettes' studies of 2009 representing aggregated part-worth utilities of attributes and attribute-levels of study 1 (N = 53) and study 2 (N = 56) and attribute importance. 132
7.4 Survey study of 2011 on the perception of nuclear waste and hazardous waste issues. 134
7.5 Survey study of 2011 concerning perceptions of nuclear waste and hazardous waste issues. 135
7.6 Survey study of 2011 on the perception of nuclear waste and hazardous waste issues. 136
10.1 Possible conditions for responsible experimentation. 196

Contributors

JOHN DOWNER is Lecturer in Risk and Resilience in the School of Sociology, Politics and International Studies, University of Bristol.

THOMAS E. DOYLE, II is Assistant Professor of Political Science in the Department of Political Science, Texas State University.

STEPHEN GARDINER is Professor of Philosophy and Ben Rabinowitz Endowed Professor of Human Dimensions of the Environment in the Department of Philosophy, University of Washington.

PAOLO GARDONI is Associate Professor in the Department of Civil and Environmental Engineering, the University of Illinois at Urbana-Champaign.

SVEN OVE HANSSON is Professor of Philosophy in the Division of Philosophy, Royal Institute of Technology (KTH), Stockholm.

KAREN HENWOOD is Professor of Social Sciences in the Cardiff University School of Social Sciences, Cardiff University.

RAFAELA HILLERBRAND is Professor of Philosophy of Engineering and Philosophy of Science at the Karlsruhe Institute of Technology and visiting researcher at Delft University of Technology.

PIUS KRÜTLI is Senior Scientist in Environmental Sciences in the Institute for Environmental Decisions, ETH Zurich.

COLLEEN MURPHY is Associate Professor in the College of Law, the Department of Philosophy, the University of Illinois at Urbana-Champaign.

JOHN NOLT is Professor of Philosophy in the Philosophy Department, University of Tennessee, Knoxville.

BINDU PANIKKAR is Postdoctoral Research Associate in the Arctic Institute of North America, University of Calgary.

NICK PIDGEON is Professor of Environmental Psychology, and Director of the Understanding Risk Research Group, in the School of Psychology, Cardiff University.

IBO VAN DE POEL is Professor in Ethics and Technology in the Department of Philosophy, Delft University of Technology.

SABINE ROESER is Professor of Ethics in the Department of Philosophy, Delft University of Technology.

RONALD SANDLER is Professor of Philosophy in the Department of Philosophy and Religion, Northeastern University, Boston.

KRISTIN SHRADER-FRECHETTE is O'Neill Family Professor of Philosophy in the Department of Philosophy and the Department of Biological Sciences, University of Notre Dame.

MICHAEL STAUFFACHER is Senior Scientist in Sociology in the Institute for Environmental Decisions, ETH Zurich.

BEHNAM TAEBI is Assistant Professor of Ethics of Technology in the Department of Philosophy, Delft University of Technology and Research Fellow at the Belfer Center for Science and International Affairs, John F. Kennedy School of Government, Harvard University.

KJELL TÖRNBLOM is Professor Emeritus in Social Psychology, affiliated with the Transdisciplinarity Lab of the Department of Environmental Systems Science, ETH Zurich.

IVO WALLIMANN-HELMER is the Director of the Program for Advanced Studies in Applied Ethics and a postdoctoral researcher in the University Research Priority Program for Ethics at the Centre for Ethics, University of Zurich.

Acknowledgments

This volume originated as a part of a bigger project to invite scholars from different fields to reflect on the sociotechnical and ethical aspects of nuclear energy in the post-Fukushima era. This idea was warmly welcomed by a great number of scholars from different fields. Social-scientific contributions will be published in a special issue of the *Journal of Risk Research* (Taebi and van de Poel 2015). Philosophical contributions were selected for this volume. Earlier drafts of some of the chapters were presented at the "Annual conference of International Studies Association" (ISA2014) in Toronto, "IEEE Ethics.2014" in Chicago, and at the "Nuclear Security, Policy and Ethics" symposium in March 2014 at Delft University; this symposium was part of The Nuclear Knowledge Summit, an official side event of the Nuclear Security Summit 2014 that took place in the Netherlands. We would like to thank the audiences of these conferences for their helpful feedback. Furthermore, we wish to thank Hilary Gaskin from Cambridge University Press for her constructive comments and guidance and two anonymous reviewers for their feedback. We further wish to thank Matthew Bunn, Christopher Clement, Rosemary Crawley, Thomas Doyle, Johan Herrenberg, Maximilian Mayer, Jeff Powell, and Andisha Sabri for their feedback and assistance.

Our work on this project was conducted at the Department of Philosophy, Faculty of Technology, Policy and Management at Delft University of Technology, and the Belfer Center for Science and International Affairs, John F. Kennedy School of Government at Harvard University. In addition to thanking these two groups, we wish to thank the Netherlands Organisation for Scientific Research (NWO). Sabine Roeser's work was funded by an NWO VIDI grant on "Moral Emotions and Risk Politics" (grant number 276-20-012). Behnam Taebi's work was funded by an NWO VENI grant on "Multinational nuclear waste repositories: ethics and acceptability" (grant number 275-20-040).

Abbreviations

ABWR	Advanced boiling water reactor
ALARA	As low as reasonably achievable
ALARP	As low as reasonably practicable
ALEPP	At Least Equal Protection Principle
AP	Accountability Principle
BFE	Bundesamt für Energie (Switzerland)
BNP	Background of Nature Principle
BWR	Boiling water reactor
CDF	Core damage frequency
CEMP	Comparative Exposure Minimization Principle
CIP	Current Impacts Principle
CNP	Concerned Neighbors of Pilgrim
CoRWM	Committee on Radioactive Waste Management
COWAM-2	Community Waste Management-2 (EU)
CRA	Capability-based Risk Analysis
CRP	Comparable Risk Principle
DECC	Department of Energy and Climate Change (UK)
DF	Distributive fairness
DLP	Dose Limit Principle
DOE	Department of Energy (USA)
DTI	Department of Trade and Industry (UK)
EHP	Excessive Harm Principle
EIS	Environmental impact statement
EISD	Energy Indicators for Sustainable Development
EPA	Environmental Protection Agency (USA)
EWA	Institute for Energy Economics (Germany)
GRP	Generator's Responsibility Principle
HDI	Human Development Index
HLW	High-level waste
HSE	Health and Safety Executive (UK)
IAEA	International Atomic Energy Agency
IARC	International Agency for Research on Cancer

List of abbreviations

ICRP	International Commission on Radiological Protection
IP	Inclusiveness Principle
IPCC	Intergovernmental Panel on Climate Change
ISS	International Security Studies
JP	Justification Principle
JRWA	Jones River Watershed Association
KASAM	Swedish National Council for Nuclear Waste
LOCA	Loss of coolant accident
LWR	Light water reactor
MADPH	Massachusetts Department of Public Health
MBP	Maximizing Benefit Principle
MEMA	Massachusetts Emergency Management Agency
MPLP	Minimal Practical Level Principle
NAIIC	Nuclear Accident Independent Investigation Commission (Japan)
NAT	Normal Accident Theory
NBP	Net Benefit Principle
NEA	Nuclear Energy Agency (OECD)
NHP	No Harm Principle
NP	Necessity Principle
NPDES	National Pollutant Discharge Elimination System
NPT	Non-Proliferation Treaty
NRA	Nuclear Regulation Authority (Japan)
NRC	Nuclear Regulatory Commission (USA)
NSAP	No Significant Action Principle
NWMO	Nuclear Waste Management Organization (Canada)
OBP	Optimal Balancing Principle
OHP	Offsetting Harm Principle
OP	Optimization Principle
OV	Outcome valence
P&T	Partitioning and transmutation
PF	Procedural fairness
PNBP	Presumptive Net Benefit Principle
PP	Publicity Principle
PPFGP	Protection of Present and Future Generations Principle
PRA	Probabilistic risk assessment
PWR	Pressurized water reactor
QALY	Quality Adjusted Life Years
RCA	Reliability-based capability approach
RY	Reactor year
SALT	Strategic Arms Limitation Talks
SEMP	Subordinate Exposure Minimization Principle
SF	Spent fuel

SFOE	Swiss Federal Office of Energy
SMHS	Southeastern Massachusetts Health Study
SRP	Special Representation Principle
TEPCO	Tokyo Electric Power Company
TMI	Three Mile Island
UBP	Undue Burdens Principle
UCS	Union of Concerned Scientists
VP	Vulnerability Principle
WCED	World Commission on Environment and Development
WHO	World Health Organization
WNA	World Nuclear Association
WTA	Willingness-to-accept
WTP	Willingness to pay
WWF	Worldwide Fund for Nature

1 The ethics of nuclear energy: an introduction

Behnam Taebi and Sabine Roeser

1.1 Introduction

On March 11, 2011, a large earthquake struck off the coast of the Fukushima prefecture in Japan. Less than an hour later, a massive tsunami wave rumbled off Japan's northwestern coast and damaged, among other things, the nuclear energy reactors in Fukushima Daiichi. While the damage to the reactors by the earthquake was relatively small and could, in principle, be managed, the ensuing tsunami exacerbated the damage substantially by deactivating all emergency cooling systems. The lack of cooling led to several meltdowns, both in the reactor cores and in the drained spent fuel pools, which again led to several explosions and release of radiotoxic material into the surrounding environment. Three and half years later, it is still unclear how long the decommissioning of the reactors and the complete cleanup of the region will take, but it will in any case take several decades (ANS 2012). The catastrophic events in Fukushima Daiichi have brought back an old stalemate concerning the desirability of nuclear energy to the forefront of controversy. While Japan is trying to avert further disaster, many nations are reconsidering the future of nuclear energy. Germany was among the countries that quickly responded to this event; the Merkel administration decided to shut down half of the older energy reactors immediately and not to extend the lifetime of the other half beyond 2022. In addition, a number of countries such as Switzerland and Italy voted against expansion of nuclear energy in referenda. Not surprisingly, the biggest influence was visible in Japan, where the entire nuclear fleet (fifty-four reactors) was eventually shut down. This made many believe that nuclear energy is dying a slow death.

The appearances are, however, deceptive. In addition to the six damaged reactors in Fukushima Daiichi, worldwide only eight other reactors have been *permanently* shut down as a result of the Fukushima Daiichi accident, and those are in Germany. The remaining forty-eight undamaged Japanese reactors are shut down *temporarily*; their future is still uncertain. It is commonly expected that Japan will reopen at least some of those reactors (e.g. Orcutt 2014; Tabuchi 2014). Japan's nuclear safety watchdog, the Nuclear Regulation Authority

(NRA), has already approved the first two reactors to go back online (Hamada and Tsukimori 2014). It seems that the NRA only pushes to shut down reactors older than 40 years; this could mean that only another handful of Japanese reactors will be permanently shut down.[1]

More importantly, projections of nuclear energy before and after the Fukushima Daiichi accidents have not changed at all. At the time that this book goes to press, 72 reactors are under construction worldwide, 174 are on order or planned, and another 299 reactors are proposed.[2] If these projections are realized, the currently operable 387 reactors in the world[3] will be joined by another 545. This represents a slight increase compared to the 540 future nuclear reactors forecast just before the Fukushima accident.[4] It is at least equally important that the number of countries with nuclear energy ambitions is vastly growing. Thirty countries currently produce nuclear energy, with the last entrant being Iran. Forty-five countries seem now to be interested in embarking on nuclear energy programs in the next decades.[5]

Hence, contrary to what one might have expected, Fukushima did not herald the end of the nuclear era. Nuclear energy is likely to play a role in the world's future supply of electricity. These observations and developments give rise to a pressing ethical question that society needs to face, namely, whether or under which circumstances nuclear energy is a desirable form of energy. It is now time to revive the field of nuclear ethics which has been dormant for some time. The challenge that this book takes up is to contribute to the academic and ultimately public debate on nuclear energy. The volume

---

[1] According to the International Atomic Energy Agency databases, Japan has only seven reactors that were built in 1975 or before. See www.iaea.org/PRIS/CountryStatistics/Country Details.aspx?current=JP (accessed September 22, 2014). It is also important to mention that some other reactors that are on "active" earthquake faults and reactors that for other reasons are unable to meet the safety standards will probably shut down too (Kyodo 2014).

[2] These figures are according to the public information of the World Nuclear Association website, which keeps track of the operational nuclear energy reactors all around the world. See www.world-nuclear.org/info/Facts-and-Figures/World-Nuclear-Power-Reactors-and-Uranium-Requirements/ (updated August 1, 2014; accessed September 17, 2014)

[3] The figure that WNA shows on its website is 435; see the last footnote. While WNA calls this "currently operable reactors" a closer look shows that the forty-eight Japanese reactors that are temporarily shut down are listed there too. WNA lists those reactors because they are still connected to the electricity grid, but they are not generating electricity. A more accurate figure of *currently operable reactors* would therefore be 435 minus the 48 Japanese reactors, which results in the 387 reactors, as mentioned in the text.

[4] On February 1, 2011, and just before the Fukushima accidents, there were 443 reactors operational, 62 under construction, 156 on order or planned, while another 322 proposed. See the WNA website: www.world-nuclear.org/info/Facts-and-Figures/World-Nuclear-Power-Reactors-Archive/Reactor-Archive-February-2011/ (updated February 1, 2011; accessed September 17, 2014)

[5] See the WNA website: www.world-nuclear.org/info/Country-Profiles/Others/Emerging-Nuclear-Energy-Countries/ (updated September 2014; accessed September 17, 2014). It is worth mentioning that the WNA are lobbyists for the world nuclear industry, which means that their opinion might be biased. Yet, there seems to be a serious interest in some new countries to start a nuclear energy programs.

addresses a wide range of ethical issues related to nuclear energy production and nuclear waste disposal. In this introduction, we first sketch a history of the field of nuclear ethics. We then provide an overview of the chapters and how they are interconnected. We conclude with some general observations and recommendations.

1.2 Nuclear ethics: a field in evolution

At the outset of this volume, Sven Ove Hansson poses the question of whether there is something to be called "the ethics of nuclear energy." It is fair to say that this field does not yet exist; as yet there is no established and well-developed field of research focusing on the full spectrum of ethical issues that nuclear energy engenders. Furthermore, the question arises as to whether we need to develop yet another field of applied ethics – or area-specific ethics as Hansson prefers to call it – that focuses solely on ethical questions of nuclear energy. Yet, we believe that this special attention to nuclear energy is more than justified. There are at least three reasons for this.

Firstly, the magnitude and the nature of harm that can occur after a possible accident with a nuclear facility are different from other technology. The catastrophic events of major accidents in the past – most notably the Chernobyl accident – bear witness to this fact. Secondly, the longevity of nuclear waste poses questions with regard to future generations. One might argue that climate change poses similar questions. This is, however, only partly true. Nuclear waste with radiotoxicity of 200,000–1,000,000 years brings new and sometimes unprecedented intricacies to the table; our species (*Homo sapiens*) is *only* 200,000 years old. Thirdly, within nuclear technology there are specific technologies – also referred to as "dual use" technologies – that are needed for the civil production of nuclear energy, while they can also be used for the purpose of nuclear weapons production. This, again, is a unique aspect of nuclear energy as compared to other energy producing technologies that do not often have such evident and potentially high impact "dual use" aspects. Furthermore, and on a related note, nuclear weapons have a unique status as compared to other kinds of weapons technology, given their major potential for destruction. Considering the nature and the magnitude of nuclear risks, a broad focus on the ethics of nuclear energy is urgently needed.

In previous decades, nuclear security and proliferation[6] risks have received serious attention in the social-scientific and philosophy literatures. To the

---

[6] In nuclear technology studies, one distinguishes between nuclear safety and nuclear security. Safety usually refers to unintentional harm or harm as a result of a nuclear accident, while security refers to intentional harm. The latter refers to both risks of theft of nuclear material for the purpose of nuclear sabotage or manufacturing a so-called nuclear dirty bomb and any other way to expose a large number of people to harmful radiation. Proliferation means both the

extent that there has been any attention to *the ethics of nuclear energy* in the past, the main focus has been on discussions of nuclear security and arms control. The literature about "nuclear ethics" emerged in the 1950s and 1960s in light of the nuclear arms race. A collection edited by Allers and O'Brien (1961), for instance, explicitly questioned the moral legitimacy of nuclear warfare. Their collection took the position of "Christian ethics," which was "an attempt to bring together some eminent thinkers from the Christian faith to discuss ... the moral problems of nuclear war" (Allers and O'Brien 1961: iii). A number of other collections focused on the development, possession, and use of nuclear arms, usually from the perspective of religious studies (e.g. Ford and Winters 1977; Goodwin 1982; English 1985; Walters 1989; Whitmore 1989). In the literature on ethics and international security, there has been a particular focus on nuclear deterrence, which is perhaps one of the most dominating features in international relations in the post-World War II era (e.g. Goodwin 1982; Nye 1986; Ardagh 1990; Barkenbus 1992). The main idea is rather counterintuitive, namely that it is by virtue of the destructive power of nuclear weapons that nuclear weapon possessing countries never attacked each other. The climax of nuclear deterrence was the confrontation between the Soviet Union and the United States in October 1962 concerning the Soviet Union's ballistic nuclear missiles in Cuba. It was – as the argument goes – the mutually assured destruction by the enormous power of both parties that prevented them from attacking one another.[7]

Despite powerful international agreements such as the Non-Proliferation Treaty (NPT), at least four new proliferators have been added to the list of nuclear weapons possessing countries, namely, India, Pakistan, Israel, and North Korea.[8] Moreover, a number of countries have openly or clandestinely pursued nuclear ambitions, either through a program dedicated to the development of nuclear weapons or as a civil program that opens the door toward a military program. As previously stated, there are a number of *dual use* nuclear technologies that are particularly troublesome. The controversies surrounding the Iranian nuclear programs vividly illustrate the complexities of this dual use of nuclear technology. While Iran keeps emphasizing its

---

dispersal of the knowledge that could lead to manufacturing of nuclear weapons and the dispersal of those weapons themselves.

[7] This is of course a very short summary of an extensive line of literature, which includes, among other things, debates on the moral legitimacy of deterrence, just war theory, as well as just defense doctrine in the nuclear age. Furthermore, there are discussions whether small yield weapons that kill fewer people might lower the threshold to nuclear war, as well as discussions on the moral imperatives of moving toward complete nuclear disarmament (e.g. Walzer 1977; Nye 1986; Hashmi and Lee 2004).

[8] It should be noted that the first three never signed the NPT, while Israel had nuclear weapons before the NPT was even completed. When the NPT was signed and ratified it was projected that there would be a far larger number of nuclear weapon states by now; however, there has actually been no net increase in the number of nuclear weapon states for a quarter century (North Korea joined the group and South Africa left it).

inalienable right to nuclear technology for civil purposes (NPT, Article 4), many countries dispute whether Iran should also develop dual use nuclear technologies. The case of Iran could gain relevance in the next couple of years because it establishes a precedent for the new countries that are planning to join the nuclear energy producing countries in the coming decades.

Of further importance is the Obama Administration's decision to revitalize its nuclear weapon program,[9] despite Obama's efforts during his first term of presidency to make nuclear disarmament a main goal of American defense policy and to substantially reduce nuclear weapons worldwide (Broad and Sanger 2014). These developments make nuclear proliferation and arms control especially relevant for academic and public inquiries. This is indeed the focus of various studies in international relations and more specifically international security. Indeed, there is an area of overlap between international relations and philosophy. This volume includes a chapter by Thomas Doyle entitled "Global nuclear energy and international security" (Chapter 11), which addresses a number of pressing moral questions, such as the legitimacy of the pressure exerted by the United States and Europe (as nuclear weapon possessing countries) on countries like Iran to abandon their dual use technologies such as uranium enrichment facilities.

However, the bulk of this volume focuses on questions of nuclear safety and risk as well as on the more fundamental issues of justice and democracy. As previously stated, most literature reflecting on the ethical and societal aspects of nuclear technology in the past decades was concerned with the military use of this technology. Some research has, however, been done to focus more on ethical issues associated with nuclear energy, mostly from the perspective of whether it is morally justified to produce nuclear energy. This is a question to which Kneese (1973) unequivocally responds in the title of his essay "The Faustian Bargain." Routley and Routley (1981) argue that considering the longevity and the toxicity of nuclear waste, nuclear energy production is morally unacceptable. A number of other authors reflected on the desirability of nuclear energy and unanimously reached the conclusion that it is ethically unacceptable to produce nuclear energy because of the inability of victims to control their fate (Hollyday 1991) and the unacceptable radiation risk that arises from nuclear energy for both the public and radiation workers (Bertell 1991). Kristin Shrader-Frechette did pioneering work in the 1990s. In addition to editing the first collection that addressed the ethical issues of nuclear energy (Shrader-Frechette 1991a), she wrote several influential

---

[9] While the recent decision of the Obama administration to revitalize nuclear weapons was portrayed as an important new development, it is, in essence, a continuation of earlier policy by both the Bush and the Obama Administration. As President Obama put it in his Prague Speech on Nuclear Weapons: "Make no mistake: As long as these weapons exist, the United States will maintain a safe, secure and effective arsenal to deter any adversary" (Obama 2009).

articles and books that addressed various ethical aspects of nuclear energy and nuclear risk (Shrader-Frechette 1980, 1991b, 1993, 1994, 2000). Among other things, she questioned the ethical acceptability of nuclear energy because of its inequitable distribution of risk (Shrader-Frechette 1991a) and for environmental justice issues associated with different steps of nuclear energy production (e.g. Wigley and Shrader-Frechette 1996). In a recent book, she argues that rather than nuclear energy, renewable energy resources are the answer to addressing the challenges posed by climate change (Shrader-Frechette 2011a). In Chapter 4 of this volume, she addresses the issues of autonomy and rights to know in the context of nuclear risk.

A number of recent works address ethical issues associated with nuclear energy production and nuclear waste disposal (Gosseries 2008; Löfquist 2008; Doyle 2010; Taebi 2011, 2012b; Roeser 2011; Taebi et al. 2012; Oughton and Hansson 2013).[10] This volume aims to make a major contribution to further establish the field of the ethics of nuclear energy by bringing together contributions on three key ethical aspects related to nuclear energy, namely, risk, justice, and democracy. The latter questions are less prominently discussed in the literature, but given their complexity and potentially far-reaching societal impact, require thorough ethical investigation. This book aims to set the scene for a comprehensive expansion of the field of nuclear ethics in light of nuclear energy's continued presence and its expected expansion.[11]

1.3   Overview of the book

The book consists of three main parts. Part I discusses normative aspects of nuclear risk. It consists of chapters that examine ethical aspects of the reliability of the available data on accidents as well as on the soundness of nuclear risk assessment methods. Furthermore, ethical issues of radiological protection principles and the influence of cultural values and gender in the acceptability of nuclear risk will be addressed. In Part II, various notions of justice will be discussed in the context of nuclear energy. This includes environmental, international, and intergenerational aspects of justice. Furthermore, the

---

[10] In addition, substantial work has been done by various national and international organizations in establishing ethical principles for governing the risk of nuclear energy and nuclear waste disposal. In particular, the work done by the following organizations should be acknowledged: i.e. the International Commission on Radiological Protection (ICRP 1977; 2007), the International Atomic Energy Agency (IAEA 1997; IAEA et al. 2006), the Nuclear Energy Agency (NEA-OECD 1995), the National Council for Nuclear Waste in Sweden (KASAM 1988, 2005, 2007) and the Canadian Nuclear Waste Management Organization (NWMO 2005); see also (Wilson 2000).

[11] This book is part of a bigger project at Delft University of Technology to reinvigorate the debate on sociotechnical and ethical aspects of nuclear energy production and nuclear waste disposal. Another part of this project is the publication of a special issue in the *Journal of Risk Research* (Taebi and van de Poel 2015).

question of how procedural justice relates to distributive justice will be addressed with a case study of nuclear waste management. Part III focuses on aspects of nuclear energy related to democracy. It discusses the justifiability of nuclear risks, both in general and in the specific context of developing countries and from a capability approach. Part III will also present a proposal to approach the introduction of nuclear technology as an ongoing social experiment whose acceptability should be continuously assessed.

Part I: Risk

Chapter 2 In "Nuclear energy and the ethics of radiation protection," *Sven Ove Hansson* focuses on one of the key areas in the ethics of nuclear energy, namely the ethics of radiological protection. Hansson argues that there is often a mismatch between *fundamental* ethics (which dominates traditional philosophy literature) and area-specific ethics. This is because of a lack of empirical links between the fundamental theories and the areas of application. Ethics of radiological protection is, however, a remarkable exception. Radiological risk can be measured and calculated rather precisely. This makes it similar to utilitarianism that works with numerical values for the measurement of moral values. Hansson uses radiation protection as a potential bridge-builder between fundamental and area-specific ethics.

This chapter covers some major issues in the ethics of radiological protection, while paying particular attention to its applications in the nuclear energy industry. Among other things, the chapter discusses the following topics: the relationship between collective and individual doses of radiation exposure, a topic that brings out the parallels between dose minimization (radiation protection) and maximization of the good; scrutinizing the legitimacy of the current practice, which applies much higher exposure limits on workplaces than in non-occupational settings; the ethical implication of the differences in radiation sensitivity between different subpopulations; the use of probability weighing in relation to the importance of low-probability disasters in nuclear risk assessment; the ALARA principle (as low as reasonably achievable) as a leading principle in radiological protection and its relation to cost–benefit analysis; the ethical implications of background (natural) radiation and risks to future generations. Hansson concludes with a list of recommendations to better understand and address the ethical issues of radiological protection.

Chapter 3 In his chapter "The unknowable ceilings of safety," *John Downer* discusses three ways in which nuclear accidents escape the formal calculus of risk assessments. He outlines the history of modern nuclear risk assessment, dating back to the US Nuclear Regulatory Commission's (NRC's) famous 1975 report: "WASH-1400." This report, for the first time, excluded meltdowns by deeming them too improbable to merit consideration – a practice that remains essential to nuclear regulation. Downer argues that there are three limitations to this approach. The first are "framing limitations," arising from the inability of reliability calculations to model all the variables that can potentially contribute to failures (including, for instance, human error). The second are "systemic limitations," arising from the emergent effects of complex, tightly coupled technical systems (due to their propensity to fateful coincidences). The third are "epistemic limitations," arising from the inherent uncertainty of the tests, theories, and models implicit in reliability calculations (which are always projections with minimal empirical data). He concludes that nuclear reliability calculations should be understood as "imperfect judgments" rather than as "objective facts," and that this has far-reaching implications for nuclear governance.

Chapter 4 Kristin Shrader-Frechette argues in her chapter "Rights to know and the Fukushima, Chernobyl, and Three Mile Island accidents" that governments and industry violate citizens' rights to be fully informed about nuclear risks. Shrader-Frechette argues that rights to know are necessary for autonomy and autonomy is necessary for human dignity. She draws on the Rossian idea that rights and duties are *prima facie* and can be overridden by other *prima facie* rights and duties. Shrader-Frechette argues that in such a case, the burden of proof is on the violator. If a *prima facie* right is not overridden, it is an *ultima facie* right. She argues that in the case of harms imposed on citizens, there is a general consensus that no explicit justification needs to be given that people have an *ultima facie* right to know about these harms (except in cases of potential mass panics). However, she argues that despite this consensus, this *ultima facie* right is continuously violated in the case of potential harms resulting from nuclear energy production. She presents and discusses data that indicate that nuclear risks and impacts from nuclear disasters at Three Mile Island, Chernobyl, and Fukushima Daiichi nuclear energy plants are more severe than is officially acknowledged. Shrader-Frechette argues that authorities intentionally misinform the public, thereby violating people's right to know and ultimately, their autonomy.

Chapter 5 Karen Henwood and *Nick Pidgeon* contribute a chapter titled "Gender, ethical voices, and UK nuclear energy policy in the post-Fukushima era." Of all socio-demographic variables, gender is the one with the most pronounced effects on risk perception, with some men in surveys tending to express less concern about risks than women. This especially holds in the case of nuclear energy and nuclear waste. In their chapter, Henwood and Pidgeon examine the ethical implications of this gendered nature of nuclear risk perception, based on a qualitative empirical study they have conducted in the UK. In focus groups where they let people discuss nuclear energy, they observed masculine marked discourses of "technocentrism," which they contrast with those stressing more caring concerns. Henwood and Pidgeon argue that presentation of knowledge claims and values as traditionally framed within the gender and risk effect literature might not always be capable of catering to epistemic diversity and the collective good. Forms of knowledge and values that are uncontested in some contexts can become controversial in others, as in the context of nuclear risk. Based on their empirical work, Henwood and Pidgeon argue that public energy discourse risks gender insensitivity, when it adopts an essentialist association between masculinity and technology on the one hand and between femininity and care on the other hand. They argue that this gender insensitivity can best be overcome by combining a technocratic approach and more "soft" approaches to risk, such as care ethics, in debates about nuclear energy.

Part II: Justice

Chapter 6 In his chapter, "The need for a public 'explosion' in the ethics of radiological protection, especially for nuclear power," *Stephen Gardiner* scrutinizes the existing principles of radiological protection. The nuclear community already acknowledges the ethical dimension of radiological protection and various standards are being proposed that are derived from explicit ethical principles. The nuclear community seems further to be satisfied about the level of maturity of these principles. Gardiner argues, however, that there are major gaps in the present system, at least when it comes to the application of these principles to nuclear energy. Following a pluralist "bottom up" approach, he introduces a number of new principles and fresh interpretations of existing ones. These new principles include three new procedural principles (Inclusiveness, Accountability, Publicity), a collective welfare principle (Presumptive Net Benefit), two minimization principles (Necessity and Comparative Minimization), and four principles of respect (Excessive Harm, Proportionality, Special Representation, Vulnerability). In particular, Gardiner's principle of publicity – which presents a duty for all people involved in nuclear energy policy to make clear to the wider public the scientific and ethical reasoning involved in justifying these policies – is of great importance for establishing public trust. With the increasing controversies in the worldwide nuclear energy debate, public trust is a vital matter. Gardiner concludes that the confidence of the nuclear community about the maturity of the currently existing radiological protection principles is premature and that there is substantial work to be done. He presents a number of alternative principles in this chapter that could be considered as a substantial first step toward a robust new ethical framework for nuclear protection.

Chapter 7 In their chapter, "Distributive versus procedural justice in nuclear waste repository siting," *Pius Krütli, Kjell Törnblom, Ivo Wallimann-Helmer, and Michael Stauffacher* focus on two key notions of justice in nuclear waste disposal, namely distributive and procedural justice, and their relative importance with respect to each other. Attitudes toward repository projects cannot be explained merely on the basis of perceived risks, trust, or technical information. Issues of justice and fairness frequently arise when burdens and benefits are to be allocated, also in case of nuclear waste disposal. A fair distribution across the various parts of a given territory for waste disposal is contingent on a number of factors such as appropriateness of the geological host formations. The process by which the specific distribution is determined and accomplished needs to be taken into account as well. Thus, justice evaluations of both the distributive outcome and the process itself, by which the outcome is accomplished, are likely to affect people's attitudes toward and acceptance of siting decisions.

They present data from a number of different studies conducted over the last eight years on site selection in Switzerland. These data suggest that a fair procedure is more essential than a fair distribution of burdens resulting from siting to a consensus about the decisions made. As a consequence, even normative assessments of the fairness of a distribution of nuclear waste must consider procedural justice as a valuable indicator of the fairness of distribution, independently of the particular shape of the distribution. In addition, contextual factors, such as the wider nuclear energy strategy of a country, may compete with procedural fairness in terms of importance. While fairness is a requirement in siting, properly addressing this issue might positively affect the acceptability of a site from a moral standpoint.

Chapter 8 In "Nuclear energy, justice, and power: The case of the Pilgrim Nuclear Power Station license renewal," *Bindu Panikkar* and *Ronald Sandler* present an ethical analysis of life extension of nuclear energy reactors. While nuclear energy is expanding worldwide and many new plants are being built, many old plants are reaching the end of their license period; on some occasions utilities choose to extend the lifetime of the reactor and, subsequently, apply for a license renewal. Panikkar and Sandler review the case of license renewal for the Pilgrim Nuclear Power Station (Pilgrim) in Plymouth, Massachusetts. Central ethical issues in decision-making on license renewals concern proper assessment of nuclear risks as well as questions regarding the distribution of risks. These need to be conducted in accordance with best practices and principles of procedural and distributive justice. Case studies are crucial because they enable us to see how and where these ethical issues arise in practice. It is important to determine the varieties of community empowerment that are necessary to accomplish responsible nuclear energy production, if nuclear energy is going to be among the energy sources in the future. The Pilgrim case is particularly worrisome because there was a lack of empowerment, even in a community that is known to be socially, politically, and economically well-resourced in comparison to many other communities exposed to risks of nuclear energy. Panikkar and Sandler conclude that the community empowerment needs to be much more substantive than it is in the Pilgrim case, because in most other cases communities will not be as resourceful and politically powerful.

Chapter 9 In his chapter "Non-anthropocentric nuclear energy ethics," *John Nolt* takes on a different perspective than most discussions of nuclear energy ethics, which are anthropocentric. Such discussions focus mainly on the implications of nuclear energy for humanity. Nolt, instead, considers the implications of nuclear energy for nonhuman life. He first presents a specific form of non-anthropocentric ethics: biocentric consequentialism. Biocentric ethics extends moral consideration to all living things, based on the assumption that any living thing can be harmed or benefited. While a deontological biocentric ethics argues for the dutiful or respectful treatment of all living things, a consequentialist biocentric ethic aims at maximizing good aggregate results. Nolt uses the latter approach as it is more easily applicable in practice, where it is not possible to treat all beings in a just, fair, or respectful way. However, as with all consequentialist approaches, this biocentric version runs into a fundamental methodological problem, the "ranking problem," related to problems with measuring and comparing well-being. For reasons of applicability, Nolt adopts an objective-list version of biocentric consequentialism that is also intergenerational. He then discusses how this account contributes to answering the question as to how large the contribution of nuclear energy should be to a morally acceptable energy mix. He argues that the harms of fossil-fuel-generated energy to both humans and nonhumans exceed in probability, severity, and spatiotemporal scale those of nuclear energy. However, the most desirable forms of energy are renewables.

Part III: Democracy

Chapter 10 In his chapter "Morally experimenting with nuclear energy," *Ibo van de Poel* focuses on the issue of uncertainty in the nuclear debate. While several decades of nuclear energy production have provided us with the knowledge basis to estimate uncertainties and risks of this technology more reliably, in several aspects nuclear energy could be called an experimental technology. More specifically, van de Poel focuses on nuclear waste disposal technologies and on new generations of nuclear reactors, with which there is only very limited operating experience, if any at all. He argues that by conceiving of nuclear energy as a kind of real-world experiment, we recognize and acknowledge the role of uncertainty and how to deal with it. Moreover, such an approach opens the possibility to deliberate on real-world experimentation, which is important for both epistemological reasons (improved learning) and for moral reasons (more responsible experimentation). Van de Poel concludes that recognizing the role of uncertainty in the debate could overcome the current stalemate between opponents and proponents of nuclear energy toward questions of conditions for responsible real-world experimentation with nuclear energy. In this way, rather than only being a debate between conflicting values, the moral debate about nuclear energy could help us to come to better normative insights.

Chapter 11 In his chapter "Global nuclear energy and international security," *Thomas Doyle* focuses on the interplay between nuclear energy production and nuclear weapons proliferation. Nuclear ethics is strongly developed around questions of nuclear security, weapons proliferation, and deterrence. The debate on nuclear ethics must, however, pay attention to the interplay of nuclear proliferation with nuclear energy development as well. While Doyle scrutinizes the key international agreement that regulates this interplay – namely the NPT – he addresses a number of central questions, such as the moral legitimacy of the pressure exerted by nuclear weapon possessing countries such as the United States on Iran and North Korea to abandon their dual use technologies (i.e. uranium enrichment or plutonium programs). Doyle develops a Rawlsian view which suggests that the state pursuit of nuclear energy is only just if it is consistent with the Principles of the Law of Peoples and the NPT non-proliferation of nuclear weapons requirement. The central political fear is, however, that if Iran or other "rogue" states were to mask nuclear weapons proliferation behind nuclear energy programs, then non-nuclear-armed liberal democratic states like Japan and Germany might be allowed to weaponize their nuclear programs on grounds of collective security. Such outcomes would most likely mark the end of the NPT. This outcome is suggested by the current US preferential treatment of the liberal nuclear democracies of India and Israel over the illiberal nuclear state of Pakistan. Doyle concludes that, from the Rawlsian viewpoint, this double standard is ethically justifiable, while from the contrary viewpoint, where liberal democracy is but one of many domestic political orders in a world of mixed anarchies, this double standard smacks of moral hypocrisy.

Chapter 12 Paolo Gardoni and Colleen Murphy contribute a chapter called "Nuclear energy, the capability approach and the developing world," in which they present a theoretical framework to evaluate the risks and benefits of nuclear energy for developing countries, and for assessing different nuclear technologies. The framework is based on a capability approach to risk as developed by Gardoni and Murphy. Following Amartya Sen, capabilities refer to opportunities that people can achieve, for example concerning education and nourishment. Gardoni's and Murphy's framework considers how nuclear energy production can pose risks for these capabilities, but how it can also contribute to their sustainable development. They first discuss general ethical aspects of nuclear energy, namely sustainability, safety, and security. They proceed to analyze these aspects from the specific context of developing countries, where people are already in an extremely vulnerable position. They then sketch a capability approach to sustainable and safe development. In the last section of the chapter, Gardoni and Murphy apply their framework to discussion of the justifiability of nuclear energy in a developing society, as compared to other sources of energy. Nuclear energy might be a more reliable energy source for developing countries than other sources of energy. However, developing countries might lack the necessary infrastructure, requiring too high entry costs to start with a nuclear energy program, given that the limited resources might be needed to be spent on more urgent investments to alleviate poverty. Also, developing countries might be especially vulnerable to natural hazards that can pose risks to nuclear energy production, such as floods. Given the potentially large-scale effects of nuclear accidents, Gardoni and Murphy argue that the international community should be involved in safety assessments.

Chapter 13 In her chapter "The role of nuclear energy in the future energy landscape: Energy scenarios, nuclear energy, and sustainability," *Rafaela Hillerbrand* argues that assessing the ethical acceptability of nuclear energy should be part of an assessment of an ethically desirable energy mix. This involves taking a long-term perspective and developing scenario analyses. Hillerbrand is critical toward current approaches to assess the sustainability of various energy sources, as they offer a lopsided ethical analysis at best. For example, measures to contribute to sustainability are often based on an aggregated approach that is at odds with individual's rights. As an alternative, she proposes to use the capability approach as developed by Amartya Sen and Martha Nussbaum. This approach has also been discussed in the previous chapter by Gardoni and Murphy in the context of developing countries, for which it was originally developed and which Gardoni and Murphy expanded to the context of nuclear energy. Hillerbrand goes a step further and introduces the capability approach in the interpretation of Sen as a possible ethical framework for addressing issues of sustainable energy supply and demand. She argues that this approach can accommodate the tension between a collective and an individual perspective. Hillerbrand goes on to argue that common approaches to sustainability assessments of energy sources are based on scenarios and models that come with high uncertainties. She concludes her chapter with arguing that this is yet an additional reason to focus more on social values, such as intergenerational equity, than is the case in conventional sustainability accounts.

1.5 Conclusion

In this introduction, we have tried to show that the topic of nuclear energy gives rise to important ethical issues that are currently insufficiently addressed in the literature. With this volume, we bring together top scholars who address a broad spectrum of ethical considerations related to nuclear energy, such as safety, proliferation, and sustainability, using frameworks based on considerations of risk, justice, and democracy. The authors contributing to this volume use approaches and concepts as diverse as biocentric consequentialism, the capability approach, gender, radiological protection, intergenerational justice, and technology as social experiment, to name just a few. Despite this diversity, what all the approaches emphasize is that the ethical assessment of nuclear energy is intricate and complex, requiring multiple perspectives and considerations. Furthermore, this volume highlights that the *ethics of nuclear energy* overlaps with a number of fields of studies such as international relations and political philosophy, social psychology, radiological protection, and gender studies. We hope that this collection of essays will be helpful for the further academic study of, and public debate about, nuclear energy. Given the moral and technological complexities as well as the predicted increase in nuclear energy production, the challenges are so pressing that philosophical and ethical reflection is urgently needed. This volume aims to provide a comprehensive overview of the most important ethical issues and how they should be addressed.

Part I

Risk

2 Nuclear energy and the ethics of radiation protection

Sven Ove Hansson

2.1 Introduction

Do we have an ethics of nuclear energy? The answer is, unfortunately: "It depends." To be somewhat more precise it depends on what we mean by having an ethics of a social sector or activity. In one sense, we have an ethics of X if there are important ethical issues concerning X. In that sense, this volume as a whole bears witness to the existence of an ethics of nuclear energy. In another sense, we have an ethics of X if there is already a reasonably well-developed and focused discourse on ethical issues concerning X. In this latter sense, we do not yet have an ethics of nuclear energy (but we may have so in the future, something this volume can possibly contribute to).

The distinction between these two senses of "an ethics of" is important since it helps clarifying the rather fragmented nature of ethical deliberations and discussions in our societies. On the one hand we have "fundamental" ethics, which dominates in philosophy departments. It is concerned with general, often rather abstract, problems such as the nature and sources of ethics, the structure of ethical statements, and whether such statements can be true or false in the same sense as factual statements. Many of these issues were discussed already by Socrates, Plato, and Aristotle. On the other hand, we have disciplines of area-specific ethics, such as medical ethics, research ethics, engineering ethics, business ethics, and environmental ethics. (I use the term "area-specific ethics" rather than the more common "applied ethics" that gives the misleading impression that work in these areas consists in applying theories from fundamental ethics, cf. Hansson [2003b].) With the exception of medical ethics, these subdisciplines are relatively new. They cover only a very small part of the human activities in which ethical issues arise. Some of the lacunae are notable. For instance, we do not have a specialized ethical discourse on traffic safety although about 1.2 million people per year are killed in road traffic accidents and another 20–50 million are injured (World Health Organization 2013). Neither do we have a specialized ethical discussion on welfare provision, insurance, building and architecture, or foreign aid, to mention just a few examples.

The reason for this is that area-specific ethics only develop when there is a devoted group of people who wish to analyze an area in an ethical perspective. In most cases when that has happened, this group consisted of members of a profession with special responsibilities in the area. With few exceptions (perhaps the most important is environmental ethics), the specialized areas of ethical discourse have been opened up as professional ethics (Hansson 2009a). In some cases, philosophers have joined in at a later stage. This has happened for instance in medical ethics. Interestingly, philosophers active in that field often call it "bioethics" rather than using the older term "medical ethics," which imparts a connection with the medical profession. (The term "bioethics" was coined by Van Rensselaer Potter II (1911–2001) in 1970. See Potter [1970] and Reich [1994, 1995].)

In other words, area-specific ethics usually originates within a profession that has the overarching responsibility for day-to-day decision-making in the area and whose decisions have clear ethical implications. There are such professions in healthcare and research, namely physicians respectively research scientists, but there is no profession with a similar role in the more fragmented area of traffic safety. This may also explain why we have no focused ethical discourse on nuclear energy. Responsibilities for the construction and management of nuclear facilities are about as dispersed among different professions as responsibilities for traffic safety.

But in one of the several professions involved in nuclear energy, namely that of radiation protection, a focused ethical discourse seems to be emerging. Several recent publications contribute to this impression, including a multi-author book with leading radiation protectors among its authors (Oughton and Hansson 2013). Even more importantly, the International Commission on Radiological Protection (ICRP), which has had a dominating role in its area since its inception in 1928, appointed a task group for the ethics of radiation protection in 2013.

The connections between area-specific ethics and the "fundamental" (or general) ethics that dominates in the teaching and research of traditional philosophy departments have usually been weak, sometimes next to non-existent. In philosophy, ethics is supposed to be based on one or other moral theory that gives us all the answers about what is right and what is wrong. Much of the philosophical debate has concerned the relative merits and demerits of various proposed such theories, including many variants of utilitarianism, deontology, rights-based ethics, contractualism, and virtue ethics. Usually it has been difficult or impossible to extract definite answers to the problems of area-specific ethics from these theories. To a large extent, area-specific ethics has therefore focused on less abstract principles that have more bearing on their specific subject matter.

One of the major reasons why the connections between "fundamental" and area-specific ethics are so weak is that some of the abstract terms used in the former area suffer from a lack of empirical correlates. In particular, utilitarianism, which has a strong role in much of modern ethics, operates with fictional numerical units for the measurement of moral value (often called "utiles" or "utils"), and extended discussions are conducted for instance on the distribution of these values among the members of a society. However, in most practical applications, these values are not matched by measurable variables in the real world. In this respect, the ethics of radiation protection is a remarkable exception. Radiation protection is concerned with reducing radiological risk, which can be measured and calculated in precise ways. This makes radiation protection an interesting testing ground for moral theories and a potential bridge-builder between fundamental and area-specific ethics. In radiation protection we can formulate our problems in terms that are commensurate with those of basic moral theories. Some of the issues and principles of utilitarian moral philosophy have been formulated independently by radiation protectors referring to radiation doses rather than utiles (Hansson 2007, 2013b, 2013c).

This close analogy between utilities and radiation doses depends on our current understanding of the dose–effect relationship of radiation exposure. About five years after Röntgen's discovery of X-rays in 1895, scientists discovered that radiation has acute effects such as skin burns. Efforts were made to keep doses well below the levels that produce these effects (Kathren and Ziemer 1980). In the 1950s, it was discovered that radiation also gives rise to long-term genetic and cancer effects. Such effects appeared to be stochastic. The probability of damage increases with the dose, and there does not seem to be any threshold dose below which these effects disappear completely (Lindell 1996). The current consensus is that regulation should be based on a linear no-threshold assumption. This means that there is no absolutely safe dose level above zero and that the probability of harmful effects is taken to be proportionate to the dose (except at very high doses). In what follows this assumption will be made as a basis for comparisons between radiation protection and moral philosophy.

This chapter summarizes some major issues in the ethics of radiation protection, paying particular attention to its applications in the nuclear industry. Section 2.2 is devoted to the relationship between collective and individual doses, a topic that brings out the parallels between dose minimization (radiation protection) and maximization of the good (moral philosophy) very clearly. Section 2.3 discusses the legitimacy of the current practice that applies much higher exposure limits on workplaces than in non-occupational settings. Section 2.4 introduces the differences in radiation sensitivity between different subpopulations and discusses the ethical implications of these differences. In Section 2.5 the use of probability weighing is discussed, in particular in relation to the importance of low-probability disasters in nuclear risk assessment. Section 2.6 is devoted to the ALARA principle (as low as reasonably achievable) for radiation doses and its relation to cost–benefit analysis. Section 2.7 discusses the regulatory and ethical implications of background (natural) radiation, and Section 2.8 extends the discussion to appraisals of risks to future generations. Section 2.9 concludes.

2.2 Collective and individual dose

Utilitarianism as a precise moral theory began with Jeremy Bentham's (1748–1832) calculus of pleasure and pain. He proposed that when assessing alternative courses of actions we should sum up all the pleasures that each of them gives rise to and deduct all the pains that it produces. Having done this for each of the alternatives, we should select that which has the highest net value of pleasure minus pain. The radiation protector has, of course, only "negative" values to deal with, and strives to minimize doses instead of maximizing pleasure. From a mathematical point of view, the difference between maximizing and minimizing is of course a triviality, namely the triviality of a minus sign.

It is a central part of the utilitarian idea that pleasures and pains should be counted the same irrespective of whom they affect. Bentham was a strong advocate of equality, and his utilitarianism went against the prevailing moral outlook of his time in claiming that every person – nobleman or commoner, rich or poor, man or woman – should count for one and no one for more than anyone else (Williford 1975; Guidi 2008). But his view has effects that are problematic from an egalitarian or otherwise justice-seeking point of view. If we just sum up all advantages and disadvantages without paying attention to whom they accrue to, then a disadvantage to one person can always be outweighed by a somewhat larger advantage to another person. This runs contrary to the idea of equality. From an egalitarian point of view, it is better to provide an underprivileged person with a certain advantage than to grant an already privileged person a somewhat larger advantage. It also runs contrary to other strongly held principles of justice. An act by which I inflict a considerable harm on myself in order to obtain an even larger benefit for myself is condonable according to utilitarianism, which seems quite sensible. But so also is an action by which I inflict that same harm on someone else in order to obtain the same benefit for myself. Examples like these have been important in the discussion on utilitarianism, as the basis for proposals to reject utilitarianism but also for various amendments of the theory intended to make it capable to deal with the problematic cases.

One of the most important alternatives to utilitarianism is deontology, or duty ethics. Deontologists such as Immanuel Kant (1724–1804) have proposed that an adequate moral theory should be based on strict moral limits that we are never allowed to transgress. A Kantian approach to radiation protection can be based on the precept that someone who causes others to be exposed to radiation is required to ensure that each individual's exposure falls below some specified dose limit. Whereas a utilitarian radiation protector would work to minimize the collective dose (the sum of all individual doses), a deontological radiation protector would instead focus on the limit for individual doses, and see to it that no single person receives a dose above that limit.

PLANT MANAGER: Unfortunately we have a task to be performed in an area with high radiological exposure. There are two ways to perform this task. Either we send in one person to do the whole job. It will take him ten workdays, and he will then receive a dose of 10 mSv. Or we can do the same thing much faster if we send in twelve persons. They can finish the whole task in one full workday, and will then receive 1 mSv each. This, of course, adds up to a total of 12 mSv, distributed among all of them. I will let you choose between the two work methods. Which do you prefer?

RADIATION PROTECTION OFFICER: There can be no doubt that I prefer the one you mentioned last. It would be unacceptable to expose a single worker to as much as 10 mSv, so from the viewpoint of justice it is much better to send in twelve workers for one day. The important thing is that nobody receives a too high exposure.

Our radiation protector appears to apply a deontological approach. For her, there is a limit between permitted and forbidden ways to treat other persons, and her duty is always to stay on the permitted side. The crucial criterion is that no one receives a too high dose. If this is how she thinks, then the sum of these doses, the collective dose, has no role in her considerations.

A week later she has a new conversation with the manager:

PLANT MANAGER: We have found a new, faster, and much less expensive way to replace used fuel in the reactor.

RADIATION PROTECTION OFFICER: Since you bring it up with me, I assume that the new work method has some implications for radiological exposure.

PLANT MANAGER: Well, yes it has. In fact, the collective dose will be 50 mSv.

RADIATION PROTECTION OFFICER: Did you say 50 millisievert? That is preposterous. This work is usually done by five persons, so they will get about 10 mSv each. That is far too much and the Nuclear Regulation Agency will never allow us to do it.

PLANT MANAGER: Do not rush into conclusions. We have found a way to perform the work that divides the dose equally among fifty persons who spend only about two minutes each in the hot region. We can then dispense with the expensive shielding and save a significant amount of money. And each worker will only receive 1 mSv. That is exactly the dose you accepted when we talked to each other last week. So what is the problem?

If our radiation protection officer is a strict deontologist, she will have to accept the new work method. But whereas uncompromising deontologists and utilitarians are easily found among moral philosophers, we would have a hard time finding a radiation protector willing to follow either of these two principles to its end. Instead, radiation protectors try to combine the two lines of thought in various ways. There is consensus in the radiation protection community that both collective and individual doses have to be taken into account, although their relative importance has been subject to debate (Wikman 2004). The commonest combined approach is first to see to it that the individual dose limits are upheld and then, as a second priority, reduce the collective dose as far as possible. This and other combined approaches are interesting also from the viewpoint of moral philosophy, since our intuitions often seem to support positions somewhere between hard-line deontology and die-hard utilitarianism. (See Wikman-Svahn et al. [2006] for a more extended discussion of how deontological and utilitarian principles can be combined in radiation protection.)

2.3 Workers and the general population

Legal dose limits differ substantially between different groups of persons (or types of exposure). Hence, the UK has a limit of 20 mSv/year for employees above 18 years, 6 mSv/year for trainees between 16 and 18 years of age, and 1 mSv/year for all other persons, i.e. the general population.[1] In the United States, the differences are even larger: The occupational dose limits are 50 mSv/year for adults and 5 mSv/year for minors, whereas the dose limit for members of the general public is 1 mSv/year.[2] Similar proportions apply in other countries. These large differences between occupational and non-occupational dose limits are not unique for radiological exposure. Large differences can also be found in the exposure limits for occupational and non-occupational exposure to toxicants (Victorin 1991).

WORKER: I am disappointed. I just found out that you do not treat people equally.
RADIATION PROTECTION OFFICER: What do you mean?
WORKER: On my way to work, I met a man who lives in a house rather close to the plant. He had been to a meeting for the plant's neighbors where you talked about radiation protection. You had told him that you apply a dose limit of 1 mSv/year to the radiation exposures that the plant may cause him.
RADIATION PROTECTION OFFICER: That is the official limit that we follow. But in practice the exposures are much lower than that, and we want to keep them that way.

---

[1] The Ionising Radiations Regulations 1999, statutory instrument 1999 no. 3232. www.legislation.gov.uk/uksi/1999/3232/contents/made.
[2] United States Nuclear Regulatory Commission (NRC), NRC Regulations Title 10, www.nrc.gov/reading-rm/doc-collections/cfr/part020/ (accessed January 14, 2014).

WORKER: So if you found out that the plant exposed him to 0.9 mSv a year you would be alarmed?
RADIATION PROTECTION OFFICER: I certainly would.
WORKER: But that is exactly the dose I received last year. And you told me it was "a fine value." How can it be a fine value for me if it would be alarming in his case?
RADIATION PROTECTION OFFICER: The difference is that your exposure is occupational, his is not.
WORKER: You just told me that the difference is that I am a worker. That is what "occupational" means. Do you now understand why I say that you do not treat people equally?

Are the differences in exposure limits between occupational and non-occupational exposures morally justified? In a 2008 paper, Anders Persson subjected such "double standards" to a careful ethical examination (Persson 2008). He based his analysis on the distinction between double standards in terms of exposure and in terms of risk. Due to differences in biology, exposure time, etc., one and the same exposure may give rise to different risk levels in different subpopulations. Consequently, different exposure limits may be required to stay below one and the same maximal risk level. The crucial moral issue is, as Persson pointed out, whether there is sufficient ethical justification for double standards concerning risks. The standards for exposures should be derivable from those for risks.

Furthermore, he noted that risks have to be weighed against the benefits arising from the same activity. Therefore, higher risks may acceptable in some activities than in others. For instance, most of us would accept larger risks in acute life-saving activities that in most other ventures. However, this applies both to the work of a professional fireman and to life-saving acts performed outside of an occupational setting. Turning to more common types of occupational risk-taking, Persson said:

Manufacturing of carcinogenic dye ingredients, mining, ocean oil drilling, and so on, are well known as risky activities, but connected to certain kinds of occupations and accepted in work life. It is also generally accepted that the public should not be exposed to such risks. But, does this depend on the occupation in question in any strict sense? I think it is more reasonable to say that these kinds of risks too are accepted because they are connected to certain beneficial activities, rather than because they are occupational. However, in most such cases, there are no corresponding non-professional activities such as those we found for firemen and founders. As a consequence of this, a justification of the double standard (occupational vs. non-occupational) of risks has to be supported by something other than a plain reference to an occupation. (Persson 2008: 165)

His conclusion was therefore that double standards in terms of risk cannot be justified. This has immediate bearing on radiation protection. According to Persson, the nature of the activity (and in particular, the benefits that it brings) can have an impact on what radiation-induced risks are acceptable, but whether the activity is occupational or not should have no such impact. It would seem to follow that radiation protectors should classify activities according to their social value rather than according to the occupational/non-occupational dichotomy.

But this is no easy way to go. The current dichotomous approach to exposure limits has the advantage of being easily implementable in practice. It is seldom difficult to determine whether a particular risk exposure is occupational or not. Classifying exposures according to their social usefulness would be a much more challenging undertaking. However, even though it may be unfeasible to base regulations on such a classification, careful ethical analysis of the social justifications of current (occupational and non-occupational) exposures can be an important contribution to radiological protection.

2.4 Sensitive individuals

WOMAN WORKER: I must talk to you. I thought you were on our side, and made sure that we all receive an equal protection against the dangers of radiation.

RADIATION PROTECTION OFFICER: That is what I try to do. What makes you think otherwise?

WOMAN WORKER: You allow us women to be exposed to larger risks than the men. And you are a woman yourself!

RADIATION PROTECTION OFFICER: There must be some misunderstanding. The same rules apply to male and female workers. I just went through last year's statistics for maintenance workers. In that group women had on average 12 percent lower doses. But that is not due to anything that I and my colleagues do. It is probably because women are somewhat more conscientious in following safety instructions.

WOMAN WORKER: I just learned that we women are more sensitive to radiation risks than men. It seems as if 0.7 mSv increases a woman's risk of cancer as much as 1 mSv for a man.

RADIATION PROTECTION OFFICER: That seems to be the case. But what do you want me to do? If we had lower exposure limits for women than for men, then the company would probably only hire men. And we both know how difficult it is for a woman to get a job in this part of the country.

According to the best available information, the cancer risk at any given level of exposure is about 39 percent higher for women than for men (ICRP 2007). Young children are even more sensitive. It has been estimated that a one-year-old infant is ten to fifteen times more likely to develop cancer due to a radiation dose than an adult who receives the same dose (Mazrani et al. 2007). There are also small minorities of the population (well below 1 percent) with inherited medical conditions making them highly sensitive to radiation (Filippi et al. 2006; Chistiakov et al. 2008).

However, neither the ICRP nor the various national standard-setting bodies have adopted different exposure limits for women and men. Instead they have set "unisex" exposure limits, basing them on the risks calculated for an average exposed individual. Such a practice can easily be justified on practical grounds, but it may be more problematic from an ethical point of view. If I am exposed to a dose that gives rise to a certain risk, can that exposure really be defended by pointing out that the risk from that dose would be smaller for an average person than it is for me? And from the risk manager's point of view: Is it defensible to treat the risk associated with an exposure as smaller than it is because it *could have been* smaller if someone else had been subject to the exposure? (Hansson 2009c)

Suppose that we decide to protect women against the radiation risks that they are exposed to (instead of the risks that some average person would have been exposed to). There are two major ways to achieve this: differentiated and unified protection. In differentiated protection, dose limits differ between men and women in such a way that the risks at the respective dose limits are calculated to be the same. In unified protection, exposure limits and other regulations are kept the same for all individuals, but they are made sufficiently strict to protect the members of the more sensitive group, i.e. in this case women. Differentiated protection usually has economic advantages, but it can also have social disadvantages such as excluding parts of the population from certain employments. Table 2.1 summarizes some factors that may legitimately have an impact on the choice between these two methods. (For more details, see Hansson 2009c.)

Table 2.1. *Factors that may have a legitimate impact on the choice between the two major methods to ensure protection of groups that are sensitive to some detrimental environmental impact, such as the carcinogenic effects of ionizing radiation.*

In favor of differentiated protection:	In favor of unified protection:
Large difference in sensitivity between the sensitive group(s) and the rest of the population.	Small difference in sensitivity between the sensitive group(s) and the rest of the population.
High marginal costs for exposure reduction.	Low marginal costs for exposure reduction.
It is easy to identify sensitive individuals.	The identification of sensitive individuals is difficult or uncertain.
Membership in the sensitive group is not privacy sensitive.	Membership in the sensitive group is privacy sensitive.
Individuals who receive special protection do not run a significant risk of social disadvantages.	Individuals who receive special protection risk unemployment or other social disadvantages.
The persons who would receive special protection are not in a vulnerable position.	The persons who would receive special protection are already subject to discrimination or otherwise underprivileged.

2.5 Low-probability events

The nuclear industry is an illustrative arena for risk management decisions, not least because this industry has to deal with a spectrum of potential negative events that differ widely in their probabilities. At one end, we have events that are almost certain to take place but have comparatively limited consequences. One example of this is the "base-line" radiation dosage that the workforce receives under normal, well-controlled conditions. At the other extreme, we have the worst possible nuclear accident, which hopefully has a very low probability but undoubtedly very large consequences. Risk managers have to deal with both these extremes and with everything that is between them. Since resources are not unlimited, priorities have to be set, and this requires some way to compare the different types of harmful events.

The standard way to do this is to measure the severity of risks in terms of the expectation values, i.e. probability-weighted values, of the harm that they give rise to. Often the harm is measured in fatalities, and the severity of a fatal risk will then be measured as the product of the number of deaths and the probability that they will actually occur. Consider the following three risks:

1. A maintenance worker is working alone in an extremely dangerous place. There is a probability of 1/2 that she will be killed by boiling water from a faulty valve.
2. If the roof falls down in the canteen at lunch time, around 100 persons will be killed. The probability of this happening is 1/200.
3. There is a probability of 1/20,000 of a major accident that will cost the lives of around 10,000 persons in the densely populated area around the plant.

According to the standard measure just referred to, these three risks all have the same severity, namely 1/2 (half the severity of a death certain to occur). Unfortunately it is common to use the word "risk" for this severity measure, so that "the risk" is said to be the same in all three cases, namely 0.5 deaths. (This usage is particularly common in the nuclear industry. It seems to originate from the influential Reactor Safety Study WASH-1400, the so-called Rasmussen report, from 1975.)

However, there is no compelling reason to consider these three risks as having exactly the same degree of severity (Hansson 2013a: 74–80). More generally, it cannot be taken for granted that the severity of the prospect of a potential harmful outcome is proportionate to its probability. In policy discussions the avoidance of very large catastrophes, such as a nuclear accident costing thousands of human lives, is often given a higher priority than what is warranted by the statistically expected number of deaths. It has been claimed that serious events with low probabilities should be given a higher weight in decision-making than what they receive if risks are judged exclusively according to their expectation values (O'Riordan and Cameron 1994; O'Riordan et al. 2001; Burgos and Defeo 2004). The latter method does not have room for risk-averse or cautious decision-making. This is problematic since risk aversion appears to be reasonable in many situations. (It may even have evolutionary advantages [Okasha 2007, 2011].)

A further problem with probabilities is that they are only very rarely known with certainty. The only clear-cut cases of known probabilities that we have are idealized textbook cases employing devices such as dice or coins that are supposed to be known with certainty to be fair. In real-life situations, even if we act upon a determinate probability estimate, we are not fully certain that this estimate is exactly correct.

In the nuclear field as well as some others, risk assessments usually depend on probability estimates made by highly specialized experts. But even when such estimates are based on the best available evidence, they may still be wrong. We know from historical experience that experts are sometimes mistaken. A rational decision-maker should take into account the possibility that this may happen again. Suppose that a proposal has been made to build a new type of nuclear reactor in the middle of a large city. A group of experts have investigated the proposal and concluded that the probability of a core damage (meltdown) in this reactor will be 1 in 100,000,000 per year. This is a very low probability indeed. However, when making a decision based on this estimate it is not sufficient to make up our minds whether or not a risk of that magnitude is acceptable. We also need to make a judgment on how reliable the estimate is. Arguably that should be the most important part of our deliberations when we are confronted with such a low probability.

Unfortunately, the uncertainty inherent in probability estimates has often been neglected, and many risk assessments have been based on the implicit assumption that all probability estimates are fully reliable. From an ethical point of view, such overconfidence is highly problematic since it may lead to the neglect of potential harmful events that should instead be at the center of our discussions.

2.6 Weighing risks against benefits

Cost–benefit analysis is a decision-aiding technique that weighs advantages against disadvantages in numerical terms (Hansson 2007). In a typical cost–benefit analysis, the various advantages and disadvantages associated with an option are all assigned a monetary value. Usually, a fixed value is assigned to the loss of a human life, and risks of losses in life are valued as fractions of that value. Hence, if the loss of a life is assigned the value $7,000,000, then the value of a risk of 1 in 1,000 of an accident in which eight people would die is

$$0.001 \times 8 \times 7{,}000{,}000 \text{ dollars} = 56{,}000 \text{ dollars}$$

In radiation protection, such weighing of risks and benefits has usually been integrated with strivings to keep doses as low as possible (not just below certain limits). This is usually expressed with the phrases "as low as reasonably achievable" (ALARA) and "as low as reasonably practicable" (ALARP) (Hansson 2013c). These phrases imply that even if exposures are below the dose limits, efforts should be made to reduce them further. ALARA is often described as a principle of optimization, by which is meant that some sort of compromise between dose reduction and cost containment is aimed for. (Whereas "ALARA" dominates in the United States, "ALARP" is more common in Europe, in particular in general workplace health and safety. Some authors have tried to make a distinction in meaning between these terms, but there is no general such difference and in practice, the two abbreviations are usually taken as synonyms. See Hansson [2013c: 144–45].)

But according to a common view of ALARA, it is not quite the same as cost–benefit analysis, since it is only intended to be applied to a part of the dose range. If the doses are very high, they have to be reduced irrespective of the costs, and there is no need for cost–benefit analysis. It they are very low, there is presumably no need for action, and therefore cost–benefit analysis is unnecessary here as well. It is in the intermediate region, with doses that are neither negligible nor utterly unacceptable, that the ALARA principle will be applied. The upper limit of the ALARA region in this model has been called the "action level" and its lower limit the "inaction level" (Hendee and Edwards 1986). Doses below the inaction level have also been referred to as "de minimis" doses. This term is derived from the legal phrase "de minimis non curat lex" (law does not concern itself with trifles). In the context of risk assessment, it expresses the view that some risks are so small that we have no reason to take action against them even if such action can be taken at no or negligible cost.

This three-leveled approach has been promoted in particular by the Health and Safety Executive (HSE) in the UK. In its influential policy document "Reducing risks, protecting people" from 2001, it divided situations involving risk into three categories: the unacceptable region, the tolerable region, and the broadly acceptable region (HSE 2001). An activity or practice falling in the unacceptable region should be "ruled out unless the activity or practice can be modified to reduce the degree of risk so that it falls in one of the regions below, or there are exceptional reasons for the activity or practice to be retained" (HSE 2001: 42). The zone at the opposite end, the broadly acceptable region, contains risks that "are comparable to those that people regard as insignificant or trivial in their daily lives" and are therefore "generally regarded as insignificant and adequately controlled." The intermediate, "tolerable" region consists of risks that "people are prepared to tolerate in order to obtain benefits" (HSE 2001: 43). It is in this region that the HSE recommends application of the ALARA principle (or in their own terminology: the ALARP principle). The limit between the broadly acceptable and the tolerable regions has tentatively been set at an individual risk of death of one in a million per year, both for occupational and non-occupational risk exposure (HSE 2001: 45). The limit between tolerable and unacceptable risks is tentatively set at one in one thousand per year for occupational risks and one in ten thousand per year for non-occupational risks (HSE 2001: 46).

This approach to ALARA is far from uncontroversial. Some radiation protectors claim that the restriction of ALARA to doses above a certain "de minimis" level is incompatible with the standard linear no-threshold assumption. If there is no safe level, then it is not clear why there should be a level below which no efforts are made to reduce exposures. "It is not reasonable to pay more than a certain amount of money per unit of collective dose reduction, but if dose reduction can be achieved at a lesser cost even at very low individual doses, the reduction is, by definition, reasonable." (Lindell and Beninson 1981: 685)

Within the scope of application for the ALARA principle, the notion of reasonableness (the "R" in ALARA) has the important role of making room for economic considerations. In an often quoted British court case it was ruled that the test of what is reasonably practicable is "not simply what is practicable as a matter of engineering, but depends on the consideration, in the light of the whole circumstances at the time of the accident, whether the time, trouble and expense of the precautions suggested are or are not disproportionate to the risk involved, and also an assessment of the degree of security which the measures suggested may be expected to afford" (Jones-Lee and Aven 2011: 877) According to one interpretation of ALARA, in the tolerable region ("ALARA region") "the value of a person-rem is constant."[3] Below that region, the value of a person-rem "tends to zero," whereas above it that value "increases sharply" (Kathren et al. 1984). This means that in its area of application the ALARA principle is "treated as being simply a restatement of the standard cost–benefit criterion that from the point of view of social welfare maximization a safety project should be undertaken only if its costs do not exceed its benefits" (Jones-Lee and Aven 2011: 879). Much in this vein, the British HSE has developed an ALARA methodology

---

[3] rem (roentgen equivalent in man) is an older unit of ionizing radiation dose. 1 rem is equal to 0.01 Sv (sievert) or 10 mSv (millisievert).

that makes use of cost–benefit analysis, but with modifications of the standard methodology to induce a certain "bias toward safety."

Due to resource limitations, a compromise must always be struck between the demands of safety and those of economy and production. For obvious reasons, such a compromise is always contestable and in need of ethical investigation. In radiation protection, such investigations will have to pay careful attention to the ALARA principle and in particular to how the "R" for reasonableness is interpreted.

2.7 Natural radiation

The word "natural" has strong, positively value-laden connotations. When we describe food, textile material, or human behavior as "natural," then that is an expression of approval or acceptance. However, it is not difficult to find counterexamples to the association between naturalness and positive value that is assumed here. Nature is full of dangers, and it is simply wrong to conclude that since something is natural, it is harmless. This fallacy has a name: *argumentum ad naturam* (appeal to nature) (Baggini 2002; Hansson 2003a, 2011a).

The fallacy comes in two variants that can be exemplified as follows:

First advertisement:
Be sure to get your daily dose of vitamin C, the natural protection against scurvy. Our product contains absolutely pure vitamin C, produced in one of the best laboratories.

Second advertisement:
Be sure to get your daily dose of vitamin C. Eat our dried camu camu berries. This is the natural way to get vitamin C, much better than the synthetic products from chemical industries.

The first advertisement exemplifies the following version of the fallacy:

X occurs naturally.
Therefore: X, whether produced naturally or artificially, is good.

The second advertisement expresses another form of the fallacy, namely:

This sample of X occurs naturally.
Therefore: This sample of X is better than artificially produced X.

The second version of the fallacy is common for instance in health food shops where it is often taken for granted that synthetic chemicals are in some way inferior to naturally occurring instances of the same molecules. From a scientific point of view, this is of course nonsense.

In discussions on radiation, this "health food store variant" of the fallacy is uncommon. But instead, the first variant of the fallacy is quite common. It comes in the form of claims that exposures of the same size as naturally occurring (background) radiation cannot be dangerous – presumably because they occur in nature. In the words of an unusually unsophisticated (but yet academic) proponent of this view:

> Unfortunately, the Japanese seem to be repeating the mistake [of over-reacting against radiation exposures of the public]. On 23 March, they advised that children should not drink tap water in Tokyo, where an activity of 200 Bq per litre had been measured the day before. Let's put this in perspective. The natural radioactivity in every human body is 100 Bq per litre, so 200 Bq per litre is really not going to do much harm. ... [T]he basis of international radiation safety regulations today, which suggest an upper limit for the general public of 1 mSv/year above natural levels. This very low figure is not a danger level, rather it's a small addition to the levels found in nature – a British person is exposed to 2.7 mSv/year, on average. My book Radiation and Reason argues that a responsible danger level based on current science would be 100 mSv/month, with a lifelong limit of 5,000 mSv, not 1 mSv/year. (Allison 2011: 194)

This is of course an absurd argumentation. The fact that something occurs naturally does not prove that it does no harm to us, and neither does it prove that it is safe to increase our exposure to it. We are all exposed to pathogenic bacteria, but in spite of being natural some of them do us considerable harm. The existence of this "background" exposure to pathogens certainly does not show that we can increase our exposure to them a hundredfold or thousandfold with impunity. Similarly, the natural occurrence of radiation is not a tenable argument for its harmlessness.

2.8 Future people

Sometimes when summarizing the advantages and disadvantages of an activity we find that they materialize at different points in time. For the smoker, the most important positive effect of smoking is immediate: She avoids the nicotine withdrawal syndrome. The most important negative effect is the risk of serious disease that will typically materialize decades later. (About half of the smokers die prematurely due to smoking, see Boyle [1997].) In climate and environmental policies, we are often concerned with measures that cost money today but have their positive effects much later. Nuclear waste management provides what is perhaps the most extreme example of such temporal discrepancies: On the one hand, energy is produced to be consumed more or less immediately; on the other hand, the potential damages from nuclear waste may materialize hundreds of thousands of years ahead.

The standard method for evaluating future outcomes is discounting, a method originally developed for money. It is based on the assumption of a positive interest rate. For example, suppose that the interest rate in a bank is constantly 3 percent, and furthermore suppose that we want to have €100,000 in ten years. Then it is sufficient to deposit €74,400 in the bank. We can therefore say that the "present value" of receiving €100,000 ten years from now is €74,400. With a similar argument, a loss €100,000 ten years from now corresponds to a loss of €74.400 today. More generally, we can "convert" the value of future money into money now using the following formula:

$$v_0(x) = v_t(x) \times 1/(1+r)^t.$$

where x is the object whose value we are converting, $v_0(x)$ its value now, $v_t(x)$ its value after t years and r the interest rate (in the example: 0.03). In cost–benefit analysis, this is the standard way to assess future risks and benefits. Suppose for instance that we discuss measures that would prevent an accident 15 years into the future in which 31 persons would die. With a 3 percent interest rate, the formula tells us to value the loss of 31 lives in 15 years the same way that we would value a loss of 20 lives today (since $31 \times 1/1,03^{15} \approx 20$).

A major problem with this approach is that it yields absurd results if we consider very long time periods. Consider, as a simple schematic example, a hypothetical choice between the following two actions:

1. Killing one person now.
2. Now performing an action that will lead to the death of the whole population of the earth, 10 billion people, in the year 2800.

If we apply discounting with a discount rate of 3 percent, the first of these actions will be worse than the second. The example is unrealistic, but it illustrates that even very large disasters will have almost zero (dis)value if they take place a couple of hundred years from now. (Lowering the discount rate only delays this effect. With a discount rate of 0.5 percent it will still be worse that one person dies today than that 10 billion people die in 4,620 years.)

It should be clear from these examples that if we apply discounting to radioactive waste management, we can in practice disregard what happens after the first thousand years or so. This runs counter to the almost universally accepted assumption, expressed in the international *Joint Convention on the Safety of Spent Fuel Management and on the Safety of Radioactive Waste Management* from 1997, that our generation has the responsibility to implement

> ... effective defenses against potential hazards so that individuals, society and the environment are protected from harmful effects of ionizing radiation, now and in the future, in such a way that the needs and aspirations of the present generation are met without compromising the ability of future generations to meet their needs and aspirations. (IAEA 1997)

In practice, the absurd consequences of discounting the future effects of nuclear waste disposal are dealt with by making a remarkably unprincipled exception:

Nuclear waste is treated differently from other environmental threats. Instead of discounting its potential future dangers, its effects far off into the future are treated as equally serious as if they were to take place today. It is interesting to compare nuclear waste with climate change in this respect. In economic analyses of climate change, both costs and effects are discounted. There are controversies on the discount rate but unanimity that it should be above zero. The difference in how the two areas assess future effects is by no means obviously justifiable.

2.9 Conclusion

The ethics of radiation protection is an emerging new field of area-specific ("applied") ethics, replete with issues and problems that are both practically relevant and well connected to more general and fundamental issues in ethics. The following is a tentative list of conclusions from this new field that may be of particular relevance for radiation protection in the nuclear industry:

1. The tolerability or acceptability of radiation doses cannot be determined based only on natural science. Ethical judgment is an unavoidable component in these deliberations.
2. The standard method that assigns weight to a potential damage in proportion to its probability does not have a firm ethical foundation. Other approaches make sense ethically, for instance approaches that assign higher weight to low-probability events with large negative consequences.
3. The uncertainty of probability estimates should always be taken into account. When we are presented with a low-probability estimate for a severe accident, it is not sufficient to consider whether that probability is acceptable. We must also ask whether the probability estimate is reliable enough.
4. Comparisons with natural radiation cannot be used to determine what radiation risks are acceptable. The fact that something is natural does not prove that it is harmless, and neither does it prove that its artificial duplication is ethically defensible.
5. There are good reasons to take both individual and collective doses into account. Focusing on only one of them can lead to ethically problematic decisions.
6. More attention should be paid to radiosensitive individuals and to the differences in radiation sensitivity between women and men. The current standard approach with its focus on average individuals may have to be replaced or supplemented with a focus on the most sensitive group.
7. The discounting of risks occurring far into the future is ethically problematic. The current practice of not discounting potential future effects of nuclear waste disposal is sound and should be continued.

For the nuclear industry and the government agencies overseeing it, these and other ethical issues are important reasons to engage in an open and respectful dialogue with the public. The ethical discussion needs to be supported by access to the best scientific information. However, science cannot settle the ethical issues and the public is right in distrusting those who claim that it can.[4]

---

[4] See also Chapter 4 in this volume.

3 The unknowable ceilings of safety: three ways that nuclear accidents escape the calculus of risk assessments

John Downer[1]

3.1 Introduction

In March 2012, the first anniversary of the Fukushima meltdowns, several US newspapers turned their gaze to the town of Tomioka, which had been evacuated as the accident unfolded. Tomioka made for a compelling photo essay. A year after the accident it was (and remains) a ghost town. Abandoned vehicles lined streets once famous for their cherry blossoms, stoplights blinked pointlessly, and weeds grew through cracks in the asphalt. Cleanup efforts were failing, and the town's exiled residents were giving up hope of ever being able to return. The New York Daily News interviewed its one remaining occupant, Naoto Matsumura, a 53-year-old rice farmer who had stayed to feed the animals that other farmers had left behind: scores of cows and pigs, and one ostrich called "Boss." His cumulative exposure to radiation had been considerable. He told reporters he did not expect to live much longer (Kennedy 2012).

Such stories were made all the more haunting (or should have been) by the under-reported release, around the same time, of the official Japanese Diet report on the accident, which offered new insights into the highest-level deliberations around the disaster (NAIIC 2012). Among the report's many findings was a singularly startling revelation: that the Japanese cabinet had concluded it might have to evacuate Tokyo City if the plant had deteriorated further, and that this almost came to pass (Fackler 2012). "We barely avoided the worst-case scenario, though the public didn't know it at the time," the chairman of the report told reporters (in Lean 2012).

The principal (and to that point largely unrecognized) danger lay in the unshielded spent fuel pool perched about 100 feet above Reactor Number 4

---

[1] The author would like to thank Charles Perrow for his comments on an early draft of this chapter, and Diane Vaughn for the invitation to Columbia University, where it was written.

(Dvorak 2012; Matsumura 2012). The report found the pool had nearly ruptured completely in the explosion that wrecked the reactor building. It further concluded that if this had happened then the 1,535 fuel assemblies the pool contained would have begun to burn uncontrollably, releasing radionuclides into the atmosphere at levels far exceeding the fallout from Chernobyl or any other nuclear event in history (Alvarez in Matsumura 2012; NAIIC 2012).

In such circumstances, Tokyo, which is about 170 miles downwind of Fukushima, would almost certainly have been lost. Tokyo is home to over 35 million people; twice the population of New York and three times that of London. Together with those cities, it is widely considered one of the three "command centers" of the global economy. The socioeconomic ramifications of evacuating it in the fashion of Tomioka are difficult to fathom. The economic consequences alone would have been apocalyptic: a financial *Götterdämmerung*. Kan Naoto, the prime minister at the time of the crisis, was perhaps not exaggerating when he told the *Wall Street Journal* that Japan's "existence as a sovereign nation was at stake" (in Quintana 2012).

From a policy perspective, it is almost unthinkable that Japan would have knowingly bet on a technology that might credibly have one day endangered its capital city. Unsurprisingly, therefore, Fukushima's construction, like those of all nuclear plants, was built on near-absolute assurances that such disasters would not happen. This is to say that in modern democracies, policy and regulatory decisions about nuclear power are predicated on two key understandings: (1) that the probability of nuclear meltdowns is *objectively calculable*; and (2) that this probability is *so low as to be negligible* (i.e. not worthy of serious policy consideration).[2] To a very large extent, in other words, states base judgments about nuclear plants on formal reliability calculations *proving* that those plants are extraordinarily unlikely to fail.

The origin of this approach to nuclear decision-making can be traced to the US Nuclear Regulatory Commission's (NRC's) landmark 1975 "WASH-1400" study of reactor safety. Earlier studies of reactor safety posed problems for nuclear proponents because they explored the consequences of major accidents and came to conclusions that were widely deemed to be untenable politically. Many observers (e.g. Rip 1986; Clarke 2005) construe WASH-1400 as the NRC's response to this problem. It ingeniously excluded meltdowns from nuclear discourse by using formal reliability calculations to demonstrate that such events were too unlikely to merit serious policy

---

[2] In a recent declaration to a UK regulator, for instance, *Areva*, a prominent French nuclear manufacturer, invoked probabilistic calculations to assert that the likelihood of a "core damage incident" in its new "EPR" reactor were of the order of one incident (per reactor) every 1.6 million years, and to conclude that the probability of a core-melt is "infinitesimal" (in Ramana 2011); see also Chapter 2 in this volume.

concern – classifying them as "hypothetical" rather than "credible" (Fuller 1976: 149–86; Rip 1986: 4–9). The study was widely criticized on its release and eventually withdrawn by the NRC, but its basic premise has remained. Probabilistic reliability calculations – used as a means of objectively establishing that reactor disasters are too improbable to merit consideration – have become a ubiquitous aspect of nuclear discourse and decision-making.

Publics and policymakers are strongly encouraged to accept such calculations at face value, as objective truths (Downer 2013). And they routinely *do* accept them uncritically, as is evinced by the observation that states consistently make choices about nuclear power that are incongruous if considered in relation to a potential disaster.

This is evident in a range of contexts. Most straightforwardly, perhaps, it can be seen in decisions about whether and where to build nuclear plants. It is probably uncontroversial to surmise, for instance, that most plants upwind of major metropolitan areas – such as Hinkley Point, about 35 miles from Bristol in the UK – would have struggled for approval if meltdowns were considered credible. Somewhat less intuitively, it can be seen in the way that states plan (or fail to plan) for nuclear incidents. Fukushima revealed gross insufficiencies in Japan's contingency planning for nuclear disasters – a shortcoming (common to all nuclear states) born of an institutionally deep-rooted confidence that such planning is fundamentally unnecessary (Clarke and Perrow 1996; Kahn 2011; Perrow 2011: 46–47). Finally, and probably least intuitively, it can be seen in the designs of nuclear plants themselves. Perrow (2007: 136), for example, argues that states would be much more reluctant to "cluster" several reactors in single facilities if they considered meltdowns possible. For even though clustering reactors offers significant economic and political benefits, it creates conditions where the failure of one unit can propagate to others, as it did at Fukushima.[3]

The widespread acceptance of nuclear reliability calculations as unproblematic facts is also evident in the academic discourses those calculations touch. Formal cost–benefit analyses of energy options lean heavily on them, for instance, either to weigh the costs (financial, social, environmental) of accidents, or (more often) to tacitly discount the possibility of nuclear accidents completely (e.g. Tengs et al. 1995; OECD 2010). No policy study comparing the social or financial costs of different energy options, for example, has formally considered the potential loss of a global financial center due to a spent fuel fire.

---

[3] The Fukushima plant was a cluster of six reactors – a planning decision that many responders must have rued when fallout from the first reactor explosion thwarted their efforts to contain some of its neighbors (Osnos 2011: 50; Strickland 2011).

In a similar vein, a substantial proportion of the academic literature pertaining to the psychological and cultural factors affecting individuals' or communities' relationship to risk is premised, to a greater or lesser degree, on the idea that nuclear hazards are *established facts* (e.g. Douglas and Wildavsky 1982; Weart 1988). Much of the "risk perception" literature, for example, has deep roots in research relating to nuclear energy and tacitly invokes official reliability calculations in demonstrating the existence of psychological heuristics that shape people's understanding of risks (e.g. Starr 1969; Slovic et al. 1982; Erickson 1991).[4] For instance, Starr's seminal (1969) finding that people will accept the probability of dying from "voluntary" risks like car accidents, at a rate a thousand times higher than "involuntary" risks like reactor meltdowns, implicitly assumes there is an empirically calculable measure of the latter against which to judge people's attitudes.

The authority of these reliability calculations remains strong, even in the face of disaster. It would be reasonable to imagine that the credibility of nuclear reliability assessments should have been undermined by the industry's history of accidents and near accidents, some of which – Windscale, Three Mile Island, Chernobyl, now Fukushima – are widely recognized and remembered. As Ramana (2011) highlights, nuclear disasters happen far more often than assessments predict. A rough calculation puts the current rate of serious meltdowns at 1 in every 3,000 reactor years.[5] Yet formal nuclear reliability calculations remain credible. Even the largest disasters, with all their visceral undeniability, have failed to compel most publics or policymakers to seriously question the reliability of nuclear reliability calculations.

This enduring faith in reliability assessment has complex foundations. In part, it can be credited to the fact that, in the wake of accidents, nuclear authorities make logical and compelling arguments for why the failed plant should be treated as an "exception" that has little bearing on wider reliability calculations (see Downer 2013). At the same time, it owes something to the inscrutability of the calculations themselves, which makes them difficult to criticize directly, combined with an institutionally and culturally entrenched deference to the technoscientific expertise those calculations represent. As Turner and Pidgeon (1997: 14) put it: "Non-engineers often seem to stand in

---

[4] Although this literature invariably treats the likelihood of meltdowns and their health consequences as established facts, it should also be noted that it sometimes questions the notion that "risk" should be defined by these factors alone. Often preferring to construe gaps between "perception" and "risk" as evidence that the latter is defined too narrowly rather than as evidence that the former is misunderstood (see Slovic 1999; Roeser 2009).

[5] This counts Fukushima as three separate meltdowns but excludes Windscale because it was a fire rather than a core melt. Other estimates put the failure rate of nuclear plants at somewhere between one in every 1,300 to 3,600 reactor years, depending on how one defines a serious failure (see Taebi et al. 2012: 203fn.).

awe of the practitioners of applied science and engineering, regarding them as inhabitants of a world where rationality reigns supreme, where alternative courses of action can be measured and rigorously compared and where science informs every decision."

Arguments about exceptionalism are not without merit, and deference to technoscientific expertise undoubtedly serves societies well in many contexts, yet both are highly misleading in relation to nuclear risk (Downer 2013). For even if disasters cannot speak for themselves, there are compelling "principled" reasons to doubt the authority of nuclear reliability calculations, none of which require a deep understanding of engineering minutiae to understand. The following three parts of this chapter will briefly outline three such arguments. They will draw on literatures from various social sciences (most prominently, the organizational sociology and science and technology studies [STS] literatures) to highlight an essential limitation of nuclear reliability calculations and explain why it necessarily undermines their credibility.

These are, in turn:

1. *Framing limitations*: Limits arising from the failure of nuclear reliability calculations to model all the variables that contribute to failures.
2. *Systemic limitations*: Limits arising from the failure of nuclear reliability calculations to recognize that "failure" as well as "safety" can be an emergent property of complex, tightly coupled technical systems.
3. *Epistemic limitations*: Limits arising from the fact that nuclear reliability calculations imply a level of certainty that is epistemologically implausible given the nature of tests, theories, and models from which they are derived.

3.2   Framing limitations

A first reason to doubt the credibility of nuclear reliability assessments lies in recognizing their scope, or more specifically their limitations: the circumscribed range of variables included in their calculations.

As discussed above, nuclear reliability assessments are presented as "all encompassing" assessments of the likelihood of a plant's failure, and they are treated that way by downstream "risk" calculations, thus allowing regulators and policymakers to ignore some potential hazards because they are "hypothetical" rather than "credible." Yet the reliability calculations underlying those assessments are not all encompassing. They are "bounded" or "framed," in the sense that their conclusions are predicated on a narrow definition of what constitutes "failure." This means that there are ways that nuclear plants can fail that fall outside the "frame" and so are not factored into reliability calculations. It further means that there are ways that nuclear plants can fail that *could not be factored into reliability calculations* even if engineers wanted them to be, simply because their probabilities are inherently unquantifiable. Nuclear reliability assessments, we might say, make all sorts of implicit assumptions about context.

To take an extreme example, no nuclear reliability assessment recognizes the possibility that a plant might be targeted by a hostile power with modern weapons in an act of war. This is because it seems almost inconceivable that nuclear plants in most modern First World nations might be subject to airstrikes, but this represents a failure of imagination. Nuclear plants are designed to last a long time, and the world sometimes changes more quickly than we imagine. Even some contemporary scholars envisage US plants being vulnerable to cyber-attacks. The point is moot, however, as it would be impossible to accurately quantify the probabilities of such events, even if regulators aspired to do so.

Nuclear engineers might argue that it is unreasonable to expect their calculations to account for such contingencies. No engineering structure could be held to such a standard, they might (justifiably) contend, and so no reliability should have to demonstrate it. This misses the point, however. The fault lies not in the nuclear reliability calculations *per se* but in the regulatory decision to treat them as assessments of the likelihood of "failures-from-all-causes" when assembling the risk assessments that inform policy.

There are, in principle, an incalculable number of such "outside-the-frame" threats to nuclear plants, and even the most exhaustive studies cannot claim to have imagined very possibility, for nuclear plants operate for decades, and who knows what the future may bring. Even today there are conspicuous threats that go unrecorded. A more realistic (or at least intuitive) contingency, for instance, is the risk of a fuel-laden airliner being hijacked by extremists and then flown into a nuclear plant. Unlike military strikes, modern nuclear assessments do recognize this risk. Rather than attempting to quantify its probability, however, they dismiss it on the claim that the hardened containment buildings around new reactors are designed to withstand such strikes.[6] Again such reasoning is moot, however, because it ignores the spent fuel pools, which lie outside of the containment building and, as Fukushima unfortunately illustrated, potentially carry far greater hazards than the reactors themselves.

By far the most conspicuous realm of "outside-the-frame" hazards lies in the organizational dimensions of nuclear plants. As the NRC itself concluded in a 2001 study (NRC 2001), nuclear reliability assessments routinely underestimate the role of human action. They assume, within certain bounds, that

---

[6] Or rather, most of them. To the best of the author's knowledge, no nuclear manufacturer is willing to assert that its containment buildings could withstand *any* conceivable aircraft impact.

the people operating or regulating nuclear plants will adhere to rules. Or, to be more precise, they assume that people will only violate those rules in predictable and circumscribed ways. In other words, the assessments embody a slew of implicit (and often explicit) caveats, such as: "given proper maintenance" or "if handled correctly."

These caveats become evident in the wake of disasters, when nuclear authorities routinely defend their reliability assessments by highlighting operator error, noncompliance, or malfeasance to claim, implicitly, that the "*calculations would have been sound if people had only obeyed the rules*" (Downer 2013). The Fukushima report to the Japanese Diet, for instance, strongly recommended that the accident be understood as a "man-made" disaster (NAIIC 2012). In doing so, it echoed reports such as the Kemeny Commission investigation into Three Mile Island and the Soviet investigation into Chernobyl, both of which pointed to operator error as the primary cause (Wynne 1983: 23; Schmid 2011: 20). Such assignations of blame serve certain institutional interests, but they highlight an essential weakness of nuclear reliability assessments. The fact that three separate disasters within forty years could credibly be pinned on organizational factors testifies to: (A) *the relevance of those factors to nuclear reliability*,[7] and (B) *the degree that reliability (and hence risk) assessments underestimate those factors*. Put simply: When reports blame people for disasters, they are saying that there are significant causes of failure that reliability assessments ignore.

Nuclear operators and authorities would contend that they pay close attention to organizational issues, and they do. Yet there is overwhelming evidence, beyond the three reports outlined above, that such issues are dramatically under-recognized by reliability assessments. Numerous studies suggest that the behaviors documented by accident investigations are unexceptional rather than aberrant, for instance (see e.g. Perin 2005; Perrow 2007). And there are principled sociological reasons[8] to believe that the reliability of complex organizations might be both fundamentally unquantifiable and imperfectible (see e.g. Wynne 1983: 23; Perrow 1999; Downer 2013: 15).[9]

---

[7] Indeed, as Wynne (1983: 23) notes, "there are countless cases where technologies have failed ... because somewhere in the social labyrinth of their enactment, people have not acted according to the designers' unrealistic assumptions and faiths."

[8] The fact that "rules" are always open to interpretation and cannot cover every exigency, for instance (Wynne 1983: 23).

[9] Over the last thirty years a large and sophisticated body of academic literature has emerged exploring how human-error, noncompliance, and malfeasance relate to accidents. Vaughan (1996), for instance, speaks of the "normalization of deviance"; Rasmussen et al. (1987) of "migration to the boundary"; and Snook (2000) of "practical drift." This discourse – of which Silbey (2009) offers a useful overview – sometimes conveys a diffuse impression, often implicit and unintentional, that human behavior is a manageable problem: "something akin to noise in the system" as Silbey (2009: 342) puts it. Human failings are a problem that has proven stubbornly

42   John Downer

This is all to say that there are potential causes of meltdowns that assessments *do not* quantify; there are potential causes of meltdowns that assessments *cannot* quantify; and it is impossible to quantify how many there are of each. Organizational failures, terrorists, and airstrikes are just a tiny subset of the countless possibilities that reliability calculations cannot hope to wholly capture. When assessments of nuclear risk treat reliability calculations as if they were absolute probabilities of a plant failing for any cause; therefore, the effect is to exclude a host of unmeasured variables from public discourse (Lash and Wynne 1992: 4; Deutch and Lester 2004).[10]

3.3   Systemic limitations

A second reason to doubt the credibility of nuclear reliability assessments lies in recognizing the system-level probabilistic implications of minor contingencies: an argument famously outlined by Yale sociologist Charles Perrow in his book *Normal Accidents* (1999, originally published in 1984).

Perrow describes his book as a "first attempt at a 'structural' analysis of risky systems" (1999: 62). It outlines what he and others have come to call Normal Accident Theory (NAT). As with Perrow's book, NAT is a broad argument with many facets and interpretations, some related to power and structural incentives, others to organizational difficulties. For the purposes of this chapter, however, I will focus on one argument in particular: the argument that *some* accidents in complex systems – the eponymous "Normal Accidents" – are unforeseeable and unavoidable because they stem from coincidences that are too improbable to predict in advance.

At the heart of this claim is a deceptively simple but nevertheless profound insight: that accidents caused by very improbable confluences of events (which no risk calculation could ever anticipate) are *statistically probable* in systems where there are *many opportunities for them to occur*. It is initially tempting to see this as a restatement of "Murphy's law," the old engineering adage that "Anything that can go wrong, will go wrong," but it is more profound than this – it is a systems-level rethinking of what it means for something to "go wrong."

To understand this we must first understand that, in the real world, no complex sociotechnical system can function without small irregularities and deviances from "Platonically perfect" operation. Each nuclear plant, for

---

resilient to sociologists' proscriptions, however, and few accident theorists claim that they can be reduced to the levels implied by nuclear reliability calculations.

[10] As Silbey (2009: 345) puts it, our "allegedly empirical analyses become solipsistic, focusing exclusively on the methods and epistemologies that are internal to technological instrumentalism."

instance, must tolerate minor irregularities, unexpected events, and small component failures: spilt milk, small sparks, blown fuses, late buses, misplaced notes, stuck valves, obscured warning lights, and so on. Engineers might not like these events, but eliminating them entirely is impracticable, and so they instead construe them as a fundamental design premise. This is to say that nuclear engineers (and regulators) assiduously account for Murphy's Law on the "component" level by thinking about safety on a "systems" level.

The reliability of nuclear plants is premised on the logic that a system consisting of many interconnected and closely responsive elements can be more reliable than any of the individual parts themselves. When engineers assert that nuclear plants are ultra-reliable systems, in other words, they are not suggesting that plants never have stuck valves or faulty warning lights, they are saying that plants are designed to accommodate the many vagaries of normal technological operation. Each of their critical components (and subsystems) is integrated into a larger system with redundancies and other safeguards that ensure that no single failure could conceivably lead to a disaster. Nuclear plants have many layers of redundancy. For a plant to melt down, therefore, it is not sufficient that just one of its critical elements fails. So must that element's backups, and so must their backups, and so on. The reasoning of nuclear reliability assessments, therefore, is that if the chance of one element failing is low, then the chance of all its backups and safeties failing at the same time is so improbable that it is virtually impossible: It would be a billion-to-one coincidence, more worthy of a Hollywood screenplay than a formal reliability assessment.

Seen from a Perrovian perspective, however, this logic is incomplete, and the proof of this is in the accident record. He argues that the accident records of nuclear plants and other complex sociotechnical systems show that fateful "Hollywood" coincidences happen far more often than the logic of systems engineering would predict. Most famously, for instance, he points to the 1979 accident at Three Mile Island (TMI). By his account, the incident began when leaking moisture from a blocked filter inadvertently tripped valves controlling the flow of cold water into the plant's cooling system: a small, entirely unremarkable failure, which was progressively exacerbated by a series of increasingly unfortunate coincidences. Redundant backup valves should have intervened but were inexplicably closed. This should have been clear from an indicator-light, but the light was obscured by a tag hanging from a switch above. A tertiary line of technological defense, a relief valve, should have opened but did not, while a malfunctioning indicator-light erroneously indicated that it had. And so forth (for details, see Perrow 1999: 15–32). None of these failures were particularly noteworthy in themselves, he argues; it was simply that complexity colluded with cruel coincidence and the reactor's controllers understandably struggled to comprehend its condition in time to prevent a catastrophic meltdown.

Perrow reconciles the failure-proof logic of systems engineering with the failure-prone record of complex technologies in practice, by intuiting that *failure*, as well as *safety*, can be understood on a systems level. His argument can be broken into two related parts.

The first is the observation that systems are considerably "messier" in practice than they are in theory. He points out, for instance, that elements in a system (even functionally unrelated elements) can influence each other in unexpected ways, with the failure of one causing the failure of another (e.g. by exploding, catching fire, or draining a common resource). Hence, the failure-rates of different elements in a system are not straightforwardly "independent."

The second is the observation that elaborate systems like nuclear plants have many more of what we might call "avenues of coincidence" than simple systems. As technologies become more complex and connected (or "coupled"), Perrow argues, the number of elements they contain expands, as does the number (and importance) of the links (anticipated and unanticipated) between those elements. This, in turn, multiplies the sources of unexpected events and the chances of those events combining in unpredictable ways to produce what he calls "Normal" (or "System") Accidents.[11]

Perrow's argument, ultimately, is that accidents can arise from the fabric of the systems themselves. The elaborate sociotechnical networks that engineers create to make reactors safe, come with unrecognized probabilistic costs. The redundancies and other systemic elaborations on which nuclear safety assessments (and nuclear safety itself) are premised represent what Arthur (2009) calls "structural deepening." They make systems more complicated and interconnected, and, in doing so, they create more opportunities for misadventure (Downer 2011b). The odds against Hollywood-esque scenarios, where a succession of small events in perfect synchrony cascades inexorably toward an unforeseeable disaster, might be in the order of billions-to-one and far too insignificant, in isolation, to affect a reliability calculation. But where

---

[11] There is relatively little that engineers can do to limit such accidents. Efforts to learn from Normal Accidents to prevent their reoccurrence offer little comfort. Partly because where there are a billion potential "billion-to-one sequences" that might instigate an accident, then it is logical to anticipate an accident but not the same accident twice. The exact confluence of faulty valves, miswired warning lights, and errant tags implicated in TMI might never realign if the same plant ran, unaltered, for ten thousand "groundhog" years. And partly because Normal Accidents offer few lessons with broad applicability, they do not challenge common engineering understandings and theories about the world. The errors that combine to produce them are rarely surprising in themselves. A stuck valve usually reveals little about valves, for example, and would do almost nothing to challenge the engineering underlying their design. Valves sometimes stick; this is why they come with warning lights and redundancies.

potentially dangerous systems have millions of interacting elements that allow for billions of unexpected events and interactions, then seemingly "impossible" billion-to-one coincidences are only to be expected (i.e. they are normal).[12] So it is, he explains, that trivial but irrepressible irregularities – the background static of normal technological practice – when taken together, have inherent catastrophic potential in certain kinds of systems.

Nuclear reliability calculations are blind to this. Indeed, NAT, when construed in this way, offers in-principle reasons to believe that Normal Accidents *necessarily* elude quantification. The events that combine to trigger them are not unusual enough in themselves to constitute a "signal" or "deviance" that is distinguishable from the innumerable other idiosyncrasies of a typically functional technological system. And given that they are billion-to-one coincidences, it is impossible to say which anomalies and interactions will be involved. So even if, with hindsight, experts might identify the specific factors that contribute to a specific Normal Accident, they cannot enumerate them in advance, no matter how rigorous their practices. The Normal Accident occupies a blind spot in our technologies of control. Formal reliability calculations cannot hope to capture the multiplicity of seemingly trivial eventualities inherent in a nuclear plant or the probability of them combining in ways that make them "non-trivial," and this should have far-reaching implications for the credibility of nuclear reliability calculations. "The Normal Accident cannot be prevented" writes Perrow (1984: 176). It cannot be predicted either.

3.4 Epistemic limitations

A third and final reason to doubt the credibility of nuclear reliability assessments lies in recognizing the uncertainties inherent in the knowledge on which they rest.

Soon after the publication of WASH-1400, the NRC's pioneering probabilistic study of reactor safety, a member of an official panel convened to review the report wrote of it that "many of the underlying facts, which must be known to accurately predict the course of an accident, are lacking [hence] the quantitative estimates of the probability of the various accident chains must be viewed with some reservations" (Okrent 1978: 17). This one comment makes explicit a facet of nuclear reliability assessments that is obvious in principle but easily forgotten in practice: that they are wholly dependent on *theoretical models* of the technologies about which they speak.

---

[12] As Churchill once wrote in respect to a naval mishap: the terrible "ifs" have a way of accumulating.

To see the significance of this, we should first understand that there are *no statistically relevant failure-data that regulators can use to "infer" the reliability of nuclear plants*. In other words, we cannot see how reliable reactors are by studying their performance (see e.g. van de Poel 2011: 286). The extraordinarily high reliability required of such plants, combined with the relatively small number of them in operation (around 400 in 2011), and the great diversity of their designs[13] (which limits the relevance of one plant's performance to the performance of others), means that the service lives of different designs would count for very little in a statistical sense. Even if we were to accept the tenuous arguments of nuclear regulators that past accidents have no bearing on other reliability assessments (see Downer 2013) and treat the industry's reliability record as flawless, then nuclear reliability calculations could be off by orders of magnitude and we would not know from the historical record.[14] Nuclear plants, as van de Poel (2011) puts it, are "social experiments."

We should further understand that without statistically relevant failure-data from which to extrapolate, calculations of *how often* nuclear plants might fail come to hinge entirely on understandings of *why* they might fail. Since experts cannot *test* the reliability of nuclear plants empirically, in other words, they must *derive* it theoretically, and to do this they rely on models of *how* plants work (or fail to).[15] Implicit in these models are a vast array of scientific and technical knowledge-claims: a spectrum of "facts" pertaining to everything from the frequency of possible earthquakes in a particular region, to the way that different materials fatigue, and much else besides. These knowledge-claims are "fractal" in the sense that the closer one looks the more there is to know. Knowledge about the fatigue behavior of a specific metal pipe, for instance, must be tempered by knowledge about the way that metal behaves under different kinds of stress (radiological, heat, pressure, age, etc.), which in turn requires knowledge about the stresses to which it will be subject, and so on.

The accuracy of a plant's reliability calculations (and the reliability of the plant) hinges on the accuracy of these knowledge claims, and even small

---

[13] At the broadest level, reactors can be divided into "types," such as Pressurized Water Reactors, Boiling Water Reactors, Pressurized Heavy Water Reactors, Gas cooled Reactors, Molten Salt Reactors, and others. These types can then be divided into "generations" (the industry regularly divides Pressurized Water Reactors into three generations, for example). Even reactors of the same type and generation are "bespoke" in that they are tailored by the manufacturers to suit specific local conditions, such as seismic requirements – a process that creates significant variation between otherwise "identical" plants.

[14] Especially since official accounts of nuclear accidents routinely encourage us to treat them as "unique" and "unrepresentative" (see Downer 2013).

[15] In many ways, designing a reliable nuclear plant and assessing that plant's reliability are essentially the same problem.

errors in the latter can be highly destabilizing for the former.[16] A small theoretical shift in the science of geology, for example, might have large ramifications for the study of seismology, and even larger ramifications for the nuclear reliability calculations (and plant designs) that invoke seismic assumptions. The silent promise of nuclear reliability assessments, we might say, is that the "underlying facts" on which they draw have been established well enough to support the conclusions drawn from them. As those "facts" increase in number and intricacy, however, and as the conclusions drawn from them become more precise and exacting, the less plausible this promise becomes. Given that nuclear reliability calculations draw on a wide range of complex facts to make very exacting claims, therefore, there are strong reasons to doubt their credibility.

The idea that nuclear plants (and their assessments) are built on uncertain and evolving knowledge-claims should not be surprising. The oldest nuclear plants in operation today, for instance, have designs premised on seismic estimates that pre-date the general acceptance of plate tectonics and continental drift by the scientific community – a fact that probably goes some way toward explaining why the earthquake that felled Fukushima was fifteen times more powerful than the maximum shock envisaged by its designers.[17] Nuclear engineering is not exceptional in this respect. Many empirical studies of high-technology engineering in other spheres have concluded that the discipline's orderly public image routinely belies a "messy reality" of real technological practice, where experts frequently operate with high levels of ambiguity and routinely make uncertain judgments based on unproven theories (e.g. Turner 1976: 379; Rip 1986; Vaughan 1996; Turner and Pidgeon 1997: 14).

It is tempting to see such uncertainty as a solvable problem, requiring only an unprecedented degree of rigor on the part of nuclear engineering – an unprecedented willingness to verify every fact. Yet modern philosophers, sociologists, and historians of science reject, on principle, the idea that any knowledge claims are, or could be, determined completely and unambiguously (e.g. Kuhn 1962; Bloor 1976; Collins 1985). Their arguments – applied specifically to engineering knowledge by scholars such as Pinch and Bijker (1984) and MacKenzie (1996) – suggest that technological "facts" are best understood as hypotheses, which contain fundamental ambiguities even when subject to the most rigorous tests and experiments.[18]

---

[16] Another way in which they might be considered "fractal."
[17] Or consider the accident at Three Mile Island, which illustrated the truth of a posited zirconium–water reaction that some scientists had deemed impossible (one of whom was the principal advisor to the Governor during the accident) (Perrow 2011: 51).
[18] Petroski (1992: 104) makes an analogous argument from within engineering.

Among the observations used to support this claim is that tests and experiments are always imperfect *representations* of the real world (e.g. MacKenzie 1990, 1996; Pinch 1993; Krohn and Weyer 1994; Downer 2007). They do not reproduce the world exactly, only re-create it in key respects. Ideally, tests and experiments reproduce the variables that "matter" and ignore the rest, but determining which is which can be complicated. To say that laboratory tests have demonstrated that a simple steel pipe can withstand the stresses of a magnitude 5.0 earthquake, for instance, is to say that the laboratory simulation of the earthquake was "adequately similar" to a real-life earthquake for the test to be meaningful.[19] Yet implicit in this claim are a vast number of ancillary questions about representativeness. Not only must the tester consider the many nuances of a 5.0 earthquake, for example, but they must consider the pipe itself. Will its age affect the test? (Tests that examine a new pipe might not capture the performance of a pipe that has been in place for thirty years.) What if it has been subject to low-level radiological bombardment or an acidic environment? What if it contains manufacturing imperfections? What if it has been damaged by routine maintenance? In principle, there is no end to such "what if" questions. Every technological test is "theory-laden," therefore, in that it contains myriad theoretical judgments about representativeness, and it is ambiguous to the extent that the tester cannot be certain those judgments are accurate.

It is easy to imagine that the esoteric misgivings of epistemologists have little practical bearing on the kinds of knowledge invoked by engineers. Critics of such "constructivist" accounts of technical knowledge often argue that the judgments embedded in facts only have meaningful ramifications at the frontiers of theoretical knowledge where there is heightened uncertainty. For even if it is true, in an austere philosophical sense, that there are judgments and uncertainties invested in even the most basic knowledge claims, it is clearly foolish to question most established "truths." Such critics further point out that engineering rarely works at the theoretical frontier. It is more concerned with *application* than with *discovery*, they argue, and, as such, has long been comfortable with theories that "work" even if they are not strictly speaking "true." (Newtonian mechanics, for instance, is perfectly adequate for most terrestrial ballistics calculations.)

Constant (1999) offers the clearest articulation of this argument. He concedes that "absolute truth" is an elusive concept, but points to engineering's pragmatic concerns to suggest that the epistemic ambiguities are largely irrelevant to our understanding of technical systems. Unlike scientific theories, he says, most of our artifacts are continuously being tested, and, as he bluntly

---

[19] Or, alternatively, that the testers understand the peculiarities of the lab well enough to know exactly how the pipe's test performance will relate to its "real world" performance.

puts it, "most of our stuff more or less works most of the time" (1999: 336, 331). From his perspective, philosophical efforts to highlight the contingencies of engineering knowledge are making an inconsequential observation. He calls them "the intellectual equivalent of looking through the wrong end of the telescope" (1999: 331).

Arguments such as Constant's have their own limitations, however, especially in the rarified sphere of nuclear engineering. It is true that epistemological deconstructions of engineering knowledge are inconsequential in many circumstances. Yet several studies (e.g. MacKenzie 1990; Downer 2011a) suggest that there are circumstances where epistemological concerns have meaningful consequences for "real-world" engineering, and there are reasons to believe that such concerns should have considerable bearing on nuclear reliability assessments. Indeed, a strong argument can be made that, relative to most technological systems, nuclear plants have an exceptional relationship to epistemological uncertainty. This is for two main reasons:

The first reason that nuclear engineering has an exceptional relationship to uncertainty is that, unlike most engineering spheres, it *does* invoke the frontiers of theoretical knowledge. Nuclear plants invoke highly specialized processes (such as fission), materials (such as enriched uranium), and operating conditions (radioactivity; temperatures; reliability demands; etc.) with which there is limited working experience. As a result, nuclear engineers must lean more heavily on scientific models and untested assumptions than their colleagues in other spheres – there is a lesser degree to which they can be content with what "works" as opposed to what is "true." This, in turn, makes the judgments implicit in their tests and models more difficult. The science implicated in a nuclear plant is newer and more challenging than that in most other safety-critical industrial systems, in other words, and this makes mistakes more likely.[20]

A second reason that nuclear plants have an unusual relationship to uncertainty is because of the unusual degree of reliability they require. The extent to which nuclear plants invoke the frontiers of theoretical knowledge is difficult to quantify, but the reliability required of them is much less equivocal. As we saw in detail above, the reliability demands of nuclear plants are extraordinarily high. So high, in fact, that they cannot be tested

---

[20] Engineers can arguably compensate for such difficulties with generous design margins, and system-level protections such as redundancy. These techniques are themselves theory-laden, however. Generous design margins presuppose judgments about "how" a system will fail, for instance, while redundancies imply judgments about "common-mode" failures and much else besides (Downer 2011b). For an example of how both can be misleading, see Downer (2011a). Although such practices undoubtedly make systems safer, they do not therefore help quantify that safety. Their effects are already folded into nuclear reliability assessments – a process involving many questionable judgments about their efficacy.

empirically, which, again, makes nuclear reliability assessments unusually dependent on theoretical models. This dependence on models distinguishes nuclear engineering from other engineering spheres and gives it a different relationship to epistemological uncertainty. In few other systems do expert understandings of *how reliably* a system functions hinge so completely on expert understandings of *how* the system functions. A laptop manufacturer need not fully understand *how* its graphics chips fail in order to know *how often* they fail, as it will learn the failure rate empirically from service data. A reactor manufacturer has no such luxury; it must work with mean-times-to-failure of millions of years – far too long to accrue relevant service data. All its reliability assessments must be derived from its theory-laden understanding of *how* the system works, and all its assessments are only as good as that understanding. The result, inevitably, is a much higher degree of uncertainty.

The extraordinary reliability demanded of nuclear plants has a dual effect. It not only introduces an unusual degree of *uncertainty* into assessment calculations by making them more dependent on theoretical assumptions, but, ironically, it simultaneously demands from those same calculations an unusual degree of *certainty* that those assumptions are correct. This is because the higher the reliability that an assessment must claim, the more error-free its theoretical judgments must be. A reliability calculation claiming a system will fail no more than "once in every hundred hours" can afford to invoke laboratory tests that overlook unrepresentative circumstances that occur "once in every hundred thousand hours"; a reliability calculation claiming a system will fail no more than "once in every billion hours" cannot. Even the most obscure flaws in a model are more likely to reveal themselves over an extremely long time frame.

This is all to say that nuclear engineers (and those who would assess the reliability of nuclear plants) are exposed to the epistemological dilemmas highlighted by philosophers and sociologists of science in a way that few other engineering spheres can match. The result, inevitably, is there can be no credible means of demonstrating that the critical assumptions underpinning the design of a nuclear plant are accurate enough to justify the reliability that nuclear plants require. Simply put: Nuclear reliability calculations are built on models, those models are built on knowledge claims, those knowledge claims are built on tests, and those tests contain human choices, judgments, and assumptions that go beyond the available evidence. Thus, there is always a meaningful possibility that that one of the "facts" underpinning a nuclear reliability assessment is tragically erroneous, such that a real-world event will challenge a nuclear plant in a way that an essential test or model did not predict – what I have elsewhere called an "Epistemic Accident" (Downer 2011a).

3.5 Conclusion

The arguments outlined above are not expressed in the language of engineering, but, for the most part, nuclear risk experts explicitly recognize their logic. Arguments about "framing limitations," for instance, closely echo what the assessment literature often refers to as "Incompleteness Uncertainty" (e.g. IAEA 2010: 53). The arguments about epistemology, meanwhile, echo what is sometimes referred to as "Modeling Uncertainty" (e.g. IAEA 2010: 53). What the engineering literature does not recognize, however, is their significance. Having outlined the dilemmas of "incompleteness uncertainty" in a document on the application of risk[21] assessment, for instance, the IAEA simply states "It is not possible to address this type of uncertainty explicitly" and then moves on. The same document says little more about other uncertainties, except to note that they might be partially addressed by generous error margins and uncertainty studies, as if such measures would not be subject to the same shortcomings.

The simple act of registering these uncertainties covers the responsibility of most official reports, which invariably have other agendas to which to attend. As the authors of those reports would justifiably contend, proper consideration of the sociopolitical implications of uncertainty would rightly be the focus of separate studies. Those studies are never undertaken, however, despite (or perhaps *because* of) their potential significance.

Nuclear risk assessments are foundational to all policy-making around national energy options, implicated, as they are, in everything from economic cost–benefit analyses to academic theories of risk perception. Yet nuclear risk assessments have feet of clay. They are premised on formal reliability calculations, and it does not take a degree in nuclear engineering to see that these calculations are necessarily "imperfect judgments" rather than "objective facts."

The sociotechnical systems required to harness nuclear fission are complex and sophisticated. These systems must operate in an unbounded world that encompasses events far outside the traditional purview of engineers – terrorist acts, armed conflicts, "Acts of God," and much else besides. Inherent in their designs are innumerable latent coincidences – tragic "Hollywood scenarios" like Three Mile Island, which are collectively meaningful even if they are individually trivial. Those designs also embody a vast spectrum of complex knowledge-claims, many pertaining to esoteric and contested sciences. Any full calculation of the likelihood of a nuclear accident would have to itemize and quantify all of these variables. And any calculation that sought to demonstrate that accidents are so unlikely as to be negligible (relative to the prospective

---

[21] The industry prefers the term "safety."

hazards) would have to perform these tasks with an almost unimaginable level of precision. For in a context where plants must run for decades and failures can jeopardize major cities, even the most improbable coincidences, ambiguities, and eventualities become meaningful.

This high bar for performance and, more significantly, for *proof of performance*, sets the nuclear world apart from other engineering spheres. In the vast majority of engineering contexts it is impractical to consider one-in-a-billion oversights, errors, or coincidences. When calculating reliabilities on which the fates of cities depend, however, it is impractical not to. Although it is intuitive to think of nuclear plants in the same way we think of other engineered systems, therefore, our knowledge about them is meaningfully distinct. The potential dangers they pose necessitate levels of reliability that cannot be credibly established as a pragmatic matter.

A pervasive deference to the authority of reliability calculations has left modern states institutionally blind to the possibility of nuclear meltdowns. The arguments outlined in this chapter suggest that the industry's sparse, but damning accident record accurately reflects the presence of structural shortcomings in its regulatory assessments. They show that formal reliability calculations – and hence the risk assessments that depend on those calculations – are spurious. And if nuclear risk assessments are spurious, then so too are the many narratives they inform. This means the historical, psychological, and sociological investigations that invoke those risk assessments to frame the nuclear energy in relation to a tension between its "objective hazards," on one hand, and a seemingly incommensurable level "public fear" on the other.[22] It means the many cost–benefit studies that invoke formal risk claims to justify excluding accidents from their calculations. And, not least, it means the regulatory, policy, and public debates that routinely disregard existential threats to major metropolitan areas because those threats are "hypothetical" rather than "credible."

---

[22] Which, it should be noted, is far from the entirety of historical, psychological, and sociological literature around nuclear energy.

4 Rights to know and the Fukushima, Chernobyl, and Three Mile Island accidents[1]

Kristin Shrader-Frechette

4.1 Introduction

Virtually all democratic nations, international organizations, and labor and consumer groups affirm the public's right to know any information that could cause serious harm. This negative right is a protection against any person or group who might attempt to withhold, misrepresent, or manipulate information that is necessary for people to protect themselves. Yet, official government, industry, and UN International Atomic Energy Agency (IAEA) pronouncements – about the 2011 Fukushima (Japan), 1986 Chernobyl (Ukraine), and 1979 Three Mile Island (US) nuclear accidents – have misrepresented information about the severity and consequences of all these accidents. As a result, they have violated citizens' rights to know and therefore likely increased the death and injury rates associated with these accidents. This (chapter (1) outlines the basic scientific-medical facts about the three nuclear accidents; (2) illustrates official IAEA–government–industry misrepresentation of accident-caused health harms at each location; (3) argues that mainly because of IAEA, government, and industry misrepresentation of the accident harms, they violated citizens' rights to know; and (4) suggests some of the reasons that this misrepresentation has occurred.

4.2 The right to know

In 2006 in Iceland, Sunshine Press began WikiLeaks, the internet non-profit organization that publishes news leaks and secret or classified information. In 2010, WikiLeaks achieved its first great triumph when *The New York Times,*

---

[1] Parts of this chapter rely on K. Shrader-Frechette. 2012. Nuclear Catastrophe, Disaster-Related Environmental Injustice, and Fukushima. *Environmental Justice* 5 (3): 133–139 and Shrader-Frechette, K. 2011. *What Will Work: Fighting Climate Change with Renewable Energy, Not Nuclear Power.* New York: Oxford University Press: 130–160.

The Guardian, Der Spiegel, Le Monde, and *El País* published parts of secret military cables between the US State Department and diplomats that documented "collateral murder," deaths of innocent civilians because of US wars in Iraq and Afghanistan. It also released classified videos showing US Army helicopters that killed journalists in the streets of Baghdad. In 2011 WikiLeaks published damning secret files concerning treatment of detainees in the Guantanamo Bay prison. In 2012 it released millions of emails concerning the Texas company Stratfor, which, for contracted fees, provides "global intelligence." In 2013 WikiLeaks published infamous cables from then-US-Secretary-of-State and later Nobel Laureate, Henry Kissinger, which confirmed his unethical, illegal, and unconstitutional activities, especially in other nations (Roberts 2011).

In response to these WikiLeaks activities, a Norwegian politician claimed its founders had helped "redraw the map of information freedom," and he nominated them for the Nobel Peace Prize. Although the US government has attempted to prosecute WikiLeaks officials, a *New York Times* editorial affirmed that people have "a right to know what is being done in their name" (Roberts 2011).

Although ethicists and politicians may disagree about whether WikiLeaks' leaders were justified in their attempts to protect citizens "rights to know," these rights themselves are beyond dispute. They are a central part of democratic theory, medical ethics, economic theory, and consumer policy. Rights to know are essential if people and governments are to recognize the principle of autonomy, essential to personhood. They are also essential to personal or governmental assignment of praise and blame, freedom or punishment, because autonomy is the capacity of a rational individual to make an informed, uncoerced decision. Hence for ethicists, autonomy is the main basis for determining moral responsibility and accountability for one's actions and omissions.

Kant and many ethicists likewise affirm that what creates the core of human dignity is autonomy, the ability to make one's own decisions, the ability to impose an objective moral law on oneself. However, this ability is contingent on having full information and hence a right to know. Thus, according to basic ethical theory, autonomy is necessary for human dignity and rights to know are necessary for autonomy. It thus follows that, when these rights to know are violated, human autonomy is jeopardized, as in the infamous Nazi medical experiments. This horrifying and exploitative experimental treatment of Jews, Roma, leftists, and political prisoners violated both the subjects' physical integrity and their personal autonomy – because personal autonomy requires that people have rights to know what potentially harmful things are done or will be done to them by others – so that they can attempt to protect themselves and to give or withhold consent.

In international human rights law and in biomedical ethics, autonomy is typically understood as self-determination, and self-determination obviously requires rights to know the potential risks and harms that others might impose on oneself (e.g. Merlo et al. 2007). However, because no rights are absolute, completely unfettered by considerations such as claims to other rights (e.g. Richardson 2004), all rights are *prima facie*. That is, they put the burden of proof on the potential violator, but they can sometimes be overridden by more important duties or considerations. Thus the exercise of rights, including rights to know, always requires *ultima facie* justification. That is why a citizen might have *ultima facie* rights to know what chemicals some industry is releasing in his neighborhood, but a criminal might not have *ultima facie* rights to know the address of witnesses who have testified against him in court.

4.3 Rights to know about nuclear-accident threats

Because both international and national law, at least in democratic societies, recognize rights to know pollutant harms imposed on citizens, often for the profit of polluters (e.g. US Environmental Protection Agency [EPA] 2013), no ethics justification is required to affirm this *ultima facie* right. Indeed, virtually all democratic societies affirm the specific "right to know" of community members who might be threatened by releases of toxins (Ashford and Caldart 1996, 2008). Because these rights are often necessary to protect lives, health, and personal autonomy, it is difficult to imagine many circumstances in which rights to know environmental harms can be overridden – except perhaps in cases in which full disclosure might cause mass panic and thus even greater numbers of deaths.

Indeed, the IAEA, affiliated with the UN and charged with both promoting nuclear energy and protecting people from it, explicitly affirms the public's right to know about nuclear-related harm. In the face of radiological threats and reactor accidents, it explicitly affirms the public's right to know (IAEA 2002: 3; 2012: 16).

Given the clear defensibility of rights to know about environmental threats to life, given explicit, self-imposed IAEA mandates to recognize the rights to know of the public, and given IAEA duties to monitor and correct the nuclear-related behavior of both industry and nation-states, has the IAEA kept its word? Has it recognized and protected citizens' rights to know about threats posed by nuclear accidents? Consider the 2011 Fukushima (Japan), the 1986 Chernobyl (Ukraine), and the 1979 Three Mile Island (USA) nuclear accidents. The remainder of this (chapter (1) outlines each of these three catastrophes, (2) reveals the erroneous government, industry, and IAEA information about these accidents, (3) argues that this nuclear disinformation has violated nuclear victims' rights to know, and (4) suggests some of the reasons that might explain these violations. Consider first the Japanese nuclear accident.

4.4 The 2011 Fukushima, Japan accident

Until March 11, 2011 atomic energy supplied about 30 percent of Japanese electricity. By May 2012, all Japanese commercial nuclear reactors were closed (Inaiima and Okada 2012). Despite massive citizen protests, some began to go back online (Associated Press 2012). By mid-2013, however, only two Japanese reactors were operating (Koike et al. 2013). What happened?

Beginning on March 11, 2011, multiple earthquakes and a tsunami hit Japan. They left nearly 16,000 dead; more than 3,000 missing; more than 6,000 injured; and still more to die from radiation-induced cancer from damaged Japanese nuclear reactors (Johnston 2012). After flooding cut cooling water to the Fukushima Daiichi reactors, radioactive fuel pools, nuclear plant fires, three reactor meltdowns, extremely intense radioactive releases, and at least four explosions occurred. They spewed radioactive contamination around the globe. Roofs and walls blew off several reactors. Gaping holes appeared in radioactive containment. Nuclear fuel melted through thick steel-and-concrete reactor bottoms. Plant radiation doses soared to 500 millisievert (mSv)/hour, roughly a million times higher than normal background radiation. Data from the United Nations International Agency for Research on Cancer (IARC) predict that after only two hours, these doses would cause all the cancers of those exposed. Massachusetts Institute of Technology (MIT) nuclear engineering PhD, Kenichi Ohmae says that "from the amount of fission material released and from the size of the hydrogen explosions," the core melts and containment catastrophes were "undeniable." Yet, the Japanese government denied the meltdowns for three months and denied radioactive-containment destruction for six months (Ohmae 2012).

The Fukushima utility, Tokyo Electric Power Company (TEPCO), was a partner in the cover-up (Taira and Hatoyama 2011; Funabashi and Kitazawa 2012; Normile 2012; Wang and Chen 2012). Nine months after the accident began, in late 2011, TEPCO announced the three melted reactors were in "cold shutdown." Yet months later, high radiation levels still prevent workers from entering the entire plant (Nishikawa 2012). Even outside the buildings, TEPCO says radiation levels could kill someone within 15 minutes (Saoshiro and Layne 2011). In 2013, more than a year after the cold-shutdown claim, radioactively contaminated water continues to leak into the Pacific. The cooling system for four radioactive fuel ponds at three reactors suddenly failed for 30 hours, threatening massive radiation releases. Months after the cold-shutdown claim, a leaking reactor gushed 8.5 tons of radioactive water and was not stopped for another month. The science journal *Nature* says the severely damaged reactors and radioactive fuel pools will continue leaking radioactivity "for another few years at least ... TEPCO must continue to [actively] inject water at the rate of around half-a-million liters a day." The eventual cleanup will take many decades, but given still-lethal radiation levels, no one knows when it can begin (Brumfiel 2011). Such a situation seems hardly a cold shutdown.

Late in 2013, more than two years after the catastrophe began, Japanese nuclear engineers say it remains a catch-22 because all alternative ways of removing damaged nuclear fuel rods could kill many people. "If you hoist them up in the air, huge amounts of radiation will come out ... and people nearby will die" (Dutzki and Madsen 2012; Whitney 2012; BBC News Asia 2013). Yet, not removing them will also kill many people when the damaged facility collapses entirely. Former US nuclear-industry Vice-President Arnold Gunderson warns this collapse could "destroy the world environment and our civilization," creating "a disaster worse than the three [Fukushima] reactor meltdowns ... People should get out of Japan and residents of the West Coast of America and Canada should shut all of their windows and stay inside" (Whitney 2012).

Did Japanese and nuclear authorities tell the truth about the Fukushima accident? Or did they violate rights to know of accident victims? On one hand, more than two years after the accident, several hundred thousand people are still displaced from their homes. Unremediated, radioactive soils contaminate areas of Tokyo, 200 miles away, including some playgrounds and schools. In the USA, such soils would be considered radioactive waste, dug up, and shipped to waste management sites (Gunderson 2012). Physicians for Social Responsibility, winners of the 1985 Nobel Peace Prize, says continuing Fukushima radiation releases could be several times greater than those from Chernobyl. Fukushima cesium releases, alone, already are more than those from 168 Hiroshima bombs. The pro-nuclear US Nuclear Regulatory Commission (NRC) likewise warns that Fukushima threats and "catastrophic explosions. ... could persist indefinitely" – one reason the international scientific community and US government recommended a Fukushima 50-mile-radius, 2-million-people evacuation (Shrader-Frechette 2011a, 2012; von Hippel 2011; Foster 2013).

On the other hand, the Japanese government, financially responsible for cleanup, used a 12-mile-radius, 130,000-people evacuation, and claimed it was safe. The government also says stress, not radiation, is the accident's main consequence: "If you live in an area outside of the [12-mile radius] evacuation area, you do not need to worry about ... receiving any radiation at all ... If you worry too much about radiation, it causes mental and physical instability" (Japanese MEXT 2011). Obviously, however, people outside the 12-mile evacuation area received much higher radiation doses than normal – which is why the international scientific community urged Japan to increase its evacuation area. Obviously, also, it is false to say no dangerous radiation would be received outside the evacuation zone, both because of contamination in areas such as Tokyo and because there is no safe dose of ionizing radiation (National Research Council/National Academy of Sciences 2006). Denying the claims of the international scientific community, the Japanese government likewise says Fukushima released only about one-tenth as much radiation as Chernobyl. Yet Fukushima had three times more meltdowns, four times more explosions, and much more radioactive fuel than Chernobyl (von Hippel 2011).

The World Health Organization says the Fukushima area, and especially children, will experience up to a 70 percent increase in some solid cancers, breast cancers, and thyroid cancers – all known to be radiosensitive cancers (Albert 2013). Yet, the main international nuclear-industry lobby group, the World Nuclear Association (WNA), continued the misrepresentation of the Japanese accident, and IAEA said nothing. WNA wrote that people living near the damaged Fukushima atomic energy plant "received such low doses of radiation that no discernible health effect" is expected. Instead, the nuclear industry said that "widespread exaggerated fears of the risks posed by contamination ... the stresses of ... the Fukushima nuclear accident, have emerged as the biggest factors in ill health for Japanese people" (World Nuclear News 2012).

4.5 The 1986 Chernobyl (Ukraine) accident

Similar official denials of harm took place after the 1986 Chernobyl accident. On April 26, 1986 an explosion and fire occurred at the Chernobyl nuclear plant in Ukraine, which was then part of the Union of Soviet Socialist Republics or Soviet Union. The accident released massive amounts of ionizing radiation into the atmosphere, especially over Belarus, Ukraine, and Russia, and these radionuclides quickly spread over much of Europe and later around the globe. More than 500,000 workers – most without dosimeters and protective equipment – worked to contain the radioactivity and prevent a more massive catastrophe (Shrader-Frechette 2011a).

However, the official Soviet Union casualty count for the Chernobyl accident was thirty-one deaths, and the IAEA claimed that the accident caused at most fifty to fifty-six fatalities (IAEA 1991; WNA 2008). Contrary to this IAEA Chernobyl claim, a UN public-health investigation called the Chernobyl accident "the greatest technological catastrophe in human history" (Savchenko 1995: 11). Because of the long half-lives of many of the radionuclides, the investigators warned that the radioactivity released by Chernobyl would never disappear completely from the biosphere

(Savchenko 1995: 5). They said that during 1986–90, 30 km from the reactor, only 4 years after the accident, there was a 50 percent increase in the average frequency of thyroid disorders, malignancies, and neoplasms. Leukemia increased by 50 percent, and there were major increases in the rates of miscarriages, still births and children born with genetic malformations (Savchenko 1995: 65). Less than six years after the accident, already there was a hundredfold increase in thyroid cancers in Belarus, Russia, and Ukraine (Henshaw 1996: 1052; Rytömaa 1996). Scientists documented a doubling of germline mutations in children born only eight years after, and 400 km away from, the Chernobyl accident (Dubrova et al. 1996, 2006). Twenty years after the accident, the journal *Nature* documented a doubling in breast cancer in the most heavily Chernobyl-exposed areas of Belarus and Ukraine, and an excess of several thousand Chernobyl-induced cancers in the three nations most affected by Chernobyl; yet because of the long cancer latency, full Chernobyl cancers will not appear for at least another twenty years (Williams and Baverstock 2006; Shrader-Frechette 2011a).

Even more disturbing, Chernobyl caused massive genomic instability. This is the phenomenon in which ionizing radiation not only increases mutation rates in the exposed somatic cells, but also causes elevated mutation rates many cell divisions – and generations – after the initial radiation damage (Barber et al. 2006; Hatch et al. 2007). These delayed transgenerational effects of ionizing radiation also cause increased cancers and many other damaging health effects in later generations – in people not even exposed to the offending radiation (Dubrova 2003; Dubrova et al. 2008; Shrader-Frechette 2011a).

Given the preceding Chernobyl health effects, it is troubling that the IAEA could claim no more than fifty Chernobyl fatalities. It knows that the radio-nuclides deposited by the Chernobyl accident have half-lives from tens, to hundreds of thousands, to millions of years. These airborne, soil-borne, food-borne, water-borne, and ingested radionuclides will cause serious long-term effects and will continue to re-expose citizens for centuries, especially given that millions of people are still living in contaminated areas, especially in Belarus (Hohenemser et al. 1986). This ongoing contamination will add to very long-term human and environmental radiation doses (Cardis et al. 2003; WHO 2006a, 2006b). These health effects will be substantial, despite the fact that many nations still impose Chernobyl-caused quarantines on local crops and farm animals, often because of cesium-137 contamination. For instance, sheep in the UK are quarantined; likewise reindeer in Finland, Norway, Russia, and Sweden (Wright et al. 2003; IAEA et al. 2006: 25; Beresford et al. 2008). Berries, mushrooms, and fish in many European countries are likely to be quarantined at least until 2050 (Nisbet and Woodman 2000; Kritidis and Florou 2001; Anspaugh 2007). At the current time, biologists continue to show reduced numbers of animals near Chernobyl, as a function of radiation dose, a fact indicating that the accident's effects on animals has been massive (Moller and Mousseau 2009; Shrader-Frechette 2011a).

Given the preceding food chain, genomic instability, and other health effects, some scientists say total Chernobyl-induced fatal cancers may rise to about 475,000 (Zakharov 1988; Gofman 1995: 1–2). If one ignores cancers caused by ongoing mutations in future generations, a reduced Chernobyl-fatality count might be like that published in *Nature*: 125,000 deaths (Campbell 1996). Just from cesium-137, a single radioactive isotope of the hundreds of types of radioisotopes released at Chernobyl, the nuclear-industry research group (the Electric Power Research Institute) and the US Lawrence Livermore Laboratories calculate between 17,400 and 51,000 additional, fatal, Chernobyl-induced cancers, just in this generation (Anspaugh et al. 1988; Smith 2007). Obviously, therefore, the IAEA claim of fifty Chernobyl fatalities is false (Shrader-Frechette 2011a).

4.6   The 1979 Three Mile Island, Pennsylvania accident

Similar information problems beset the March 28, 1979 US nuclear accident in Dauphin County, Pennsylvania, the worst accident in US commercial nuclear power plant history. The partial meltdown at the Three Mile Island (TMI) plant resulted in both intentional and unintentional releases of radioactive gases such as xenon and krypton, as well as radioactive iodine into the environment.

Although the US government and nuclear industry claim "no member of the public died" because of Three Mile Island, virtually all university medical scientists who have studied the case disagree (Herbst and Hopley 2007: 138; WNA 2008). They say it has killed and will kill thousands of people prematurely. Four years after the accident, epidemiologists agree that a 64 percent cancer-incidence increase occurred within 10 miles of the plant (Hatch et al. 1990; Talbott et al. 2003). Nevertheless, epidemiologists disagree about what caused this increase. Holding the majority position, nuclear-industry-funded scientists say stress has caused the deaths. Holding the minority position, independent university and medical scientists say radiation caused most of them.

Because the industry radiation monitors went off-scale because of high doses, and because the utility claimed that many other monitors were somehow "lost," stress-hypothesis proponents typically accept the industry and government assumptions that the Pennsylvania nuclear-accident radiation doses were no more than 100 mrem. This is about one-third of annual background radiation. Consequently, they deny that this level of radiation had any impact on overall mortality (Hatch et al. 1990; Hatch et al. 1991; Talbott et al. 2003). Instead, as occurred at Fukushima and Chernobyl, industry scientists say accident-related stress likely caused nearby cancer and mortality increases (Hatch et al. 1990; Hatch et al. 1991; Susser 1997; Walker 2004: 235; Levin 2009). Scientists supported by nuclear-industry monies from the Three Mile Island Health Fund – mainly at Columbia University and University of Pittsburgh – support the stress position, perhaps because industry spokespeople must approve their study assumptions and protocols (Hatch et al. 1990, 1991; Susser 1997; Talbott et al. 2000, 2003).

Radiation-hypothesis proponents, independent university and medical scientists, who are not funded by the nuclear industry, typically reject industry–government assumptions of low Three Mile Island doses. Consequently they hold the minority position when they say radiation, not stress, likely caused the agreed-upon, increased fatalities (Wing 1995, 2003; Wing et al. 1997; Shrader-Frechette 2011a). These scientists are mostly physicians or epidemiologists working for governmental or nongovernmental agencies or for institutions such as the University of North Carolina (Wing et al. 1997; Wing 2003; Shrader-Frechette 2011a).

For at least four reasons, the radiation-hypothesis proponents appear to be correct about the cause of the devastating TMI-area health harms. That is, at least four reasons suggest that TMI radiation has caused the massive cancer, infant-mortality, and child-retardation increases after the 1979 accident.

1. Most of the post-TMI cancers were radiosensitive cancers, those known to be caused by ionizing radiation. If stress had caused most of these cancers, there would be no reason for most of them to be radiosensitive.
2. Disproportionate numbers of the TMI cancers were respiratory, caused by inhalation of hazards. Yet the TMI releases were radioactive noble gases – precisely material that can be inhaled. If stress had caused most of these TMI cancers, there would be no reason for them to be disproportionately respiratory.
3. TMI cancer increases persisted and were documented hundreds of miles downwind, all the way into the state of Maine, something that easily could have been caused by well-documented, downwind increases in TMI radiation, from hundreds of miles away. Yet people living so far away from TMI, in Maine, had no reason to have stress-induced cancer, particularly because stress proponents claim that the level of cancer/stress is proportional to geographical closeness to the reactor, and people living hundreds of miles away are not close.
4. People living only several miles upwind of the reactor had no cancer increases, yet if proximity to the reactor is the surrogate for stress, and stress caused excess TMI cancers, these upwind people should have had cancers. Yet they did not. However, because these upwind citizens, very

close to TMI, nevertheless were not exposed to TMI radiation, the absence of increased radiation could easily explain the absence of their cancers (Shrader-Frechette 2011a).

4.7 Nuclear-accident violations of rights to know

Given the preceding details about the Japanese, Ukrainian, and US nuclear accidents, is it reasonable to conclude that industry, government, and the IAEA covered up accident harms, perhaps in part to avoid liability losses, industry shutdown, negative publicity, paying for citizen relocation from accident areas, and economic harm to the affected regions? Cover-ups and violations of rights to know seem plausible because of other government and industry denials of nuclear-accident harm. Because one cannot see, hear, feel, touch, or taste ionizing radiation, nuclear core melts often can be covered up. This is what occurred, for instance, in Los Angeles. Industry and government covered up this Santa Susana meltdown until cancer increases, years later, nearby forced release of secret reports (Smith 2007; Shrader-Frechette 2011a: 110–60).

Nuclear-accident cover-ups and violations of rights to know also are consistent with the fact, for instance, that the UN's World Health Organization (WHO) says seven million people are receiving or eligible for benefits as Chernobyl victims, living in radioactively contaminated areas (WHO 2006a, 2006b). They are like the nearly two million Japanese living in Fukushima-contaminated areas from which the international scientific community recommends evacuation. Yet the WHO would not classify these people as victims, if only fifty people had died because of Chernobyl, as the IAEA claims.

Contradicting the WHO, the main international commercial nuclear lobby group, the WNA, blames nuclear-accident victims for their health problems. It says Chernobyl's "ionizing radiation killed only a few occupationally exposed people ... The Chernobyl fallout did not expose the general population to harmful radiation doses ... Psychosomatic disorders ... were the only detectable health consequences among the general population ... Panic and mass hysteria could be regarded as the most important" (WNA 2009). In 2014, the WNA again blamed the victims for stress, claiming Chernobyl's "biological and health effects ... cannot be attributed to radiation exposure ... and are much more likely to be due to psychological factors and stress" (WNA 2014; Giel 1991; Rich 1991). In other words, the nuclear industry blamed the victims of Chernobyl, suggesting their own supposed psychological instability caused their ailments, not radiation.

Is such blaming and denial reasonable? It is not, in part because a prominent international physicians group, winner of the Nobel Peace Price, disagrees. It says Fukushima radiation releases could be several times greater than those from Chernobyl. Even before the radioactive releases stopped, Fukushima cesium releases, alone, equaled those from 168 Hiroshima bombs. The pronuclear US NRC says Fukushima threats and "catastrophic explosions ... could persist indefinitely" – one reason the international scientific community and US government urged a 50-mile-radius, 2-million-people evacuation after the accident (Shrader-Frechette 2011a: 130–60; von Hippel 2011; Foster 2013).

IAEA, government, and nuclear-industry claims, about the trivial nature of the Fukushima, Chernobyl, and TMI nuclear accidents, err for at least eight reasons.

1. As the US National Academy of Sciences confirms, the scientific consensus is that there is no safe dose of ionizing radiation, no matter how small; 35 electronvolt is enough to disrupt DNA and begin the cancer process, and even normal background radiation causes cancer (National Research Council/National Academy of Sciences 2006).
2. For more than thirty years, repeated scientific studies in England, France, Germany, Scotland, the UK, the USA, and elsewhere have confirmed that even normally operating reactors, without accidents, cause nearby cancer increases, especially among children. These normal radiation releases are much smaller than those from the Fukushima, Chernobyl, and TMI accidents (Heasman et al. 1986; Clapp et al. 1987; Forman et al. 1987; Gibson et al. 1988; Gardner et al. 1990; Michaelis et al. 1992; Morris and Knorr 1994; Viel et al. 1995; Watson and Sumner 1996; Busby and Scott-Cato 1997; Viel and Pobel 1997; Mangano 2000, 2002, 2006, 2008; Guizard et al. 2001; Baker and Hoel 2007; Kaatsch et al. 2008; Mangano and Sherman 2008; Spix 2008).
3. As the US National Academy of Sciences confirms, the scientific consensus, based on universally accepted, empirically confirmed, radiation dose–response curves, is that health effects of ionizing radiation are linear, proportional to dose, with no threshold for harm (National Research Council/National Academy of Sciences 2006). This dose–response curve clearly confirms thousands of premature Fukushima, Chernobyl, and TMI casualties.
4. The New York Academy of Scientists affirmed that because of long-term induced genetic defects, cancers, and other diseases, Chernobyl will cause one million premature casualties (Yablokov et al. 2009). According to University of California scientists and physicians, Chernobyl premature cancer fatalities, alone, will be roughly 475,000 (Zakharov 1988; Gofman 1995).
5. Consistent with the findings of the New York Academy of Sciences, the WHO confirmed that the Chernobyl accident released about 200 times more radiation than did the Hiroshima and Nagasaki bombs (WHO 1995). Although the two types/circumstances of radiation exposure were somewhat different, because bomb radiation has caused thousands of premature

fatalities, Chernobyl radiation has caused and will cause hundreds of times more deaths than the bomb radiation.

6. Consistent with the WHO and New York and US National Academy of Sciences findings, twenty years after the accident, respected journals like *Nature* already documented a doubling in breast cancer in Chernobyl-exposed areas of Belarus and Ukraine – and an excess of thousands of Chernobyl-induced cancers in the three nations most affected by Chernobyl; yet because of the long cancer latency, full Fukushima, Chernobyl, and TMI cancers will not appear for at least another fifty years (Williams and Baverstock 2006).

7. Scientists have confirmed genomic instability – the fact that ionizing radiation not only increases mutation rates in exposed somatic cells, but also causes elevated mutation rates that will continue to occur many cell divisions and generations after the initial radiation damage (Barber et al. 2006; Hatch et al. 2007). These delayed transgenerational effects of ionizing radiation will also continue to cause increased cancers and other damaging health effects in later generations, in people not even exposed to the offending radiation (Dubrova et al. 2003, 2008). As one scientist put it, the health effects of Chernobyl's – and other – ionizing radiation will never end, at least not until/unless natural selection and adaptation eliminate these mutations (Savchenko 1995: 5).

8. The radionuclides deposited by the Fukushima, Chernobyl, and TMI accidents have half-lives from tens, to hundreds of thousands, to millions of years. Airborne, soil-borne, food-borne, water-borne and ingested, these radionuclides will cause serious long-term effects, will continue to re-expose citizens for centuries, especially because millions of people are still living in areas of "wide-scale contamination" where ongoing radioactive contamination will harm health for centuries (Hohenemser et al. 1986; Cardis et al. 2003; WHO 2006a, 2006b).

For all the preceding reasons, the IAEA, government, and nuclear industry erred when they said the Fukushima, Chernobyl, and TMI accidents caused no, or trivial, health harms. But if they erred when they misled the public about the consequences of serious nuclear accidents, obviously they violated citizens' rights to know about the hazards they faced. As a result, at least some people probably did not protect themselves as well as they could have done, given correction information about radiation hazards.

4.8 Why there are nuclear-accident violations of rights to know

The preceding data concerning the three major nuclear accidents suggests that the famous US essayist and poet, Ralph Waldo Emerson, was right. He warned that "money often costs too much"; because people frequently seek money as an end, not a means, money can cost them their character, their family, their education, or their happiness (Emerson 1904: 380). The preceding violations of citizens' rights to know, in the face of deadly nuclear accidents, suggest that polluters' desire for money also may be costing them their ethics – and costing the rest of us our health.

What causes polluters to force the rest of us to pay such a high price for their harms? Apart from greed and expediency, one factor is lack of liability. Many polluters are not legally and financially liable for the harm they cause. In the case of nuclear fission, the vast majority of nations do not make nuclear plant owners legally liable at all for any of the harm they cause, even because of deliberate safety violations. Even in the USA, only 1–2 percent of damages from a worst-case nuclear accident are insurable by law; the government gave the nuclear industry protection from liability and, as a result, citizens arguably lost their rights to due process – and to compensation from harm (Shrader-Frechette 2011a, Ch. 2). Moreover, even where polluter liability exists, theoretically, it often cannot be used in many practical cases. This is because, if government does not fund studies to assess the effects of various pollutants, then there often is inadequate evidence, both to make appropriate regulations, and to charge polluters with environmental crimes. Therefore, polluters typically lobby politicians to avoid funding pollution assessments. As a result, for example, only 7 percent of high-production volume chemicals used in US manufacturing and agriculture have ever been assessed for developmental effects or toxicity to children (Landrigan 2001).

Some of the additional factors that cause and worsen environmental pollution include polluters' tendencies to lie about pollution and to blame the victims for the harms, as already illustrated with Fukushima, Chernobyl, and TMI. Polluters often blame the victims because, given a cancer or disease "cluster" in some location, those guilty try to divert blame from themselves. To do so, they must propose another cause of the local pollution. Mounting an ad hominem attack, they try both to discredit their accusers and to divert attention from their own guilt. Blaming victims' alleged mental illness or instability, polluters also focus on an alleged cause of harm that is very difficult to measure or evaluate. Hence polluters can escape responsibility.

Blaming the victim also is often expedient for polluters, because their victims usually do not understand much science. Frequently victims cannot easily explain how or why some pollutant made them ill, especially when polluters manipulate the relevant science to suit their own purposes. That is, polluters often use special-interest science, "science" that has predetermined conclusions and that is done by those focused on protecting their profits, not determining truth (Shrader-Frechette 2007, Chs. 2–3). Special-interest science is performed or funded by industries, special interests, who seek private profits, not public goods like health or unbiased knowledge. They fund scientists to give them what they want, including incomplete, biased "science" affirming that the funders' pollution or products are safe or beneficial. This fact has been repeatedly confirmed for pharmaceutical and medical-devices research, energy-related research, and pollution-related research (Krimsky 2003; Shrader-Frechette 2007, Chs. 2–3; 2011a, Chs. 1–4). It explains why so many industries fund special-interest science. After all, such "science" helped US cigarette manufacturers avoid regulations for more than fifty years. It also explains why fossil-fuel industry "science" denies anthropogenic climate change, and why the nuclear industry, its lobbyists, and governments tied to it attempt to claim erroneously that nuclear fission is cheap, low carbon, plentiful, and able to supply reliable base-load electricity. All these government, industry, and IAEA claims are false. They are false because they rely on flawed, special-interest science, just as accounts of the Fukushima, Chernobyl, and TMI accidents rely on special-interest ethics, ethics that ignores the rights to know of nuclear-accident victims (Shrader-Frechette 2007, 2011a).

4.9 Conclusion

The 2011 Fukushima (Japan), the 1986 Chernobyl (Ukraine), and the 1979 Three Mile Island (USA) nuclear accidents were deadly, and they resulted in the deaths of many people. This chapter has outlined each of these three nuclear accidents; revealed the flawed government, industry, and IAEA information about these accidents; argued that this nuclear disinformation has violated nuclear victims' rights to know; and suggested some of the reasons that might explain these violations of citizens' rights to know. What remains is for all citizens to become informed and active. Citizens must demand their rights to know. Otherwise they cannot protect themselves from deadly technologies.

5 Gender, ethical voices, and UK nuclear energy policy in the post-Fukushima era

Karen Henwood and Nick Pidgeon

5.1 Introduction

How to account for our perceptions of technological, environmental, and health risks has been a focus of empirical, theoretical, and philosophical inquiry within the field of risk research for almost forty years. From this work we know that socio-demographic variables such as age or class do not consistently predict either risk perceptions or the acceptability of nuclear risks. The clear exception to this rule is gender, with a longstanding finding being that male respondents in surveys tend to express lower levels of concern than women when asked about their perceptions of a range of environmental and technological hazards. This gender and risk perception relationship appears particularly pronounced for people's perceptions of nuclear power and radioactive waste as well as other risks, for example those posed by chemicals, which hold the potential for local contamination (Davidson and Freudenburg 1996). Given these findings, it is surprising that none of the traditional accounts of nuclear ethics (e.g. Nye 1986; Shrader-Frechette 2000) take account of the issue of gender or the gendered nature of our understanding of nuclear risks.

In the present chapter we explore how an account we have developed of the gendered nature of risk perceptions might throw light on contemporary ethical and philosophical debates about nuclear energy, a matter that has become of particular policy concern in the UK post-Fukushima. Our argument is that the topic of gender and nuclear ethics is impossible to understand without in-depth consideration of the sociocultural processes leading to the gendering of knowledge displays and epistemic subjectivity in contemporary life, alongside the need to address more fragmented and plural identities. In advancing these arguments, and in contrast to much of the established survey-based research in this field, we draw on theoretical and qualitative interpretive work within discursive social psychology, social studies of science and technology (STS), and associated discussions of justice and care ethics within gender theory. This allows us to create a theoretical synthesis for approaching the gender–risk relationship in relation to nuclear power. We see this relationship as arising from cultural and identity work conducted within readily circulating discourses, and the struggles for recognition of differences in ethical positioning they create. Such an analysis shows that a better understanding of the complexly gendered nature of environmental and risk perceptions has an important role to play in current ethical discussions and philosophical reflections on nuclear energy.

5.2 UK energy policy and public risk perceptions: the devil's bargain

The UK commissioned the world's first commercial nuclear reactor at Calder Hall in Cumbria and greatly expanded its reactor program after the Suez Crisis in 1956 amidst concerns about national energy independence (Welsh 2000). This nuclear dawn proved to be short-lived, however, with the accidents at Three Mile Island and Chernobyl leading to unprecedented levels of public opposition. Rising concerns about nuclear economics also followed in the wake of the privatization of the UK's electricity supply industry in the 1990s, leading to an effective moratorium on the commissioning of any new nuclear capacity in Britain.

In more recent years the debate about nuclear energy in the UK has taken a different turn, with the country adopting the most ambitious decarbonization targets in the world and a commitment in the 2008 Climate Change Act to an 80 percent cut in carbon emissions by 2050. This constraint, alongside a lack of progress in bringing forward genuinely radical low carbon solutions, means that nuclear power has once more attracted policy attention, with current scenarios envisaging 16–75 GW of new nuclear power in Britain by 2050 (DECC 2011).

This increased attention to nuclear options has brought with it attempts to reframe the technology within policy discourses. Framing is one of the means by which policy domains become defined and rendered manageable (Jasanoff 2005). Bickerstaff et al. (2008) observe that from about 2000 some industry representatives, senior UK politicians, and scientists had begun to advocate the low carbon credentials of nuclear energy (also Teravainen et al. 2011). While such discourses are not particularly new (pro-nuclear interests in Germany had advocated them long before this; Weingart et al. 2000), the increasingly urgent need to secure low carbon energy has seen them re-emerge.

In seeking to explore this issue, Bickerstaff et al. (2008) report that in a series of focus groups with members of the public in 2002 discussing both climate change and radioactive waste disposal, participants became more ambivalent and less antagonistic about nuclear power as an energy source when it was explicitly positioned alongside climate change. Nevertheless, few in the groups wholeheartedly supported climate change mitigation through new nuclear build, with participants eventually arriving at the conclusion that the nuclear option represented the lesser of two evils – a *devil's bargain* in the face of the potentially greater risks of climate change. In effect, such support reflected only an ambivalent or "reluctant" acceptance (see also Pidgeon et al. 2008). Furthermore, this discourse was accompanied by a questioning of the risk–risk trade-off implied and a desire to explore other policy framings, alongside a preference for a varied and sustainable energy strategy incorporating investment in renewable energy and reduced demand.

Public acceptability of energy options, not just nuclear power, is important not only because in a democracy policies must remain sensitive to the views of the electorate (Pidgeon 1998), but also because public and interest group opposition had significantly impacted upon the siting processes for both power stations and radioactive waste disposal in the past (Pidgeon and Demski 2012). In its inquiry *Energy – The Changing Climate* the UK Royal Commission on Environmental Pollution concluded: "we do not believe that public opinion will permit the construction of new nuclear power stations unless they are part of a strategy which delivers radical improvements in energy efficiency and an equal opportunity for the deployment of other alternatives to fossil fuels" (2000: 20). The UK government stated in 2003 that, while not including proposals for the construction of new nuclear capacity, it did not exclude the possibility that such an option might be revisited in the future, and that this might indeed "be necessary" to meet the nation's carbon targets (DTI 2003: 12). This statement signaled openly the *political reframing* of nuclear power as a potential component of the UK's future energy strategy. This was followed five years later by a direct endorsement of the technology in *A White Paper on Nuclear Power* (DBER 2008) and publication of industry nominated sites for new nuclear stations. The stage had therefore been set for the UK to include nuclear power in the future generating mix.

Butler et al. (2013) recount how the immediate policy response to the Fukushima Daiichi disaster in March 2011 varied in different countries: either (1) amplification of risk and withdrawal of policy support (e.g. in Germany, Japan, Italy, and Sweden) or (2) a safety review, then attenuation of risk, followed by continued support (e.g. the UK and USA). Similarly, the impact upon public opinion has varied, with an immediate fall in support in many countries. However, in Britain that fall proved only temporary, such that by December 2011 support had returned to levels seen just prior to the accident. In other countries such as Switzerland (Siegrist and Visschers 2013) and the United States (Joskow et al. 2012) attitudes also appear to have remained remarkably resistant to change. However, aggregate findings can obscure more subtle underlying patterns. There is evidence that people who formerly accepted nuclear power in the UK have now become more uncertain since

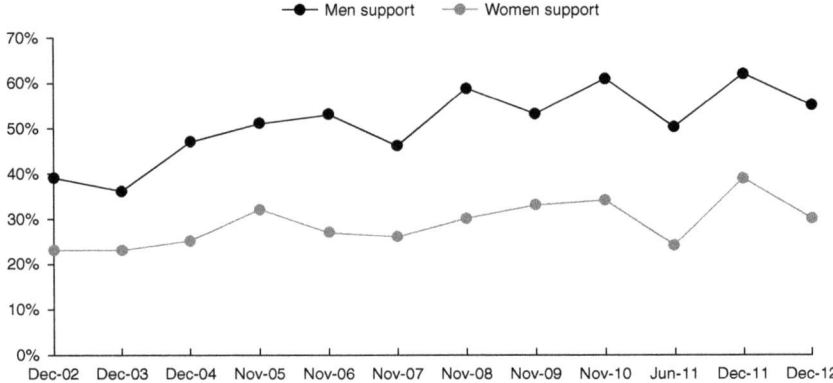

Figure 5.1 British public views on replacement of nuclear power station. (Source: Ipsos-MORI, Nuclear Industries Association.)

Fukushima (Poortinga et al. 2013), while the average response obscures a large and consistent gender gap (Figure 5.1).

The data series shown in Figure 5.1, routinely updated at the annual conference of the UK's Nuclear Industries Association, served to ignite a policy debate about its significance. In the summer of 2011 the University of Birmingham Policy Commission was set up to consider Britain's nuclear energy future (Hunt 2012). In its draft chapter on public attitudes, the commission pointed to evidence of both the gender gap in acceptability, alongside the observation that women's average self-reported knowledge about nuclear was lower than that of men. The initial conclusion in the draft report was that it would be helpful if the government could increase science education for women and girls! Having initially provided evidence to the commission, the current authors had the opportunity to point out some of the problems with this line of argument, in that it runs the risk of reproducing the idea that men and women view nuclear differently simply because of some fundamental (but unexplained) difference between the genders. We also know that promoting greater knowledge of a technology or risk, the so-called "deficit model" of science communication (Irwin and Wynne 1996; Sturgis and Allum 2004), does not necessarily lead to greater public acceptance, while research on risk perceptions finds that levels of knowledge typically fail to explain gender differences in responses (Davidson and Freudenburg 1996; Hitchcock 2001). As a result, a more nuanced conclusion was published by the commission in its final report:

A range of variables are important in the relationship between the public and an understanding of the nuclear industry, e.g. income, gender, political ideology, cultural values and trust in the information source. Consequently it cannot be automatically presumed that more information will lead to greater acceptance. [The report goes on to conclude that ...] A greater emphasis on developing an awareness of energy in schools and opening up the nuclear debate could help with engagement in the nuclear industry and energy generation. *However, a better understanding of the diverse values around care, relationships, environmental protection and futures needs to be taken seriously.* (Hunt 2012: 97 emphasis added)

5.3 Fathoming the complexity of risk governance and nuclear ethics

The "public understanding of risk program," as broadly framed, is testimony to the possibilities that exist for academics and the policy community to work collaboratively on matters of public concern that are subject to risk governance in modern societies. This should not be taken to imply that the subject of risk governance lacks controversy, or that investigating this will necessarily resolve the many ethical questions involved. Real questions exist about opportunities for addressing the question "where do the controversial matters of risk governance lie?" and the possibilities that can be brought into play for paying attention to questions of risk ethics. Equally, the social science community does not always acknowledge the intractability of the problems facing governments when contemplating hard choices about how we should live in the face of depleting energy resources, and potential imposition of new limits on societal organization and everyday functioning (although for a useful website on how such shifts are manifesting themselves to academics and other stakeholders involved in energy demand reduction interventions; see www.energybiographies.org).

In terms of elucidating the intractable nature of issues of risk governance, there is much to be gained from the environmental governmentalities field, which explores possible shifts in regimes or forms of governance in order to understand their specific and cumulative effects on ecological systems, climate change, environmental citizenship, and ethics. It draws on literature incorporating "(s)ocial constructivist and discourse analytical perspectives on climate change that is capable of highlighting the extent to which climate change is a social product of discursive struggles rather than a naturally given problem" (Oels 2005: 185). Highlighting discursive struggles is important as a research strategy in that it seeks to address the consequences of different problem framings, as well as attending to configurations of state and corporate power. In so doing, interpretive practices and claims are introduced about the conflictual basis of environmental politics as a discursive space, and how scientific research too is implicated in this space.

In this field, discussions of social transformation are predicated on clarity of critique and pursuit of interpretive claims as objects of knowledge. For example, cost–benefit analysis can be critiqued for the way that it "obscures moral issues of equity and responsibility" and the emphasis on globalism for the way it "disempowers local solutions" (Oels 2005: 185), criticism which has also been made within the risk ethics fields (Asveld and Roeser 2009) and directed at the related technologies of risk assessment and analysis (see Okrent and Pidgeon 2000; Pidgeon and Butler 2009). We would concur that these are both important objects of knowledge. Our argument, however, is for further exploration of matters of epistemology and ethics that are implicated in such claims.[1] Specifically, we search for insights from empirical study of how gender positions and discourses lead to differences in perceptions of the acceptability or otherwise of nuclear technology for the production of energy, while considering nuclear power as one among other, related components of climate change and resource depletion risks.

5.4 Gendering risk: conceptual issues

Gender is a matter that is both difficult to fathom and yet has to be taken fully into account by academic risk researchers and policymakers. A messy and complex issue (Benschop et al. 2012), it cannot be approached simplistically within research programs that recognize how, as well as posing scientific questions, risk has moral, cultural, evaluative, affective, and aesthetic dimensions (Tulloch and Lupton 2003), and that both are necessary to understanding matters of public concern. Questions of identity and environmental controversy are of longstanding significance in the academic field of risk perceptions research (Douglas and Wildavsky 1982; Joffe 1999; Satterfield 2003; Henwood and Pidgeon 2013) and among nongovernmental organizations seeking to influence policy (Compton and Kasser 2009). Particularly important within risk and identity studies is the realization that there are different ways of framing questions of risk (Henwood et al. 2008b; Henwood et al. 2010). Within the science and society research community, extensive knowledge of risk framing has led to the realization that the dictum "the public should be educated to understand the science" is a route to impoverished risk governance practice (e.g. Rayner 2004). This realization is testimony to the need for sensitivity to questions of identity and identity related values (such as stressing the importance of social inclusion and acknowledging diversity), as part of the wider practice of public accountability in science.

Earlier, we noted the very extensive, well established literature on gender and risk perception, which has identified complex empirical effects (Davidson and Freudenburg 1996; Hitchcock 2001). Such studies typically utilize quantitative survey methodologies to elicit judgments reflecting the cognitive and

---

[1] See also Chapter 3 in this volume.

social psychological determinants of beliefs about risk: the so-called "psychometric" paradigm (see e.g. Pidgeon et al. 1992). A frustration often expressed with this literature is that it fails to offer properly theorized explanations of why the observed relationship between gender and risk perceptions might occur. Recently, and in response, attempts have begun to identify models from the risk literature for elucidating theoretical explanation (Wester 2012). Nonetheless, efforts to explain patterns of risk perception in individual (gender) difference terms continue to dominate, even in the face of little empirical support. Three often-repeated proposals are that women might be less familiar with science and technology than men; that men are more concerned about their external role as economic providers whereas women with children are more concerned about health risks; and that women tend to be more distrustful of government, science, and technology, something which is related to increased environmental concern.

One explanation that does gain some empirical support, according to Davidson and Freudenburg, is the "safety concern hypothesis": This is attributed to women's role as nurturers and carers of their family unit, which is extended to their local community and hence invokes a greater concern for both. According to Flynn et al. (1994), observed gender "differences" are due to a small group of men within their sample who hold much lower risk perceptions than other demographic groups, the so-called "white male effect." This observation has been related to more general discussion of identities and societal vulnerability (Satterfield et al. 2004) together with questions about how to research diverse relationships between gender and marginality (Henwood 2008).

A critical distance is taken from explaining such observed patterns in individual (gender) difference terms within the field of gender research, where the understandings they foster are typically seen as limited by simplistic interpretations. Merely observing a gender-related difference in a quantitative dependent measure as ipso facto saying something so obvious about men and women that one can report a statistically significant gap without further comment, and without acknowledging its implications for understanding experienced risks, gender norms, and stereotypes, is a highly misleading interpretive practice (Hare-Mustin and Maracek 1990). Explaining the significance of gender does not mean automatically treating masculinity and femininity as different variables, of a social and/or psychological nature, that function as causal antecedents or effects. Rather it involves rendering problematic the commonplace assumptions held within particular cultures about what it is to be a woman or a man (Henwood et al. 2002), and how this can underpin or warrant asymmetries in power between women and men.

A related set of concerns, encompassing more of the scope of gender studies, are the wide-ranging efforts that have been made to understand why gender apparently exerts such a powerful influence within society, set alongside contemporary thinking which tends to eschew essentialist or fixed accounts of gender "differences." Rather, researchers ask what empirical findings about sex and gender difference might mean, how they relate to controversy about men and women's positions in society, and how they are related to people's life-projects. Such research seeks to arrive at more contextual, cultural, and depth psychological views of masculinity and femininity as cultural binaries (e.g. Frosh 2002), while recognizing that gender and cultural binaries can operate interpretively in ways that hide as much as they highlight (see e.g. MacCormick and Strathern 1992). Reflecting these concerns, Gustafson (1998) has pointed out that the traditional "gender differences" explanations of the risk and gender effect might be limited by the exclusive use of evidence drawn from quantitative surveys, and so has recommended a more interpretive qualitative approach to analyzing how men and women construct understandings of risk issues.

5.4.1 An interpretive, qualitative approach to inquiring into gender and risk perception

Research practice in many fields of interpretive social science involves a more philosophical concern for the relevance of moral questions about risk (Roeser et al. 2013). One influential approach involves considering the role played by gender discourses and subject/identity positioning in the ways both men and women understand and interpret social and scientific issues in everyday life (see e.g. Fisher and Davis 1993), with a particular concern to avoid essentializing or fixing accounts of gender "differences" (Wetherell 1986; Henwood et al. 1998). In the course of studying discourse dynamics, people are construed as historically situated subjects whose ways of invoking and reworking meanings complicate the social, cultural, and intergenerational transmission of gender and other social/identity categories (Wetherell 1996; Finn and Henwood 2009; Coltart and Henwood 2012). At the same time, such discourse research focuses upon the ways in which people constantly create and claim subject or identity positions for themselves and others in the course of social interaction. How identity positions are sustained or discarded as an emergent feature of social interchange, in ways that are accepted or disputed by others in that interaction, can also become a focus of study as such identity positions provide possible sites and means of self perception and reflection.

Such qualitative social psychological work is concerned with what has been called the "most worldly of all our interpretive practices" (Denzin 1997: 250) that involve asking the types of questions that carry meaning in everyday life. What might empirical findings about sex and gender difference mean? How do they relate to men and women's changing positions in society, and how is it possible to account for the pace (often slow) of cultural and psychological change? For Lohan (2000), working in the field of social studies of science and technology (STS) such social psychological sources (e.g. Segal 1997) have raised questions about how – in breaking down binary oppositions – spaces can be opened up to create "tolerance" of gender difference as a form of anti-essentialist practice. Lohan invites researchers to attend to the workings of sociopolitical understandings as a means of analyzing how culture and power operate to hold differences in place. Obvious points of connection exist between such theorizing and ways of formulating questions, and helping to make sense of empirical findings on gender and risk. One example considered in our own work concerns the examination of gendered "moral voices" (e.g. Gilligan 1982), as ways of encoding and communicating conventional dichotomies between women and men in perceptions of risk and its acceptability (Henwood et al. 2015).

These theoretical developments articulate with the proposal by Gustafson (1998) that a more theoretically nuanced, interpretive qualitative approach is needed to understand gendered construction of risk issues. They articulate closely with a conceptually novel approach that we have developed to foster inquiry in the gender and risk domain, called *effects made by gender* (Henwood et al. 2008a), by which we mean drawing on a synthesized framework (that is capable of further development) for conceptualizing gender within social and philosophical theory. We use this framework to interrogate the ways in which pervasive gender categories, codes, and discourses define everyday realities, including the taken for granted "truths" of risk perception. Insights generated through this research are presented in Section 5.5.

Alongside theory from discursive social psychology, our theoretical synthesis or theoretical platform draws upon the work of Faulkner, in the STS field. Faulkner (2000a, 2000b) discussed technology–gender relationships as social and cultural constructions, shaped by changing historical circumstances and sociopolitical processes, and functioning as regulatory mechanisms or norms of discourse and conduct. Faulkner places importance on the durability of modernist cultural associations between masculinity and technology – and especially as part of the conviction that social progress is attributable to technological development and its economic role within industrial capitalism. Faulkner argues that processes of gendering at play in technological work (e.g. computer software engineering) result from these associations, and further specific links to cultural and psychological themes of control, mastery, and domination (also known as masculine hegemony), which together constitute engineering and technology as a powerful nexus of masculine culture. As part of the workings of this cultural nexus, regulatory ideas of gender (in)authenticity exercise people to show themselves to be appropriately gendered (or not) when expressing interest in, or associating themselves with, science and engineering domains. Faulkner sees masculine culture operating through such a regulatory norm of gender (in)authenticity as explaining women engineers' reluctance to admit that they enjoy technology too much since it detracts from their female identity. Faulkner's approach therefore sees certain forms of technology as culturally gendered in perception, which, we argue, pertains to the gender-risk effect as originally established in relation to large-scale technological or environmental hazards.

In explaining gender–culture–technology–risk relations, it matters that gendered associations (e.g. between large-scale technology and masculinity) are symbolic positions – arising through the workings of tacit knowledge, expectations, thought and reflection, imaginative understanding, subject positioning, figurative meaning, but with individuals rarely taking up such a clear position in any practical context. For Jeanes (2007: 554) regarding gender as a norm means looking at how it "operates in social practices as an implicit (though occasionally explicit) standard of normalization: a norm that is difficult to read and discernible most clearly in the effects it produces."

In our own analytical work, we have endeavored to make visible such difficult to discern effects while taking the view that, once brought to one's attention, they are likely to appear as commonsensical – even to exist everywhere. In addition to the work of discursive social psychologists, and Faulkner (as discussed above), our work has drawn on the feminist philosophical work of Scheman (1993) and her notion of epistemic subjectivity. This refers to taking on an identity as an authority on a subject in discourse, or conversely hesitating over expressing personal authority or pleasure in the activity of knowing. Scheman proposes that, while widely and legitimately contested within philosophy, recognizably masculine epistemic frameworks often remain culturally placed as the "best positions to know" (1993: 4). A relevant example in the sphere of risk knowledge is the tendency for groups exerting powerful influences within society to place epistemic authority in technical–rational approaches to understanding and managing risk problems, rather than in worldviews stressing practical values of responsibility and care as part of broader social and ecological considerations. Following Scheman's argument, different forms of knowing may lead people to construct risk problems in ways that are recognizably gendered. Accordingly, this analytical insight provides an original strategy for investigation. Epistemic subject positioning is a potentially significant issue in public evaluations of nuclear power, discussions of environmental/energy policy and ethics, and the gendering of risk perceptions.

5.5 Explaining the gender-risk effect: findings from a UK study

With the benefit of an Economic and Social Research Council supported project (Pidgeon et al. 2007), we sought to overcome the criticisms in

Section 5.4 of explanations of the empirically substantiated gender-risk effect. Having developed our conceptual synthesis out of wider theorizing about gender, and taking a qualitative empirical approach, we conducted a discourse analytic study of dynamic, sociocultural (and to some extent, deeper psychological) aspects of processes of epistemic and identity positioning as manifest in social interactions occurring among focus group members (Henwood et al. 2015).

Returning to original focus group transcripts where the devil's bargain frame was first identified in public discourse (discussed in Section 5.2), we analyzed various aspects of cultural and identity work in these data, which took the form of extensive discussions about environmental and technical risk issues. Radioactive waste [RW], nuclear power [NP], and climate change [CC] were the specific topics discussed in a subset of four of these groups. Although these topics would be expected to produce the gender-risk effect in surveys, the focus groups themselves were not planned with this in mind.

The women and men who took part in the study were average citizens (not experts in energy or technology) and occupied a range of occupational and social positions. For one of the groups, professionally qualified men and women were interviewed together, and the groups discussing nuclear power and climate change were all mixed gender. Sustained group discussions took place over the course of two meetings of two hours on consecutive evenings. For many reasons, including the way focus group methodology is highly interactive for participants, the data took a very different form to discrete, decontextualized statements about who perceives the most risk as collected in surveys.

In what follows, we present fragments of the gendered nature of the conversations, including where women engage with a technological viewpoint and men a care point of view in a non-essentializing way. We have selected extracts of data to illustrate the interpretive analysis we developed in two main studied topic areas.

5.5.1   Epistemic subjects: positions, knowledge, and risk

A pro-technoscientific epistemic form was commonly articulated across the risk issues by some participants who endeavored to speak authoritatively about science and technology. A number of the men in the focus groups, from early on, took up apparently authoritative and confident positions, as actual, aspiring, or potential knowers – as people who are interested in talking from a perspective of knowledge about the matters under discussion. By contrast, while it was far rarer among the men, the women overtly expressed doubts, hesitancies, and uncertainties. Our analysis not only portrayed this strikingly gender differentiated pattern, but showed how taking an essentialist view of it belies the operation of cultural work and identity dynamics involved in creating and contesting power-knowledge claims and gender hierarchies.

For example, in response to Ethan's repeated claims that technoscientific ways of resolving safety issues with radioactive waste make its management unproblematic, Elizabeth objects by drawing attention to the inherent uncertainties involved when making such long-term claims.

> ETHAN: We can't carry on just storing it at the power stations, something's got to happen and they can't make their minds up. Why not bury it in a mine or something or salt mines like the Swedes do, 300 years under store. You know, you could think about, you've got 300 years to think about it. . . . they case it in glass and put it in stainless steel drums and put it in the salt mine . . . and they could still bring it out and do something else with it, when they know how to sort of cope with it better. So I mean, I can't see the problem.
> ELIZABETH: How do they know it's safe in 300 years?
> ETHAN: Pardon?
> ELIZABETH: How do they know it will be safe in 300 years? (Cromer,[2] RW and NP)

Elizabeth's remarks are counterposed to Ethan's repeated claims that technoscientific ways of resolving issues with radioactive waste from nuclear power stations makes management of the risk unproblematic. Her remarks discredit the position he had taken up as a technocentric epistemic subject by pointing to the detectable flaws in his argument, and effectively shut down the exchange between the two conversationalists at this point in time. Overall, the effect of the exchange is to bring two very different kinds of epistemic position into conflict. What is also interesting about this (and other similar) instances of talk is the way Elizabeth's position is not overpowered by the established gender pattern assuming superiority of technical risk and safety practices. In other examples, along with pointing out flaws in technocentric arguments, wit (sarcasm, irony, flippancy, and ridicule; see Parkhill et al. 2011) was another highly effective epistemic form discursively deployed by both men and women in efforts to disallow knowledge and identity claims that seemed to activate forms of gender dualism.

Our analysis of the data on epistemic speaking, or identity positions, points to an ingrained association between knowing, as a form of masculine subjectivity, and technocentrism, which configures a culturally recognized form of masculinity. Speaking in culturally authoritative ways on scientific and technological matters, may create the possibility of powerful, identity-affirming positions in encounters if they succeed in bolstering a desired, gender authentic form of epistemic subjectivity: in the case of masculine subjectivity, this would

---

[2] The names of towns where the focus groups took place appear first inside the brackets followed by acronyms indicating discussed topics.

be one connoting mastery and control. However, as we have seen, this kind of epistemic positioning can occasion moments when gender identities are contested in discourse-power relations, and where epistemic plurality is articulated and valued within displays of different forms of knowing.

5.5.2 Technocentrism, responsibility, and care

The ways in which women and men often spoke differently about technology, risk, and the environment was also considered in relation to the ways in which they constructed their ideas out of cultural repertoires (specific ideas, arguments, risk and value framings, subject forms) made available by popular, gender-marked discourses of technocentrism, responsibility, and care. At the center of a masculine marked discourse (termed technocentrism) was the establishment of the modernist, world-making, and risk-controlling power of technology, confidently articulating the value of technologies and grand technological visions operating across extended scales of technology, geography, and time. As part of a gender binary, it was both distinct from, but also coexisted with, a feminine marked discourse attaching importance to a range of different matters such as individual and collective responsibility as a safeguard against possible harm, the value of small-scale technologies and efforts at remediating the effects of large-scale technological risks, and generally perceiving a role for affect, morality, self–other connections, and a concern for future generations in everyday, societal, and political decision-making about risk.

The idea of countervailing and coexisting discourses that can be gender-marked resembles Gilligan's (1982) ideas about how it is possible for women and men to speak in different moral voices: an abstract, universalistic, voice underpinned by the application of rules, logic and reason (on the one hand), and a more contextual, relational, and concrete/particularistic voice about how actions can be appropriately guided by a concern for others (known as a moral voice of responsibility/care) (see also Sevenhuijsen 1998). In our study, technocentric and care discourses, similar in kind to Gilligan's abstract–concrete moral voice binary, contributed as meaning-making resources to identity processes within the matrix of culture–technology–identity relationships (in our terminology, creating "effects made by gender"; Henwood et al. 2008a). We were able to study the dynamic role played by discourses of care/technocentrism both with regard to the ways in which women and men displayed their understandings of risk in the focus group setting, and in (de)stabilizing what might otherwise have been taken for granted as truths about the gendering of risk. Care discourses were evident, following a binary gender logic, when women objected to technological solutions to risk problems on the grounds of their epistemic failings (as too risky), as illustrated in the next quotation from Beth (where she is primarily concerned with contamination from nuclear power stations, and people dying from a catastrophic accident).

BETH: Nuclear power . . . I just see it as being negative. . . . if you hear anything about it, it's either costing a lot of money or there's waste that they're dumping in the sea, or there's leakages, I mean you've just got to look at Chernobyl. . . . how many were at Chernobyl? And they're still dying of cancer now. (Norwich, Professionals, RW and NP)

But, with equal conviction, technology's use was endorsed within care discourses. This happened where technological possibilities and intended benefits were perceived (e.g. as useful for risk remediation), by taking action to modify behaviors and practices that had been constructed as risky. Nuclear power was talked about in this way but at this point we can better exemplify our argument by referring to a different technology discussed by other groups in this series. Genetic modification simply to improve the aesthetics or taste of a food gained support only very rarely from women (and also men), while its use for the purpose of improving nutritional content of foods was seen as beneficial, for either their own children, or less fortunate individuals in Third World countries. A further pattern emerged when technologies or behavioral change were said to be futile, and women responded vehemently to this by deploying discourses of responsibility and care:

OLIVIA: if each local authority had a target to produce their own . . . over the next 50 years or whatever, just small things like building houses with solar panels, places . . . wherever there is water and what have you to make use of . . . we could make one of those. It doesn't have to be a huge solution surely.
CHRISTOPHER: Unfortunately we're not all blessed with having a nice fast stream going through the garden are we?
OLIVIA: We've all got roofs that we can put solar panels in. (Cromer, CC).

According to Faulkner (2000a, 2000b), gender dualistic discourse and positioning – in her case in relation to the identity work regarding notions of gender authenticity, symbolically guards against threats to gender identity. Faulkner's work is concerned with configurations linking masculinity with technology and with understanding engineering identities. Her work also promotes the idea that gender – functioning as a regulatory norm of conduct – may not fully explain its effects in producing highly invested (i.e. psychologically and emotionally committed) identity formations (also called – especially in the feminist cultural studies and psychosocial literatures – subjectivities). Likewise in our study, the regulatory powers of technocentrism, and the countervailing and coexisting notions of care, gave rise to cultural and identity work potentially deepening the mode of regulation of men and women's conduct and subjectivities (Masco 2006).

Our study was concerned with people talking about technical, environmental, and social risk issues in everyday life, not in an occupational setting such as engineering or nuclear industries, and we witnessed instances of increasingly invested, or emotively charged, conflictual encounters which seemed to be related to a perceived erosion of boundaries between technological and care as valued speaking/identity positions and epistemic forms of knowing. In such instances, there did seem to be a possible identity protective role for participants in the way they spoke or reacted to the epistemic speaking positions taken up by others in connection with the importance, or otherwise, of practices of technological world-making and risk-taking culture. Sometimes this took the form of distancing oneself from hubristic, hegemonic forms of masculine identity. For example, Joshua seems to distance himself from such a position when alluding to human beings as the "second plague" because of their dominance and responsibility for harming the planet.

JOSHUA: You [moderator] asked who was the planet for. Is it for humans, or is there a bigger meaning? So perhaps what's wrong with the planet is the humans. Get rid of all the humans.
ABIGAIL: And then it will be alright.
JOSHUA: And then it will be alright.
JACOB: Where will I be? [Laughs]
JOSHUA: Well I suppose if I have to sacrifice myself I think to save the whole earth [laughs]. We're the second plague aren't we? That's one way to look at it. (Heysham, CC)

Our observations suggest that enjoyment of hegemonic cultural forms of masculinity as part of identity formation within the social, political, and economic institutions of late modern societies (as emphasized by Faulkner) can be a complex phenomenon. Regarding the study of gender and the perceptions of risk, its significance may lie in opening up the possibility that gendered, binary thinking rests on a contestable value base, and that when displayed it is part of the struggles for recognition that take place within gendered discourse.

5.6 Gender, risk, and policy-making: a question of nuclear energy or nuclear ethics?

In keeping with the orientation of the present volume, the arguments advanced in this chapter can revitalize and strengthen ethical analysis of nuclear issues in the twenty-first century where diverse identities, interests, aspirations, and conflict dynamics bear upon risk, energy, and environmental decisions and policy. Hansson (2012) stresses that a variety of approaches are needed for approaching normative risk assessments in such contexts.

Some seek to establish new philosophical principles for analyzing the continuing deployment of nuclear technology, for example, strengthening the no harm duty and balancing obligations to future generations with contemporary social interests (Taebi 2011; Taebi et al. 2012). Doyle (2010) has initiated mapping ethical landscapes by highlighting morally justified differences of motivation and conflicting obligations at different levels of ethical analysis. But this is methodologically complex work involving studying how ethical disagreements about nuclear issues emerge in particular contexts, and discussing their significance in policy and public realms. The present chapter, by developing theoretical understanding of the gender–risk relationship in everyday settings, and presenting empirically informed and enriched ethical analysis, starts to elucidate such methodologically complex work.

Our findings concern when, why, and how the empirical gender-risk effect was reproduced in group discussions, as a means of fathoming the complexity of gender and risk. The approach taken in the study involved considering discursive struggles over epistemic values and identity (or subject) positioning. A number of matters of controversy emerged in the groups relating to the way different epistemic positions came into play, resulting in a patterning of discourse response around conflicting arguments. Epistemic diversity was mobilized as one among other discursively articulated values and spoken identity positions. Analysis focused upon occasions where technoscience and care ethics were discussed and, from other less culturally archetypal and recognizable kinds of values, we have started to introduce the importance of mutual recognition (see also Benjamin 1988). This patterning of talk would be expected in contexts where democratic values, attaching importance to disparate voices, come into play. In this sense, what our analyses have shown is not remarkable. But there are important implications when such values are part of discussions about things that matter to people (Sayers 2011), and where the epistemic and other value positions in question are connected to matters of wider policy relevance (Pidgeon 1998). Of particular concern to us in this chapter are effects that are made – or mobilized – when different issue framings linking to matters of gender are heard to communicate attenuated or amplified perceptions of risk. Our reported findings suggest that, while in certain contexts prevalent forms of knowledge and values may appear as legitimate or dominant, they may appear in others to be opportunistic, supporting one particular group or set of subjective interests, in the thrall of identity dynamics, and thus unlikely to work in an appropriately motivated fashion for a diverse populace or for the collective good. This "effect made by gender" applies equally to care values and technoscientific ones, suggesting that matters of energy and risk policy are not best approached within either of these frames singly.

A wider issue to which our inquiries speak is what gets omitted from discussions of technology, energy policy, and environmental futures, when and why. Buck et al. (2014), considering the implications of ecofeminism for geoengineering, have problematized the use of gendered metaphors and discourse in science and policy, and lack of consideration for those who need to be concerned about risk effects either because they are more likely to be vulnerable to them or benefit less from risk adaptation measures. Our own analyses of gendering processes in risk perception likewise engage with some of the same science metaphors (e.g. hubristic attitudes to nuclear power), showing how they can bolster the durable association between masculinity and technology as part of historically constructed realities. However, our study also brings to light epistemic and identity processes by which such associations are re-invoked, re-imagined, and reworked in everyday talk – exploring, in particular, how the deepening hold of gender as a form of culturally ingrained and fluid subjectivity holds out different possible interpretations of this long-established cultural association. One way in which our study closely aligns with conclusions drawn by Buck et al. is in cautioning against adopting a fundamentally technocratic approach to creating large-scale system wide interventions for guiding energy transitions and environmental risk management. Alternative, soft energy pathways are capable of avoiding unnecessarily (Parisi 1977) and thoughtlessly (Buck et al. 2013) going down risky and uncertain pathways.

Nuclear energy – as we have argued– is not a fixed object of knowledge, but diversely framed over time. Questions of nuclear risk have loomed large in the landscape of public perceptions at certain time periods (e.g. the Cold War) and are awakened in response to everyday incidents prompting awareness of hazards (Parkhill et al. 2010), but they do not currently figure in UK nuclear energy frames. Rather, the technology's future role is being determined through its connection with securing energy in the immediate and long term for the population at large, along with achieving decarbonization targets. Moreover, a clear commitment remains in UK policy discourse that public understandings of environmental and technological risk issues, including risks associated with nuclear technology for the purpose of energy production, are trumped by the objective science of risk should they diverge from it. So it is here where it makes good sense to bring in the gender-risk conundrum from the shadows to center stage. Buck et al. (2013) argue for the need to entertain support for a risky technology all the time it has possible merit in a resource limited and carbon emissions threatened world. They also cover what a concern for gender dimensions can bring to the foreground when "what gets attention" in policy and public awareness are technologically advanced, bold and risky methods, at the expense of gentler, more natural solutions with fewer uncertainties and known risk. This raises the question "how can gender enhance scientific, technological and risk discourse, and not simply reject such research, in order to consider its possibilities for remediating harm?" Part of the answer is that such discourse needs to change to avoid a gender insensitive research trajectory. Our own research contributes to thinking through how public energy discourses risk gender insensitivity.

Acknowledgments

Writing this chapter was in part facilitated by grants from the Economic and Social Research Council (RES - 160 - 25 - 0046) and the US National Science Foundation (SES 0938099), We wish to thank Karen Parkhill and Dan Venables.

Part II

Justice

6 The need for a public "explosion" in the ethics of radiological protection, especially for nuclear power[1]

Stephen M. Gardiner

Nuclear energy is at a crossroads. While some concerned about climate change urge a rapid expansion of nuclear power to facilitate a shift away from fossil fuels (e.g. Caldeira et al. 2013), others argue for a decisive rejection of nuclear energy, especially in the wake of Fukushima and ongoing difficulties with the storage of long-lived nuclear waste (e.g. Yucca Mountain). Interestingly, much of the argument on both sides is overtly ethical, highlighting obligations to the most vulnerable and to future generations.

The nuclear community accepts that its work raises ethical questions and promotes various standards, based on explicit ethical principles, to address them. Given its influence on national and international energy policy, this system is likely to come under increasing scrutiny in the years ahead, as the debate between pro- and anti-nuclear positions intensifies. Still, on the whole, the community appears satisfied with its current approach. For instance, after an important report by the International Commission on Radiological Protection (ICRP), one commentator declared that "the system of protection established by and large in its present form several decades ago has reached a certain level of maturity [such that] *no major changes to radiological protection regulations ... should be necessary*" (Wrixon 2008: 161, 167; emphasis added), while ICRP itself stated that it expected publication "to lead to a *clear understanding and wide acceptance*" of its approach (Clarke and Valentin 2009: 98).[2]

In my view, such confidence is premature, at least when it comes to nuclear energy.[3] Serious questions persist about how the current principles are

---

[1] This chapter extends some arguments from (Gardiner 2005, 2006b, 2008). I thank Christopher Clement, Carole Lee, Alex Lenferna, Sabine Roeser, Behnam Taebi, Per Wikman-Svahn, and participants at the ISEEH workshop in Budweis in June 2014 for their comments. The views expressed are my own.
[2] While subsequent commentary on Fukushima led by the ICRP Vice-Chair largely reflects this consensus, it does raise worries about the rationale for the ICRP's numbers and its public accessibility (See ICRP Task Group 84 2012: 9; González et al. 2013).
[3] Radiological protection covers more than nuclear energy; still, many of my concerns apply more broadly.

formulated, understood, and implemented, and there are also major gaps in the present system. As a result, a new approach is needed to protect nuclear policy from several standing threats. Here I pursue a pluralist, "bottom up" strategy for identifying guiding principles of nuclear ethics, resulting in the introduction of a number of new principles and fresh interpretations of existing ones. My proposals challenge the existing system by raising specific alternatives. Nevertheless, my intent is not to deliver a robust new ethical framework for nuclear protection, but rather to reopen an important debate. Hopefully, others will take up the challenge and offer more considered proposals that improve both on the existing system, and my tentative emendations.[4] My main point is that there is work to be done, and a case to answer. Of special importance is my new principle of publicity. This responds to a worrying mismatch between how the existing principles appear to outsiders, and how they have sometimes been interpreted in policy. This problem threatens to undermine both the system itself and public trust in it.

6.1 Standing threats

Nuclear energy policy involves several pronounced asymmetries, resulting in a number of standard threats to its integrity that an ethical approach should seek to neutralize.

6.1.1 Epistemic asymmetry

The first asymmetry involves knowledge. The scientific and technological aspects of nuclear energy are significant, pervasive, and complex. They affect how we understand nuclear approaches both in isolation and in comparison to other energy sources. This raises difficulties for anyone trying to make an ethical assessment of nuclear energy, but the obstacles are more pronounced for outsiders than insiders. Consequently, one standing threat to ethical decision-making is that of a *retreat* (and perhaps exit) of nonexperts from the policy debate. As disputes among experts become difficult to follow (even opaque) to most people, this encourages the ceding of nuclear policy to a technical elite.

Such a retreat poses several ethical problems. First, there are questions of justification, including of procedural justice and political legitimacy. For instance, to the extent that those affected are excluded from the making of decisions (in fact or in effect), this casts doubt on the justifiability of those decisions.

Second, there is a risk of selection effects. For example, to the extent that insiders have distinct values relevant to decision-making (e.g. a preference for quantitative approaches, technological optimism), these are likely to have a disproportionate influence.

---

[4] See also Oughton and Hansson (2013) and Shrader-Frechette and Persson (2001).

Third, the policy discourse itself may become distorted. For instance, retreat may encourage bias in the *framing* of policy questions, so as to implicitly favor some concerns over others, obscuring the full range of ethical considerations and possible solutions from the wider public. Such distortions may not arise intentionally (for example, they may occur due to inadvertent selection bias). Still, an ethical nuclear policy would protect against them. It would also guard against more robust forms of distortion, such as regulatory capture and outright corruption.

6.1.2 Spatial asymmetry

The second pronounced asymmetry is spatial. Nuclear energy programs typically have different implications for individuals and populations, depending on where they live and work, so that costs and benefits are distributed unevenly. For instance, exposures to potentially harmful radiation are likely to differ between populations close to nuclear power plants and those far away, and between those who work in the plants and those who do not (Shrader-Frechette 2002, 2011a, 2013). The standing threat here is of injustice, and its relevance is well-documented. Many empirical studies in the environmental justice literature suggest a strong correlation between exposure and membership of populations that are historically disadvantaged (e.g. as classified by race, ethnicity, and socioeconomic status; cf. Wigley and Shrader-Frechette 1996).

6.1.3 The temporal asymmetry

The third asymmetry is temporal. Costs and benefits can be (and are likely to be) dispersed across time. The most obvious cases are intergenerational. A characteristic threat is that of a tyranny of the contemporary, a collective action problem similar too but harsher than the traditional tragedy of the commons (Gardiner 2011). Specifically, the temporal position of the current generation allows them to impose costs on future people that they ought not to bear and to deprive them of benefits, opportunities, and background entitlements that they ought to have. Moreover, the risk of such "buck-passing" is iterated: The temptation to take advantage of its privileged position arises for each generation. Consequently, iteration threatens accumulation: the imposition of escalating burdens on the further future. As generations further off are exposed to more predecessors, the effects on them are compounded and may become severe or even catastrophic. The threat of such a tyranny is highly relevant to nuclear policy given worries about long-term nuclear waste and genetic effects.

A basic question of nuclear ethics is whether current regulatory policy is adequate to meet these three asymmetries (epistemic, spatial, temporal) and their associated threats (retreat, environmental injustice, temporal buck-passing). At first glance, it appears well-placed to do so. Over several decades, the nuclear community has developed an elaborate system of nuclear protection and appears well-satisfied with that system. However, I will now raise a number of serious concerns, and suggest some improvements. As an ethicist, my focus is on the content of these principles and how they have been interpreted over time.

6.2 A methodological pluralism

6.2.1 On principles

A common approach to addressing standing threats in public life is by promoting sets of ethical principles and standards based on those principles. Ethical principles can play a number of roles. For instance, sometimes they are employed to *justify* more concrete ethical claims; on other occasions they are used to *explain* why such claims are made; and on still further occasions they provide *guidance* on how decisions should be made. Ethical principles can also take various forms. For example, some aim to be *decisive* in either the justification or guidance they offer, while others are intended only to *identify* relevant concerns that may potentially be outweighed or even silenced by other factors; similarly, some attempt a comprehensive, *all-things-considered* evaluation of a situation, while others consider only aspects.[5]

The fact that principles can function in various ways sometimes causes confusion in public discussion, including in the nuclear setting. So, let me be clear about my approach. First, my principles are intended mainly as aids to deliberation. They identify ethically relevant features of the policy context and are in the spirit of what are sometimes called "principles of moral salience" (Herman 1993). Second, these principles have a fairly modest status: For example, each evaluates only some aspects of a situation rather than providing an "all-things-considered" judgment; even in situations where only one principle is relevant, this does not necessarily make it decisive; and we should not assume that each principle picks out features that are always morally relevant in the same way (cf. Dancy 2004). Third, as aids to deliberation, the principles are always subject to further deliberative scrutiny, both as regards their individual content and their collective adequacy. The process of identifying and refining such principles is open-ended.

The principles fit into a methodologically pluralist approach. Rather than invoking a single moral theory as the basis for nuclear ethics, they identify a range of ethical concerns to be taken into account. Such pluralism is a natural default position in the sense that such concerns have status before we come to

---

[5] Partial evaluations can be decisive (e.g. certain rights violations).

wider theory and that any theory that seeks to bring order to nuclear ethics should seek to explain, justify, or replace these principles. One advantage of this approach is that it allows nuclear ethics to proceed on a less controversial basis, avoiding unnecessary partisanship about ultimate principles as far as possible. Another advantage is that it avoids misleading descriptions of principles in partisan terms, as often happens in radiological policy.[6]

My approach will also be "bottom up" rather than "top down" (Cf. Beauchamp 2003). Instead of deducing the relevant principles from some externally determined set of values, it works from principles, problems, and omissions already present in existing discussions of nuclear ethics. One reason to proceed in this way is a concern for epistemic modesty. Often, the range of considerations that a strong ethical theory should seek to integrate and justify are best gleaned from the real context in which they are intended to operate rather than from more abstract sources. A second reason is theoretical modesty. In a historical context where we have complex but competing ethical theories, driving public policy through a single moral theory seems premature and (arguably) inappropriate. Instead, to the extent possible, one should focus on areas of agreement. A "bottom up" approach facilitates that.

6.2.2 ICRP principles

I begin with the foundational ethical principles put forward by the ICRP. These ground much regulation of nuclear energy, including the fundamental safety principles of the International Atomic Energy Agency (IAEA) and the policies of national, regional, and multinational groups, such as the United Nations, the Nuclear Energy Agency of the OECD, and the European Union.[7] Though they govern a range of different situations, I will focus on the nature of the principles themselves, and (to the extent that it makes a difference) on how they are

---

[6] For example, one should resist claims such as (a) "inevitably, radiological protection ... will require *a balancing* between these two ethical principles [i.e. utilitarianism and deontological ethics]," or (b) "no practical protection work can be based on an absolute application of one principle [i.e. utilitarianism or deontology] alone" (Clarke and Valentin 2009: 105). On (a), strictly speaking, utilitarianism claims that maximizing happiness is the *single* ultimate principle of morality. It is therefore monistic in a way that rules out "balancing," and differs from more modest pluralist principles which assign ethical importance to welfare but allow for other values. On (b), a purely utilitarian approach is possible (and, as we shall see, seems to have been practiced in the past); moreover, there is no reason to think that deontological considerations could not effectively govern nuclear policy all by themselves (e.g. if such considerations mandate that some forms of nuclear power are currently impermissible whatever their advantages for collective welfare).

[7] The IAEA includes the ICRP principles as principles 4–6 of its safety principles, and in introducing the latter states that "the distinction traditionally made between nuclear safety and radiation protection is hardly justifiable at the conceptual level" (IAEA 2006 et al.: vii).

applied to public exposure in the production of nuclear power and waste management.

The ICRP states that the primary aim of its recommendations is "to contribute to an appropriate level of protection for people and the environment against the detrimental effects of radiation exposure without unduly limiting the desirable human actions that may be associated with such exposure" (ICRP 2007: 41). To its credit, the commission is well aware that this aim "cannot be achieved solely on the basis of scientific knowledge on radiation exposure and its health effects," but requires "value judgments about the relative importance of different kinds of risk and about the balancing of risks and benefits" (ICRP 2007: 41). Acknowledging this, it seeks to make its value judgments clear through the announcement of three principles.

These principles are best understood in light of their history.[8] They first appear together in the ICRP's landmark report of 1977. As formulated then, they state:

- *Justification Principle* (JP): No practice shall be adopted unless its introduction produces a positive net benefit.
- *Optimization Principle* (OP): All exposures should be as low as reasonably achievable, economic, and social factors being taken into account.
- *Dose Limit Principle* (DLP): The doses to individuals shall not exceed the limits recommended for the appropriate circumstances by the commission.

Our main question concerns how well these principles address the asymmetries and standing threats identified earlier.

6.3 Procedural principles

Let us begin with the epistemic asymmetry and the threat of retreat, including the problems posed by procedural justice, selection effects, and distortion. Surprisingly, given that such issues are well known in other areas, the ICRP principles fail to address them. Indeed, the three principles are silent on procedural issues more generally.

To fill this gap, I propose three new principles of radiological protection. I do not suggest that they are adequate or exhaustive. Instead, they are offered only as reasonable additions that are at least as plausible as the original three principles, so that serious reasons would be required for rejecting them. Of course, the new principles may require emendation, and further principles may be required. Such discussion is to be welcomed. My point in proposing new principles is to stimulate further debate and so facilitate the development of a more comprehensive and robust framework.

---

[8] See Clarke (2003); Clarke and Valentin (2009); Gardiner (2008).

6.3.1 Inclusiveness

My first principle concerns inclusiveness:

Inclusiveness Principle (IP): Development, implementation, and enforcement of policies involving nuclear energy should be done by representatives of a diverse group of stakeholders and the wider public, paying special attention to the most vulnerable.[9]

Promoting inclusiveness involves explicit attempts to ensure broad participation in decision-making, especially by those heavily affected by a policy, those historically under represented, or those whose views tend to be marginalized (e.g. women, minorities, the poor, children).

Inclusiveness is a common strategy for addressing institutional biases, and is widely recognized to be important for both epistemic and ethical reasons. On the epistemic side, research shows that both inclusive deliberation and inclusive communities in science enhance knowledge production (Longino 1990, 2002; Lee and Schunn 2011). In ethics, inclusiveness is seen as a first step toward procedural justice, and an important component in securing justification for regulative activities (Schlosberg 2007).

In recent years, the ICRP has shown some concern for increasing the size of the circle involved in deliberation on nuclear protection. For example, since 2002 it has circulated draft proposals and allowed for public comment. In the wake of Fukushima, it has also supported the nuclear community's organization of a number of major regional conferences. Nevertheless, the commission remains markedly exclusive when it comes to its own make-up. It is an independent group, selects its own members, restricts membership to those of "scientific merit," and explicitly rejects the idea of membership based on other grounds, including those based on representation "of any country, organization, or other entity" (Clarke and Valentin 2009: 27). On the face of it, this approach is strikingly out of step with the principle of inclusiveness and so requires justification.

The commission claims its approach protects its "independence and scientific integrity" from "special interest groups and other outsiders with vested interests," and from "covert criticisms aimed at gaining outside control of its membership and/or its policies" (Clarke and Valentin 2009: 27). To some extent, these concerns are legitimate. An ethical approach would not sanction the ICRP becoming a narrowly partisan political body, or merely the instrument of a small set of powerful industry players.

Still, the commission's stance remains debatable. First, it is questionable that such a rigidly exclusive policy is necessary for the purpose of protecting the

---

[9] Cf. (EPA 2014). I intend "policies" in the broad sense that include laws and regulations. Although the ICRP is not in a position to implement or enforce its proposals, it promotes ethical principles that apply to these activities.

ICRP's integrity. Other options for limiting unduly partisan or commercial influences deserve consideration, including increasing diversity.

Second, it is not clear that the commission's current procedure is adequate to protect itself from corrupting influences. Self-selected groups are themselves subject to bias, and it is unclear what (if any) protections are in place to ensure that distortions do not creep into the commission's selection process.[10] For instance, given that the ICRP is officially in the business of making value judgments and generating ethical principles, one might question the exclusion of all nonscientists, including *experts from other disciplines* (such as ethics and law) and *representatives of affected populations and the wider public*. The commission's approach appears implicitly to regard only scientists as having the relevant qualifications for deliberating on these matters; yet this presumption seems unjustified and unjustifiable.

Third, the issue of inclusiveness is relevant to the serious background issue of whether and why the ICRP pronouncements should be taken to have any *authority*. From an ethical point of view, the very idea that a self-appointed and unaccountable group can dictate the basics (including the foundational ethical principles) of nuclear policies that affect many millions of people requires some elaboration and defense. One question is what gives such a group the right to set itself up in this role; another (more important) question is why others, and especially representative institutions such as governments, should take its pronouncements seriously. Though such questions might be answered, the principle of inclusiveness imposes a significant burden of proof on such answers and on the ICRP to provide them.

6.3.2 Accountability

This leads us to my second principle:

Accountability Principle (AP): Those who develop, implement, and enforce policies involving nuclear energy should be accountable to the wider public and especially those directly affected.

The key thought behind this principle is that those who subject the wider public to policies that have the potential to have serious affects on them are answerable for this and especially to those directly affected. This is a central tenet of modern democratic political philosophy and a mainstream thought in the political traditions of most nations.

---

[10] For example, while the commission's current make-up reflects a limited diversity of science disciplines and geographical origin, it is unclear whether this is the result of internal policy or happenstance, and whether there is anything in place to ensure that it will be maintained over time.

As it stands, the ICRP appears to stand outside of standard mechanisms of accountability. The best that can be said is that many of the organizations that employ the ICRP recommendations are themselves subject to various mechanisms (e.g. through connections to representative and democratic institutions), so that the system as a whole is not immune from wider scrutiny. Still, it remains true that the commission itself is not directly accountable. Moreover, it is also not clear that the accountability of other organizations is a sufficient check on the overall system. For instance, the ICRP may provide political cover for other organizations by presenting itself as a purely "scientific" body whose recommendations are grounded in ethical principles, and to whom such matters can be "outsourced." Given this, there is a risk that its presence may *undermine*, rather than encourage, wider accountability mechanisms.

6.3.3 Publicity

My third principle concerns publicity (cf. Gardiner 2008; Shrader-Frechette 2013):

Publicity Principle (PP): Those involved in the development, implementation, and enforcement of policies involving nuclear energy have a duty to make clear to the wider public (and especially those directly affected) the *full* scientific and ethical reasoning involved in justifying these activities in terms that are both accurate and readily accessible.

The IAEA expresses a concern for accessibility to nonspecialists, but applies this only to responsible decision-makers, such as those "at senior levels in government" (IAEA et al. 2006: viii). In my view, this goal is too limited. By contrast, although it does not suggest a *principle* of publicity, the ICRP seems open to the basic idea, since it announces a commitment to the related thought that "the basis for, and distinction between, scientific estimations and value judgments should be made clear whenever possible, so as to increase the transparency, and thus the understanding, of how decisions have been reached" (ICRP 2007: 41). Moreover, the commission has taken steps to act on this commitment by publishing many of its materials, and creating a mechanism for public comment.

Still, there remains room for improvement. In my view, the ICRP should raise its commitment to transparency and public understanding to the level of an explicit principle. In the long run, this would help to increase public trust and aid both the commission and other organizations in holding themselves accountable to these ideals. More substantively, instead of "transparency," the commission should embrace the more robust ideal of publicity. Specifically, I take the commitment to publicity to involve an *active* duty to engage with the wider public and seek their participation, rather than (say) merely a passive duty not to shield what one is doing from outside scrutiny.[11] Given the knowledge asymmetry and threat of retreat, there are strong grounds for embracing this more robust ideal.

Concrete steps that could be taken toward fulfilling the more robust ideal range from the modest to the fairly ambitious. First, at the modest end, the commission could produce "executive summaries" of its reports for the general public and make its documents freely available on the web, rather than leaving them behind paywalls that tend to limit access to specialists. Second, it could make efforts to explain its approach in public venues, and especially in settings that make them accessible to those most affected. Third, at the more ambitious end, the commission could commit itself to promoting wider public participation in nuclear decision-making by facilitating public deliberation both within traditional venues and more broadly, especially around the issue of the appropriate norms and their implementation (see also Oughton and Hansson 2013). Such efforts are visible in other areas where scientific matters are of public concern, such as climate change, genomics, and genetically modified food. I propose that they also be taken here.

My most important suggestion is that the ICRP commit to making its scientific and ethical reasoning *fully* accessible to outsiders (as publicity demands). This commitment is necessary because the current system is at risk of being *only superficially transparent*. Most notably, the key element of the ICRP's current approach is its public recognition that its decisions involve value judgments, and its efforts to be clear about what these are and how it makes them. The three foundational principles play a prominent role in this effort. At first glance, they are reassuring. They appear to express reasonable and widely shared ethical concerns (for net benefit, minimization of exposure, protection of individuals); and this suggests a pluralist, comprehensive, relatively uncontroversial, and nonpartisan approach to radiological ethics. Unfortunately, this appearance is misleading. As we shall see, the three principles are open to interpretation in ways which not only could undermine publicity, but in practice have actually done so. Specifically, rather than facilitating a clear understanding of radiological decision-making, the principles sometimes pose a barrier to that understanding, especially for outsiders. Most seriously, in some cases, they may not merely *obscure* the underlying justificatory practices, but actually *misrepresent* them. This poses a serious threat to the radiological system and especially to public trust. It therefore provides extra

---

[11] Even if the existing commitment might be read as endorsing such an ideal, it is in the spirit of publicity to be clear.

reason for incorporating a principle of publicity and encouraging the nuclear community to apply that principle vigorously.[12]

Let us pursue this matter by examining how the system has operated historically, focusing first on the threats posed by spatial asymmetry.

6.4 Collective welfare principles

At first glance, the ICRP appears to announce a pluralistic system of regulation, responsive to three separate concerns.[13] Moreover, each principle appears to reflect a relatively uncontroversial (even commonsensical) ethical value that is morally and politically nonpartisan, and likely to be widely endorsed. Unfortunately, there is a mismatch between this impression and how the principles have often been understood.

6.4.1 Justification

The justification principle is frequently seen as the "cornerstone" of the system of radiation protection. In its original (ICRP 1977) version, it states:

Justification Principle (JP): No practice shall be adopted unless its introduction produces a positive net benefit.

The JP poses something of a puzzle. Competing understandings of it have been put forward, and different ones seem to have been dominant in different periods. This is important not just for historical reasons, but because it provides an insight into the apparent malleability of the overall system from the point of view of regulatory authorities. Such malleability is of ongoing concern in light of the standard threats to radiological ethics, especially in the nuclear setting.

6.4.2 Maximizing cost–benefit

Let me begin with a traditional view of the principle as it operated in the initial period after its introduction (1977–90). According to leading ICRP figures, the justification principle was originally interpreted as reflecting a maximizing approach aimed at achieving the greatest net benefit.[14] This suggests:

---

[12] Alex Lenferna suggests to me that it may also imply the need for an independent and accountable review body.
[13] The ICRP suggests at some points that the principles represent and have historically emerged from different philosophical traditions in ethics – utilitarianism, Kantian deontology and Aristotelian virtue ethics – and so reflect a theoretical pluralism. However, see note 6.
[14] There is some ambiguity (and apparently disagreement) about whether the JP or the OP (or perhaps the two in combination) grounded this commitment. The JP account has some credibility because of its name, and because it was initially introduced to clarify the OP. However, ICRP Secretary Christopher Clement tells me that he thinks that no professional would now

Maximizing Benefit Principle (MBP): Unless it produces *the maximum net benefit*, a given nuclear practice is not justified, and so should not be permitted.

In addition, the MBP was itself understood through the procedures of standard economic cost–benefit analysis (CBA), yielding the more specific:

Maximizing Cost–benefit Principle (MCBP): Unless it produces the maximum net benefit *as understood through the methods of standard economic cost–benefit analysis*, a given nuclear practice is not justified, and so should not be permitted.

For instance, former ICRP chairman Roger Clarke describes the 1977 recommendations as involving a "classical use of cost–benefit analysis" and reflecting a "utilitarian" ethics, associated with philosophers such as Jeremy Bentham and John Stuart Mill. For example, he states:

The principles of justification and optimization aim at doing more good than harm and at *maximizing the margin of good over harm for society as a whole*. They therefore satisfy the *utilitarian principle of ethics*, whereby actions are judged by their overall consequences, usually by comparing in monetary terms the relevant benefits (e.g., statistical estimates of lives saved) obtained by a particular protective measure with the net cost of introducing that measure. (Clarke 2003: 42)

Traditionally, we are told, the approach was operationalized through the concept of a collective dose. The commission would endeavor to calculate which total dose of radiation to all humans affected by a given practice would maximize net social benefit understood in standard cost–benefit terms. Moreover, the same strategy was used to determine the content of the other two principles. Specifically, not only was optimization interpreted in terms of maximization of benefit, but dose limits were derived from the individual's "average share" of the collective dose, as justified by maximizing net benefit:[15]

In 1977, the establishment of the dose limits was of secondary concern to the CBA and use of collective dose. This can be seen in the wording used by ICRP in setting its dose limit for members of the public. Publication 26 states: "The assumption of a total risk of the order of 10^{-2} Sv^{-1} would imply restriction of the lifetime dose to the individual member of the public to 1 mSv per year. The Commission's recommended limit of 5 mSv in a year, as applied to critical groups, has been found to give this degree of safety and the Commission recommends its continued use." In a similar manner the dose limit for workers was argued on a comparison of average doses and therefore risk in the

---

interpret the JP as either the MBP or MCBP. Still, he also believes that a maximizing interpretation of optimization is widespread. (See Section 6.5.2.)

[15] Intriguingly, Clarke's more recent history suggests the more pluralistic view that the dose limit principle was retained on deontological grounds, Still, the claim that it was operationalized in terms of collective dose remains (Clarke and Valentin 2009: 104).

workforce with average risks in industries that would be recognized as being "safe," and not on maximum risks to be accepted. (Clarke 2003: 42)

One advantage of the traditional interpretation is that it makes sense of the title "justification." The initial framing of the three principle system implies that the JP is only one of three foundational principles, and so might suggest that all three are principles of justification. However, the utilitarian principle claims to be the ultimate principle of ethics, in terms of which all activities are to be justified. Hence, if the JP represents utilitarianism, it is natural to think that the other (optimization and dose limit) principles are derivative and so concern implementation rather than justification.

Still, the traditional interpretation has significant disadvantages. First, utilitarianism is a controversial ethical theory. Most notably, because of the focus on overall outcomes, utilitarian approaches are often criticized for being insensitive to the importance of distributive concerns and the value of the individual (e.g. the "separateness of persons" objection), and in ways that lead it to endorse violations of individual rights and other kinds of injustice. For example, according to one classic case, if the numbers worked out, a simple utilitarian approach would require a surgeon to take all the major organs from one healthy patient (killing him in the process) in order to save five others needing transplants. Consequently, on the traditional reading the three principle system seems especially vulnerable (given spatial and temporal asymmetry) to the threats of environmental justice and intergenerational buck-passing.

Second, the traditional approach employs a controversial account of benefit and how to integrate it. For instance, standard economic cost–benefit analysis is rejected not only by nonutilitarians (such as rights theorists), but also by many utilitarians, who doubt that application of standard economic cost–benefit methodology is the way to produce the best outcomes in the long run. Specifically, many utilitarians would claim that standard economic cost–benefit analysis fails to capture the right kinds of costs and benefits (e.g. because of the focus on market prices), or treats them in morally problematic ways (e.g. by incorporating discount rates that reflect pure time preference on the part of the current generation). For such reasons, most philosophical utilitarians favor indirect forms of utilitarianism, where utility is best promoted through other means, such as procedural justice, rights, and principles of fairness in distribution. Consequently, the claim of standard economic cost–benefit analysis to *represent* utilitarianism is overstated (Gardiner 2011).[16]

Third, the Publicity Principle is violated. For one thing, what initially appears to be a pluralistic ethical system turns out to be decidedly monistic: The three

---

[16] Such objections also cast doubt on employing the MCBP to represent the value of welfare within a more pluralist approach.

principles are all driven by a single background value, that of utility. For another, the MCBP is a very odd interpretation of the wording of the JP and so seriously misleading to outsiders. Let us explore this by considering an alternative interpretation.

6.4.3 Net benefit

In my view, the JP is naturally read as asserting a *side constraint* on practices that involve the possibility of radiation exposure (Gardiner 2005, 2008).

Net Benefit Principle (NBP): Unless it produces a positive net benefit, a given nuclear practice is not justified, and so should not be permitted.

The NBP is very different from the maximizing cost–benefit principle. For instance, the MCBP is comparative, whereas the NBP is noncomparative: The MCBP makes judgments between competing projects all of which produce positive net benefit, whereas the NBP only identifies such projects. Moreover, maximizing net benefit is much more demanding than merely securing net benefit and so plays a stronger role in constraining policy choice.

While net benefit is a more modest principle than the MBP, it can play still a notable role. First, the NBP presents itself as a "gatekeeper" principle that is decisive in a limited domain: It explicitly rules out projects that produce net costs or break even on costs and benefits. Thus, the other principles (OP and DLP) become relevant only if the NBP is satisfied.

Second, as a "gatekeeper," the NBP is non-trivial. For instance, a common dispute in nuclear policy concerns whether nuclear energy projects satisfy the net benefit requirement once the full lifetime costs of nuclear plants and disposal of nuclear waste are factored in (e.g. under what is sometimes called "full-cost accounting"). Specifically, some argue that current nuclear practices do not promote a net benefit when subject to a proper long-term evaluation and that the net benefit requirement cannot be met given current technology (Shrader-Frechette 2011a).

Nevertheless, third, at least in principle, the NBP leaves plenty of room for other principles to play a role, since it does not present itself as decisive outside of its limited domain. Most obviously, the NBP provides no guidance on how to choose between projects all of which produce net benefits. Less obviously, satisfying the NBP is not enough to establish that a given project is permissible all things considered. Instead, it leaves open the possibility that a project may still be found impermissible on other grounds.[17] On non-traditional

---

[17] Counterintuitively, this implies that a project may satisfy the justification principle and yet not be justified. See Sections 6.5–6.8 (especially Sections 6.5.3–6.5.5, 6.6.3–6.6.5, 6.7.2, and 6.8.2–6.8.7).

interpretations, this allows for a (non-derivative) justificatory role for other principles of nuclear protection.

The net benefit interpretation has some significant advantages over the maximizing approach. As well as providing a literal reading of the original JP, it initially appears relatively uncontroversial, and is friendly toward the pluralistic impression suggested by the three principle system.

Nevertheless, significant issues remain. The first concerns how to interpret and operationalize the NBP. Here, the central issues are what to count as benefits and costs, and how to integrate these into a calculation of "net benefit." Most notably, given the issues with the MCBP, it is far from clear that a standard cost–benefit approach is warranted. For instance, even fans of CBA in other contexts often balk at applying it to complex intergenerational and environmental problems. For example, full-cost accounting over very long time scales (of at least hundreds and probably many thousands of years) seems required, yet it is far from clear that standard economic CBA has the conceptual or technical resources to do the job accurately or responsibly. This worry is a major one in related problems involving the long-term future, such as climate change, where estimates of net benefit vary by orders of magnitude, and where this is *largely because of* disagreements about foundational conceptual questions related to ethics (Gardiner 2011).[18] In such settings, standard CBA is likely to be indeterminate, so that specific analyses are prone to be more reflective of the views of the analyst than anything else. This not only renders the process vulnerable to corruption, but also threatens paralysis if CBA is our only guide.[19]

There are also more general issues about the robustness of a net benefit approach. On the one hand, a net benefit condition may turn out to be unduly permissive. For example, by comparison with energy policies that result in catastrophic climate change, or in the face of significant positive discount rates, very many projects might satisfy an NBP. The NBP may thus provide an illusion of serious "gatekeeping" where none exists. Among other things, this would leave a large justificatory gap. If very many projects would produce net benefits, the NBP alone would provide grounds for choosing among such projects and further reasons would be required to make the decision. In practice, then, the NBP might be construed so as to give very large discretion

---

[18] Cf. Hansson's suggestion that radiological protection should not follow climate economics in adopting long-term discounting; See Chapter 2 in this volume.

[19] Similarly, a calculation of net benefit must be made against a specific baseline. However, it is unclear what the relevant baseline should be. For instance, if an expansion of nuclear power is being advocated as a response to the threat of climate change, it will likely make a significant difference whether the net benefit assessment is done against a baseline of the current market costs of fossil fuel sources, or one including the long-term environmental costs of those sources, or one reflecting a rival package of nonfossil fuel sources, and so on.

to decision-makers to choose on other grounds. Arguably, this would violate the principle of publicity: It would present the NBP as central to justification when in fact its role is marginal.

On the other hand, the NBP may also turn out to be overly restrictive. Notably, it rules out the possibility that, in some situations, societies may be willing to countenance nuclear policies that result in a net cost. Yet some may be willing to accept a net cost in order to achieve other objectives (e.g. energy independence, a landscape free from windmills). Moreover, some may even be willing to take on extra burdens in their energy policy in order to address further ethical issues. For example, they may feel obliged to take on projects that are more burdensome for them in order to correct for a wider injustice, including climate injustice (Gardiner 2006a; Taebi 2011). For example, a nation might come to the conclusion that it should take on a costly nuclear energy project because it has exceeded its fair share of cheaper energy sources (such as fossil fuels), and taking on the extra burden is a way of making up for that overconsumption.

Among other things, this last worry reflects the fact that NBPs (like the MBP, MCBP, and utilitarianism) are ultimately exclusively forward-looking. They therefore implicitly reject substantial backward-looking considerations, such as ethical perspectives concerned with justice and rights, to the extent that these do not also have a forward-looking rationale. Since the NBP is a decisive principle, it may therefore rule out important ethical concerns.

6.4.4 Offsetting harm

Interestingly, more recent ICRP reports appear to endorse a version of the NBP rather than the earlier MBP. For instance, the 2007 report rephrases the original JP to yield:

Offsetting Harm Principle (OHP): Any decision that alters the radiation exposure situation should do more good than harm.

It then explicitly interprets this as meaning that a relevant radiation activity "should achieve sufficient individual or societal benefit to *offset* the detriment it causes" (ICRP 2007: 88).

Still, this endorsement of net benefit over a maximization approach is not unequivocal. The commission also offers a specific rationale:

Sometimes, the radiation detriment will be a small part of the total. Justification thus goes far beyond the scope of radiological protection. It is for these reasons that the Commission only recommends that justification require that the net benefit be positive. To search for the best of all the available alternatives is a task beyond the responsibility of radiological protection authorities. (ICRP 2007: 89)

Apparently, then, the ICRP resists maximizing due to epistemic concerns and worries about responsibility: because it believes that it lacks the expertise and authority to make judgments about nonradiological costs and benefits. However, this suggests that the commission would endorse a maximizing approach if these obstacles could be overcome; indeed, its rationale appears to encourage organizations with wider knowledge and a more extensive remit to do just that.

Both the OHP and the ICRP's rationale raise further questions. Let me mention just three. First, the offsetting principle is controversial: It assumes that inflicting harm can be justified if it brings about more good; yet sometimes we endorse a rival "do no harm" principle. Of course, on other occasions we are willing to trade off some kinds of costs against some kinds of benefit. Still, "harm" is often used in a more restricted way than "cost," where part of the point of the restriction is that harms are more morally serious, and in a way that prohibits some kinds of trade. For example, many refuse to trade off the harms inflicted on animals through testing cosmetics against the benefits to consumers. Presumably, similar worries arise in the nuclear case with (for example) trading off the health risks of radiation against luxury consumer goods. Given this, the offsetting principle fails to confront at least one aspect of the threat of environmental injustice.

Second, moving to the rationale for the OHP, it is not obvious why the commission thinks it retains a responsibility to promote a robust side constraint *on collective welfare grounds* in cases where the radiation issue is small compared to the other social and ethical considerations. Presumably, some will argue that in such cases wider welfare considerations overwhelm even a modest net benefit requirement. This casts doubt on the status of ICRP's recommendations based on the JP.

Third, more generally, the ICRP's sudden modesty is a little misleading. The commission worries that its limited knowledge and role restrict the kinds of ethical principle it should endorse and promote. Yet it does not question its self-imposed mandate to offer principles and make such judgments. Indeed, it continues explicitly to promote one specific collective welfare standard (the OHP), and may be implicitly promoting another (the MCBP) to governments and other organizations. Not only is it unclear what gives the commission the expertise, competence, or authority to do so, but its modesty appears to be selectively applied. For example, as we shall see, when it comes to setting individual dose limits, the ICRP simply asserts its own authority as its warrant.[20]

---

[20] Similarly, the IAEA explicitly states that it is "desirable that all States adhere to and advocate" its principles, and that they "provide support for States in meeting their obligations" (IAEA et al. 2006: viii, 2).

6.4.5 Presumptive net benefit

In light of this discussion, it is unclear whether some form of the NBP should be retained. Still, if it is retained, I propose that it be regarded as at most a presumptive, rebuttable principle, rather than as decisive. This allows for the fact that other ethically relevant factors, such as rights, can matter more than net benefit. I also suggest that it be made clear that it is only such factors (usually, presumably, to be represented by other principles) rather than just any consideration that can override net benefit. On this reading, net benefit imposes a burden of proof on nuclear projects rather than an absolute constraint:

Presumptive Net Benefit Principle (PNBP): Unless it produces a positive net benefit and causes no serious harm, a given nuclear practice is not justified and so should not be permitted *unless it furthers some other specified, and more ethically important, purpose.*

6.5 Minimization principles

6.5.1 Optimization

Let us turn now to the second principle:

Optimization Principle (OP): All exposures should be as low as reasonably achievable, economic and social factors being taken into account.

As with justification, some writers claim that in practice optimization is the central principle of radiological protection. So, how is it to be understood?

Traditionally, the OP is often read as endorsing utilitarianism. Sometimes (as above) it is seen as simply derivative of the JP understood as the MBP. On other occasions, however, it is interpreted as expressing the MBP in its own right, so that the OP is read as the primary principle of radiological protection in light of which the other two are to be understood.

6.5.2 Optimal balancing

In particular, optimization is often thought to require an "optimal balancing" of doses and costs, such that "it would be undesirable to deviate in either direction: Higher doses should be avoided since they can be cost-efficiently reduced, and lower doses since they would involve indefensible costs" (Hansson 2013c: 145):

Optimal Balancing Principle (OBP): Exposures should be optimized so as to maximize net benefits.[21]

---

[21] Hansson describes the OP as "some sort of compromise between dose reduction and cost minimization" applied to one part of the dose range, and thinks an interpretation of "reasonable" is needed; see Chapter 2 in this volume. Jones-Lee and Aven (2011) think of optimization as

Again, this traditional interpretation strikes me as in violation of the Publicity Principle. As stated, the original OP is most naturally read as an *exposure minimization* principle: Exposures should be minimized according to some notion of the "reasonably achievable" and in light of a holistic social and economic evaluation. This is most plausibly understood as expressing a high priority on avoiding exposures. Yet maximizing net benefit may involve no attempt to minimize exposures. Indeed, under some circumstances, the OBP could justify *maximization* of exposure in the collective and individual dose relative to other options, so long as the benefits of such exposure were large enough.[22] However, this seems a perverse interpretation of a principle whose wording focuses on exposure minimization. At best, it is a very oblique way to express an MBP; at worst, the OBP could even be seen as an extreme violation of publicity, namely *disinformation.*

6.5.3 Subordinate minimization

A more obvious reading of the OP is that optimization requires the "lowering of doses as far as possible" (Hansson 2013c: 145). This claim is itself open to interpretation. One option understands it as a subordinate principle that kicks in when a project has been justified in other ways:

Subordinate Exposure Minimization Principle (SEMP): Exposures should be minimized as far as is possible among projects that have satisfied the other ethical principles.[23]

So, for example, those adopting a NBP might employ an exposure minimization principle to choose between projects that pass the net benefit test, or to adjust the exposures of a project that has already been approved on net benefit grounds. Exposure minimization then becomes an independent but subordinate goal: Although projects that satisfy other principles are permissible in isolation, the SEMP licenses us to make judgments between them or in how they are to be managed. Plausibly, this suggests a very different outcome to the MBP. If minimizing exposures is expensive in terms of net benefit, then the SEMP would tend to drive down overall benefits and favor projects with low net benefits relative to others.

"simply a restatement of the standard cost–benefit criterion" within that range. Arguably, the IAEA description of optimization encourages this, since it insists that "the resources devoted to safety ... have to be commensurate with the magnitude of the radiation risks and their amenability to control," and emphasizes factors (number affected, magnitude of dose, etc.) that suggest cost–benefit calculation (IAEA 2006 et al.: 10).

[22] Incidentally, the same applies to net benefit principles.
[23] This may be the spirit of the constrained application view discussed by Hansson; see Chapter 2 in this volume.

6.5.4 Comparative minimization

Exposure minimization might also be understood as a primary principle, directing that particular nuclear projects are permissible only if they minimize exposures. The most natural interpretation would be that exposures must be socially and economically necessary *all things considered*, comparing all other policy options (including non-nuclear options) for achieving the same social ends. In other words:

Comparative Exposure Minimization Principle (CEMP): Exposures are impermissible if alternative policy options would achieve the same social and economic ends with less exposures.

On one reading, this comparative principle reflects an opportunity cost argument and so addresses one weakness of the NBP, its lack of comparative assessment (cf. Wikman-Svahn 2012: 264). Notably, it helps to fill the justification gap left by the NBP, but without resorting to a maximizing approach.[24]

6.5.5 Necessity

Still, arguably, a more specific exposure minimization principle would be more faithful to the original wording of the OP, where the focus is not on comparative benefits, but rather on exposures themselves. The OP suggests that exposures are special in a way that warrants a burden of proof against them and that this justifies a minimization strategy. The most obvious reason for this would be because of the threat of harms to health, including negative genetic effects. The thought would be that exposures should be minimized because such "costs" have a more serious status than (say) the normal benefits of nuclear energy and the costs of other energy sources.

This interpretation might be made more visible by announcing a further principle of nuclear protection:

Necessity Principle (NP): Exposures are permissible only to the extent that they are necessary to achieve sufficiently important social ends that cannot be reasonably achieved in other ways.

The NP combines the opportunity cost consideration with the idea that the ends that justify exposure must be of the *right status* to justify the risks.[25]

---

[24] Christopher Clement tells me that both the OBP and CEMP are widespread.

[25] The IAEA's fundamental safety objective "to protect people and the environment from harmful effects of ionizing radiation" (IAEA 2006 et al.: 4) initially suggests a much stronger prohibition on harm. This is immediately softened in the accompanying text, which declares that the objective must be achieved "without unduly limiting" radiation activities. Still, this raises major publicity worries about the objective, especially if optimization is understood as the OBP. The necessity principle at least provides a plausible reading of the softening without eviscerating the objective.

The NP might initially strike some nuclear advocates as draconian. However, on closer inspection explicit focus on the status of different kinds of goods seems to facilitate the right kind of discussion. On the one hand, in picking out the category of the "sufficiently important," the NP allows us to raise the important ethical question of whether some goods (such as health and in particular reducing the risk of cancer) are worth sacrificing purely for the sake of at least some kinds of other goods (e.g. luxury goods produced through nuclear energy). On the other hand, it does so without denying that there might be some goods that do satisfy this requirement (e.g. the alleviation of severe poverty or catastrophic climate damages).

Arguably, both considerations (opportunity cost and special status) are important to the early debate about the expansion of nuclear power. By making them clear in a principle, the NP therefore focuses discussion in a way that the existing ICRP principles do not, at least as usually interpreted. As well as being a serious contribution to nuclear ethics in its own right, this is helpful when it comes to satisfying the Publicity Principle. It helps the OP mean something that many would have initially taken it to mean, based on surface grammar and common-sense morality.

6.5.6   "Anything goes"

The availability of numerous interpretations of the OP poses a serious ethical challenge. According to a recent review:

In practice, optimization is applied in a wide range of ways: from being seen as a frame of mind ("have I done all that I reasonably can?") and simple improvements of work processes, to complex decision-aiding methods, such as cost–benefit analysis. (Wikman-Svahn 2012: 260)

One worry is that that optimization ceases to become any kind of guide to decision-making, and especially one useful for overcoming the standing threats of injustice. A deeper concern is that the OP may in effect license an "anything goes" approach, malleable enough to accommodate whatever ends practitioners might wish. This magnifies the threats of injustice and possible corruption. Either way, the various manifestations of optimization create large challenges for transparency, consistency, and publicity.

6.6   Individual protection

The principles discussed so far focus on the collective level. None therefore addresses the central worry about collective welfare approaches: that they tend to sacrifice individuals, and in particular are insensitive to considerations of justice and rights. For just this reason, the ICRP has, since the 1990s, presented itself as moving away from the traditional "utilitarian" approach and toward a greater concern for respecting individuals. This is manifested in more attention being paid to the dose limit principle, and the introduction of the concept of dose constraints.

6.6.1 Dose limits

The dose limit principle states:

Dose Limit Principle (DLP): The doses to individuals shall not exceed the limits recommended for the appropriate circumstances by the Commission.

On the face of it, this principle is peculiar. Importantly, the DLP reveals neither the rationale for its limits, nor how they are determined. In addition, though it raises the expectation that the ICRP will set limits for individuals, the DLP does not mandate this: It could be read as asserting only that *if* the ICRP recommends limits, these should not be exceeded.

6.6.2 Authority

As worded, the primary message of the DLP is merely to assert the *authority* of the ICRP to set limits for individuals:

Authority Principle (AUP): The ICRP has the authority to set dose limits for individuals that nuclear projects should accept.

This principle raises three basic issues. First, there is the general background problem (mentioned earlier) that it is far from evident why other actors should accept the authority of the ICRP, given that it is self-appointed and apparently unaccountable.

Second, it is puzzling that the ICRP feels the need to assert its authority specifically with respect to dose limits for individuals *in a separate principle*. If authority must be asserted, should it not also be asserted for justification and optimization? Why not also assert parallel authority principles in those areas?

Third, and most seriously, a bare appeal to authority seems particularly misplaced in this setting. The DLP is supposed to be one of the three foundational ethical principles of nuclear policy. Yet, interpreted as the authority principle, the DLP offers *no explanation, justification, or even guidance* for the ICRP's approach, including to the commission itself. Instead, it seems more of a placeholder for a useful principle than an ethical principle in its own right.

Given these issues, I suggest that the authority principle be rejected.

6.6.3 Excessive harm

The fact that the ICRP mandates limits for individuals and that the DLP is one of the three basic principles does suggest a foundational moral concern for protecting individuals as such from excessive exposures. Indeed, an authoritative ICRP history states that "the principle of applying dose limits *aims to protect the rights of the individual not to be exposed to an excessive level of harm*, even if this could cause great problems for society at large," and that the principle "therefore satisfies the deontological principle of ethics, also called "duty ethics," proposed primarily by Immanuel Kant" (Clarke and Valentin 2009: 95). Thus, one way to generate an appropriate dose limit principle would be to replace the authority principle with:

Excessive Harm Principle (EHP): Individuals have a right not to be exposed to an excessive level of harm, even at the expense of large social interests.

Such a reading is also suggested by the IAEA's interpretation of the dose limit principle: "measures for controlling radiation risks must ensure that no individual bears an unacceptable risk of harm" (IAEA 2006 et al.: 10). The crucial question then becomes how to understand the concept "excessive harm."[26]

6.6.4 No harm

There have been dose limits since the earliest days of the ICRP. Initially, these were seen as setting a threshold of exposure that would prevent deterministic effects, specifically understood as tissue reactions. (These were high by current standards.) If the thought was that individuals would not be harmed by exposures under the threshold, this suggests:

No Harm Principle (NHP): Individuals have a right not to be exposed to harm.

Unfortunately, by the time the three principle system was introduced in the 1970s, it had become clear that the threshold view of harm was inadequate. By then, it was understood that exposure to radiation also has stochastic effects, such that no level of exposure is "safe" (all exposures carry some risk of negative health effects, "there is no threshold for the risk of cancer" [Wikman-Svahn 2012: 260]), and the risk increases with additional exposures. Consequently, if "excessive" harm means "no harm," then nuclear projects that increase exposure are ruled out.

Proponents of nuclear power view this requirement as unreasonably strict. In particular, they argue that some risks are too trivial to be considered, and that

---

[26] Intriguingly, the IAEA states that its principle is insufficient to "ensure the best achievable protection" and therefore requires supplement with optimization. This encourages minimization readings of optimization, making the OBP even more misleading.

the magnitude of the risks is relatively low. They therefore propose other accounts of "excessive" harm.

6.6.4 Comparable risk

One such principle is:

Comparable Risk Principle (CRP): Individuals have a right not be exposed to a level of risk of harm from exposures that is not comparable with risks faced in other areas of life.

It is usually rejected because risks in other areas are hard to compare and because the comparison often seems inappropriate (e.g. since other risks are often chosen by those so exposed).

6.6.5 Background of nature

Another principle that has seen favor is:

Background of Nature Principle (BNP): Individuals have a right not be exposed to a level of exposure beyond those found in nature.

This is also usually rejected these days because it involves a naturalistic fallacy: an inference from what is the case to what ought to be the case (Wikman-Svahn 2012; see also Hansson's Chapter 2 in this volume).

6.6.6 Pragmatism

Of late, the attempt to identify a distinct principle for individual dose limits seems to have been abandoned. According to a recent review, the current ICRP recommendations employ "a multiattribute assessment of risks," but "the final choice seems to be based on *pragmatic* considerations" (Wikman-Svahn 2012: 261).

Pragmatic Principle (PGP): Doses to individuals shall not exceed limits determined on pragmatic grounds.

Pragmatic approaches are sometimes warranted. Nevertheless, such an approach to dose limits does little to assuage worries about the standing threats of spatial and temporal injustice. For one thing, it encourages worries about transparency, publicity, and "anything goes." For another, arguably, a pragmatic approach stands in tension with the presentation of the principle as representing a Kantian approach that emphasizes "the *strictness* of moral limits" (Clarke and Valentin 2009: 95).

6.7 Equity

The idea of an excessive level of harm plays a role in another component of the ICRP approach apparently intended to protect individuals, the concept of the dose constraint.

6.7.1 Dose constraints

Oddly, rather than being introduced as a new principle, this concept was simply added to the OP in the 1990s. The expanded version of the OP states:

[The ALARA optimization] procedure should be constrained by restrictions on the doses to individuals (dose constraints), or on the risks to individuals in the case of potential exposures (risk constraints) so as to *limit the inequity* likely to result from the inherent economic and social judgements. (Clarke and Valentin 2009: 97; emphasis added)

On the face of it, dose constraints address one aspect of the standing threat of environmental injustice. In setting an upper limit on how much extra risk individuals can be expected to bear for a given project, they suggest that no one should be expected to take on more than their "fair share" of the burdens of nuclear activities.

Unfortunately, dose constraints seem insufficient to block environmental injustice, and inadequate to capture the idea of a "fair share." One problem is that such constraints may still be satisfied even when those subject to the highest exposures derive *no benefit at all* from the project (i.e. the benefits are all for others). Less dramatically, they are also compatible with cases where those most exposed receive minor benefits compared to others (e.g. power plants in rural areas that mainly fuel distant cities).

6.7.2 Proportionality, special representation, and vulnerability

To address such problems, we might suggest two principles:

Proportionality Principle (PRP): Those exposed must be reasonably expected to receive at least a proportional benefit.

Special Representation Principle (SRP): Those disproportionately exposed are entitled to special consideration in the structuring of nuclear policy.

One implication of these principles may be that the ICRP should replace its past "representative man" and current "representative person" standards for radiological protection with one that focuses on those known or suspected to be more vulnerable to exposure, such as women and children (Wikman-Svahn 2012; Hansson, Chapter 2 in this volume; cf. Shrader-Frechette and Persson 2001). Indeed, this point suggests a third, more general principle than the SRP:

Vulnerability Principle (VP): Special consideration should be given to protect populations that are especially vulnerable to exposure.

6.8 Intergenerational principles

Let us turn now to temporal asymmetry and the standing threat of a tyranny of the contemporary.

6.8.1 Intergenerational buck-passing

To see that threat more clearly, consider a simplified (and highly idealized) model. First, imagine a sequence of non-overlapping generations.[27] Second, suppose that each generation must make decisions about goods that are *temporally dispersed*. One type – "front-loaded goods" – is such that their benefits accrue to the generation that produces them, but their costs are substantially deferred and fall on later generations. Another type – "back-loaded goods" – is such that their costs accrue to the generation that produces them, but their benefits are substantially deferred and arise for later generations. Third, assume that each generation has preferences that are exclusively *generation-relative* in scope: They concern things that happen within the time frame of the generation's own existence.

In such a situation, each generation has some reason to engage in "buck-passing." It can secure benefits for itself by imposing costs on its successors and avoid costs to itself by failing to benefit its successors. Moreover, absent other factors (e.g. moral convictions) this reason may be decisive. Since any given generation is (by hypothesis) concerned only with what happens during its own time, it has a standing concern for intragenerational benefits and costs, but no obvious concern for intergenerational costs and benefits. Buck-passing is thus the default position.

Other things being equal, buck-passing raises serious ethical questions. First, there is a substantive worry: Each generation is likely to *oversupply* front-loaded goods and *undersupply* back-loaded goods relative to reasonable ethical norms. This is clearest in the case of front-loaded goods. It seems unethical for an earlier generation simply to foist costs on a later generation with no consideration for the latter's interests (e.g. without any compensation). However, buck-passing is also relevant for back-loaded goods. On the (modest) assumption that, other things being equal, any given current generation has an obligation to engage in at least some back-loaded projects (e.g. some with extremely low present costs and

---

[27] Elsewhere I argue that complicating the model with generational overlap does not undermine the basic problem (Gardiner 2009, 2011).

extremely high future benefits), then each generation will fail in its duties to the future if it fails to invest in such projects.

Second, there is a structural worry: Later generations are subject to the arbitrary (and apparently unaccountable) power of earlier generations.

The substantive and structural worries are unsettling enough when considering buck-passing by a single generation. However, when multiple generations are in play, they threaten to become profound. For one thing, if buck-passing is iterated (i.e. if each generation succumbs), then the accumulation of effects makes severe or catastrophic outcomes more likely, especially in the further future. For another thing, the bad behavior of earlier generations may even pressure otherwise decent generations into buck-passing behavior. For instance, a later generation faced with severe impacts may (perhaps correctly) feel licensed to impose otherwise unacceptable burdens on the further future out of a right of self-defense. In short, taken to extremes, a tyranny of the contemporary threatens a dangerous downward spiral in social conditions, material and ethical.[28]

One area in which the possibility of intergenerational buck-passing seems especially relevant to nuclear policy is long-term nuclear waste. Nuclear energy initially appears to have the characteristics of a front-loaded good: While its production is directly beneficial for the current generation, the waste generated creates threats of harm to future generations as well as costs of storage, maintenance, and disposal.[29] Let us turn to how the current system addresses such threats.

6.8.2 Protection

The IAEA's principle 7 states:

Protection of Present and Future Generations Principle (PPFGP): People and the environment, present and future, must be protected against radiation risks. (IAEA et al. 2006: 12)

This suggests that future people have standing as primary subjects of radiological protection as well as present people.

The corresponding ICRP principle goes further in granting at least equal standing for future people, and potentially even greater protection:

---

[28] The features of the situation also make it more difficult to resolve than more familiar collective action problems, such as the prisoner's dilemma and tragedy of the commons.

[29] Similarly, the prevention of genetic effects appears to be a backloaded good. Such prevention imposes costs on the current generation, in terms of more expensive safety protocols; yet it benefits future people.

At Least Equal Protection Principle (ALEPP): Individuals and populations in the future should be afforded at least the same level of protection as the current generation (ICRP 1998, 2013).

How are these principles to be interpreted? The ICRP reemphasizes its three principle system. This raises many of the issues already identified, and suggests the need for additional principles (e.g. necessity, vulnerability, special representation, proportionality). However, the IAEA offers further guidelines.[30]

6.8.3 Current impacts

One thought is:

Current Impacts Principle (CIP): Radioactive waste shall be managed in such a way as to assure that predicted impacts on the health of future generations will not be greater than relevant levels of impact that are acceptable today (IAEA 1995: 6).[31]

At first glance, the CIP appears to block at least some buck-passing, since it suggests that the health of future people be treated according to the same standards as that of current people. Unfortunately, this conclusion is too quick.

First, the CIP allows a form of intergenerational buck-passing. Historically, health standards for current people have been set in accordance with the idea of the amount of health risk worth taking on *in order to realize some economic benefit*. However, this threatens to make the situation for current and future people asymmetric. For the current generation, the question is how much of a health risk they are willing to accept for the sake of a given economic benefit that accrues *to them*. Hence, the underlying rationale is one of *compensation*: Current people take on a risk in the expectation of receiving some benefit. However, future generations are probably being asked to accept a given level of health risk for the sake of benefits that accrue largely to current people.[32] So, the rationale of compensation does not apply.[33]

Consider the following parallel. Suppose I am away on a business trip. You call me to say that my office is on fire. I scream, "No! The signed photograph of me with Cristiano Ronaldo is in there." I beseech you to save it; you refuse. In response, I retort, "You are being unreasonable – if I were there, I would be willing to take the risk of dying from the rampaging fire in order to save my precious picture." This response is unconvincing. Perhaps you should be

---

[30] The ICRP mentions other principles in passing, such as precaution and sustainable development, but I will not discuss them here (ICRP 2013).
[31] Principle 4 of the IAEA safety fundamentals of 1995. Interestingly, this principle is not present in the 2006 report.
[32] I set aside the nonidentity problem; but see Gardiner 2011, ch. 5.
[33] This suggests violations of the proportionality and vulnerability principles.

willing to take some risks on my behalf; but this is not one of them. The fact that I would be willing to take such a risk on my own behalf does little to change that.

A second problem with the CIP involves a related asymmetry. The principle appears intended to specify a condition under which future people can be called upon to assume costs for the sake of the current generation, but not vice versa. In other words, it is concerned with the production of front-loaded goods, not back-loaded goods. Unfortunately, this is predictable in a tyranny of the contemporary: Buck-passing generations will not be interested in back-loaded goods.

6.8.4 Undue burdens

The IAEA also promotes, and has recently emphasized, a further principle:

Undue Burdens Principle (UBP): Radioactive waste shall be managed in such a way that will not impose undue burdens on future generations. (IAEA 1995: 7; IAEA et al. 2006: 12)[34]

Unfortunately, as stated, the UBP is ambiguous: "undue" might mean either "excessive" or "inappropriate." If it means "excessive," then there remains room to pass on some kinds of burden to future generations, so long as one does not surpass the threshold of excessiveness (e.g. even without compensation). This might be avoided if "undue" means "inappropriate." However, then we need some account of what this means, and this requires rather than indicates some principle of intergenerational ethics. Fortunately, the IAEA offers further guidance.

6.8.5 Minimal practical level

First, it advocates minimization:

Minimal Practical Level Principle (MPLP): Generation of radioactive waste must be kept to the minimum practicable level. (IAEA 2006 et al.: 12)

This claim echoes the ICRP's OP (the IAEA's principle 5 in 2006), raising problems of interpretation familiar from earlier, including the important question of the Necessity Principle.

6.8.6 Generator's responsibility

Second, the IAEA makes a claim about responsibility:

---

[34] In 1995, this is principle 5; by 2006 it has become an interpretation of the PPFGP.

Generator's Responsibility Principle (GRP): Generations that produce waste have to seek and apply safe, practicable and environmentally acceptable solutions for its long term management. (IAEA 2006 et al.: 12)

The content of this principle is a little unclear.

6.8.7 No significant action

However, third, the IAEA goes on to make a claim that implies a fairly strict understanding of "undue burden," and a correspondingly strong responsibility for the current generation:

No Significant Action Principle (NSAP): Where effects could span generations, subsequent generations have to be adequately protected without any need for them to take significant protective actions. (IAEA 2006 et al.: 12)[35]

This principle places *all* the significant burdens of addressing nuclear waste on the current generation. At first glance, it thus imposes a very demanding standard of adequate protection for future generations, and one that both signals awareness of the compensation issue and diffuses it. As with other radiological principles, the appearance is of a very cautious and restrictive approach.

Unfortunately, on closer inspection matters are much less clear, and worries about a mismatch between appearance and reality resurface. To begin with, there are problems of application. First, an honest deployment of the NSAP is likely to render much nuclear waste production impermissible. It is all very well to *say* that the current generation should take responsibility for the waste. However, in practice this is at least very difficult, and probably impossible. Some waste remains dangerous for thousands, hundreds of thousands, and even millions of years. Neither technical nor institutional solutions are (yet) available through which the current generation can ensure safety over such time periods. Consequently, it appears inevitable that serious responsibilities will fall on future people. If so, the No Signigicant Action Principle appears to rule out nuclear projects.

Second, this raises worries about how the NSAP is actually interpreted and implemented in practice. Given the tyranny of the contemporary, the current generation faces a temptation to interpret the principle in a way that underplays the burden it ought to assume. (Plausibly, this also raises the threat of *de facto* violations of the publicity, vulnerability, and other principles.[36]) Such worries are alive in the current policy setting where nuclear projects are ongoing and the

---

[35] "The management of radioactive waste should, to the extent possible, not rely on long term institutional arrangements or actions as a necessary safety feature ..." (IAEA 1995: 7).

[36] E.g., arguably the IAEA's "to the extent possible" is misleading if the potential for protection is very limited.

whole issue of long-term storage of waste remains in limbo, even as more waste accumulates (e.g. Vandenbosch and Vandenbosch 2007, 2015).

There are also theoretical issues. Consider just two. First, the inference from equal consideration to the NSAP looks questionable. For instance, presumably it is possible for at least some (e.g. proximate) future people to benefit from the present generation's investment in nuclear energy (e.g. if it reduces the magnitude of harmful future climate change) and in such cases perhaps the present generation need not be responsible for all of the associated costs. Some will argue that failing to recognize this may lead to an underinvestment in nuclear technology by present people, adversely affecting the future.

Second, despite its apparent strictness, the NSAP underplays our responsibility to the future. For one thing, if (as now) strict responsibility cannot be fully discharged yet the current generation proceeds with nuclear projects anyway, further intergenerational principles (e.g. of compensation and redress) seem needed. For another, current obligations may go far beyond even a very strict responsibility for waste. For instance, the focus of most existing principles seems to be on projects involving front-loaded goods (benefits now, risks deferred). Yet nuclear ethics (and energy ethics more broadly) may require serious investment in back-loaded projects, which have costs now, but exclusively benefit future people (e.g. massive research into safer reactors, nuclear fusion, renewables, etc.). Plausibly, however, we think such concerns should be addressed, principles of intergenerational radiological ethics are needed that highlight them, rather than leaving the issues obscured behind the rhetorical flourish of the "no significant burden" principle.

In conclusion, although the various ICRP and IAEA principles initially appear to diffuse the tyranny of the contemporary, this appearance is deceptive (cf. Vandenbosch and Vandenbosch 2007; Taebi 2012a). At best, they simply impose some upper limits on the amount of intergenerational buck-passing that can occur. This might be valuable, but does not suffice to eliminate the phenomenon altogether. At worst, they perpetuate a dangerous illusion of robust protection. Either way, additional principles are required.

6.9 Conclusion

I have argued against the view that the existing international system of radiological protection has already reached "a level of maturity such that no major changes should be necessary" by critically examining its ethical basis in the setting of nuclear power. In doing so, I suggested a range of interpretations of and alternatives to various ICRP and IAEA principles. My personal favorites include the three new procedural principles (Inclusiveness,

Accountability, Publicity), a collective welfare principle (Presumptive Net Benefit), two minimization principles (Necessity, and to a lesser extent Comparative Minimization), and four principles of respect (Excessive Harm, Proportionality, Special Representation, Vulnerability). Though these suggestions require more elaboration and defense, hopefully they demonstrate the limitations of the current system and so help to reopen an important debate. Most notably, my arguments should make clear the importance of the (new) principle of publicity, especially for establishing public trust. As the debate about nuclear energy intensifies, this is a vital matter.

7 Distributive versus procedural justice in nuclear waste repository siting

Pius Krütli, Kjell Törnblom, Ivo Wallimann-Helmer, and Michael Stauffacher

7.1 Introduction

When civil use of nuclear power was introduced in the late 1950s, it was meant to provide current and future societies with positively valued resource electricity. Decades later it was evident that electricity production in nuclear power plants produced harmful nuclear waste as a by-product. In contrast to electricity, nuclear waste is negatively valued. Strong resistance against potential repositories for nuclear waste emerged when implementers initiated site selection processes and site exploration. The reasons for opposition were manifold: inappropriate top-down decision-making procedures (e.g. Rosa and Clark 1999); perceived high risks of radioactive leakage (e.g. Slovic 1987); lack of trust in implementers in particular (e.g. Kasperson et al. 1992); fundamental opposition to the use of nuclear power in general (e.g. Rosa and Freudenberg 1993); violation of ethical norms (e.g. Shrader-Frechette 2000); values (e.g. Sjöberg and Drottz-Sjöberg 2001); and the so-called NIMBY (Not In My BackYard) attitude (e.g. Kraft and Clary 1991).

Justice issues emerged during the early stages when people realized that safe storage of nuclear waste is very problematic and cannot be easily resolved. Justice in its *distributive* sense concerns questions about what is a fair share of a particular (tangible or intangible, positive or negative) social resource that is allocated or exchanged. The focus can be on intergenerational and/or intragenerational justice, which, in turn, represents a mismatch between the outcomes of the profiteers of nuclear energy and the affected future generations (Shrader-Frechette 1980; Kasperson 1983; KASAM 1988), as well as between the outcomes of the profiteers and parts of the present generations.

Procedural justice issues were mostly neglected until the 1990s, when responsible institutions began to realize that open-ended, transparent, stepwise, and participatory processes were indispensable prerequisites to making progress in finding geologically suitable sites (e.g. National Research Council

2001). The handling of nuclear waste needs technical and managerial skills to secure safe storage in appropriate facilities. Further, it is impractical or impossible to *distribute* the waste equally or equitably among the members of a given society. Thus, given that nuclear waste is not very amenable to a just distribution, the question instead arises if and to what extent a fair site selection *procedure* may affect perceptions of distributive justice.

The purpose of this chapter is to shed light on justice issues by focusing the relation between procedural and distributive justice issues, theoretically as well as empirically. For this purpose, we use the example of nuclear waste repository site selection processes in Switzerland. The chapter is organized into six sections. Section 7.2 contains an overview of discussions about distributive and procedural justice in social psychological and normative research. Section 7.3 provides the reader with information about radioactive waste management and its pertinent and emerging justice issues. Section 7.4 reviews evidence of procedural and distributive justice controversies in the context of repository site selection processes in Switzerland. In Section 7.5, findings are discussed from both social psychological and normative perspectives. Section 7.6 concludes the chapter with some theoretical and practical implications.

7.2 Distributive and procedural justice

Social psychological justice research makes a distinction between two major domains: distributive and procedural justice. Distributive justice refers to the evaluation of the outcome of an allocation process, and procedural justice concerns the allocation process itself. Similarly, in normative theory there is a distinction between a procedural and a substantive understanding of justice. Theories of the first kind argue that any outcome of a fair allocation procedure is just. In contrast, according to substantive theories of justice the distributive outcome is the main concern of justice. While social psychological theories and research results are designed to show under what conditions distributions are subjectively perceived as just, normative investigations aim at vindicating distributions as just.

The social psychological approach to distributive justice is a development based on exchange theory (Thibaut and Kelley 1959; Homans 1961; Blau 1964). Exchange theory focuses on the initiation, maintenance, and termination of social relationships. In this view, people form and maintain relationships because they find it rewarding to do so, based on the types and amounts of reward they receive and provide in return. The relationship is often terminated when one (or more) of the exchange partners is under-rewarded, becomes dissatisfied, and/or experiences injustice. This insight contributed to the development of equity theory (Adams 1965), which focused on the perceived similarity or dissimilarity between the ratios of outcomes to inputs for two persons. Equity exists when the ratios are perceived to be similar and inequity when not. Thus, a situation is viewed as equitable if person P's inputs of 20 hours of work are awarded $1,000 and person O receives $500 for 10 hours of work. Although P's and O's inputs are not equal and their outcomes are not equal, their respective hourly pay is equal, namely $50/hour. This principle can be traced back in history to Aristotle and his primary formal justice principle of "proportionate equality" (2012).

Elaborations and a more encompassing view of distributive justice occurred when social psychological researchers began to realize that justice is multifaceted, i.e. may be conceived in terms of many additional principles than equity (e.g. Deutsch 1975; Leventhal 1976; Mikula 1980; Törnblom and Jonsson 1985). In particular, two additional principles, equality and need, became the focus of theory and research. Thus, equity, equality, and the need principles were considered the major distributive justice rules.

These three rules or principles of just distribution find their equivalents in normative theory and are justified in normative justice research. Egalitarian theorists, in particular, claim that "there is something which justice requires people to have equal amounts of" (Cohen 1989: 906).[1] Equal distribution is considered the default option that underlies all distributive issues. It is the only distributive outcome not in need of justification, since all human beings have an equally legitimate claim to the social resources to be distributed. Thus, any deviation from equal distribution requires justification, which, in turn, may assume different forms. Option luck, for example, may justify unequal outcomes (Dworkin 2000). Other justifications could be arguments from need or desert and equity, respectively (Tugendhat 1993). Arguments referring to needs, however, must not necessarily be constrained by a presumption of equal distribution. So-called sufficientarians argue that an individual is more in need the more her social and economic circumstances are below a level sufficient to allow a decent human life or meeting basic needs (e.g. Casal 2007). Equity entitlements, on the other hand, can be evaluated against a standard of desert. All who contributed to a common good deserve as much benefits as is appropriate in accordance with their contribution to the produced outcome (e.g. Miller 1999). As such, these conceptions of the three principles of just distribution, as legitimized in normative theory, mirror their conceptions in social psychological research.

Social psychological discussions focusing on *procedural* fairness emerged in the early 1970s. Thibaut and Walker (1975) investigated the differences

---

[1] If it is accepted that justice requires equality of something then one of the most important tasks is to define the currency of justice. Cohen, for example, proposes to equalize access to advantage. Others argue for equalizing resources and still others for equality of capabilities (cf. Sen 1992; Dworkin 2000).

between adversary (US system) and non-adversary (European tradition) trials. They found that a trial where judge and jury were two distinct bodies was perceived as fairer than a system where the dispute resolution process leadership and decision-maker were in the hands of one and the same person. In other words, it is not only the fairness of a distributive outcome but also the procedural conditions under which an outcome is accomplished that enhances its acceptance.[2]

Studying the interaction between procedural and distributive justice, social psychological justice scholars are still trying to determine (1) under what conditions justice evaluations are based on the distribution of outcomes, and under what conditions evaluations are based on the procedure (i.e. the decision-making process by which the distribution of outcomes was accomplished), and (2) when both the distribution and the process are relevant and salient for an overall judgment of fairness, if one of the two is more important than the other or if they are equally important. When both are relevant, some researchers suggested that a procedurally just allocation (i.e. when the person is given a voice in decisions) may mitigate reactions to an unfavorably unjust distribution (the "fair process effect" – see Folger et al. 1979). However, these two aspects of justice are frequently interdependent, and the significance of each will vary with the situation to be judged (e.g. Sweeney and McFarlin 1993; Brockner and Wiesenfeld 1996).

For some reasons, the interdependence of distributive and procedural justice has not received much attention in normative theory. In fact, the commonest normative theories of justice are divided into procedural and substantive outcome oriented views while neglecting the respective other part of justice in the sense that it only receives "instrumental" attention. In Rawlsian terms (Rawls 2005), pure procedural views of justice argue that it is the fairness of a procedure and only its fairness that makes a distributive outcome just. Libertarians argue that any distributive outcomes resulting from fair conditions for the exchange of social resources must be accepted as legitimate (e.g. Nozick 1974). Outcome oriented normative theories of justice, by contrast, argue that the goal of any distribution should be a state of affairs that can be judged as just according to one or several principles of justice (as mentioned above). According to these theories, allocation procedures play a minor role in the realization or approximation of this goal (Miller 1999; Rawls 2005). In consequence, the fairness of procedures is predefined by the just outcomes to be reached, but they have no value independent of the just outcome – which is in sharp contrast to what social psychological discussion suggests (cf. Lind and Tyler 1988).

---

[2] For a more comprehensive analysis of procedural fairness, see Lind and Tyler (1988).

Viewed from the perspective of substantive theories of justice, this does not mean that the fairness of a procedure cannot be assessed independently of the outcome to be reached. Proponents of outcome oriented theories of justice would likely side with Miller (1999) who argues that an allocation procedure is fair only if it may be characterized by the following four features. First, it must ensure equal consideration of all claiming a social resource. A procedure would be unfair if it were biased against some claimants but not others. Second, a distributive procedure is fair under the condition that it uncovers all relevant and only relevant information for the social resource to be distributed. If a distributive procedure only considers part of relevant information to reach a just outcome, it is ill-suited to reveal how a social resource should be distributed. Third, it must be transparent. A fair procedure must make accessible to all the rules and criteria applied to distribute the social resource in question. Fourth, it must display adequate respect for individuals considered as claimants. A procedure might lead to a just outcome but make it necessary that individuals reveal humiliating facts about their current state of affairs. All these features are in line with what social psychological justice theory suggests (e.g. Leventhal 1980).

A further and more or less neglected aspect of justice in normative theory has been proposed by Törnblom and Vermunt (1999). Their Total Fairness Model integrates outcome valence (positive or negative) as a third factor (besides procedural and distributive fairness) that may affect people's fairness judgments. The distributive (DF) and procedural fairness (PF) factors were dichotomized into fair versus unfair (+DF vs. −DF and +PF vs. −PF) and outcome valence (OV) into positive versus negative (+OV vs. −OV). This facet design allowed eight situations to be generated and then rank ordered in terms of likely subjective justice perceptions ranging from the most unjust situation (−DF/−PF/−OV) to the most just situation (+DF/+PF/+OV).

Regardless of scholarly disputes in both social psychological and normative (social) justice research, we argue that the distinction between distributive and procedural fairness is pertinent in the context of many social issues such as nuclear waste disposal. We now turn to this issue in more detail in Section 7.3.

7.3 Nuclear waste management featuring justice issues

Three types of justice issues are especially crucial in discussions of nuclear waste siting. (1) *Intergenerational justice*, i.e. a proactive (rather than reactive) distributively just allocation of risks and benefits to present and future generations.[3] This entails short and mid-term operational and managerial considerations (e.g. operation, monitoring, and closure activities that are needed for decades to come – up to hundreds of years after a complete shutdown of

---

[3] On intergenerational justice, see also Chapter 6.

nuclear power plants), as well as assessments and considerations of long-term risks with potentially leaking repositories. (2) *Intragenerational justice* referring to (a) an uneven distribution of waste within a given society based on safety-technical constraints, i.e. issues of *distributive justice*, and (b) the site selection processes to find the best (safest) site, i.e. issues of *procedural justice*. Intergenerational problems will remain as long as the waste is there, but this problem is not the focus of this chapter.

For safety and managerial reasons nuclear waste has to be stored centrally. This might be considered unfair from a moral standpoint, concerning distributive justice, as all members of a given society benefit equally or equitably from electricity produced in nuclear facilities, while a minority is forced to shoulder the burden of waste disposal. If all have equal access to a social resource, they should also shoulder the burden of its negative externalities to an equal amount and if some consume more of a social resource they should pay more to neutralize negative by-products.[4] On the other hand, it could be argued that centralization is the most efficient solution and minimizes burdens and risks for the greater number of people (utility principle). But whether it can be justified to overturn justice issues in the name of overall aggregate utility is a question which many and most prominently Rawls answered in the negative. If all members of society have to be viewed as having equal rights then it is illegitimate to discriminate the rights of some in the name of the greater utility for all (Rawls 2005). Thus, how to find the "best" host site, given several geologically favorable areas, is an issue of not only technical importance but of procedural justice as well, because a large part of the problem has to do with the process of making a decision about the allocation (siting) of the waste. It means weighing greatest utility (minimized burdens and risk) for all with concerns of outcome justice. Again the inextricable juxtaposition of distributive and procedural justice becomes salient.

7.4 Evidence from the Swiss repository site selection processes

In this section we discuss the Swiss site selection approaches with a special focus on issues of fairness.

7.4.1 Phase I: 1972–2002 featuring the former Wellenberg project

Switzerland started its nuclear waste management program in 1972. First approaches to find an appropriate site failed. While attempts for low- and intermediate-level waste failed due to inappropriate top-down management

---

[4] Both these principles are prominent in normative research on climate ethics. While the first principle is similar to the so-called "beneficiary-pays-principle," the latter could be identified with the so-called "polluter-pays-principle" (cf. Gardiner 2004; Caney 2005; Page 2008).

approaches that faced strong local resistance, efforts in the context of high-level waste failed due to geological reasons (Flüeler 2006).

A long-lasting process concerning an earlier site named Wellenberg (low- and intermediate-level waste) in the Swiss Canton of Nidwalden was terminated in 2002. The results of cantonal votes resulted in rejection, despite the fact that a number of project modifications were executed between 1995 (when the first voting took place) and 2002 (the year of the second vote). The host municipality Wolfenschiessen voted in favor of siting twice, while the closest neighboring municipalities Dallenwil and Oberdorf strongly rejected the project twice. An inappropriate process may have contributed heavily to the outcome. At this time the implementer (Nagra[5]) was provided with the dual role of process-owner and technical body. This may have forced Nagra in 1986 to accept the offer by the Canton of Nidwalden government to extend exploration activities and reconsider Mount Wellenberg as a potential repository host site although the Wellenberg was not shortlisted in Nagra's earlier narrowing down (Flüeler 2006).

Data from a case study (Scholz et al. 2007; Krütli et al. 2010) conducted in 2006 using multiple methods (media analysis, survey, focus groups, in-depth interviews) supported the proposition that fairness matters in the context of nuclear waste siting. A survey in the Canton of Nidwalden ($N = 532$, response rate: 31%) on radioactive waste issues such as risk/benefit, emotions, trust, information, attitudes, and fairness, for example, indicated the importance of fairness issues (see Figure 7.1). Procedural issues such as "transparency/traceability of procedure," "alternative site options," "early and comprehensive information," "participation options," and "means for consultations with alternative expertise" were highly rated (4.04–4.52 on a 5-point scale, 1 = "not at all important," 5 = "very important"). Interestingly, there were substantial differences between proponents and opponents of the repository project Wellenberg regarding "participation options" and "means for alternative expertise provided." This difference may indicate that there are different views on how much "voice" should be given to concerned people.

Information about distributive preferences regarding how to allocate repositories (assuming that a number of potential host sites meeting geological requirements are available) were collected via endorsements of options (items) such as: "Repository hosted by region with highest electricity consumption"; "No repository in region already burdened with nuclear power plants"; "Several repositories spread over a favorable area"; and "Repository in area with lowest population density." These four items rated significantly lower (2.54–3.26 on a 5-point scale, 1 = "do not at all agree," 5 = "strongly agree") (see Figure 7.2) than procedural issues as shown in Figure 7.1. Interestingly, the

---

[5] www.nagra.ch/en

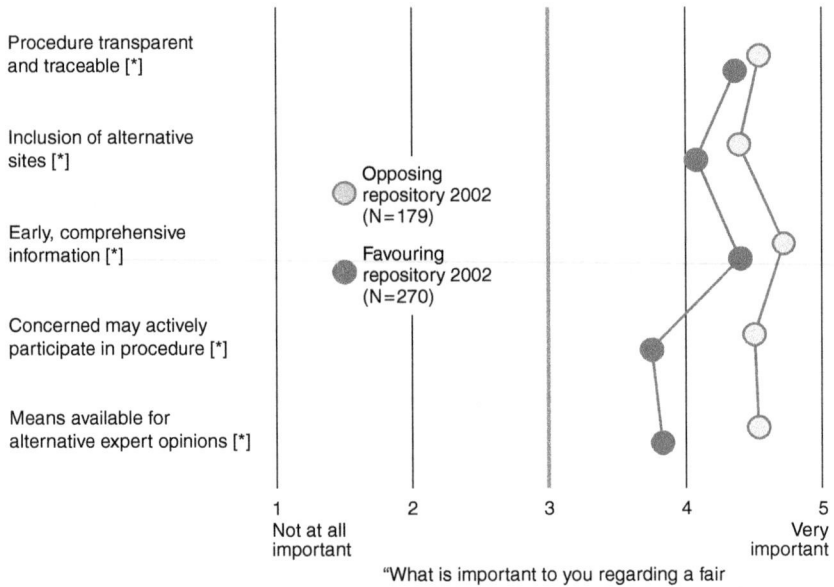

Figure 7.1 Survey data from the Swiss Canton of Nidwalden in 2006 on respondents' perception of procedural fairness issues in repository siting for nuclear waste. Source: adapted from Krütli (2007: 63; see also Krütli et al. 2010).
* $p < .05$ (pairwise t-test, 2-tailed)

option "lowest population density" is clearly favored. Yet no significant differences were obtained between proponents and opponents of a repository.

It is notable that a Swiss-wide survey ($N = 2,428$; response rate: 46%) revealed the same pattern as shown in Figures 7.1 and 7.2 (cf. Stauffacher et al. 2008).

The most striking result of the survey in the Swiss Canton of Nidwalden, however, is shown in Figure 7.3. Respondents of the municipality directly adjacent to the potential host community of a repository, Dallenwil, reveal a distinct pattern in their perception of the siting process fairness. They considered themselves significantly less fairly treated and less involved in the procedure than respondents from all other municipalities in the canton. How come? Participants of focus groups in the case study mentioned above reported repeatedly that (1) the planned repository would have affected residents of the community of Dallenwil directly due to transportation and noise during the construction phase; (2) they would not have received the same attention by the implementer as the siting municipality Wolfenschiessen; (3) in contrast to

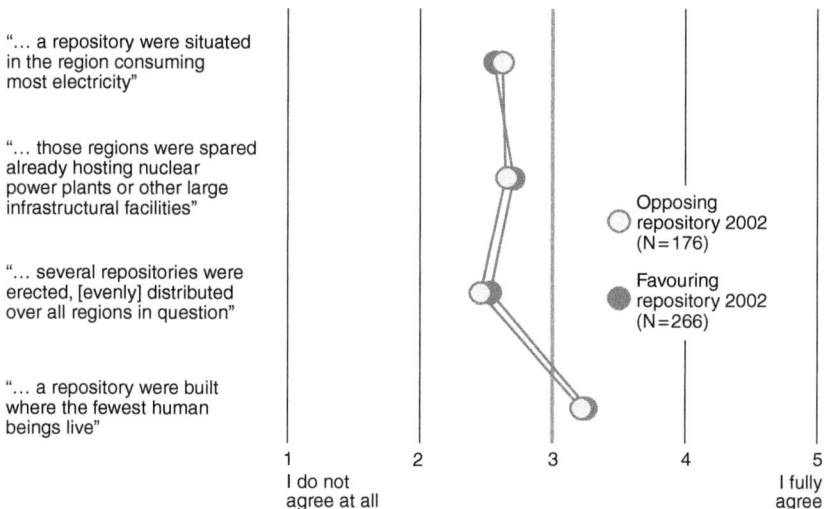

Figure 7.2 Survey data from the Swiss Canton of Nidwalden in 2006 on respondents' perception of distributive fairness issues in repository siting for nuclear waste. Source: adapted from Krütli (2007: 59).

Wolfenschiessen no compensation was foreseen for Dallenwil in the case a repository would have been built in Wolfenschiessen; and (4) information and negotiation activities were concentrated to the potential host site Wolfenschiessen and the capital municipality Stans (Krütli 2007; see also Krütli et al. 2010).

A final outcome to be presented here concerns the respondents' perception of procedural versus distributive justice. A fair process is in general considered more meaningful than a fair distribution. The item "Any outcome would be accepted if it resulted from a fair procedure" scored significantly higher than the other two items (see Table 7.1).

In summary, there is evidence from survey data (as well as from other studies using local media analysis, focus groups, and in-depth interviews) that fairness matters. There is even a clear trend in people's perceptions indicating that procedural issues are more meaningful than distributive issues in the repository siting process. The following statement in the questionnaire of a survey respondent who is an opponent of the repository project may illustrate these findings: "Only in dialogue with all stakeholders can a solution be found."

Table 7.1. *General perception of procedural vs distributive fairness (in the frame of nuclear waste). Source: adapted from Krütli (2010: 17). Data are from a survey in Switzerland (2007) and in the Swiss Canton of Nidwalden (2006) on the topic of radioactive waste. 5-point scale (1 = "do not at all agree"; 5 = "fully agree").*
* $p < .00$ (pairwise *t*-test, 2-tailed); **$p < .00$ (pairwise *t*-test, 2-tailed)

Item	Swiss-wide survey 2007, N = 2,298		Survey in the Swiss Canton of Nidwalden 2006, N = 522	
	Mean	SD	Mean	SD
Procedure does not matter, outcome has to be fair	3.09*	1.15	3.13**	1.12
Any outcome accepted if resulting from a fair procedure	3.67*	.95	3.75**	.87
It depends: if a lot is at stake the outcome counts, if not the procedure	2.77*	1.05	2.82**	.97

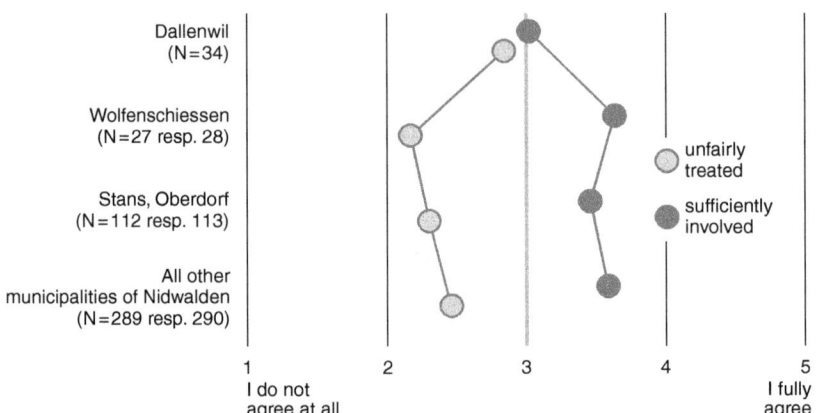

Municipal comparison of opinions "sufficiently involved" und "unfairly treated", respectively, in the Wellenberg process (place of residence in 1995)

Figure 7.3 Survey data from the Swiss Canton of Nidwalden in 2006. Respondents of Wolfenschiessen's directly adjacent neighboring municipality Dallenwil feel less fairly treated and less well involved in the process. Source: adapted from Krütli (2007: 65; see also Krütli et al. 2010).

7.4.2 Phase II: 2003 until today, new stepwise approach

In 2003 Switzerland changed the Nuclear Energy Act. The new act does not allow a cantonal referendum for nuclear facilities anymore. Parallel to the revision of the Nuclear Energy Act and as a further consequence of the events of Wellenberg, the Swiss Federal Office of Energy (SFOE) prepared a new repository site selection concept (BFE 2008). A major change regarding the procedure concerned the clear allocation of responsibilities. While Nagra, the Swiss implementer, is responsible for all safety related technical issues, the Swiss Federal Office of Energy is the responsible body for the (participatory) process.

This delegation of responsibility consists of a three-stage procedure over 12 years designed to systematically screen (and narrow down) geologically favorable areas. The whole procedure is characterized by the primacy of safety and consultative participation of the regions under consideration. There are currently (2014) six siting regions under consideration for hosting a repository for low- and intermediate-level waste, high-level waste, or for both. The major part of Switzerland is out of consideration due to unsuitable geological conditions (see Figure 7.4). This makes the realization of distributive fairness very difficult or impossible, making the necessity of procedural fairness even more salient and pertinent.

The new site selection procedure in Switzerland draws from flaws of the Wellenberg project and from project failures as well as new approaches in other countries such as UK, Sweden, and Germany (e.g. AkEnd 2002; KASAM 2005; CoRWM 2006). It is, moreover, guided by recommendations of international bodies such as the Nuclear Energy Agency (NEA 2004) and the International Atomic Energy Agency (IAEA 2003) as well as research institutions such as the US National Research Council (National Research Council 2001, 2003). They all have in common that they consider open, transparent, stepwise, and participatory site selection processes (i.e. fair procedures) a must (cf. COWAM 2 2007). Data from own studies may illustrate this.

Two vignette studies using conjoint analysis technique (e.g. Gustafsson et al. 2007) and conducted in 2009 analyzed the importance of three aspects (attributes) of a siting process: procedural fairness (PF), distributive justice (DF), and outcome valence (OV). The design of the vignettes followed the Total Fairness Model of Törnblom and Vermunt (1999) proposing that the evaluation of the fairness of a situation is a function of PF, DF, and OV. These attributes were represented by three levels (each derived from relevant justice literature, the siting concept of SFOE, and own insights from previous studies of the issue at hand): PF (fair, mid-fair, unfair), DF (just, mid-just, unjust), and OV (positive, mid-positive, negative). This design with three attributes and three attribute-levels each provides 27 combinations of alternative decision

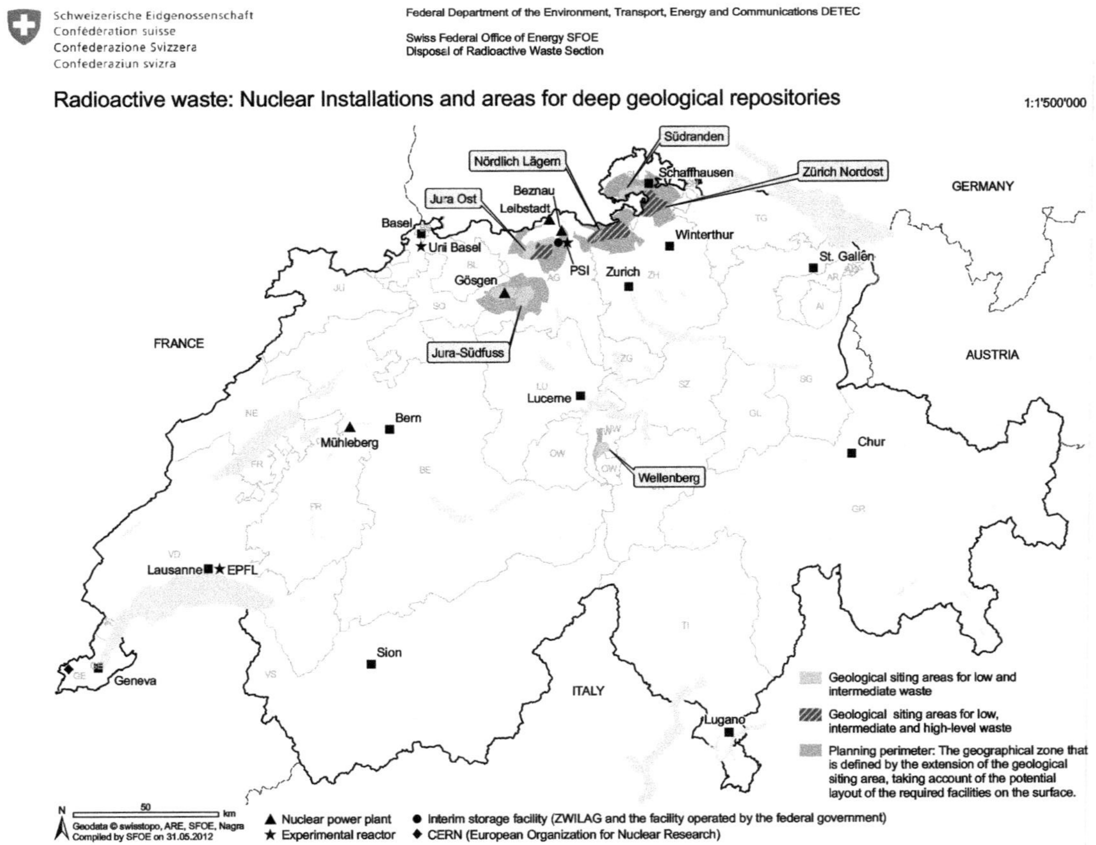

Figure 7.4 Repository siting areas with favorable geological conditions under consideration (current state, 2014). Source: BFE (2013).

Table 7.2. *Example of a vignette representing an unfair procedure (procedural justice, −PF), an mid-fair distribution (distributive injustice, +/−DF), and a negative outcome valence (−OV). Source: Krütli et al. (2012: 87).*

The site selection procedure is not regulated; restricted information is provided; the affected population cannot actively participate in the decision-making process, participation in panel discussions only; administrative bodies represent interests of the population; substantive issues are delegated to experts.

A site has to be selected out of several regions providing (similar) appropriate safety conditions; in this final site selection step voluntariness is the core criterion, i.e. the region willing to take the depository will be selected; the Swiss Federal Council takes the decision.

No geological repository for radioactive waste will be built, the waste will be stored on surface sites for unlimited time; the power consumption increases due to continuing electrification; for that reason it was recently decided to increase nuclear capacity (new power plants); simultaneously renewable energy systems will be promoted.

---

situations (vignettes), representing realistic decision situations of the current repository site selection process in Switzerland (cf. BFE 2008). A reduced design comprising nine vignettes represents a sufficient set to be assessed by participants (cf. Backhaus et al. 2006). Two more vignettes were included to check the validity of the statistical model. A total of 109 volunteers participated (Study 1, $N = 53$ people from academia; Study 2, $N = 56$ people from the general public). Participants ranked all eleven vignettes (see Table 7.2, for an example) according to their personal preferences. Rank 1 represents the most preferred vignette while rank 11 represents the least preferred one.

Computation provides estimates of part-worth utilities of all attribute-levels and the importance of all three attributes (for details see Krütli et al. 2012). Part-worth utilities of attribute-levels vary positively or negatively from a basis utility, which corresponds to the average rank of the vignettes. Importance of attributes corresponds to the range of attribute-levels within the attribute. That is, the greater the range the more important an attribute is. All attributes sum up to 100%. Results of the two studies showed the same general pattern: Situations (vignettes) including fair procedures (+PF), just distributive rules (+DF), and positive outcome valence (+OV) provided positive part-worth utilities and vice versa (see Table 7.3). While a fair process resulted in highest positive part-worth utility values (Study 1: 1.04; Study 2: 1.35), negative outcome valence (−OV) resulted in highest negative ones (Study 1: −1.73; Study 2: −1.77). Negative outcome valence refers to a situation where no geological repository will be built (waste will be stored on surface for an indefinite time-range), while new nuclear power plants will be built and renewable energy will be promoted. Distributive issues were of minor relevance, while OV turned out to be the most important attribute

Table 7.3. *Major results of vignettes' studies of 2009 representing aggregated part-worth utilities of attributes and attribute-levels of study 1 (N = 53) and study 2 (N = 56) and attribute importance. The column on the very right indicates p-values of t-test (2-tailed) of means of attribute importance. For further explanations see text. Source: Krütli et al. (2012)*

Attribute	Attribute-level	Part-worth utilities of attribute-levels		Attribute importance [%]		p-value
		Study 1	Study 2	Study 1	Study 2	
Procedural fairness (PF)	Unfair	−1.14	−1.24			
	Mid-fair	.10	−.11	30.38	34.22	.32
	Fair	1.04	1.35			
Distributive fairness (DF)	Unjust	−.34	.05			
	Mid-just	−.13	−.21	22.86	18.27	.13
	Just	.47	.17			
Outcome valence (OV)	Negative	−1.73	−1.77			
	Mid-positive	.70	.76	46.76	47.51	.86
	Positive	1.03	1.01			

(Study 1: 46.76%; Study 2: 47.51%; see Table 7.3) followed by procedural fairness (Study 1: 30.38%; Study 2: 34.22%) and distributive fairness (Study 1: 22.86%; Study 2: 18.27%). This means that subjects, as expected, followed the general assumptions of the Total Fairness Model of Törnblom and Vermunt (1999), i.e. +PF, +DF, +OV is preferred to −PF, −DF, −OV. Subjects' rank orders were most heavily influenced by the valence of the outcome (OV) followed by procedural fairness (PF), while the fairness of the distribution (DF) was of very minor (if any) importance.

In a representative survey study targeting the Swiss German population conducted in 2011 ($N = 3,082$, response rate 41%) we replicated the results of the before mentioned studies. A major goal of the study was to analyze how people perceive *nuclear* waste versus *hazardous* waste[6] in terms of risks, trust,

---

[6] Hazardous waste is understood as non-radioactive material which cannot be further used. Examples of hazardous waste are batteries, heavy metals, fluorescent tubes, metal-bearing sludge, mineral oil mixture, filter ash from incineration etc. Hazardous waste has to be disposed at surface sites or in old mines.

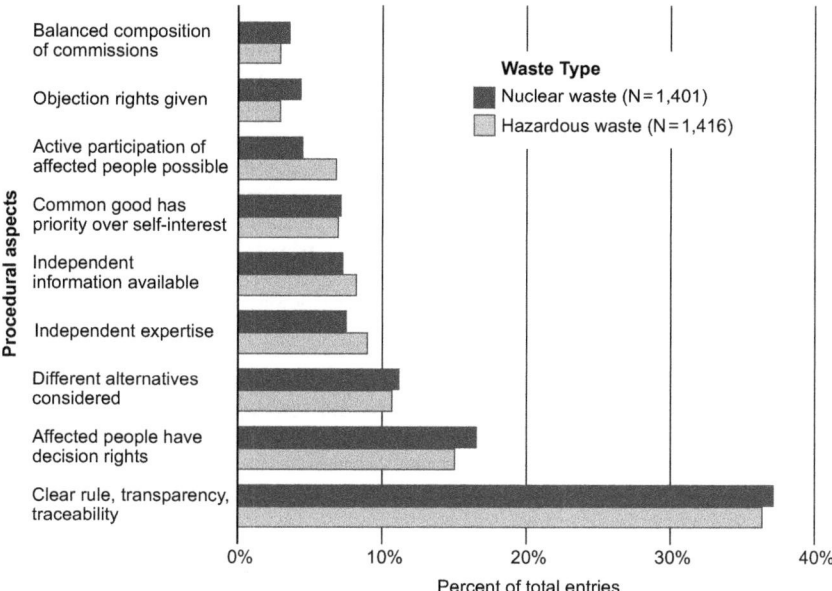

Figure 7.5 Survey study of 2011 on the perception of nuclear waste and hazardous waste issues. Importance of procedural fairness aspects (political process, planning process, etc.) is shown.

management, information, etc. A number of justice issues were included in the questionnaire. We used two separate questionnaires, one targeting nuclear waste and the other hazardous waste. People were asked to rate nine items representing procedural aspects. All of them scored 3.75–4.45 on a 5-point scale (1 = "not at all important"; 5 = "very important"). The question was of a general kind ("In general, how important are the following aspects in a X process?" where X = political, planning, etc.). Item "clear rules, transparency, traceability" scored highest (4.45 on a 5-point scale). The high scores for procedural issues, particularly for the item "clear rules, transparency, traceability," conformed to the results of earlier studies as presented above (see Figure 7.1). Furthermore, respondents had to select the most important option ("Which one of the previously mentioned procedural aspects is, in your eyes, the most important one?"). For both waste categories the aspect "clear rules, transparency, traceability" was clearly top ranked with 37 percent of total entries (see Figure 7.5), followed by "decision rights" (15.9%) and "alternatives considered" (10.9%). This distinct preference for "clear rules, transparency, traceability" is interesting as it shows that in general people do not primarily claim "voice" or "decision power" (all of which one can hear in the field of nuclear waste) in a decision process where safety is most important and technical issues are pertinent. Likewise it is pertinent that the rules

Table 7.4. *Survey study of 2011 on the perception of nuclear waste and hazardous waste issues. The table shows an example of a pair of vignettes to be evaluated (in terms of fairness) by respondents.*

Procedure [unfair]: hardly any rules; little information available; no options for participation of affected population; no budget for independent expertise available.	Procedure [fair]: clear rules; comprehensive information; affected population has options for participation; budget for independent expertise available.
Final selection of site (safety-technically comparable alternative site regions) [just]: site meeting different criteria (conflict potential, ecology, and other infrastructure facilities).	Final selection of site (safety-technically comparable alternative site regions) [unjust]: site with lowest population density.
Deep geological repository [positive]: will be built (referendum); above ground interim storage facilities will be closed.	Deep geological repository [negative]: will not be built (referendum); nuclear waste will be stored above ground for an indefinite time.
Vignette A: ☐	Vignette B: ☐

have to be clear (of how to select a repository), and the procedure has to be transparent and traceable.

In the same survey people were asked to pairwise compare two situations (vignettes) of a site selection process including three attributes PF, DF, and OV on two attribute-levels each. While attribute-levels of PF and DF correspond to fair/unfair those of OV corresponds to repository yes/no. This design with three attributes and two attribute-levels each provides eight potential situations resulting in 28 different pairs to be compared, respectively. Each respondent was provided with two randomized pairwise combinations (see Table 7.4, for an example) to be assessed in terms of fairness ("Which situation do you consider more fair?").

Computation of aggregated data shows that situations (vignettes) featuring a fair procedure received top rankings (Table 7.5). Very similar to previously obtained patterns, a fair process resulted in the highest positive part-worth utility values (.89/.83, cf. Table 7.6). The most negative part-worth utility ($-.89/-.83$) lies in the PF attribute, indicating that under the given design PF is the most important attribute. While +OV (part-worth utility: .29/.36) represents a situation where a geological repository will be built, $-$OV (part-worth utility: $-.29/-.36$) represents a situation where no geological repository will be built. Distributive issues are, again, of minor relevance (part-worth utility: $+/-.14/ +/-.19$). Results also confirm the general assumptions of the Total Fairness Model of Törnblom and Vermunt (1999) as shown above. Furthermore, subjects' preferential rankings of the perceived procedural fairness of the situations clearly overshadow the rankings of OV. This is in contrast to the vignette studies described above (cf. Table 7.3). In this

Table 7.5. *Survey study of 2011 concerning perceptions of nuclear waste and hazardous waste issues. Percentages refer to the number of vignettes totally shown versus selected by respondents. Example: the top ranked vignette of the nuclear waste frame (fair; just; yes) was selected by respondents in 624 cases out of total 789 cases (79%) while the bottom ranked one was selected in 146 cases out of total 785 cases (19%). GR = geological repository.*

Preference of vignettes based on individual pairwise comparison [%]	Nuclear waste (hazardous waste)		
	attribute / attribute-level		
	Procedural fairness	Distributive justice	Outcome valence
79 (82)	Fair	Just	GR yes
71 (69)	Fair	Unjust	GR yes
62 (60)	Fair	Just	GR no
53 (51)	Fair	Unjust	GR no
33 (38)	Unfair	Just	GR yes
27 (30)	Unfair	Unjust	GR yes
22 (22)	Unfair	Just	GR no
19 (16)	Unfair	Unjust	GR no

survey study OV was significantly revised. Perhaps the absence of information about the energy strategy may account for weaker preference for OV.

In summary, there is a clear dominance of the weights assigned to PF over DF in the context of safety considerations pertaining to nuclear waste disposal. However, procedural aspects compete with the perceived valence of the outcome (OV) and contextual factors such as future alternative energy sources. Survey data from *pairwise vignette comparisons* are consistent with data from *vignette ranking* studies.

7.5 Discussion

The purpose of this chapter was to discuss the significance of fairness issues in repository site selection processes for nuclear waste. Our major focus was on how stakeholder endorsements are affected by their perceptions of procedural and distributive justice as well as by the valence of the final outcome of the selection process.

Results from the studies described in this chapter strongly suggest that procedural fairness matters. Data clearly indicate that procedural issues are perceived to be more meaningful than distributive issues in the context of the repository siting process. Respondents considered clear rules, transparency, and meaningful information to be the most important procedural factors ahead

Table 7.6. *Survey study of 2011 on the perception of nuclear waste and hazardous waste issues. Aggregated part-worth utility estimates of attribute-levels and attribute importance of both framings nuclear waste and hazardous waste are shown. The utility estimates of the attribute-levels vary positively or negatively from the basis utility. The total utility of a vignette is calculated (additively) by the constant and the part-worth utilities of the attribute-levels of all attributes of the corresponding vignette). Note that attribute importance sums up to 100%.*

		Part-worth utility estimate		Attribute importance [%]	
Attribute	Attribute-level	Radioactive waste	Hazardous waste	Radioactive waste	Hazardous waste
Procedural fairness (PF)	Unfair	−.89	−.83	67.56	60.07
	Fair	.89	.83		
Distributive fairness (DF)	Unjust	−.14	−.19	10.52	13.80
	Just	.14	.19		
Outcome valence (OV), geological repository/disposal facility	Negative (No)	−.29	−.36	21.92	26.13
	Positive (Yes)	.29	.36		

of "voice" and "decision power." Furthermore, "process violations," as shown in the Wellenberg case, tend to have a "long memory," i.e. people may remember violations of procedural aspects for a longer time, as compared to violations of distributive aspects.

A problem-free distribution of nuclear waste can only be achieved if necessary technical safety requirements are guaranteed to be met, no matter which distributive rule is applied (e.g. equality, equity, need). Thus distributive justice principles (that determine who is entitled to what and in what amount) are likely to play a minor role for those concerned with or affected by nuclear waste issues. However, the site selection process becomes more salient and gains in importance, especially when a region at the receiving end is forced to accept the waste for underground storage. Therefore, the perceived fairness of the decision-making procedure that determines the deposit siting is crucial (clear rules, comprehensive information, etc.). Safety considerations will guide the entire process, which, in turn, will affect the perception of procedural fairness. If one cannot convincingly show in a transparent way that the chosen site is the best alternative from a safety perspective, the procedure will most probably be perceived as unfair. This is a tightrope walk inside a highly politicized battlefield where heated discussions about the civilian use of nuclear energy are carried out. It may well be the case that the intended outcome will not be reached, even if both the distribution and the procedure are perceived as fair.

Viewed from a normative perspective, it would certainly be a mistake to derive normative requirements from the empirical results described above, as an *ought* cannot be deduced from an *is* (Hume 2000). Empirical results do not allow for normative claims about whether or not it is appropriate (e.g. in the context of social issues like nuclear waste repository siting) to consider procedural justice more important than distributive justice. However, it would also be unwise to ignore the relevance of procedural fairness for the perceived fairness of a distributive outcome, especially when distributive justice is not possible to accomplish.

More generally, normative theory should at least consider the following three aspects, all fleshing out the context-sensitive interdependence of procedural and distributive justice.

First, since data suggest that in cases where a just outcome distribution is impossible, a just procedure might increase the likelihood that the perceived distributive injustice is still accepted. Normative theory should explore under what conditions it can be argued that this is an option. In the case of nuclear waste siting, it is considerations of safety or aggregate utility that seem to make the accomplishment of a just distribution impossible. But whether it is considerations of safety or aggregate utility alone that account for a situation in which distributive justice is impossible to accomplish seems to warrant clarification in the context of normative theory. It seems that normative theory would benefit from explorations regarding the conditions under which (e.g. for what kinds of social issues) distributive procedures may be judged as more weighty than distribution outcomes for fairness assessments of a situation.

Second, data also indicate that, in the case of nuclear waste siting, it is important for the acceptance of a distributive outcome that the distributive procedure (of the decision-making process) is fair, regardless of how just the outcome is considered. Thus, concerning some distributive issues, it seems to be necessary to assess what a fair procedure should be independent of what a just outcome would be. Based on data from the above-mentioned nuclear waste siting studies, the procedural justice aspects of transparency and traceability took priority over distributive justice considerations (as, again, distributive justice was not possible to accomplish). But whether or not, from a normative point of view, transparency and traceability can always be justified to be more important than other procedural aspects when defining fair procedures is a question for further investigation. Thus, the question of what procedural aspects should become relevant in what kinds of social issues seems to be another desideratum requiring further and context-sensitive normative investigation.

Third, if it is the case that some social issues demand fair procedures, because a just distributive outcome is impossible, it becomes necessary to show in what way the respective distributions can be viewed to be normatively justified. According to libertarians, a fair procedure justifies any kind of distributive outcome as just. In contrast, substantive theories of justice argue, that it is only the fairness of a distribution that justifies its acceptability, while the distributive procedure is merely a means to reach this goal. But since it seems that only for some issues (e.g. those in which a just distribution is not possible to accomplish), reliance on procedures alone is justified. Acceptability of the outcome distribution depends on the social issue at stake and cannot be determined by framing all questions of justice in procedural or in substantive terms. Therefore, the nature of normative justification of a distribution is likely to vary with the social issue at stake. Thus, normative theory should be able to explain why different social issues require different justifications for a given distributive outcome.

Taken together, these three points suggest that normative theory should take into consideration that for some social issues, such as the case of nuclear waste siting discussed here, it seems prudent to leave it an entirely open question what a just outcome would be. In other words, we should leave it to fair procedures rather than any vision of distributive justice to decide outcomes. In the case of these social issues, fair procedures would only call for as much transparency and traceability of distributive decisions as possible but leaving it to (technical or other) experts what the best distributive decision is. In the case of social issues for which expertise cannot be as distinctively assigned, as in the case of nuclear waste repository siting, fair procedures would demand that all parties involved regard each other's comparable interests as equally legitimate for the decision made (Scheffler 2015). Viewed from a democratic theoretical perspective equal substantial decision power for all should be ensured (Schuppert and Wallimann-Helmer 2014).

However, as data indicate, these normative ideals may be challenged on the basis of safety considerations, which, in turn, allow the technocratic approach more weight. Procedural fairness in the form of an acknowledged (critical) voice may act as a challenge during the decision-making process of the technical community. It may therefore contribute to improved safety standards and to the fulfillment of democratic standards in form of a fair process. From a long-term time perspective, this is crucial as the "best" current (or intragenerational) solution of the waste disposal problem that meets present-days' technical and societal needs may also be the best solution for future generations. Thus, since from an empirical perspective procedural fairness is a necessary – although not sufficient – condition for the acceptance of waste storage siting decisions, it becomes important to further explore in what sense it also contributes to the moral acceptability of these decisions.

7.6 Outlook

Subjective evaluations of the total fairness of a situation are contingent upon individual characteristics (age, sex, values, etc.) as well as social, cultural, and contextual factors. The nature of the allocated resource and the valence of the outcome (in our case negative outcome) are other factors that may affect fairness judgments. The specific context/issue relevant to our studies (e.g. nuclear waste deposit safety considerations) turned out to affect the importance of fairness considerations. Future studies are needed to map the conditions under which disagreements and conflicts may emerge about (a) safety considerations; (b) the amount of "voice" (and other procedural factors) that affected people should be granted in decisions about negative (as well as positive) outcome allocations; (c) the distributive principles (or their combinations) that are considered most appropriate for the allocation of social resources that are not divisible; and (d) how the nature and importance of the allocated resource (and other "contextual" factors) may affect justice conceptions.

A future research program may thus focus on the relative weights and importance of safety and fairness considerations, respectively, for decisions about how nuclear waste repositories ought to be selected. We may use a facet design to exemplify the generation of a systematic and comprehensive research framework containing a large number of mutually related studies involving four major variables: (a) safety issues (e.g. transport, repacking, long-term storage), (b) procedural principles (e.g. voice, transparency, consistency), (c) distributive principles (e.g. equity, equality, need), and (d) social resources (e.g. information, services, money). This incomplete set of variables generates a $3 \times 3 \times 3 \times 3 = 81$ factorial design, allowing the construction of a large number of studies focusing on comparisons of the relative weights of safety versus fairness, where importance ratings for different combinations of procedural, distributive, and resource aspects would be compared to importance ratings for each type of safety consideration.

Further, social psychological theory (*what is*) and normative theory (*what ought to be*) are largely detached from each other. Considering the often artificial separation between various disciplines (and their mutual isolationist tendencies), this is understandable. However, various disciplines would benefit from each other's viewpoints and accumulated knowledge. We have aimed for an interdisciplinary research approach in which the represented disciplines are social psychology, and normative political theory. Our research program may also be characterized as transdisciplinary in that various stakeholder perspectives are incorporated and contributed to the studies, respectively. Hopefully, our research may not only make theoretical contributions but also provide ideas that might benefit attempts at resolving social problems that emerge in the context of selecting repositories for nuclear waste.

Acknowledgments

A special thanks goes to Behnam Taebi and Sabine Roeser, editors of this book, for inviting us to contribute a chapter to this important volume. We would also express our thanks to Sandro Bösch for his help with all the figures and to Dario Pedolin for his support with data analysis. Finally, we would like to thank an uncountable number of respondents, interview partners, critical readers, informants, and other supporters of our studies on radioactive waste. Without their willingness to voluntarily complete questionnaires, answer requests, participate in workshops and focus groups, we would not have been able to produce our study results.

8 Nuclear energy, justice, and power: the case of the Pilgrim Nuclear Power Station license renewal

Bindu Panikkar and Ronald Sandler

8.1 Introduction

Social and environmental evaluation of nuclear energy requires assessing it over the course of its life cycle. Close to five decades after the first commercial nuclear generator became operational in 1968, many of the first wave of reactors[1] are approaching the end of their design lives. Nevertheless, they continue to function and be profitable, and many have applied for licenses to operate past their design life. For example, since 2000, the United States Nuclear Regulatory Commission (NRC) has approved extensions for 73 of the 104 nuclear energy plants in the country, and 29 more will be up for renewal before 2023 (GAO 2013). These renewed licenses will in turn expire starting 2023. NRC expects license renewal applications for reactors beyond 60 years by 2018 or 2019 (Dolley 2014), and in a 2008 joint workshop between NRC and Department of Energy (DOE) they explored future technical and research requirements to continue beyond 60 years (NRC and DOE 2008). Relicensing, like original plant sitings, are contentious for reasons to do with community and environmental health and impacts (risk assessment). They are also cases in which issues of justice are prominent, including the distribution of benefits and burdens (distributive justice) as well as recognition and standing in decision-making processes (procedural justice).[2] They thereby raise issues of energy, authority, and responsibility. This chapter examines the social, ethical, and environmental claims made in response to license renewal and continued operation of plants at the end of their design lives. However, many of the issues apply, *mutatis mutandis*, to plant siting generally. The focus of the chapter is the Pilgrim Nuclear Power Generator (Pilgrim) in Plymouth, Massachusetts.

---

[1] First generation nuclear reactors were proof-of-concept reactors. Almost all operational nuclear energy reactors in the world are second generation reactors (Goldberg and Rosner 2011).
[2] See also Chapter 7 on procedural justice.

In January 2006, Entergy Corporation, Pilgrim's current owner and operator, filed a license renewal application with the NRC to extend the operation of Pilgrim Nuclear Power Station (Pilgrim) past its original 40-year license. The NRC approved this application on May 29, 2012, giving Entergy a 20-year license extension for the plant (NRC 2014a). As a result of community contentions on license renewal, Pilgrim underwent a record-length license review, taking six years rather than the typical two and a half (Corcoran 2011).

The licensing process assesses the feasibility of extensions; it examines if an industrial project satisfies all regulatory requirements and does not pose undue risks to human health or the environment. Because of what is at stake with licensing and license renewal, the process is often highly contentious, as it was with Pilgrim. It is filled with debates and disputes on regulatory authority, rights, the value of nature, risks and benefits, and justice.

Risk assessment or an environmental impact statement are primary tools used in the United States and elsewhere for decision-making in license renewals, as well as to set regulatory standards and enforcement mechanisms. Calculated risks are based on known hazards, their magnitude and probability of occurring as well as cost–benefit analysis. The risk consequences are largely viewed from a non-fatalistic viewpoint (Renn and Rohrmann 2000) which may be of particular concern when assessing an aging reactor. Perceiving, interpreting, and acting upon risk involve not only scientific and economic factors but also social, political, and legal factors. The sociopolitical factors are central to understanding modern technological risks since calculability itself and the construction of security (or safety) is a social endeavor that has subjective and contextual elements, which are subject to a high degree of uncertainty and contestation (Beck 1992; Dean 1999; Lash 2000); see also Chapter 3 by John Downer in this volume. Many governments are making concerted efforts to engage the public with regards to technological development, even at the level of permitting (Hagendijk and Irwin 2006). However such democratic endeavors are often a hotbed of fierce debates and contestations or "technopolitics" in framing of risks and benefits and in governance of technologies (Schrader-Frechette 1991c ; Freundenberg and Pastor 1992; Bauer 1995; Gottweis 1998; Gieryn 1999; Jasanoff 2005; Sunder Rajan 2005).

One way to understand social debates and social movement is as a set of collective beliefs and opinions in a population that suggests changing some perceived unethical or harmful elements within a society. Social and cultural rationalities that build beliefs and opinions are informed not just by science, but also tradition, values, attitude, emotion, and needs (Freudenburg and Pastor 1992; Renn 1998; Gieryn 1999). Central to understanding differential risk perception in a society is the variance in ethical values, what actors consider to be "good," and what value they attach to pieces of information. Renn and

Rohrmann (2000: 14) define risk as "the possibility that human actions, situations or events might lead to consequences that affect aspects of what humans value." The central source of concern for the community members in the Pilgrim case is how economic development is prioritized versus consideration of community, nature, and future generations. Thus, what is contested is not only what the risks are of the facility (i.e. the assessment of the risks), but crucially whether they are acceptable (i.e. whether an aging facility is safe for continued operation as it is and if it needs improved safety mechanisms based on the new technology available). Safety and acceptable levels of risks are not just technological and scientific components but also issues of power, control, and trustworthiness (Freudenburg and Pastor 1992; Gottweis 1998).

Risk, in the case of Pilgrim, may be higher than usual because Pilgrim is an aging plant; it has many intrinsic disadvantages and limitations such as its design, the Mark 1 boiling water reactors. While relicensing takes aging into consideration, it does not require the use of better safety mechanisms in place based on better technology available. While extended operation offers benefits for some, or even for society at large, it does so while imposing a huge burden of risks on others (Freudenburg and Pastor 1992). This imposition of risk on one group by another is often at the heart of technological risk conflicts and is the source of concerns regarding distributive justice, including intergenerational justice (Perrow 1986). It can be used and misused by different social and political actors, and can perpetuate existing distributional inequalities and unequal power relationships (Michaels 2005; Frickel and Moore 2006; Krimsky 2010). Hence, they are also cases in which issues of recognition and standing in decision-making processes (procedural justice) are prominent. They thereby raise issues of power, authority, and responsibility.

Social and environmental evaluation of nuclear energy requires assessing it over the course of its life cycle. Given the importance of the social, political, ethical, and economic networks in shaping science and technological development, understanding the concerns associated with decision-making in nuclear energy licensing requires a detailed case study. What follows is such an examination. It is a study of the various social, legal, and policy claims made by different stakeholders in response to license renewal and continued operation of Pilgrim Nuclear Power Station (Pilgrim) in Plymouth, Massachusetts.

To explore and document the social discourse around the Pilgrim license renewal and its continued operation we conducted close to thirty in-depth interviews with key community members, industry officials, scientists, and town and state officials, and examined hundreds of community documents and websites, media reports, legal briefings and scientific articles. We also attended community meetings, flotillas, town hall hearings, and policy hearings at the Massachusetts State House to understand the varied contexts within which the community seeks accountability and justice in improving Pilgrim's safety. Pilgrim offers an exceptional case study that enables us to understand how community members have attempted to promote transparency and accountability in industrial practices on justice-based grounds, as well as the power dynamics and structures in which they have worked. In many respects, the Pilgrim case is emblematic of the challenges to participatory justice and decision-making surrounding nuclear energy facilities from permitting to management to end-of-life.[3]

8.2 Pilgrim's first forty years

Pilgrim Nuclear Power Generator, a Mark 1 boiling water reactor, stands on the rocky western shores of Cape Cod Bay in Plymouth, Massachusetts. When it was built in 1972, the primary reasons for situating a reactor in this historic town were the availability of land close to water and the low population density. The latter no longer holds true, as Plymouth's population has more than tripled since the 1970s. Bechtel Corporation constructed Pilgrim under the ownership of Boston Edison Co. and started its operation in 1972. In 1999, Louisiana-based Entergy Corporation bid Pilgrim for $80 million, of which $67 million was paid for nuclear fuel. It was the first time a US nuclear energy plant was sold in a competitive bidding process (Salpukas 1988; Werlin 2008). Today, Pilgrim generates 680 megawatts of nuclear energy; Massachusetts State Nuclear Profile shows that Pilgrim generates close to 14 percent of the total electric energy produced in Massachusetts (EIA 2012). However community members contest this statistic, as the information they obtained from NSTAR, a utility company that supplies retail electricity and natural gas to Massachusetts indicates that maybe as little as 5 percent of the energy used in Massachusetts is sourced from nuclear energy.

Community contentions against relicensing Pilgrim have stemmed partly from its 40-year-long operational history and its design limitations, which are discussed in what follows.

Concerns about Pilgrim's Mark 1 reactor design and its once-through cooling system arose right from the beginning. As early as 1972, Dr. Stephen Hanauer, an Atomic Energy Commission safety official, recommended the discontinuation of all Mark I designs (Hanauer 1972; Mosk 2011) as the containment structure around the reactor core is small and would be unable to withstand increased pressure in the event of a cooling system failure (Zellor 2011). In 1986, Harold Denton, a top NRC safety official, estimated that there was a 90 percent chance of failure of the Mark I pressure containment system if the fuel rods were to overheat (Yang 2011). In response to this design flaw, most

---

[3] See also Gardiner's "Publicity Principle' in Chapter 6 in this volume.

Mark 1 reactors, including Pilgrim, installed direct torus vent systems in 1988 to reduce the vulnerability of boiling water reactor (BWR) Mark 1 containments to severe accident challenges (NRC 1989). However, Pilgrim does not have filters on these vents, so in an emergency situation the surrounding communities could be exposed to large amounts of radiation released directly from the reactor core, a problem which became salient after the Fukushima nuclear disaster (Borchardt 2011; Lochbaum 2012).

Besides the design flaw, early history recorded by long-term community resident, Mary Lampert, show that Pilgrim also began operating without an augmented off-gas treatment system, which reduces the radioactivity in the reactor and minimizes the sludge build-up in the reactor vessel. The augmented off-gas system was installed only in late 1974; until then, the reactor was potentially venting higher levels of radioactive particulates into the environment. In addition, Pilgrim was using defective fuel during the first few years, and the reactor had to be shutdown in 1973 due to fuel channel box damage, which may have increased these radioactive releases into the environment (UCS 2006a, 2006b).

A survey of documents obtained through the Freedom of Information Act by Daniel Burnstein and local public documents from the Plymouth Public Library by Ellen B. Cargill (unpublished) as well as reports by the Union of Concerned Scientists shows multiple spent resin spills that may have flowed through the storm drain into Cape Cod Bay throughout the late 1970s and 1980s (UCS 2006a, 2006b). In December 1983, Pilgrim was shut down for an entire year to replace cracked recirculation system piping. The piping was intended to last the entire 40-year life of the plant but it lasted little more than a quarter of that time. In 1986 the plant had to be shut down again when a design flaw was discovered in the Standby Gas Treatment System (Commonwealth of Massachusetts Senate 1987; UCS 2006a, 2006b). With these series of equipment problems and scrams, Pilgrim was rated the second worst nuclear plant in the country (Darst 1988; Wald 1988). Some of the key issues included problems with the instrumentation monitoring of the core, dry well vacuum breakers, leaks in the instrument air system, weld leaks on the reactor head spray pipe, an oil leak from a pipe in main turbine hydraulic control system, valve failures, insufficient water in the feed water system, and failure of the main transformer (UCS 2006a, 2006b).

The events happening at Pilgrim throughout the 1980s initiated widespread community resistance to Pilgrim. As a result, the Massachusetts Governor Michael Dukakis pushed for a cancer study in the area, which resulted in the Southeastern Massachusetts Health Study (SMHS). SMHS conducted by the Massachusetts Department of Public Health (MADPH) found a fourfold increase in leukemia among residents of certain towns within a 20-mile radius of the plant (Morris and Knorr 1990). A written testimony by Prof.

Dick Clapp, who was part of a federally funded epidemiologic feasibility study shows that "Pilgrim had over-exposed more of its workers (to higher levels of radiation) than any other commercial nuclear plant in the US" (Clapp et al. 1987; Clapp 2014). The number of excess leukemia deaths over a ten-year time period was estimated to be "90 times greater than that predicted by data from other radiation studies" (Morris and Knorr 1990). These reports further galvanized demonstrations and protests against reopening Pilgrim. The Pilgrim Alliance, a group of 300 local activists, sponsored a non-binding referendum in Plymouth and Kingston to shut Pilgrim down. Ted Bosen, an attorney and Pilgrim Alliance member, reflected "Fifty-four percent of [Plymouth's] residents, at a time when Pilgrim paid for 25% of financial revenue, voted to shut it down." However, after the replacement of the failed transformer, which cost a billion dollars, the reactor was connected back to the grid in mid-1989 (UCS 2006b).

At the same time, MA Emergency Management Agency (MEMA) declared that emergency plans for a nuclear disaster in Plymouth were ineffective (Commonwealth of Massachusetts Senate 1987). Some of the key activists, such as Lampert, began to work on emergency planning issues. Citizens at Risk Cape Cod which later evolved to Cape Downwinders (See http://capedownwinders.org) has taken this task on wholly as there is no evacuation plan for the Cape even if Cape residents were identified as an at-risk population within the Ingestion Pathway Zone. Cape Downwinder members, Diane Turco and David Agnew, point out in an in-person interview that within the existing evacuation plan, the bridges that lead out of the Cape would be closed, and Cape residents would be trapped on the Cape with no shelters or any emergency plans in place, which was also made apparent in the remarks made by the Massachusetts Emergency Management Agency Director, Kurt Schwartz at the Barnstable County Regional Emergency Planning Committee (Schwartz 2012).

Community resistance to Pilgrim also revolved around its once-through cooling system. Pine duBois, the founder of The Jones River Watershed Association (JRWA) in Kingston, Massachusetts (See http://jonesriver.org) was particularly concerned about Pilgrim's impact on the ecosystem of Cape Cod Bay. She shared that when Pilgrim sought permission from the state in the 1970s to use Cape Cod Bay as a water source for cooling, Massachusetts mandated a closed-cycle system. Pilgrim's owners successfully challenged the state's mandate and installed the cheaper, once-through system that it has currently. Pilgrim takes in over half a billion gallons of seawater a day from the Cape Cod Bay and discharges heated (by up to 30–40 °F) and polluted water at high velocity, scouring the sea floor and creating a thermal plume, sometimes covering an area up to four square miles (EcoLaw 2012b). This intake harms and often kills fish, plankton, fish eggs, and larvae by "impingement" and "entrainment" (trapping the marine life on intake screens or sucking them through the plant's pipes). Studies done in the 1970s and 1990s show a drastic reduction in rainbow smelt, winter flounder, and cunner populations. They also demonstrate a 15 percent reduction in copepods (a type of zooplankton that right whales feed on exclusively), loss of haddock eggs and larvae, and loss of pollock eggs and from impingement and entrainment (NRC 2007).

Meg Sheenan, an attorney and founder of EcoLaw, a local public-interest law firm based in Cambridge, Massachusetts, notes that the Environmental Protection Agency (EPA) has been regulating entrainment since 1974 and impingement since 1980 under Clean Water Act through the National Pollutant Discharge Elimination System (NPDES) permit process, but these laws also require that the location, design, construction, and capacity of cooling water intake structures reflect "the best technology available" to minimize adverse environmental impacts. The NPDES permit to control water pollution was issued after licensing and has been essentially unchanged since it was first issued while risk monitoring and assessment technology has vastly improved (EcoLaw 2012b).

8.3 The relicensing process

Many of the activists and groups who protested Pilgrim in its early days are still the key players contesting relicensing and its continued operation today. In 2005, a year before Pilgrim applied for the license extension, Lampert started Pilgrim Watch to contest the license renewal. The Pilgrim Watch website offers the most thorough analysis of Pilgrim's risks and the legal contentions it has initiated with the NRC against Pilgrim relicensing (see http://pilgrimwatch.org). Lampert's goal was to get a website so people can understand the issues. For Lampert, relicensing was a way to draw public attention back to Pilgrim. "That's what I knew was going to be the positive outcome of relicensing. I knew full well, nobody wins relicensing. I don't care whether you're Attorney General or a pretend lawyer. You aren't going to win."

By happenstance, Lampert met Molly Bartlett, an attorney with a degree in environmental law. Lampert knew the subject matter and Bartlett knew the legal side and this two-member team initiated many of the contentions against the relicensing of Pilgrim (see http://adams.nrc.gov/wba/).

Pilgrim Watch filed five sets of contentions initially with relicensing in 2006, three with regard to aging and two with regard to environmental impacts of extended operation (NRC 2011b). Some of these contentions were heard but eventually overturned. Amidst relicensing, the Fukushima Daiichi nuclear disaster in Japan struck, adding a twist to the relicensing of Pilgrim. Additional contentions were filed following the inadequate hearing and based on the lessons learned from the Fukushima disaster (NRC 2011a).

Because Pilgrim bears the exact same design as the Fukushima reactor, the event aroused broader citizen interest in Pilgrim, resulting in the formation of Pilgrim Coalition (see www.pilgrimcoalition.org), their outreach has now resulted in over 500 members and affiliated with 28 organizations in and around the state.

While Pilgrim Watch dealt with the NRC, the JRWA and EcoLaw petitioned the EPA. Early 2012, ten months after the Fukushima disaster, EcoLaw began working with the JRWA to investigate Pilgrim's environmental violations.

In January [2012] we started going through all the files at EPA. We spent a long time at EPA, and then started making Freedom of Information Act requests of DEP, tried to figure out who was minding the store. We pulled out the permit and it was expired. The law allows them to administratively continue the permit, so it has been administratively continued. Pretty sad. Nobody's minding the store. Nobody. In the meantime, Entergy complies with a 17-year-old standard. (duBois, Interview)

An official at the Massachusetts Coastal Zone Management stated that the NPDES permit review conditions were previously enforced by an administrative technical committee, and the permit required a committee of fifteen people to provide feedback to the EPA and Boston Edison about whether they were meeting standards and whether any changes were needed in the permit. However, this committee was disbanded when Entergy bought the plant from Boston Edison in 1998. Leading up to the relicensing, the community groups redoubled their efforts around the NPDES permit and petitioned to MADEP, EPA, NRC, Entergy, and National Marine Fisheries Service (EcoLaw 2012a). Pine duBois believes that bringing attention to the expired NPDES permit under the Clean Water Act has increased public awareness of the issue.

A related issue that sparked concern among community members was the leaking of tritium at above the levels of concern into the groundwater, identified as a result of installing ground water monitoring wells in 2007 (Massachusetts Department of Public Health 2013). To date, Entergy has not been able to locate the source of the leak, and the matter remains under investigation. Similarly, Pilgrim has been leaking tolytriazole and sodium nitrate (corrosion inhibitor) into the Cape Cod Bay (EcoLaw 2012a).

Locally at the town level, the Freeze Pilgrim Committee, started with the goal of increasing community involvement among Plymouth residents, began working on a referendum, much like the one the town had successfully passed in 1987. Under the guidance of Attorney Bosen, the committee turned the legislation that Senator Markey filed after Fukushima into a referendum:

We the People of Plymouth, Massachusetts, direct the Plymouth Board of Selectmen to call upon the NRC to immediately suspend all further action on the application of the Entergy Corporation for renewal of its license to operate Pilgrim pending the full implementation of all safety improvements recommended by the NRC as a result of lessons learned from the failures of similarly designed reactors in Fukushima, Japan.

In a town meeting on March 12, 2012, exactly a year after the Fukushima disaster, the memorandum was passed. Although it was non-binding, it received media coverage, and larger organizations (such as Union of Concerned Scientists) and state officials became involved. Bosen reflected:

Let's put it this way, it doesn't affect the licensee whatsoever. Who it's impacting, and it's clear that it is impacting our elected public officials who now see huge numbers that they didn't see before, didn't believe were there. [It] unified our entire state. State rep, state senator, and governor, two state reps, everybody represented a piece of Plymouth in some way, came out not only for the referendum and all of the issues in it, they went beyond it. They said, the dry cask storage has to be in place before that's relicensed because it is not safe ...

This referendum in turn set a precedent for other communities to follow. Led by the Cape Downwinders, all of the fifteen towns on the Cape (Sandwich, Bourne, Falmouth, Mashpee, Yarmouth, Dennis, Brewster, Harwich, Chatham, Orleans, Eastham, Wellfleet, Truro, Barnstable, and Provincetown) have endorsed a memorandum to shut Pilgrim down and presented the petitions to Governor Patrick requesting that the NRC shut down Pilgrim on the grounds that it violates public trust and safety. Martha's Vineyard just recently voted to shut the plant down.

Despite the success of the campaign, Pilgrim was relicensed on May 29, 2012 without meeting any of the safety guidelines from the lessons learned in Fukushima, without a valid NPDES permit, without addressing the community contentions and requests from the state officials.

David Tarantino, an Entergy spokesperson, believes that although the contentions filed by the community tremendously delayed the license renewal and cost Entergy millions of dollars in legal expenses, none of the contentions prevailed because none of them were legitimate concerns. He thinks that the activists do not represent the community as a whole:

You have to realize also that in recent surveys 68 percent of the people in this country support nuclear energy. And you listen to a very small percentage of people. They had this big rally, they had 30 people there. If there is this much public opposition, it's kind of like the chicken littles of the world, running around saying the sky is falling, and it's their lifetime. They've done it for twenty years. I've worked with the same people for twenty years and they're persistent. It is primarily Mary Lampert from Duxbury. Now we have Meg Sheehan and she's moved into the territory, but Mary Lampert was the prime mover and as I say I give her credit for being persistent. I'll give them that and they work hard and they're true believers. But it's not a widespread movement. And that's even in Massachusetts, which is a little bit of a liberal state. You go down south or out in the southwest, people love the nuclear energy plants because they provide jobs.

To Tarantino, the activists sensationalize and submit inaccurate information to the media. He thinks that if activists were to "play straight," they would be more valuable.

8.4 Post relicensing

After the relicensing in October 2012, EcoLaw filed an intent-to-sue with the EPA for Clean Water Act violations (2012a). EcoLaw focused on two provisions under the Clean Water Act that are of particular significance to Pilgrim: that they must meet effluent limits that will "assure the protection and propagation of balanced indigenous populations of shellfish, fish, and wildlife" and that the cooling water intake structure itself must be designed so that the "location, design, construction, and capacity reflect the best technology available for minimizing adverse environmental impact." Another basis for the contention was the disbanding of the expert committee, which was required by permit. The EPA has yet to present its revised draft permit for a public hearing. Community groups are hoping that closed-cycle cooling will be required, as opposed to the once-through cooling system that Pilgrim uses currently.

The Pilgrim Coalition members under the leadership of State Rep. Sarah Peake (Democrat, Provincetown) and State Rep. Jim Cantwell (Democrat, Marshfield) have also presented two legislative bills: (1) to expand the EPZ from the current 10 miles to 20 miles in order to include Cape Cod in Emergency evacuation planning (Senate Bills H.2045 and H.1906), and (2) to increase the funding that Entergy provides for environmental monitoring to the MADPH from the current $180,000 to an amount no less than $400,000 (Senate Bills H.1907 and H.2046). The bills address the fact that the Commonwealth has insufficient funds to be able to perform its legislatively required monitoring, surveillance and emergency response planning. While these bills were heard at the Massachusetts State House, no further action has been taken.

Post relicensing, community contentions have also involved factors that were not reviewed in the license renewal, such as the storage of spent fuel rods. Pilgrim's spent fuels pool is now beyond capacity, and rods must be moved to dry cask storage by its next refueling in 2015 in order for it to continue operating. In December 2012, William Maurer, a resident of Falmouth, spotted construction on the Pilgrim site, which later was identified to be foundations for the construction of dry cask storage. The construction was started without seeking any special permit from the Town of Plymouth Zoning Board. While the NRC regulates all radiological matters, the state and municipalities retains jurisdiction over zoning.

In the summer of 2013, in a packed town hall, EcoLaw, representing eighteen community members from the Town of Plymouth, petitioned the zoning board to require a special permit to construct dry cask storage, just as any resident in the community would be required to obtain a special permit to build on his/her property. After two heated hearings at the Plymouth Town hall in late July and August, the residents ultimately lost the bid in a three–two vote. According to the ruling, the special permit Entergy obtained in 1967 to build the reactor was sufficient to build dry casks, even though dry casks were not part of the special permit review in 1967. Local bylaws and history are not clear on the matter. Previously, Pilgrim was required to get special town permits to build a parking lot and a weather tower. The dry cask ruling was based on the fact that dry cask ensures more safety than current storage, and that nuclear waste and its storage falls under "accessory use" characteristic of the industry (EcoLaw 2013; EcoLaw vs. Entergy 2013). Community member Diane Turco believes that it is a crime that the citizens of the community have no input or oversight into something that will remain in the community forever, even after the plant is shut down.

The Concerned Neighbors of Pilgrim (CNP) was born late in the summer of 2013 following the debates around dry cask construction. Their mission is to "ensure that the dry cask nuclear waste storage facility is built and operated to the best possible standards" (see http://concernedneighborsofpilgrim.org). The group's concerns stem from the fact that the current dry cask construction plans were approved based on generic assessments and not site-specific risks. The dry casks are being built only 100 feet from the coastal zone and about 25 feet above mean sea level without any corresponding studies on the impacts of climate change and sea level rise on the facility, which could place the casks in the way of harsh elements and a future flood zone. Additionally, there is no transparent monitoring of temperature and radiation emissions required with the construction. The dry cask's two vents are prone to corrosion from exposure to the elements. To improve safety, they want an earthen berm to be built as a barrier between the dry casks and the bay. They want the concrete pad moved to higher ground, and they want a site-specific environmental impact statement (EIS) done before construction for the dry casks begins. To address these concerns, Article 33, a non-binding warrant article, was submitted by the CNP to the town officials to impose fees on Entergy for storing spent fuel in cooling pools, require careful monitoring for dry casks, forbid the company from accepting spent fuel from other nuclear generators, and to launch a study on the impacts of rising sea levels on Pilgrim. This Article was later reshaped and put on the ballot question with the help of the Board of Selectman (Miano 2014). A majority (82 percent) of the residents want Pilgrim to transfer all the spent fuel to dry cask as soon as possible (Mand 2014). The group also took the matter to Massachusetts Land Court, which was heard on March 14, 2014 (Bostek vs. Entergy 2014). The land court rejected claims by the plaintiffs on the environmental and health concerns but accepted the claim that the residents living close to Pilgrim have offered sufficient evidence that the new dry cask storage will harm their property values. Encouraged by this decision, the plaintiffs are filing a lawsuit arguing that Pilgrim and its nuclear waste storage casks have hurt property values in the area (Burrell August 2014a).

Since its relicensing in 2012, Pilgrim has faced recurrent unplanned shutdowns, equipment failures, leaky safety valves, and maintenance issues that hint at a possible repeat of the events that happened at Pilgrim in the 1980s. In 2013, Pilgrim exceeded industry averages for unplanned shutdowns; it was offline for 33 days due to seven unplanned scrams and three related events (NRC 2014a).

Following these multiple shutdowns in 2013, Pilgrim has come under increased NRC scrutiny; the NRC allows only one unplanned shutdown per year. Pilgrim's performance rating was lowered, placing it among fifteen other underperforming nuclear reactors in the country that require more federal oversight (Legere 2013). Early in 2014, the NRC further downgraded its performance rating to "degraded," putting Pilgrim among the nation's seven worst performers (Burrell 2014b). Pilgrim is also listed as having nine out of eleven risk factors that might lead to early shutdowns or retirements (Cooper 2013). A new report commissioned by the Pentagon also highlights Pilgrim at high risk for a terrorist strike (Burrell 2013). The declining cost of natural gas and the increasing operating costs of nuclear plants may lead to an increasing likelihood of early retirements of some nuclear energy plants in the future (McMahon 2013). Pilgrim's financial viability is also under severe pressure from market forces and Entergy is in the process of streamlining and laying off several employees (Mand 2013). US Senators Edward Markey (D-MA) and Bernie Sanders (I-Vt.) are demanding to know why the NRC staff was directed to refrain from requesting financial information from Entergy about the company's financial ability to operate its fleet of reactors (Markey 2013). Senator Dan Wolf (2014) and Massachusetts Governor Deval Patrick have recently called for the shutdown of Pilgrim Nuclear Power Reactor if it does not comply with health, safety and environmental regulations (Metzger 2014).

8.5 Discussion

Pilgrim clearly illustrates how concerns about power, participation, and control play out in discourses on waste management, use of best technology, monitoring, access to information, oversight, and risks to the environment and health in licensing and relicensing decisions. The community's perception is that the decision-making processes regarding risk (what the risks are and how they are managed) are inadequately inclusive, thereby failing to satisfy procedural justice, as well as that the results of those decisions do not fairly distribute the risks and benefits, thereby failing to satisfy distributive justice (see also Chapter 7 by Krütli et al. in this volume).

Community dissent to the representation of risks by the nuclear industry has been a central source of conflict. They have challenged it in two main ways. First, they have challenged the corporate construction and representation of science and their relaxed standards of measurement and monitoring (e.g. the risks to the aging structure, limitations in Mark 1 designs, safety mechanisms and monitoring needed, the ecological impacts of the cooling system, and the design and storage of nuclear waste). Second, they have challenged the adequacy of regulatory safety standards, oversight, and enforcement. The community does not trust the nuclear industry and the nuclear regulatory bodies to accurately portray risks, as they believe that their priority is maximizing near term energy production and economic profits. They believe the corporation uses the least required standards and the cheapest technology available within those requirements to address risks associated with an aging reactor and the construction of nuclear waste storage in perpetuity.

If people are going to be exposed to significant risks, then it seems that (1) they ought to be adequately informed about those risks, (2) they ought to be included in a meaningful way in decision-making about them, (3) individuals and the community ought to receive full and equal political standing, and (4) industry needs to be socially responsible to fulfill and maintain a respectful community–industry relationship. This has become a bedrock conception of justice within environmental justice communities. If these conditions are not met, then individuals and communities are disempowered and politically marginalized, which puts them in a position where they can be exploited or exposed to unwarranted risks or burdens for the benefit of others (Westra and Lawson 2001; Schrader-Frechette 2005; Sandler and Pezzullo 2007; Schlosberg 2009). The primary goal of community dissent was to initiate and address procedural justice, which involves participatory or democratic decision-making. Procedural justice is crucial for respecting the value of individuals and communities, and it provides a bulwark against distributive injustice, i.e. outcomes where the risks and benefits are not fairly distributed. In this case, the problematic distribution of risks was thought to be both contemporaneous, e.g. the industry resistance to use best available technology to improve safety mechanisms in Mark 1 designs (such as vents), the lack of adequate ecological protections, and the absence of disaster preparation for Cape Cod, as well as intergenerational risks, and the lack of longitudinal climate change consideration in the construction of the on-site dry cask storage for spent fuels rods. As discussed above, relicensing, to many of the community members who are concerned about the safety of the present and future generations, did not address these concerns. In fact, relicensing reviews by the NRC do not examine many important areas, including spent fuel storage, site-specific environmental impact assessments, accurate modeling of emergency planning based on real-life scenarios, and impacts of severe accidents. They thereby fail to take the life cycle perspective necessary for comprehensive social and ecological evaluation. They are considered to be unjust because those who are benefitting from the practices – i.e. the corporation that does not need to spend additional resources for on-site evaluation, new technologies, or disaster planning – are passing the burden of the greater risk to others – i.e. current and future residents as well as the nonhuman environment. Moreover, they are doing so without their consent and in the absence of an agreed-upon compensation or benefit-sharing. Thus, not only are the considered risks and costs contested, so too are the weighting given to them (and who bears them) as well as that not all ethically relevant factors are considered (Taebi and Kadak 2010) including non-anthropogenic ethical issues (see Chapter 9 by Nolt in this volume).

Issues of oversight and enforcement are also prominent in the Pilgrim case, as with nuclear energy generally. NRC is supposed to revise their environmental regulations and guidance for license renewal every ten years but it has not been changed since first issued in 1996 (GAO 2013). The Massachusetts Attorney General sought to have the safety of spent fuel pools (environmental and terrorism risks) considered in the relicensing review, but the NRC rejected both (GAO 2013). A testimony submitted by Richard Webster (2008), Legal Director of Eastern Environmental Law Center, to the Subcommittee on Clean Air and Nuclear Safety Committee on Environment and Public Works, reveals that the NRC's systems for ensuring safety at old nuclear plants are "opaque, legally and scientifically flawed, burdened with unjustified assumptions, and counter-productively exclude much useful public participation" (GAO 2013). A 2002 survey showed that 47 percent of the NRC's employees are also afraid to speak out about safety issues because they fear doing so would jeopardize their jobs, and that employees were concerned that pressure from the industry is greatly undermining the agency's ability to oversee safety.

The community attempted to remedy these procedural, distributive and regulatory concerns by promoting corporate accountability, social responsibility, and transparency by means of community appeals, petitions, and legal suits, as well as by seeking changes in the governance of science and technology, reducing power imbalances and increasing democratic decision-making by getting elected officials involved and seeking policy resolutions at the state and federal level. However, the power imbalances are substantial. Despite considerable resources, organization commitment and support from elected officials, as well as operating within a context of strong institutions and respect for law, activists have had very limited success in having their concerns addressed – e.g. relicensing, ecological impacts, fuel storage, and emergency planning. This activist community has considerable expertise, knowledge, skills, access, and social capital in comparison to many communities affected by nuclear energy worldwide, as well as in comparison to most environmental justice communities. It is not an economically or politically marginalized community. Nevertheless, structural factors, including policies and oversight mechanisms, as well as the resources that Entergy has at its disposal and the information that it controls has made their concerns difficult. In fact, in 2004 NRC reformed the procedural rules on public participation in nuclear energy plant licensing and relicensing to make it even harder for citizens to raise concerns about safety. Relicensing limits public participation to begin with because its reports are often highly technical, and citizens need experts to interpret it. The scientific, technical, and legal experts required to do such work are huge expenses even for wealthy communities to afford. It is also difficult to locate problems in an application when the standards are constantly changing and the community has only 60 days to submit their contentions for adjudication while applicants have many years to prepare an application.

At the heart of almost all of these conflicts – what is behind them and drives them – are contrasting values. David Agnew reflects, "I really think it's principle more than anything else. I just don't think it's right that a for-profit corporation can pollute the biosphere, pollute the planet's genetic material." Bill Maurer frames it simply: "I do not like being lied to." Demand for corporate transparency and accurate representation of risks are clear signs that the community is demanding a certain ethical conduct and accountability from the corporations; something demanded by communities affected by nuclear energy around the world. As Norman Pierce, a concerned neighbor of Pilgrim puts it, "Politics are how we are made safe or unsafe" (Mand 2014).

8.6   Conclusion

Nuclear energy is expanding rapidly worldwide. New plants are being built, while old plants are having their lives extended. Pilgrim today (and nuclear energy globally) is promoted as an answer to combat climate change (Ailworth 2013) and thereby as a benefit to future generations. However, nuclear waste requires perpetual management and maintenance, including in emergency situations and in the face of climate change. Central to the ethics of nuclear energy is risk assessment, risk management, risk decision-making, and risk distribution. These need to be conducted in accordance with best practices and principles of procedural and distributive justice. However, what those practices and principles are is itself contested. Case studies are crucial to the ethics of nuclear energy because they enable us to see how and where these issues arise in practice, the different conceptions of justice and attitudes about risk that are operative, and the barriers to accomplishing nuclear energy that could be ethically acceptable. In the Pilgrim case, we see the emphasis that the community places on procedural justice, future generations, and ecological systems, as well as the enormous power differential in play between communities and industry as a result of regulatory and political structures. If the ethics of nuclear energy is not all or nothing – if the question is not "should we endorse nuclear energy?" but "under what conditions and in what forms should we endorse nuclear energy and its continued operation?" – then it is necessary to determine the varieties of community empowerment that are necessary to accomplish responsible nuclear energy. It certainly needs to be much more substantive than it is in the Pilgrim case, which involves a community that is itself socially, politically, and economically well-resourced in comparison to many communities exposed to the hazards of nuclear energy.

Dedicated to Wedge Bramhall (1952–2014) for his tireless advocacy on Pilgrim issues, his deep sense of justice and courage to speak up for the truth. We also wish to thank the editor Behnam Taebi offering valuable inputs and guidance on this report. Lastly, we would like to thank Emily Viggiano for helping us with some of the interviews, transcription, and editing.

9 Non-anthropocentric nuclear energy ethics

John Nolt

9.1   Introduction

Most discussions of nuclear energy ethics are anthropocentric – that is, concerned with the implications of nuclear energy for humanity. This chapter takes a broader view, considering also its implications for nonhuman life, independently of us. It is divided into three parts. The first part introduces non-anthropocentric ethics and characterizes the particular version – a form of biocentric consequentialism – that I will use to illustrate the differences between anthropocentric and non-anthropocentric approaches. The second part applies a simplified form of biocentric consequentialism to the question "how much of our electricity should be generated by nuclear sources?" The third part summarizes the conclusions of the second and notes that they would not differ much had I used other non-anthropocentric ethics instead.

9.2   Non-anthropocentric ethics

Traditional ethics are anthropocentric; they prescribe actions or policies that respect humans, promise to promote human welfare, or the like. They tend also to be short term, considering only people who are now alive and perhaps the next few generations. Yet contemporary human actions, including the use of nuclear technologies, pose dangers to both human and nonhuman beings for far longer than the next few generations. Our technological power thus threatens to outstrip our discretion.

In response, some theorists have sought to increase the breadth and objectivity of ethics by expanding moral consideration to nonhuman life, to the distant future, or, more rarely, to both. This chapter attempts to do both, tracing the implications of long-term non-anthropocentric ethics for nuclear energy production.

An ethic is a general account of moral responsibilities. *Anthropocentric* ethics regard harms or benefits as morally significant only insofar as they are, directly or indirectly, harms or benefits to humans. *Non-anthropocentric* ethics regard harms and benefits to some nonhuman living things as morally significant independently of how they affect humans. Thus, for example, an ethic that condemns cruelty to animals merely because it upsets us, demeans us, or promotes violence against humans is anthropocentric. An ethic that also regards cruelty as wrong because of how it affects the animals is non-anthropocentric. Similarly, an ethic that values ecosystems merely for the services they provide to humans is anthropocentric. An ethic that values their well-being directly is not.

Anthropocentrism is to non-anthropocentrism as egoism is to altruism: the former pair for the human species, the latter pair for human individuals (Nolt 2013b). Non-anthropocentric ethics are, in other words, generalizations of anthropocentric ones. They retain moral consideration for humans but broaden it to include some nonhuman entities.

The sheer novelty of non-anthropocentric ethics may render them suspect. How could traditional ethics have missed so much? Part of the answer is that traditional ethics didn't miss that much. They were largely adequate for traditional ways of life. We need to enlarge the scope of ethics now because of the historically recent escalation of human knowledge and power.

The tradition was, however, hampered by ignorance. At the time it took shape, humans were still regarded as radically distinct from all other life on earth. It was therefore natural to posit a sharp moral divide at the boundary of the human species. But, since Darwin, justifications for that divide have been steadily eroded.

There is another reason why traditional ethics overlooked the moral importance of nonhuman life: Every human group – as the histories of tribalism, racism, nationalism, and the like attest – has always regarded its members as uniquely or especially morally significant. Given this history, a tendency to deny the moral significance of nonhumans is a predictable consequence of human nature.

9.3   Variations in scope

Non-anthropocentric ethics differ in scope. The broadest, *biocentric* ethics, extend moral consideration to all living things. Biocentric ethics are founded on the assumption that any living thing can be harmed or benefited. Trees, for example, benefit from rich soil, adequate sunlight, and regular rain and are harmed by disease, injury, and excessive heat or cold. Living things can be harmed or benefited because they have their own genetically "programmed" purposes. These purposes are products of species-specific evolutionary adaptations. In primates, for example, including humans, a primary purpose of the forelimbs is to grasp and manipulate objects. In most birds their chief purpose is to power and support flight. Some broad purposes – e.g. procuring nutrients, respiring, maturing, and so on – are common to all, or almost all, organisms, though, of course, each species accomplishes them in its own way. What facilitates the organism's autopoietic (self-maintaining) functions is good for it; what hinders these functions is bad for it. Harm and benefit in this sense are objective, factual conditions, independent of human cognition or appraisal (Nolt 2009).

Artifacts, too, can be said to be harmed or benefited – but only derivatively, via human valuing. Sharpening a knife, for example, is good for it, but only by enhancing its utility for human purposes. An artifact's purposes are all assigned to it by humans; it has no purposes of its own. Consequently ethics takes no interest in harms to artifacts, except insofar as those harms affect humans. Non-living natural objects, such as rocks, likewise have no purposes of their own. Thus though they can be destroyed, they cannot be harmed. Ethics therefore takes no interest in non-living things, unless they make some difference to a living thing.

The term "living thing" is ambiguous. It may refer just to individual organisms, or, in addition, more broadly, to such collective entities as species or ecosystems. Biocentric ethics are often classified as individualistic or holistic, according to whether their concern is primarily for individuals or collectives. Holistic biocentrists hold that collectives can, like individual organisms, be harmed or benefited (Rolston 1988, chs. 4–6; McShane 2004).

Some non-anthropocentric ethics are narrower in scope than others. *Sentientist* ethics, for example, give moral consideration only to sentient beings – that is, animals capable of suffering or enjoyment (Singer 2002; Varner 2012, ch. 5). Sentience is a plausible criterion of moral considerability; *human* suffering is obviously morally significant, and mere absence of a human genome seems a paltry reason to withhold concern from sufferers.

Sentientists do not deny that non-sentient living things can be harmed or benefited. But they insist that since non-sentient organisms can have no positive or negative experiences, they have in themselves no moral significance. Biocentrists reply that although they cannot appreciate their own welfare, nevertheless it can and should matter morally to us.

9.4 Variations in aim: deontology versus consequentialism

Independently of their scope, non-anthropocentric ethics can also vary in aim. As in ethics generally, the two most prominent orientations are deontological and consequentialist. Deontology typically advocates dutiful or respectful behavior toward individuals (and sometimes collective entities such as nations), while consequentialism promotes aggregate welfare. (The third most prominent form, virtue ethics, often, though not always, presupposes one of the other two. For reasons of space, it will not be considered here.)

Deontological ethics are codified as rules, conformity with which is deemed right and violation of which is deemed wrong. Moral action aims at what is right, as defined by the rules, rather than at what is good, as determined by results. Hence deontologists downplay consequences of actions, regarding them as irrelevant or secondary to the moral assessment of the actions. Adherence to the rules is paramount and must be maintained even if greater good can be achieved by harming or disrespecting some individuals. Deontological biocentric ethics insist, in theory at least, on dutiful or respectful treatment of all living things (Taylor 1986).

Consequentialist ethics, by contrast, aim at maximizing good results. Actions are assessed not by their conformity with rules, but by their aggregate consequences for all individuals affected. The more widely benefit exceeds harm, the better the action. Harm to individuals matters only insofar as it detracts from aggregate welfare. Sentientist consequentialist ethics regard the welfare of an individual as morally significant only if it is consciously experienced by that individual (Singer 2002: 7–8). Biocentric consequentialist ethics count the welfare of any living thing, regardless of whether it is conscious, as to some degree morally significant (Attfield 1991).

Because there is considerable variation among non-anthropocentric ethics, it would be tedious to consider the ramifications of all variants for nuclear energy policy. Moreover, their differences from one another are in this context less important than their collective differences from anthropocentric ethics. Therefore I will consider nuclear energy policy in the light of just one representative form of non-anthropocentric ethics: biocentric consequentialism.

For illustrative purposes, the inclusiveness of biocentric ethics is an advantage; for more can be gleaned by considering a broader ethic than a narrower one. Though biocentric ethics regard all living things as having some moral status, they may accord special consideration to sentient animals and even greater consideration to animals with highly developed cognitive capacities – including humans. Thus they share many of the same concerns as sentientist and anthropocentric ethics.

Among biocentric ethics, consequentialist versions are most readily applicable to nuclear energy policy. Deontological theories suffer from conflicting implications. To address the conflicts, they need further rules governing exceptions to rules and still further rules governing restitution when rules are violated. Thus rules proliferate unsettlingly. This problem is inordinately exacerbated in biocentric ethics, which vastly increase the number and kinds of entities that must be respected. Paul Taylor, for example, in his seminal work on biocentric deontology (1986) provides well over a hundred pages of rules and their justifications. But nearly all of this material is controversial, and the resulting system seems unworkable in practice. This is not just a fluke of Taylor's system. Deontology and biocentrism are, in general, ill-suited to one another, for it is impossible to be just, fair, or respectful to all living beings. There are too many of them. In respecting some, we must treat others as mere objects or means – those that they eat, for example, or those with which they complete for resources.

Consequentialist biocentrism, by contrast, aims not to respect each living thing, but rather to promote the good of life as a whole. It does not object to harming some individual organisms, if this promotes the greater good. Hence, in that respect at least, it is more practical.

Like many consequentialist ethics, however, it does not provide a reliable way to measure or rank overall consequences of the available choices on a single scale from better to worse. As a result, there may be no best outcome, and hence no single right action. I call this the *ranking problem*.

9.5 The ranking problem

Jeremy Bentham defined the best action as the one that produces the greatest pleasure with the least pain for all affected. For Bentham, the ranking problem is manifest as the doubt that pleasure and pain have well-defined quantities – or that, if they do, these are knowable or can be aggregated.

Welfare economists have devised an elegant, if controversial, solution. Instead of defining welfare as pleasure and the absence of pain, they define it as degree of preference satisfaction. The strength of a person's preference for any good can, they assume, be empirically measured by the amount of money that person is willing to pay for that good. To find the overall value of any given policy, then, one need only determine how much money its potential beneficiaries would be willing to pay to enact it, and subtract from that the amount of money that its opponents would accept in compensation for accepting it. In theory, at least, the result is a linear ranking of outcomes. This elegant solution is popular among policymakers, particularly as a source of numerical inputs to cost–benefit analyses.

But such numbers are not accurate measures of actual human welfare. For one thing, since willingness to pay is a function not only of preferences but of wealth, at best the numbers indicate not preference strength *simpliciter* but wealth-weighted preference strength. They are, in other words, biased in favor of the rich.

Moreover, preference satisfaction itself, no matter how measured, is not the same thing as welfare. Economists typically measure consumer preferences, and these differ from considered values, whose realization may more closely reflect actual welfare (Sagoff 1988). People's preferences are, moreover, frequently shaped by propaganda and advertising, and are thus often opposed to their actual interests. Often, too, people benefit from outcomes for which they had no preferences, and sometimes they benefit more by eliminating preferences (for, say, excessive consumption) than by satisfying them. For all these reasons, welfare and preference satisfaction are quite distinct. Therefore, whether measured by willingness to pay or by something else, aggregate preference satisfaction is not the same thing as welfare or the general good (Hausman and McPherson 2009). Thus the economists' solution to the ranking problem does not in fact solve it, but merely changes the subject.

Recognizing this, some policymakers have attempted to formulate more adequate welfare measures. An example is the Human Development Index (HDI) (UNDP 2013), which is grounded in the capability approach that has been developed by economist and Nobel Prize-winner Amartya Sen and philosopher Martha Nussbaum (See also Chapter 12 by Gardoni and Murphy and Chapter 13 by Hillerbrand in this volume). Designed as a measure of the level of development for a region, the HDI, which combines longevity (a proxy for health) with measures of education and living standards, is also a rough indicator of human welfare. Its chief advantage over the economic conception is that it regards welfare as a matter of objectively measurable conditions, not satisfaction of subjective preferences, which must be questionably inferred from some indicator of willingness to pay.

Notions of welfare which, like the HDI, analyze welfare into certain universal and objective conditions are known as *objective-list* conceptions. In addition to health, adequate wealth, and education, other conceptions include such goods as security, employment, political freedom, etc. Sometimes pleasure and the absence of suffering are also regarded as objective goods, but in that case care is needed to avoid the objections raised against Bentham's view.

For objective-list conceptions of welfare, the ranking problem lies largely in the fact that the welfare components are not all measurable on the same scale. They cannot, for example, all be reduced to dollar amounts. Overall welfare comparisons must therefore either integrate these components into a single linear scale, assigning each some prescribed weight (which is the method of the HDI) or else use multidimensional scales. The first method introduces arbitrariness. The second increases the difficulties of comparison and decision-making.

9.6 Biocentric consequentialism

The most workable form of biocentric consequentialism, in my view, is a straightforward generalization of anthropocentric objective-list consequentialism (Nolt 2015: 172–83). Three main ideas underlie this generalization: (1) there is one component of welfare – which, to a first approximation, is health – that is applicable to all living organisms; (2) not all living things are capable of all of the components; and (3) two organisms capable of the same welfare component are often capable of it to different degrees. Because the consequentialist aim is to promote overall welfare, it follows that organisms that are capable of only one or a small number of the components of welfare, and only to small degrees, have small moral significance in themselves – though they may be ecologically significant for other organisms. Plants, bacteria, fungi, and insects are typical examples. Likewise, organisms that are capable of many of the components of welfare, each to a high degree, have high intrinsic moral significance. Humans, of course, are the best example.

The ranking problem haunts biocentric consequentialism with a vengeance. Not only does the biocentric version, like the simpler anthropocentric one, have to deal with not-always-commensurable welfare components, but in some cases values for a single welfare component are not in all cases comparable across species (Nolt 2013a). Thus it is in general not possible to obtain numerical, or even linearly ranked, aggregate welfare values for the outcomes of a given action. This hampers, but is not fatal to, decision-making. Even if there is no full ordinal ranking of outcomes, they will in general be partially ordered. Hence many possible choices can be eliminated as clearly worse than others. At worst, then, we may have to choose arbitrarily among the remaining options (Hsieh 2007). Elsewhere I have argued that in many cases we can do better than that. Values incomparable with one another may nevertheless be comparable to other values in ways that illuminate decision-making (Nolt 2015: 178–83, 237–40). Still, there is no denying the complexity and difficulty of biocentric objective-list consequentialist ethics.

Not all of that complexity may be needed, however, for a general, illustrative discussion of the global problem of nuclear energy over broad expanses of time. In what follows, I will employ just two crude proxies for biocentric welfare values. In the human case, assuming a fixed population, welfare is typically high when the mortality rate is low and vice versa. Thus for humans I will use mortality rate as a rough negative indicator of aggregate welfare. Casualty rates, which include illness and injury, are more accurate where some choices cause many injuries but few fatalities. However, for the long-term, large-scale consequences to be considered here, there is little reason to think that this is the case, and fatality estimates are often all that is available, so mortality rates will have to serve. The product of mortality rate and population is, moreover, a better measure of aggregate welfare where population size varies; but, to avoid complication, I'll generally ignore population differences here.[1] Even for a fixed population, of course, low mortality is not

---

[1] The complications have to do with a number of problems raised by Derek Parfit – in particular, the so-called Repugnant Conclusion and the non-identity problem. These are of less concern in non-anthropocentric ethics than in anthropocentric ethics, see (Nolt 2015: secs. 4.5, 4.6.2, 5.12 and 6.9.)

identical with high aggregate welfare. I am merely assuming that the correlation between the two is in our actual situation good enough for the illustrative examples I will offer here.

We might use mortality rates for nonhuman individuals, too, except that they are far more fine-grained than would be useful and also are not well known. Instead, I will use a suitable notion of biodiversity loss (loss of species richness, perhaps) whose rate is (in our actual situation) high when aggregate nonhuman welfare is low, and vice versa. Again I'm not claiming that low biodiversity loss *equals* high nonhuman welfare. And certainly biodiversity itself is a problematic concept (Maier 2012). But I think that this rough proxy will do for illustrative purposes.

My aim is not to provide a thoroughgoing analysis of the nuclear energy problem, but merely to apply a simplified biocentric objective-list consequentialist ethic to the broad features of that problem and draw some general conclusions. A more thoroughgoing analysis would, among many other improvements, analyze welfare into a more detailed list of components.

Since I know of no non-arbitrary way to compare biodiversity loss with human mortality, I will not attempt to integrate these two measures into a single linear scale, but rather will treat each as a more or less separate dimension of value. When one policy yields a lower level of one and at least as low a level of the other, then I count it as better. When one policy ranks higher in one dimension and lower in the other, my crude analysis will define no relative ranking.

My decision procedure will be formally the same as in cost–benefit analysis: list the policy options and their possible consequences, consider the value and probability of each consequence, and choose an option whose expected value is at least as high as any with which it is comparable. (The expected value for an option is the sum for each of its consequences of that consequence's value times its probability.) The main difference is that I am using objective welfare values (expressed as rates of mortality and biodiversity loss), rather than monetary values. This procedure might in practice need to be modified by considerations of justice, equity, and so on, particularly in the human case, but again for reasons of space I will leave these considerations aside here.

In contrast to standard economic approaches, which reduce all values to satisfaction of contemporary human preferences, this non-anthropocentric approach values the objective welfare of humans and nonhumans, both present and future. In the crude version illustrated here, all economic matters are in effect assimilated into a single measure: mortality rates. In a less crude version, human welfare would be resolved into several objective components, perhaps along the lines of the HDI, and biodiversity might be similarly articulated into several measures of nonhuman welfare.

Biocentric consequentialism differs not only from economic approaches, but from those anthropocentric forms of environmental ethics that value biodiversity for its non-economic benefits to humans – ecosystem services, scientific importance, aesthetic value, recreational potential, and the like. Biocentric consequentialism, even in the attenuated form just described, accounts for the value of some such benefits (since some presumably reduce human mortality), but it also values the welfare of nonhumans themselves – even those that do not benefit us in any way.

The difference between biocentric and anthropocentric ethics shows up most starkly in the case of human extinction. If we knew, for example, that the human species would be extinct by the end of this century, but that much of the rest of life would continue, this would not change biocentric concern for the welfare of nonhumans beyond 2100. But an ethical anthropocentrist can see nothing of moral significance in post-human times. He is like an ethical egoist, who, valuing nothing but his own welfare, can see nothing of moral significance beyond his own death. The profound moral shallowness of anthropocentrism is thus illuminated by analogy with the evident moral shallowness of egoism (Nolt 2013b).

9.7   Temporal range

In addition to its anthropocentrism, traditional ethics had a second limitation: It applied only to contemporaries or near-contemporaries – that is, at most, to the next few generations. So long as the predictable effects of human actions extended no further, that was good enough. But today we knowingly produce climate change, long-lasting nuclear wastes, ocean acidification (from our carbon emissions), and similar phenomena whose long-lived effects will predictably be felt millennia hence. Thus the temporal range of our ethic must be long.

In their anthropocentric forms, long-term ethics – known as *ethics of future generations* or *intergenerational ethics* – emerged only in the late twentieth century. The most influential work has been that of Parfit (1984, part IV), but the literature is large and growing (see e.g. Partridge 1980; De-Shalit 1995; Dobson 1999; Gardiner 2003; Mulgan 2006; Gosseries and Meyer (2009).[2]

Intergenerational ethics deal with future people – people who at a given time are not alive, but will be later. (People who could exist but never do are not future people.) Like the term "foreign," "future" characterizes, not the kind of a thing, but rather the point of view from which it is described. From the viewpoint of our homeland, we are not foreigners. But from the viewpoints of people of other lands, we are. Similarly, from our temporal viewpoint we are

---

[2] On intergenerational justice, see also Chapter 6 in this volume.

not future people, but from the viewpoints of our predecessors we are. People who are "future" are therefore not, as such, inherently different from us, and mere futurity is no better reason for moral discrimination than mere foreignness. For intergenerational ethics, the welfare of future people counts no less than the welfare of people today.

This egalitarianism contradicts the contemporary economic practice of discounting all future harms and benefits by a standard annual rate, so that all values, both positive and negative, shrink toward zero the farther from us they occur into the future. This practice has been justified in various ways, the most prominent of which assume that the values of future events are determined only by the preferences of present people – as assumption which from an intergenerational viewpoint discriminates unjustly against future people. For an account and critique of the various justifications for discounting, see Parfit (1984), Appendix F.

Certain forms of intergenerational ethics are sometimes said to be unfair to, or excessively demanding of, present people (Mulgan 2006, especially ch. 10). Whatever the theoretical merits of that claim may be, demandingness is no threat in practice. Since causation operates only from past to future, future people cannot impose demands on the present. Therefore intergenerational ethics are at best an effort at moral *self*-restraint by those parties in an asymmetrical relationship who hold all the power. The historical evidence – consider, for example, the last two decades of climate negotiations – suggests that there is little chance that these parties will impose excessive or unfair demands upon themselves.

Preference utilitarians, and among them many economists, may object that we cannot act on behalf of future people since we cannot know their preferences. But ethics based on objective-list, rather than preference, conceptions of welfare are not vulnerable to that criticism.

The ethic used in this chapter is not only long-term, like intergenerational ethics, but non-anthropocentric. It may therefore be understood with equal accuracy either as a non-anthropocentric generalization of an intergenerational ethic or as a long-term generalization of a biocentric ethic. For biocentrists, whose concerns transcend current humanity, there has never been any reason to consider discounting the future in favor of the human present.

Expanding the temporal range of biocentric ethics has a fortuitous side effect: It helps to resolve the tension between individualistic and holistic variants. Take the holistic notion of species welfare, for example. Conservation biologists say that a species is doing well if its population is numerous, genetically diverse, widely distributed, and subject to no major global threats. At bottom, this means that it is doing well if there are likely to be many healthy organisms of that species far into the future – that is, if the aggregate welfare of future individuals of that species is likely to be high.

Species welfare can thus be regarded as aggregate individual welfare for present and future species members. Holism and individualism are thereby reconciled. Conversely, when we extrapolate individualistic biocentric ethics into the distant future, it quickly becomes impossible to consider specific individuals and we must think in terms of species welfare – and, more generally, of overall biodiversity (Nolt 2015: 178–81, 202–04). This is a further reason to use biodiversity as a rough proxy for nonhuman welfare.

Having now characterized an especially simple version of long-term biocentric objective-list consequentialism, I will next apply it to the problem of nuclear energy.

9.8 The problem of nuclear energy

By "nuclear energy" I mean electricity generated by nuclear reactors. Nuclear reactors produced about 5.7 percent of the world's energy and 12.9 percent of its electricity in 2010. Fossil fuels produced, by comparison, about 80 percent of the energy and 67.4 percent of the electricity (IEA 2013a: 6, 24). The problem to be dealt with here is: How much of our electricity *should* come from nuclear sources?

To answer, I will survey the potential outcomes of various energy policies, assess the harms and benefits of those outcomes (indicated as rates of mortality and biodiversity loss), estimate the probabilities of the outcomes to determine a rough expected value for each policy, and choose a policy whose expected value is maximal – or at least as high as any with which it is comparable.

The chief *benefits* of any form of energy production are improvements to human life made possible by the generated electricity. No form of energy production much benefits nonhumans, apart from the companion animals of humans, and none significantly enhances biodiversity. Since the human benefits (expressed here as reductions in mortality) are essentially the same for each energy source, the discussion below ignores benefits and compares just potential harms – to both humans and nonhumans.

9.9 Potential harms of nuclear energy

The most pervasive hazards of nuclear energy are effects of ionizing radiation. Ionizing radiation consists of subatomic particles that are energetic enough to eject electrons from atoms upon impact. It accompanies all stages of the fuel cycle of fission reactors, from mining to waste disposal. Fusion reactors, still in the experimental stage, also produce high levels of ionizing radiation internally.

Fission reactors generate ionizing radiation directly in normal operation, but nearly all of it is contained within the reactor vessel and the heavy concrete containment structure that shields the environment from the reactor. Reactors also create radionuclides – atoms whose nuclei emit ionizing radiation. Nuclear plants can eject large quantities of radionuclides into the environment if both the reactor vessel and containment structure are breached, as happened in the Fukushima Daiichi accident and at Chernobyl. Radionuclides can also be released into the environment during mining, manufacture of reactor fuel, decommissioning, and waste disposal.

All radionuclides ultimately decay into stable, non-radiotoxic atoms. The ionizing radiation produced by a given emission therefore decreases over time. The rate of decay (measured in half-lives) varies widely, however, from isotope to isotope; hence the duration of the hazard depends on the radionuclides involved. The two radionuclides of greatest concern in the Fukushima Daiichi and Chernobyl accidents, for example, were cesium 137, which has a half-life of about 30 years, and iodine 131, whose half-life is about eight days. It takes about two centuries for 99 percent of the radiation from cesium 137 to vanish. For iodine 131 it takes about two months. Thus iodine 131 contamination from the Chernobyl emissions, which ceased long ago, is no longer significant; but in parts of Europe and the former Soviet Union levels of cesium 137 in soils and crops are still "of concern" (NEA-OECD 2002). It is still not clear when Fukushima Daiichi emissions will cease.

Though ionizing radiation is present at low levels in nature, any amount can cause biological damage; the greater the intensity and duration of the radiation, the higher the probability of harm. At very high doses ionizing radiation is lethal to all forms of life. But even at low doses, it can kill cells, disrupt cellular function, and damage DNA molecules. Some of the DNA damage is repaired by cellular mechanisms. But misrepair may cause mutations or cancer. Mutations occurring in germ cells may be passed on to progeny, though over time harmful mutations tend to be selected out of the gene pool. Radiation-induced cancers typically appear only after a latency period, which may span decades. Dose–response rates for mutation and cancer due to ionizing radiation vary considerably with species and tissue type; but, in general, the greater the cumulative exposure, the higher the probability of both (National Research Council/National Academy of Sciences 2006: 11–12).

To provide a rough sense of scale, I find it useful to classify the potential harms of nuclear energy and other energy regimes as either local or global. Since we are operating with a long-term non-anthropocentric ethic, that scale must be large. By local harms, I mean those that are confined to limited geographic regions, where they deplete at most a small fraction of earth's biodiversity and kill no more than, say, a million people. Harms larger than that are global.

All harms associated with the normal life cycle operation of a nuclear power plant (including mining, manufacture and transportation of fuel, daily operation, and on-site waste storage) are local in this sense – despite the wide distribution of nuclear materials beyond national boundaries. It might be thought that the gradual environmental accumulation of radionuclides as a result of routine worldwide employment of nuclear energy would be a global threat. But because the radionuclides decay, there is not much accumulation and the harm does not approach global scale in the sense just defined.

The big worries with nuclear energy go beyond normal operation. These include large environmental releases of stored high-level nuclear waste, destruction of power plants by accident or attack, and facilitation of the proliferation of nuclear weapons where, as, for example, in Iran, the line between energy and weapons programs may be indistinct (See also Chapter 11 by Doyle in this volume).

Nuclear power plants produce highly radioactive waste, consisting mainly of spent fuel or, where fuel is reprocessed, material from the reprocessing. Spent fuel that has not been reprocessed is especially problematic, remaining potentially harmful to humans for up to a million years, depending on the radiation standard used (Taebi 2012a). (Effects on nonhuman individuals are rarely considered.)

High-level waste is typically stored on-site at nuclear plants, but better storage methods may eventually be developed. Serious harm could result if the waste were dispersed into the environment. Though not itself explosive, it could, if commandeered, be used to make "dirty bombs" powered by conventional explosives that spread radionuclides over population centers. The likelihood of one or more large releases of radionuclides, whether accidental or intentional, is, over time, substantial; but the harm to both humans and nonhumans would almost certainly be local.

The long-term probability of a catastrophic failure of one or more nuclear reactors, due to accident or attack is, given the history of such events, not inconsiderable (Shrader-Frechette 2011a: 117–22). But even in the Chernobyl case, severe contamination was confined mostly to certain regions of Europe and the former Soviet Union, and the high-end long-term death toll estimates of opponents of nuclear energy are in the hundreds of thousands (Shrader-Frechette 2011a: 64–65). Though there were substantial biodiversity reductions locally, even the very thorough survey paper of Yablokov et al. (2009) records no extinctions. Such events are by the liberal criteria set forth above still to be classified as local.

The greatest worry with nuclear energy is that it may promote the proliferation – and hence, possibly, the use – of nuclear weapons. Nuclear weapons explosions produce not only radiation, but blast effects, fires, and atmospheric disturbances – including, for a massive exchange, nuclear winter. A full-scale thermonuclear war would significantly deplete biodiversity and kill billions of people. These effects are clearly global. But the atmospheric effects would probably dissipate within a few years, and the radiation, mostly from cesium 137 and strontium 90, both with half-lives of about 30 years, would decay to insignificance within a few centuries (Pittock et al. 1986: 14–16, 208–10).

That is the worst case. Other forms of nuclear conflict, though perhaps more probable, are less deadly. Moreover, since nuclear weapons can be developed with or without nuclear energy production, what matters for our purposes is not the long-term probability of weapons use *per se*, but rather how much that probability increases, given worldwide development of nuclear energy. It does, I assume, increase to some degree.

In sum, of the three most important threats of nuclear energy – waste releases, power plant releases, and increased nuclear weapons proliferation – only the third is potentially global in scope, but its probability may not be high. Having surveyed the potential harms of nuclear energy, we next contrast these with the potential harms of the alternatives. We begin with fossil energy sources (coal, oil, and natural gas).

9.10 Potential harms of fossil fuels

The most damaging consequences of the burning of fossil fuels are air pollution (which in the case of power plants consists of sulfates, oxides of nitrogen, particulates – and, as a secondary pollutant, ozone), ocean acidification (which threatens marine biodiversity), and climate change. Air pollution from power plants is more or less localized, but ocean acidification and climate change are long-term global effects.

Outdoor air pollution currently causes about 1.4 million deaths annually – 500,000 in China alone (DARA 2012: 256–57). Not all of this pollution is from power plants, though much of it is. Climate change kills another 400,000 (DARA 2012: 2). But since fossil-fueled power plants account for about a quarter of worldwide greenhouse gas emissions (IPCC 2007: Figure 2.1, 36), they are responsible for only about 100,000 of these. Thus the current annual death toll from fossil plants is certainly at least in the hundreds of thousands.

Even if we assume the upper-end death toll estimates for such sporadic events as occurred at Fukushima and Chernobyl, the average annual death toll from nuclear power plants is not of the same order of magnitude. It should be kept in mind, however, that fossil plants, being more numerous, generate about five times as much electricity as nuclear plants do. Still, even if we divide the average annual death toll for fossil plants by a factor of five, it exceeds that for nuclear plants.

Climate change will, moreover, continue to kill people long after we stop burning fossil fuels. Climate change mortality is expected to reach 700,000 annually by 2030 (DARA 2012: 2) and cumulative deaths will almost surely be in the tens of millions by the end of this century. The only consequence of nuclear energy production that has a significant chance of killing that many people by 2100 is proliferation-induced nuclear war. But while nuclear war might be avoided, and thus is uncertain, if we burn fossil fuels for a few more decades, those tens of millions of climate-induced deaths by 2100 are virtually guaranteed.

Climate change will, moreover, not cease at 2100. Current research suggests that elevated temperatures will persist for 23,000–165,000 years (Zeebe 2013). The death toll from a hot climate over so long a time will be much larger than a few tens of millions. Since the most important environmental radionuclides from nuclear war or nuclear accidents would decay much more rapidly than the climate would cool, a nuclear economy is nearly certain to produce far fewer total deaths than a fossil-fueled economy, even if it breeds nuclear war.

What about effects on nonhumans? If we continue burning fossil fuels even at current rates for a few more decades, climate change and ocean acidification may well produce a mass extinction – that is, loss of at least three-quarters of earth's species (Barnosky et al. 2011; Zeebe and Zachos 2013: 13). The duration of that sort of harm is long. Barnosky et al. (2011: 51) state that recovery of biodiversity from an anthropogenic mass extinction "will not occur on any timeframe meaningful to people: Evolution of new species typically takes at least hundreds of thousands of years and recovery from mass extinction episodes probably occurs on timescales encompassing millions of years." (Incidentally, I dissent from this assertion on one point: that time frame *is* meaningful to long-term non-anthropocentrists.)

If, by contrast, a nuclear economy sparked a major nuclear war, extinctions would probably occur, but no authoritative source that I know of suggests they would add up to a mass extinction (see Robinson 1979: 24–27; Harwell and Hutchinson 1985: 252–53; Westing 2013: ch. 7). And, again, it is by no means certain that a nuclear economy would lead to nuclear war.

In sum, the harms of fossil-fuel-generated energy to both humans and nonhumans exceed in probability, severity, and spatiotemporal scale those of nuclear energy. The difference is greater when viewed non-anthropocentrically than anthropocentrically, and greater still the further we look into the future. If nuclear energy and fossil fuels were our only options for generating electricity, then the answer to the question "how much of our electricity should be generated from nuclear sources?" would have to be nearly all of it – as quickly as possible.

The urgency follows from two relatively uncontroversial assumptions about climate change: (1) that the ultimate global temperature increase will be roughly proportional to cumulative total anthropogenic carbon emissions (Stocker 2013: 280); and (2) that mortality and biodiversity loss increase with temperature.

9.11 Potential harms of renewables

Fortunately, there is a third option, besides nuclear and fossil energy: solar, wind, tidal, plant-based, hydroelectric, and geothermal energy sources – collectively called "renewables." None of these have a great potential for long-term harm. Hydroelectric dams can burst, killing thousands downstream. But such events, though tragic, are distinctly local. Dams also alter the ecology of rivers, which can produce extinctions of endemic species. Windmills kill birds and so can contribute to extinctions. Careless production of biofuels could likewise deplete biodiversity. But again such effects, though they should not be underestimated, come nowhere close to the potential long-term death tolls and biodiversity losses of either fossil fuels or nuclear energy.

If nuclear energy could be used indefinitely without major accidents, and without sparking nuclear weapons use, then its long-term consequences might approximate those of the renewables. But in a volatile world such safety cannot be assured. Since nuclear energy's worst potential consequences are dire, the expected value of the nuclear option is, using our objective welfare measures, lower than that for any of the renewables. Unsurprisingly, then, the foregoing analysis favors all forms of renewable energy over both fossil and nuclear energy.

9.12 Determining the energy mix

It might seem, therefore, that the appropriate answer to the question "how much of our electricity should be generated from nuclear sources?" is almost none; we should use renewables instead. But that doesn't follow. Eighty percent of the world's energy is now generated by fossil fuels. We must reduce this figure deeply and quickly. It may be that we can do this more quickly if we develop both renewables and nuclear energy, than if we develop renewables alone. If so, then we should replace some fossil plants with nuclear plants.

We should first, however, consider a prior question: How much energy *should* we generate in total? Here the answer depends in part on global population and in part on the efficiency of our energy use. Human population and energy efficiency will both no doubt increase (the latter certainly *should*), but since these variables introduce complexities that cannot adequately be addressed in this chapter, to avoid unuseful complication I will suppose them fixed.

The question, then, becomes: "how much energy produces the most overall welfare, given these suppositions?" Since no form of power generation much benefits nonhumans and most forms have some negative consequences for both humans and nonhumans, no increase in energy production is justified unless it elevates the objective welfare of humans – without excessive harm to nonhumans. We are measuring increases in objective human welfare by reductions in mortality. Hence we should generate *at most* as much energy as contributes to reducing human mortality.

Among the world's poor, more energy would almost surely have that effect. But the rich can reduce energy use without increasing mortality and hence ought to conserve. So, since we are assuming a steady population, rich nations should generate less energy than they do now. They should not, therefore, increase nuclear capacity, except as needed to accelerate retirement of fossil plants beyond the rate achievable by conservation and renewables.

Poor nations, by contrast, should increase energy production up to the point at which more production no longer increases total welfare. But, assuming long-term biocentrism, that total includes the welfare of both humans and nonhumans, both present and future. Hence the energy source makes an enormous difference. Given the long-term global damages of fossil fuels, it is doubtful that *any* increase in fossil energy production, even in the poorest nations, would increase total long-term biocentric, or even human, welfare.

The case is less clear for nuclear energy. But in the absence of large-scale nuclear accidents or nuclear war, use of nuclear energy to alleviate poverty would probably increase overall welfare. And certainly, as in rich nations, there is justification for replacing existing fossil plants with nuclear plants if that cannot be done with renewables.

In sum, the answer of the foregoing analysis to the question "how much of our electricity should be generated from nuclear sources?" is as much as is needed to speed the retirement of fossil plants beyond what can be accomplished by renewables alone – and perhaps more where needed to reduce poverty-induced mortality.

Assuming short-term anthropocentrism, by contrast, the needs of today's poor might justify construction of new fossil plants in developing regions – by overlooking long-term consequences. But given either long-term anthropocentrism or biocentrism or both, new fossil plants are indefensible. Such agreement between long-term anthropocentrism and biocentrism is to be expected so long as long-term human welfare is strongly correlated with the welfare of nature. But if that correlation weakens, then, as the next section illustrates, these two ethics may pull in different directions.

9.13 Non-anthropocentric fusion energy ethics

Fusion is not yet a viable commercial energy source; and, by most estimates, it will not be for decades. Yet its proponents are enthusiastic. According to the European Fusion Education Network:

Fusion is a beautiful process, not only for physicists but also [as] a potential energy source ... The fuels are abundant ... The only emission consists of a puff of Helium, which in turn can be used by other factories, or to fill children's balloons. . . . Fusion does not create any long-lived radioactive nuclear waste (it produces no actinides) . . . a "melt down" is not possible. (FuseNet, 2013)

This may all be true. Suppose it is. Suppose, indeed, that fusion reactors can produce a limitless supply of safe energy. What then?

It is this very limitlessness that worries the non-anthropocentrist. For such an abundance of energy could spur accelerated exploitation of the oceans, land development, habitat destruction, and population growth – thereby inflicting enormous losses on nonhuman life.

There are, of course, anthropocentric reasons to avoid such losses. Some of us today, for example, would prefer more verdure. But over time, as artifice increases and familiarity with nature declines, such preferences may become archaic. Having a safe and limitless energy supply might eliminate most anthropocentric reasons for caution by freeing us from ecological dependencies. Eventually we might be able to fine-tune atmospheric chemistry; manufacture delicious and nutritious food directly from wastes; and, generally, remake earth into the spaceship of our dreams. True, this might not increase objective human welfare, as distinct from preference satisfaction. But, then again, it might not do anything that an anthropocentric ethic would recognize as harm.

Objective welfare biocentrism, by contrast, would limit human ambitions. It gives no moral weight to preference satisfaction without increase in objective welfare. And although it permits actions that increase objective human welfare at the expense of nonhumans (provided that no alternative action would produce higher overall welfare), it condemns such actions if there are better alternatives.

Still, biocentric consequentialist ethics need not wholly reject fusion. They, like their long-term anthropocentric counterparts, would recommend replacement of more damaging forms of energy production with fusion reactors if no better alternative were available. And if fusion reactors perform as advertised, they might even endorse a fusion economy – but with limits. Uses of energy should either be harmless to nonhumans or productive of *objective* human welfare greater than the harm that they do.

Why accept such limits? If fusion gives us unlimited energy, why not do as we please? This is not far from asking, "why be ethical?" I noted at the outset that anthropocentrism is to non-anthropocentrism at the level of species as egoism is to altruism at the level of individuals. Answers to the question "why accept a non-anthropocentric ethic?" are therefore analogous to answers to the question "why be altruistic?" The philosophical tradition gives various answers to the latter question, and many of them carry over to the former. One of the best, I think, is that altruism (or, more precisely, self-transcendence) enables one person to have hope for those who will outlive her, and hence to avoid despair at her own approaching demise. By analogy, then, non-anthropocentrism enables humanity to have hope for life itself – and hence to avoid despair even at the prospect of its own extinction (Nolt 2010).

9.14 Conclusions

A simplified long-term biocentric consequentialist ethic has led us to four main conclusions concerning nuclear energy:

1. If nuclear energy and fossil fuels were our only options for generating electricity, then we would be morally obligated to generate nearly all of it from nuclear sources – as quickly as possible. Fortunately, these not our only options.
2. Renewables are the most desirable option. Nuclear fission has a lower expected value (in terms of objective welfare, both human and nonhuman) than they do.
3. Still, nuclear fission can contribute to long-term objective welfare where renewables are not available quickly enough in sufficient quantity to reduce carbon emissions or relieve dire poverty. But its use should be limited to these purposes.
4. Nuclear fusion, if it performs as advertised, might also contribute to objective welfare; but it should not be used to increase objective human welfare at the expense of nonhumans if some alternative energy policy would produce higher overall welfare, considering both humans and nonhumans.

Conclusions 1–3 are also supported by long-term anthropocentric objective welfare consequentialism. Conclusion 4 is not. It therefore illustrates the difference between an anthropocentric and a non-anthropocentric ethic, even when both are long-term. The reason for the agreement on conclusions 1–3 is that, for now, long-term human and nonhuman welfare remain strongly correlated.

Though I have employed only a very crude conception of objective welfare in reaching these conclusions, the consequences of the various forms of energy production are so weighty that the conclusions would not be much altered, I think, had I used a more refined conception. Nor would they have changed much had I used a narrower (e.g. sentientist) non-anthropocentric conception of welfare.

Acknowledgment

I wish to thank Jenna Nolt for research help with this chapter.

Part III

Democracy

10 Morally experimenting with nuclear energy

Ibo van de Poel

10.1 Introduction: the experimental nature of nuclear energy

The past few years have witnessed a revival of the debate about nuclear energy. The greenhouse effect, alongside with technological developments that allegedly lead to safer nuclear reactors and to a reduction of the lifetime of nuclear waste have been an argument to plea for an increased use of nuclear energy. Conversely, the Fukushima disaster and the events following it have also led to serious doubts about the nuclear option. Germany has decided to phase out nuclear energy. Stress tests on existing reactors, which were done after the Fukushima disaster, showed serious weaknesses in current nuclear reactors.

My aim in this contribution is not to take sides in the nuclear debate. Rather, I am interested in the terms in which this debate is conducted. I am particularly interested in one specific aspect, namely how the issue of uncertainty is dealt with in the nuclear debate. Briefly put, my claim is that nuclear energy is still in several, although not all, respects an experimental technology and, so I will argue, recognizing this experimental nature would improve the moral debate about the desirability of nuclear energy. It would, in particular, allow us to better take into account and deal with the uncertainties, and sometimes even ignorance, that surrounds at least some aspects of nuclear energy.

It may sound strange to call a technology with which there is more than fifty years of operating experience experimental. I admit that – as regards the uncertainties and risks – nuclear energy is less experimental than fifty years ago. We might be able to make much more reliable estimates of the probability of a core meltdown than fifty years ago. A lot has been learned from the incidents and accidents that have occurred with nuclear energy over the last decades. Nevertheless, in some other aspects, nuclear energy may still be called experimental. This first and foremost applies to the issue of nuclear waste. With currently available technologies, nuclear waste will remain radiotoxic for an estimated period between 10,000 and 200,000 years, depending on the exact nuclear fuel cycle employed (Taebi and Kloosterman 2008). Measured on these time scales, the current experience with the storage and disposal of nuclear waste is negligible. An even after a hundred years, operating experience with for example geological disposal will still only amount to about 1 percent, or less of the time that the waste remains radiotoxic. So, nuclear waste storage and disposal is still a quite experimental technology. The same applies, albeit maybe to a lesser degree, to some of the new generations of reactors designs that have been developed and that are based on principles of passive or inherent safety, the so-called Gen III, Gen III+, and Gen IV reactor designs. Although these new generations of reactor designs may be promising in terms of safety, there is still only very limited operating experience with them (Taebi and Kloosterman, 2014).

By calling nuclear energy (in some respects) experimental, I do not just want to draw attention to lack of operational experience with the newer generations of nuclear reactor designs and with geological disposal of nuclear waste. My claim is broader and also relates to the institutional and normative aspects of nuclear energy. The claim is that the operation and use of nuclear energy amounts to a kind of real-world experiment.[1] I call this a real-world experiment because it is an experiment in society rather than in the laboratory, or the testing of a prototype on a limited scale. What is being tested in the experiment is not just the technical operation of nuclear energy, it also relates to broader social impacts, the institutional arrangements with respect to nuclear energy, and their normative and moral dimensions. What is, or at least could be, learned in the course of the experiment relates not only to how to better, and more safely, operate nuclear reactors, but also to other impacts, institutions, and even normative insights. Recognizing what I call the experimental nature of nuclear energy thus not only means recognizing that the technology is not yet completely finished but also recognizing that the moral debate is an ongoing debate in which new factual and normative insights may come to play a role as learning occurs. We are thus not only technologically and socially but also morally experimenting with nuclear energy.

In Section 10.2 I will discuss a number of episodes from the history of nuclear energy. My aim in doing so is to make tangible what I mean with the experimental nature of nuclear energy. I will also use the episodes in some of my later discussions in the chapter. Sections 10.3 and 10.4 will look respectively at epistemological and moral reasons for conceiving of the employment of nuclear energy in society as real-world experiment. In both cases, I will discuss reasons why I think it is insightful to conceive of nuclear energy as a

---

[1] In earlier publications, I have used the term social or societal experiment (Van de Poel 2009, 2011). In this contribution, I prefer the term "real-world experiment" to distinguish the notion from the notion of social experiments used by the Chicago School of Sociology (e.g. Small 1921) (see also discussion in Section 10.3.2). In some respects, I still think social or societal experiment catches the idea better because it stresses not only that it is an experiment in society (the real-world aspect) but also on and by society (Van de Poel forthcoming). The idea of new technology as a real-world experiment goes back to Krohn and Weingart (1987), Martin and Schinzinger (1989), and Krohn and Weyer (1994).

real-world experiment, but I will also discuss possible objections. I end with conclusions.

10.2 Four episodes from the history of nuclear energy

10.2.1 Probabilistic risk assessment and core meltdown

When the first risk assessments of nuclear reactors were done, there was neither a full-fledged theory of reactor operation nor historical accident data. The well-known Rasmussen study therefore estimated the risks of nuclear power on the basis of what has become known as probabilistic risk assessment (PRA) (NRC 1975). Although PRA has proved to be an important approach to risk assessment and safety design, it also soon became clear that PRA cannot take away the large uncertainty with respect to nuclear hazards (e.g. Lewis et al. 1978). Moreover, PRA as such cannot avoid ignorance about possible disaster scenarios without extensive operational experience.[2]

Arguably today there is extensive operational experience. It is therefore interesting to compare the historical estimates of nuclear risks based on PRA with the statistics of actual accidents. An important accident scenario in a reactor is the occurrence of reactor core damage. The probability of this scenario can be expressed in terms of a core damage frequency (CDF) per year of reactor operation, or reactor year (RY). Rasmussen's report estimated the CDF to be between 2.6×10^{-5} and 5×10^{-5}, indicating an accident probability of once every 20,000–40,000 RY. Historical data suggest, however, that the actual CDF is between 1 in 1300 and 1 in 3,600 RY (Taebi et al. 2012).[3]

In 2001, the International Atomic Energy Agency (IAEA) stated that future nuclear reactors should have a CDF of less than 1 in 100,000 RY (IAEA 2001: 73), i.e. a factor 1,000 to 3,000 safer than the current record. In the last decades new reactor designs based on so-called inherent and passive safety features have been proposed which are allegedly much safer than the current reactors. Some of these designs have already been built and some have operated for several years. Examples of such new reactor designs are the ABWR (Advanced Boiling Water Reactor) and the AP1000 (Taebi and Kloosterman, 2014). The ABWR is an improved version of the traditional boiling water reactor (BWR), which is allegedly much safer; it is in operation but not yet for a long period. The AP1000 is an improved version of the pressurized water reaction (PWR); it

---

[2] See also Chapter 3 in this volume.
[3] The number depends on what exactly counts as severe core damage and there is no agreement on that. If one only takes into the account the uncontroversial four severe core damage (one reactor in Chernobyl and three in Fukushima), the historic data suggest a CDF of once every 3600 RY. The number of 1300 is based on 11 severe accidents. Shrader-Frechette (2011b) claims that there have been as much as 26 severe core damage accidents.

is not operational yet. Still, risk assessment of these reactors and the claim that they are much safer than current reactors have to rely on PRA as there is still too limited operating experience for risk estimates on the basis of statistical data on incidents and accidents. According to my analytic framework, the new reactors can therefore still be called experimental.

10.2.2 Rapid upscaling and failure in the USA[4]

In the USA, nuclear energy boomed in the 1960s to fail in the 1970s; since 1978, no new reactor has been built in the USA. While the reasons for this failure are complex, it can at least in part be attributed to the rapid upscaling of nuclear energy technology at the time, and a neglect of the experimental nature of the technology.

In the USA, nuclear energy focused on the building of so-called light water reactors (LWRs). The first LWR for the generation of energy was built in 1957. In 1963, the first purchase of an LWR on purely economic grounds and without governmental subsidies was announced. In 1965, the first nuclear reactors were ordered by utilities without firm price guarantees of the reactor manufacturers. During 1966–67, utilities placed orders for almost fifty plants.

Between 1964 and 1974, the annually ordered nuclear capacity in the USA was larger than the total nuclear capacity installed in all preceding years (Bupp and Derian 1978). The mean capacity per nuclear plant ordered quickly rose, from about 636 MW in 1963 to 1141 MW in 1972 (Bupp and Derian 1978: 73). At no time between 1963 and 1972 was any plant in operation as large as the smallest one being ordered (Jasper 1990: 49). Due to this rapid upscaling of nuclear plants, there was scant operating experience on which the design of new reactors could be based. In addition, new safety issues were raised by the rapid upscaling of nuclear reactors. In many cases, their resolution led to design changes, added safety features, and – sometimes – retrofitting of existing reactors. As a result, ever more safety features were added to nuclear reactors.

Between the mid-1960s and the mid-1970s, cost estimates for nuclear power became increasingly less optimistic. In 1974, the estimated costs of generating nuclear energy were about five times as high as in the mid-1960s. In the same time, the estimated time to build a nuclear reactor more than doubled (Burn 1978: 31). The rising costs were partly due to the mentioned safety and regulatory problems. In 1975 the number of nuclear orders sharply declined. Some utilities were forced to cancel the construction of nuclear plants due to financing problems. After 1975, ever more reactor orders were canceled and the number of reactor orders quickly fell. Since 1978 no nuclear reactor has been

---

[4] For more details, see van de Poel (1998: 247–53).

ordered in the USA and the 1980s witnessed the cancelation of the building of nuclear plants in which already substantially had been invested.

The "failure" of nuclear energy in the United States is sometimes attributed to the accident at Three Mile Island in 1979, but the reasons are much more complex. In fact, the number of nuclear orders already started declining well before the accident (Bupp and Derian 1978). Although earlier authors (e.g. Bupp and Derian 1978; Burn 1978; Jasper 1990) use other terminology, their analysis shows that one of the reasons for the failure of nuclear energy in the USA was a neglect, or at least underestimation, of what I have called the experimental nature of nuclear energy. This led to a pace of upscaling, both in terms of number of reactors and reactor capacity that was much faster than operating experience accumulated. This in turn led to safety and licensing issues, cost overruns, and eventually public distrust.

10.2.3 The Fukushima disaster

On March 11, 2011 an earthquake and a tsunami struck Japan, which led to a partial nuclear meltdown of three reactors at the Fukushima Daiichi nuclear power plant. It was the combination of the earthquake and the tsunami that resulted in the accident. Although the combination of events at March 11 was rare, it could arguably have been anticipated, in which case it might have been possible to take (design) measures to avoid the accident (Lipscy et al. 2013). In this sense, the Fukushima disaster was probably preventable.

However, even if the scenario that occurred at Fukushima had been anticipated and design measures had been taken, the adequacy of these design measures can only be verified in a real-world experiment. One cannot test earthquake resistance in a laboratory.[5] Instead, models are built and calculations and computer simulations are done, but all of these are based on assumptions, of which the adequacy cannot be fully tested before the nuclear plant is actually operational. The real test is therefore unavoidably a real-world experiment.

The Fukushima disaster also teaches us something about the uniqueness of (social) experiments. In particular, it tells us that siting conditions (e.g. near the ocean, possibility of earthquakes) are part of the experiment, so that experience with nuclear reactors under other siting conditions is not necessarily directly relevant for decreasing the experimental nature of this specific experiment. On the other hand, the Fukushima experiment is not completely unique as it

---

[5] Tsunami resistance may be tested with scale models; for earthquakes this is probably more difficult. But even if it could be tested in the lab, one needs to rely on assumptions about similarities between the scale model and reality; assumptions that can often only be tested in a real-world experiment.

contains important lessons for other coastal nuclear plants and for the vulnerability of nuclear reactors to natural disasters (cf. Lipscy et al. 2013).

10.2.4 Nuclear waste

Nuclear energy reactors produce not only energy but also nuclear waste. As a matter of fact, at least part of this nuclear waste (also sometimes referred to as spent fuel) could be reprocessed and then be reused as fuel for (other) nuclear reactors. This is known as the closed fuel cycle; conversely, in the so-called open fuel cycle nuclear waste is not recycled but it is supposed to be immediately stored and disposed of.

Nuclear waste from the open fuel cycle remains radiotoxic for about 200,000 years; waste from the closed fuel cycle will remain radiotoxic for about 5,000–10,000 years (Taebi and Kloosterman 2008). The latter period may be reduced to 500–1,000 years with a new technology that is still under development: partitioning and transmutation (P&T). Although the closed fuel cycle has advantages in terms of the volume and longevity of the nuclear waste produced, it has disadvantages as well, especially in the short term. One of the disadvantages of the closed fuel cycle is that it increases security and proliferation risks as it will result in a larger production of plutonium, which can be used to produce an atomic bomb.

There are several available and potential technologies for the storage of nuclear waste. I will focus here on the options for the storage of high-level waste (HLW) and spent fuel (SF).[6] With respect to HLW and SF, a consensus now seems to be developing in the engineering community that deep geological storage is the best option for the long term. Although risk assessments and experiments are conducted for deep geological repositories, these are surrounded by large degrees of uncertainty and probably also ignorance about possible failure scenarios (e.g. Shrader-Frechette 1993, 2011b; Macfarlane and Ewing 2006). Currently, most nuclear waste is (temporarily) stored above the ground; so there is very limited experience with deep geological repositories and it seems no exaggeration to say that the relevant experience will stay limited for at least several decades to come, especially given the time scales at which nuclear waste remains radiotoxic.

Nuclear waste storage involves not only uncertainty about natural and engineering processes but also about human behavior. Uncertainty about human behavior is not just epistemological but also relates to what might be called the indeterminacy of human behavior: Humans are free to choose how they want to act. This is an additional and separate argument for the

---

[6] Other types of waste include low level waste (LLW) and intermediate level waste (ILW). These are usually stored above the ground or at shallow depths.

experimental nature of waste storage. It is an experiment with how future generations will deal with waste storages, like deep geological repositories, and in fact also an experiment with how we can communicate risks to future generations. For example, should we somehow sign post geological repositories and what language or symbols are appropriate for doing so?

10.3 Epistemological reasons for and objections against calling the employment of nuclear energy a real-world experiment

10.3.1 Epistemological reasons for calling nuclear energy a real-world experiment

There are two main epistemological reasons to call the employment of nuclear energy in society a real-world experiment. One reason has to do with uncertainty and lack of knowledge, the other reason with what we might learn from an experiment. I will discuss both aspects in turn below.

Uncertainty and lack of knowledge The first epistemological reason to call nuclear energy experimental is that there are still a lot of things we are uncertain about. In this subsection, I focus on the general nature of uncertainty and distinguish different kinds of uncertainty, some of which cannot be reduced before a technology is introduced in society. In the next subsection, where I discuss potential epistemological arguments against considering nuclear energy a real-world experiment, I relate these different types of uncertainty to nuclear energy.

We can distinguish between different kinds of uncertainty. One distinction that is often made is that between epistemological and aleatory uncertainty (Paté-Cornell 1996). Epistemological uncertainty is due to a lack of knowledge; conversely, aleatory uncertainty is inherent in the world, for example because natural processes may be underdetermined. In addition to epistemological and aleatory uncertainty, one might distinguish indeterminacy (e.g. Wynne 1992). I will understand indeterminacy as the situation in which the causal chains toward the future are still open so that it is indeterminate what exactly will happen. Indeterminacy may be due to human behavior but also to causal factors that we treat as external to the system under study.

While aleatory uncertainty can usually not be reduced because it is inherent in the world, epistemological uncertainty and indeterminacy can be reduced but they can in different ways.

Epistemological uncertainty can be reduced by research and other modes of investigation. Although epistemological uncertainty can in principle be reduced before a technology is introduced in society, in practice this often turns out to be difficult or practically impossible. Here it is relevant to distinguish between different levels of epistemological uncertainty (Walker et al. 2003):

- Statistical uncertainty: We know the scenarios that might occur and their probabilities.
- Scenario uncertainty: We know the scenarios that might occur but cannot meaningfully attach probabilities to each of the scenarios.
- Recognized ignorance: We do not know certain things and we are aware of this lack of knowledge ("known unknowns").
- Unrecognized ignorance: We are unaware that we do not know certain things ("unknown unknowns").

Indeterminacy is often only resolved once something is done. This is the case because indeterminacy is due to the openness of causal chains, and these chains will only be closed if people act or if an indeterminate factor becomes determinate. In many cases, the introduction of a technology involves indeterminacy because how a technology is actually introduced in society and what social effects materialize will depend not just on the design of the technology, but on how people exactly implement the technology, how they use it, how it is regulated, etc. Although we might sometimes be able to make more or less reliable predictions about how these indeterminacies will be resolved, in many cases there is a remaining degree of uncertainty as long as people have not actually acted and causal chains have not been closed. This remaining uncertainty can only be resolved by actually introducing a technology in society because only then the indeterminacy ends and actions and consequences become determinate. Indeterminacy can therefore not be fully reduced before a technology is introduced in society. This is in fact a main reason, although not the only one, that the introduction of technology in society has an experimental character.

Improved learning through deliberate experimentation While the first epistemological reason to call a technology experimental is related to uncertainty and lack of knowledge, the second epistemological reason is related to what we can learn from an experiment. Once we recognize something as an experiment, it offers the possibility to learn from it. Recognizing the experimental nature of a technology is the first step not only toward more deliberate experimentation but also toward improving learning and attempting to reduce the costs of learning (van de Poel forthcoming).

Deliberate experiments offer increased possibilities for learning for two reasons. First, they allow for more systematic observation and for monitoring, so that, for example, unexpected effects are earlier detected. Second, they allow for (shorter) feedback loops between the outcomes of a real-world experiment (like certain social impacts) and the set-up of the experiment. For example, if certain undesired consequences materialize (think of a nuclear meltdown in the case of nuclear energy), the set-up of the experiment may be adapted or the experiment may be stopped.

Deliberate experimentation can not only improve learning but it can also reduce the social costs of learning. Monitoring and feedback loops already reduce the costs of learning because it takes less time to observe certain effects (monitoring) and one can quicker act on unexpected effects (feedback loops). In addition, the experiment may be scaled up in such a way that the possibilities to learn in each step of upscaling are optimized while the social costs of learning are kept limited because if an undesirable social consequence occurs, it only occurs at a relatively limited scale.

Elsewhere (van de Poel forthcoming) I have argued that sound real-world experiments with technology should further at least three kinds of learning, i.e. learning about the impacts of a technology (e.g. the safety and health effects), learning about the proper institutions to embed a technology in society (e.g. forms of regulation or risk governance), and normative learning (e.g. learning about which moral values and norms are at stake and should be upheld in the development and governance of a technology).

10.3.2 Epistemological objections against considering nuclear energy a real-world experiment

I will now consider three possible epistemological objections to the idea that the employment of nuclear energy in society constitutes a real-world experiment.

First epistemological objection: Nuclear energy is no longer experimental The first epistemological objection is that nuclear energy is, after more than fifty years of operating experience, no longer experimental. This is to some extent true. As we saw in the description of PRA and core meltdown, we might be better able to estimate the probability of severe core damage now than in the past. As we have seen, this suggests that the actual probability of severe core damage is most likely larger than initially thought. It has been argued that new generations of nuclear reactors, the so-called Gen III, Gen III+, and Gen IV reactors, will reduce the CDF because they are based on passive or inherent safety features. Such safety features are intended to assure that the nuclear reaction in a reactor automatically stops if something goes wrong, rather than relying on active safety features that stop the nuclear reaction. However, these reactor types are still experimental, as I have argued above. Also in relation to nuclear waste and earthquake resistance, nuclear energy still has important experimental features.

Nuclear waste is probably the most experimental aspect of nuclear energy as it involves a high degree of epistemological uncertainty as well as indeterminacy. It involves a high degree of epistemological uncertainty because it involves not just statistical uncertainty, and scenario uncertainty, but also ignorance. The reason why it involves ignorance is that we most likely do not know all routes through which a nuclear waste repository might fail over the coming centuries and millennia. In so far as this is recognized, it is a case of recognized ignorance. But in so far as it is neglected in risk assessment, we might speak of unrecognized ignorance. There are also other unknowns, for example, how future generations will deal with stored nuclear waste. It should be noticed that the uncertainty about how future generations will behave is not only due to epistemological uncertainty but also due to indeterminacy. There is a principled limit to the degree to which we can know the behavior of future generations, as this behavior is still indeterminate. This gives the dealing with nuclear waste a clearly experimental character.

Second epistemological objection: Real-world experiments are uncontrolled experiments and therefore not real experiments A second objection runs as follows: Real-world experiments are not real experiments; they are at best experiments metaphorically speaking. A main difference between real-world experiments and traditional experiments is that real-world experiments do not take place in the laboratory. A main reason why traditional experiments are done in the laboratory is that it is a controlled setting that allows for controlling the independent variables in an experiment, and therefore, in scientifically establishing cause–effect relationships. According to this objection, real-world experiments are not real experiments because they are uncontrolled and therefore they are inappropriate for finding cause–effect relationships. While I concede that real-world experiments are uncontrolled, I will argue below that that is not a conclusive reason for not calling them experiments as we might still learn from them.

But let us first look at why control is so central in the traditional notion of experiment. Control is often seen as essential for the possibility of establishing cause–effect relationships in experiments (cf. also Woodward 2003). To establish causal relations in an experiment, one needs to assure that what one observes is the relation between the independent and dependent variables in which one is interested. This can be done by keeping constant or eliminating the possible causal factors in which one is not interested. Controlled experimentation allows for such factors to be kept constant or eliminated, while in uncontrolled experiments it is usually impossible to keep intervening factors constant or to eliminate them. In this respect, the artificiality of the laboratory is often seen as advantageous for doing experiments because it offers better control. As Webster and Sell write:

The greatest benefits of experiments reside in the fact that they are artificial. That is, experiments allow observation in a situation that has been designed and created by the investigators rather than one that occurs in nature. Artificiality means that a well-designed experiment can incorporate all the theoretically presumed causes of certain phenomena while eliminating or minimizing factors that have not been theoretically identified as causal (Webster and Sell 2007: 11).

According to various authors, an experiment without control cannot properly be called an experiment. Webster and Sell for example state that "a study is an *experiment* only when a particular ordering occurs: when an investigator controls the level of independent variables *before* measuring the level of dependent variables" (Webster and Sell 2007: 8).

In reviewing the literature on experiments, Gonzales observes that for many authors "experiment" and "controlled experiment" are more or less synonymous (Gonzales 2010: 27). Nevertheless, he also notes that there are various notions of experiment that do not presuppose control. This includes notions like natural experiment, social experiment, real-life experiment, and quasi-experiment. Natural experiments are natural events like an earthquake or volcano outburst which do not normally happen but, when they happen, allow for the observation of phenomena that can normally not be observed (cf. Gonzales 2010). The notion of "social experiments" has been used in various ways, but the usage of the Chicago School of Sociology in the early twentieth century comes close to the social counterpart of natural experiments: interesting social phenomena that occur spontaneously and may be observed as they happen (e.g. Small 1921). The term "real-life experiment" has been used by authors like Krohn and Weyer (1994). It refers to the fact that some effects or hazards of a new technology only become clear when they are actually introduced in society. The notion of quasi-experiment has been used in the social sciences (e.g. Campbell and Stanley 1966). It refers to the fact that we can use the occurrence of uncontrolled variation to experimentally find out the effect of a variable. For example, if we are interested in the effect of class size on student performance, we might use the variation of class size that exists in a country to study how it affects student performance.

This brief overview shows that the notion of "experiment" has also been used to refer to uncontrolled experiments. However, it might be objected that in all these cases the notion of "experiment" is used improperly. More specifically, it might be objected that these notions of experiment blur the distinction between experiments and observations. For example, an earthquake allows for interesting observations, but there is no value added by calling it a "natural experiment," so the objection might run. There is certainly a grain of truth in this objection. However, we might distinguish between experiments and mere observations in other ways than requiring the presence of a controlled environment to speak about an experiment. We might, for example, require some form of intervention or manipulation that creates the phenomenon we are interested in (and hence allows for observation of it) to properly speak of an experiment. If we would do so, natural and social experiments would not count as real experiments because they rely on spontaneously occurring events. Also quasi-experiments would not be real experiments according to such a criterion, as the phenomena are not, or at least not necessarily, the result of an intervention. Real-life experiments, or real-world experiments as I will call them, are real experiments according to this criterion, as the phenomena studied are the result of an intervention, i.e. the introduction and employment of a technology in society.

It might, however, be objected that the new criterion might help us to distinguish real-world experiments from mere observations, but that the uncontrolled character of real-world experiments nevertheless makes it impossible to learn from these experiments. After all, scientists aim for controlled experiments because they make it possible to establish cause–effect relations. I think this possible objection does not hold for several reasons. First, the learning that takes place in real-world experiments is not only, or even primarily, learning about causal relations. As pointed out earlier, in real-world experiments one can learn about social impacts (impact learning), about the proper institutions to embed a technology in society (institutional learning), and about relevant moral issues, norms, and values (normative learning). Institutional and normative learning in particular do not necessarily require the establishment of causal relations. Second, the learning in a real-world experiment is primarily aimed at better introducing a technology in society rather than at producing general knowledge about cause–effect relations (as is often the aim of laboratory experiments). When we introduce a new technology in society as a real-world experiment, we want to learn about this specific technology in a more or less specific context. A real-world experiment is in fact often more appropriate for this kind of learning than a laboratory experiment. Laboratory experiments that take place in a controlled setting can be used to test hypotheses derived from a theory, and to establish causal relationships, and they can be replicated more readily than real-world experiments. In this way, the internal validity of the outcomes of an experiment (or a series of experiments) is increased. However, this comes at a cost; the artificiality of the laboratory setting raises questions about external validity as it is unclear whether the results from laboratory experiments can be generalized to situations outside the laboratory settings (Millo and Lezaun 2006; Walker and Willer 2007). So, while real-world experiments score less on internal validity, their external validity is larger, and if we want to learn about how to improve the employment of a technology in society, this external validity is of prime importance. All in all, we may conclude that real-world experiments offer opportunities for learning, albeit other opportunities than controlled experiments.

In the case of nuclear energy, it is rather clear, I think, that the employment of nuclear energy technology is not and cannot be a *controlled* real-world experiment. For example, for obvious ethical reasons, we would not test out the hypothesis that a loss of coolant accident (LOCA) leads to meltdown in an operating reactor (or even in a test or research reactor). Similarly, if we have good reasons to suspect that a certain organizational culture at a nuclear plant or a certain style of regulation would increase the chances of a serious accident, we would not do an experiment in which we deliberately create cases of such organizational cultures or regulatory styles and systematically compare them with a control group of reactors with what we think is a more effective organizational culture or regulatory style.[7]

Still, the employment of nuclear energy amounts to an uncontrolled real-world experiment, from which a lot can be learned (especially if it were done more deliberately) and from which a lot has indeed already be learned. The history of PRA and core meltdown (Section 10.2.1) has shown that now more reliable estimates of CDF are possible. Moreover, the incidents and accidents that have happened in the past have contributed to insights incorporated in the new generations of reactor designs. Also in the case of the Fukushima disaster, it is clear that a lot can be learned from an uncontrolled experiment, in terms of reactor siting, organizational culture and regulation (Section 10.2.3). Some of these things might have been impossible to learn in laboratory experiments or computer simulations, and in that respect the real-world experiment has a larger external validity. Of course, that in itself does not settle the question of the desirability or acceptability of such experiments, a question that I will discuss in Section 10.4.

Third epistemological objection: The experimental nature of nuclear technology has already been recognized According to this objection, the experimental nature of nuclear technology has already been recognized. Again, there is a grain of truth in this objection as there are signs of at least a tacit recognition of the experimental nature of nuclear energy. As in many hazardous industries, there are systems, like the International Reporting System for Operating Experience (IRS), for reporting and sharing information on nuclear incidents and accidents.[8] This may be interpreted as an awareness that something that is not yet known can be learned from such events. Similarly, the stress tests that were done after the Fukushima disaster in for example

---

[7] Note that the situation might be different if we do not have reasons to expect beforehand that one organizational culture is less effective than another. Then such a controlled experiment may be ethically defensible under certain circumstances.

[8] www-ns.iaea.org/reviews/op-safety-reviews.asp?s=2&l=15#irs (accessed January 14, 2014). See also: www-ns.iaea.org/tech-areas/emergency/incident-reporting-mechanisms.asp (accessed January 14, 2014).

Europe may be seen as recognition that Fukushima was not only a disaster but also a kind of experiment from which lessons can be drawn for other reactors.

Although these are indeed signs of at least the implicit recognition of the experimental nature of nuclear energy, there are also examples that show that in many respects the experimental nature of nuclear energy has not yet been recognized. We have seen that that the "failure" of nuclear energy in the USA was partly due to a neglect of the experimental nature of nuclear energy. But also today the experimental nature of nuclear energy is not generally recognized. For example, many current risk assessments of new types of nuclear reactors or of nuclear waste facilities suggest a degree of accuracy in predicting risks that shows an unawareness of the experimental nature of these technologies. In addition, in the moral debate the experimental nature of nuclear energy is not really recognized; this is an issue to which I now turn.

10.4 Moral reasons for and objections against calling the employment of nuclear energy a real-world experiment

10.4.1 Moral reasons for calling nuclear energy a real-world experiment

Let me now turn to the moral reasons for recognizing the experimental nature of nuclear energy. My main argument is that recognizing the experimental nature of nuclear energy improves the moral debate. I will discuss below four more specific reasons why I think that conceiving of the employment of nuclear energy as a real-world experiment improves the moral debate: (1) it explicitly recognizes the role of uncertainty in the debate; (2) it shifts the debate away from the stalemate between opponents and proponents of nuclear energy; (3) it provides for a moral framework based on the notion of responsible experimentation; and (4) it recognizes the dynamic and ongoing character of the moral debate and the possibility for moral learning.

Recognizing uncertainty in the moral debate Moral debates about technology often have a hard time dealing with the role of uncertainty (Sollie and Düwell 2009). There is a tendency to discuss technologies as if they are completely known and as if their characteristics are given, rather than something to be (partly) discovered or (partly) to be designed. As Hansson (2003c) has pointed out, most traditional ethical theories have difficulties dealing with uncertainty and risks. Hansson also suggests that we should perhaps not so much focus on the acceptability of risks but rather on the acceptability of actions like risking, risk-taking, and risk-imposing (Hansson 2003c: 302). I think that recognition of the experimental nature of nuclear energy would well fit the shift proposed by Hansson. Rather than discussing inherent risks (and other disadvantages) of nuclear energy technology, it would place the focus on the question whether it is worthwhile to risk certain things by experimenting in society with nuclear technology.

For example, in the case of nuclear waste, we should not primarily ponder whether the risk in terms of probability and consequences is acceptable, but rather pose the question whether an experiment with nuclear energy that might have benefits for the current and future generations justifies putting at risk the life and health of especially future generations, and the risk that we leave them with diminished opportunities to fulfill their needs, while recognizing that not doing the experiment might also pose risks in terms of opportunities for future generations. One obvious complication here is that we cannot ask future generations for their consent with such an experiment.

It should be noted that conceiving of the employment of nuclear energy as a real-world experiment also implies recognition that we cannot express all uncertainties in terms of risks. If we define risk as probability times (undesirable) consequences, as is often done in the technological risk assessment literature (cf. Hansson 2009b), we can calculate risk in cases of statistical uncertainty, but not in cases of scenario uncertainty, and cases of (recognized or unrecognized) ignorance. As I have argued above, nuclear energy also involves these types of uncertainty, especially in the case of nuclear waste disposal, and in my view the moral debate should recognize our limited ability to express uncertainties in risks. Recognizing the experimental nature of nuclear energy is instrumental in doing so.

Shifting the moral debate away from the stalemate between opponents and proponents of nuclear energy Conceiving of nuclear energy as a kind of real-world experiment would shift the debate away from discussions about the inherent acceptability of nuclear energy to a debate about the acceptability of experimenting with nuclear energy (van de Poel 2011). Of course, a first question then would be if *any* experiment with nuclear energy in society can be morally acceptable. It seems to me that there are two possible arguments why experimenting with nuclear energy in a real-world experiment is unacceptable: one referring to catastrophic hazards and the other referring to the time scale of nuclear hazards.

The argument from catastrophic hazards would say that the mere possibility of catastrophic hazards makes it unacceptable to do real-world experiments with nuclear energy. The potential of catastrophic hazards is obviously a serious concern in the case of nuclear energy technology, but I don't think it provides a conclusive argument against experimenting with nuclear energy in society. To the best of our current knowledge, the most catastrophic scenario for nuclear energy is a core meltdown in a nuclear plant. The historical cases of Chernobyl and Fukushima suggest that such a scenario has very detrimental effects, but it is not obvious that the consequences are so catastrophic that they entail strong enough reasons to ban any real-world experimentation with nuclear energy. That would, it seems to me, very much depend on other concerns like the expected benefits, available alternatives, and the exact set-up of the experiment.

A second possible argument would go as follows: Experimenting in society with nuclear energy introduces hazards on very long time scales, and we have a moral obligation not to harm future generations, and therefore a moral obligation not to introduce these long-term hazards. This argument draws attention to considerations of intergenerational justice and our moral obligations to future generations. These are indeed very important considerations in the moral debate about nuclear energy. I doubt, however, whether they provide a conclusive reason against experimenting with nuclear energy in society. It seems to me that many new technologies, and especially energy technologies, create hazards and the possibility of harm for future generations. Fossil fuels, for example, contribute to global warming, which clearly might harm future generations. Again, it is not obvious that the argument provides a conclusive reason for banning any real-world experiment with nuclear energy.

If, as I believe, real-world experiments with nuclear energy are not inherently morally unacceptable, the question shifts to the conditions under which we would consider such experiments acceptable. I think this is a much more fruitful question for the moral debate about nuclear energy than a sole focus on the moral acceptability of nuclear energy. It opens up the possibility for a more constructive debate and toward improved social experimentation with nuclear energy.

A moral framework for responsible experimentation   Conceiving of nuclear energy as a real-world experiment is also helpful in developing a moral framework to judge the acceptability of such experiments. Such a framework could draw on the existing ethical literature of experiments with human subjects. Even if a real-world experiment with nuclear energy is not primarily an experiment on human subjects, it involves human subjects in a number of ways. First, humans can obviously be harmed if something goes wrong in the experiment (like a meltdown or leakages from a geological repository). Second, humans are essential in the operation of nuclear energy in society (as operators of the technology but also, for example, as regulators) and also in that sense they are part of the experiment.

In bioethics, four principles have been formulated that are central in judging the acceptability of experiments with human subjects: respect for persons (moral autonomy), beneficence, non-maleficence, and justice (e.g. Beauchamp and Childress 2001). These principles have been further specified in the context of medical treatment and experimentation. In the context of real-world experiments, a new specification of the four principles is needed because real-world experiments are different from the experiments on human subjects that are the central focus in current research ethics and in medical ethics. Real-world experiments are different in two main respects. First, as they are experiments in the real-world it is usually much harder to delineate who are the experimental subjects than in traditional experiments. Not only may many more people be involved, but the boundaries of the system in which the experiment takes place are often more fuzzy, so that it is not always entirely clear beforehand who are subjected to the experiment and who not. Second, real-world experiments will often involve higher degrees of uncertainty than traditional experiments.

Table 10.1 suggests a number of more specific conditions for responsible real-world experimentation, most of which I have argued for in earlier publications (van de Poel 2009; Jacobs et al. 2010). The conditions can be justified in terms of the four general ethical principles of bioethics: respect for persons (e.g. conditions 9–12), beneficence (condition 8), non-maleficence (conditions 1–7), and justice (condition 13–14).

These conditions are not only helpful in judging the acceptability of real-world experiments with nuclear energy; they can also be used to improve the set-up of such real-world experiments. One can, for example, decide to (better) monitor consequences (condition 2), or can create possibilities for people to withdraw from the experiment (condition 12).

Moral learning and experimentation If we take the experimental nature of nuclear energy fully serious, we should acknowledge that finding the right moral framework for responsible experimentation is part of the experiment. Not only may we learn experimentally what moral issues are at stake in the debate about nuclear energy, we might also learn about the adequacy and applicability of certain moral norms and values, like the four bioethical principles that are at the foundation of the conditions proposed in Table 10.1.

The idea of moral experimentation has especially been elaborated in John Dewey's pragmatic philosophy. Dewey sees existing moral principles as tools to deal with moral issues (Dewey 1957: ch. 7). Although such tools have proven their usefulness and adequacy in the past, they may not be the best to deal with new issues. To test out these moral tools, we need to experiment with them. This would mean that the bioethical principles of respect for persons, beneficence, non-maleficence, and justice, and the more specific conditions in Table 10.1 that are based on these four principles, may guide the initial set-up of a real-world experiment, while at the same being subject to the ongoing

Table 10.1. *Possible conditions for responsible experimentation*

1. Absence of other reasonable means for gaining knowledge about hazards
2. Monitoring
3. Possibility to stop the experiment
4. Consciously scaling up
5. Flexible set-up
6. Avoid experiments that undermine resilience of receiving "system"
7. Containment of hazards as far as reasonably possible
8. Reasonable to expect social benefits from the experiment
9. Experimental subjects are informed
10. Approved by democratically legitimized bodies
11. Experimental subjects can influence the set-up, carrying out, and stopping of the experiment
12. Experimental subjects can withdraw from the experiment
13. Vulnerable experimental subjects are either not subject to the experiment or are additionally protected
14. A fair distribution of potential hazards and benefits

experiment. We might learn new things by applying the principles and the conditions, on the basis of which we might have to reformulate the principles or conditions. In other words, real-world experiments provide us not only with new empirical insights but also with new normative insights.

If we recognize that the real-world experiment with nuclear energy is also a moral experiment in the sense explained above, we are also able to do justice to the fact that, in the moral debate about nuclear energy, we might get to know, or might develop new arguments, or that existing arguments may turn out to be unwarranted. One example of the latter is the argument that nuclear energy leads to a totalitarian state, as it requires strict governmental control to contain the safety and security issues it raises. This argument was made popular through Robert Jungk's book *Der Atom-Staat* (1977), but has also been suggested by others (e.g. Winner 1980). Almost forty years of experience later, this argument has lost a lot of its appeal. It is true that nuclear proliferation is a yet uncontrolled hazard, and there may be no reasons to be optimistic about the world's ability to tackle this issue; at the same time, there is as far as I know no empirical evidence that the use of nuclear power has led to the establishment of totalitarian governments.

All in all, conceiving of nuclear energy as a real-world experiment that also involves moral experimentation allows us to do justice to the fact that the moral debate about nuclear energy is an ongoing debate in which new normative insights may arise, rather than just a clash between existing normative principles or systems. This allows for a much more constructive take on the moral debate.

10.4.2 *Moral objections against considering nuclear energy a real-world experiment*

I will now discuss three possible moral objections against considering nuclear energy a real-world experiment.

First moral objection: Conceiving of nuclear energy as real-world experiment short-circuits the moral debate According to this objection, saying that nuclear energy is a moral experiment entails saying it is morally unacceptable. It might be true that some people, especially some opponents of nuclear energy, would immediately draw the conclusion that "nuclear energy is unacceptable" from the proposition "nuclear energy is experimental." However, this conclusion is too fast. As argued above, I believe that moral experiments with nuclear energy are not inherently unacceptable; moral acceptability very much depends on how one experiments.

But even if one were to conclude that any experiment with nuclear energy is unacceptable, the objection does not hold. If we have good reasons to believe that nuclear energy amounts to a real-world experiment and that such experiments are morally unacceptable, we have good reasons to believe that nuclear energy is morally unacceptable. There is nothing wrong with such a line of reasoning.

Second objection: Conceiving of nuclear energy as real-world experiment does not answer the question whether nuclear energy is acceptable According to this objection, the original question of whether nuclear energy is acceptable is not answered by answering the question of whether it would be acceptable to experiment with nuclear energy. For example, Martin Peterson has argued that "a good answer to the new question about the acceptability of a social experiment may not be a good answer to the original question whether we should accept the new technology. The two questions do not address the same issue" (Peterson 2013: 350).

Peterson assumes here that the question about the acceptability of a technology is the central question to be answered by an ethical inquiry. In the case of nuclear energy, this assumption boils down to the assumption that the moral debate on nuclear energy is primarily about the moral acceptability of nuclear technology. The underlying issue here is what question is, or what questions are, appropriate to ask in the moral debate about nuclear energy. First, I would like to stress that there are several relevant moral questions. There are moral questions about what fuel cycles or what type of nuclear reactors to employ, questions about siting of nuclear reactors, questions about how to dispose of waste, questions about responsibilities to future generations, and many more. So there is not one central or most appropriate question in the moral debate about nuclear energy.

One might object that even pondering all these questions presupposes that nuclear energy is not inherently morally unacceptable. As explained above, in my approach, the question of inherent acceptability would boil down to the question whether *any* conceivable experiment with nuclear energy would be unacceptable, and, as explained above, I believe this does not result in a conclusive argument against nuclear energy. But more importantly, I have two reasons for thinking that we should pose the relevant moral questions in terms of the acceptability of experimenting rather than in terms of inherent acceptability of nuclear energy. First, any reasons that would count as reasons for the inherent unacceptability of nuclear energy would also count as reasons against experimenting with that technology. So no relevant reasons are banned or concealed. Second, the focus on the experimental character draws attention to the importance of uncertainty. In doing so, it also helps to recognize that nuclear energy is still a developing technology, witness the proposed Gen III, III+, and IV reactor designs. A focus on the inherent acceptability of nuclear energy would tend to treat the technology as given and unchanging, while my approach explicitly acknowledges that nuclear energy is an innovative technology that may change its "character."

Third moral objection: The question whether it is acceptable to experiment in the real world with nuclear technology is hard to answer A third objection is that my proposal to conceive of the use of nuclear energy as a social experiment does not make the relevant moral questions easier to answer. This objection has again been voiced by Martin Peterson: "It is a mistake to think that it is easier to adjudicate whether a social experiment is ethically permissible than it is to adjudicate whether a new technology is ethically acceptable. Our understanding of research ethics is no better than our understanding of ethics in general" (Peterson 2013: 349).

It might be true that the question about the acceptability of experiments with nuclear energy is hard to answer, but that is hardly an argument against my view. We do not choose certain moral questions because they are easier to answer than others; we choose them because they are more appropriate in a certain situation or context. Some questions better highlight the morally relevant features in a situation than others. In the moral debate about nuclear energy, it is important to highlight, among other considerations, the roles of uncertainty and ignorance. Conceiving of nuclear energy as real-world experiment is helpful in this respect. Even if that were to lead to questions that are hard to answer, it is not a reason not to pose those questions.

10.5   Conclusions

I have argued for recognizing the experimental nature of nuclear energy in the moral debate about this technology. I have given both epistemological and moral reasons for doing so. By conceiving of nuclear energy as a kind of real-world experiment we, first of all, recognize the role of uncertainty and are better able to deal with it. Second, it opens the possibility to deliberate real-world experimentation and to better modes of experimentation, which is important for both epistemological reasons (improved learning) and moral reasons (more responsible experimentation).

I have further argued that conceiving of the introduction and employment of nuclear energy in society as a real-world experiment offers genuine possibilities for improving the moral debate about this technology. It helps us to recognize the role of uncertainty in the debate, and in this way, it may also help to shift the debate away from a stalemate between opponents and proponents about the inherent (un)acceptability of nuclear energy toward questions of responsible real-world experimentation with nuclear energy. I have offered a moral framework for discussing the moral acceptability of real-world experiments with nuclear energy and for setting up such experiments more responsibly. I have also argued that if we conceive of the employment of nuclear energy as a real-world experiment, this moral framework is itself the subject of experimentation; that is to say: By employing the framework for discussions and for improving real-world experiments, we test the framework at the same time, and this moral experimentation may lead to new normative insights. This helps us to see that the moral debate about nuclear energy is not, or at least should not be, just a debate between conflicting moral views and systems but also a debate in which we can come to better normative insights.

Acknowledgment

This chapter is part of the research program "New Technologies as Social Experiments: Conditions for Morally Responsible Experimentation," which is supported by the Netherlands Organisation for Scientific Research (NWO) (project code 277 - 20 - 003).

11 Global nuclear energy and international security

Thomas E. Doyle, II

11.1 Introduction

The catastrophic effects of the 2011 Fukushima Daiichi nuclear plant meltdown in Japan reignited grave concerns about the short- and long-term risks of nuclear energy generation on diverse human and natural environments. Most of the authors in this volume are concerned about the ethical implications of such sustained nuclear energy programs. I share their concerns, and, as a political scientist and theorist, I would also like to emphasize that, from the early days of the atomic age, it was understood that the spread of nuclear energy capabilities could lead to the spread of nuclear weapons programs. Nuclear weapons offer insecure states the promise of an ultimate deterrent against (nuclear) aggression, although they also induce deep insecurities about nuclear accident or warfare. Some scholars believe that states with nuclear energy programs are more likely to pursue nuclear weapons (Fuhrmann 2009), while others maintain that nuclear energy programs are often the result of nuclear weapons aspiration (Bluth et al. 2010). Either way, the debates on nuclear ethics must pay attention to nuclear weapons proliferation as much as to nuclear energy development. The specific questions that motivate this chapter are:

1. To what extent is the pressure exerted by the United States and Europe on Iran and North Korea to abandon their uranium enrichment or plutonium programs morally legitimate?
2. What is the relationship between justice, global nuclear energy, and international security?
3. What are the implications in terms of justice and security for any state's continued pursuit of nuclear energy after Fukushima Daiichi, especially those that run afoul of institutional demands within the nuclear nonproliferation regime?

This chapter begins by briefly discussing various conceptions of international security and their relation to conceptions of international ethics or morality. It then summarizes the history of the Nuclear Non-Proliferation Treaty (NPT) regime in light of the three motivating questions above. This section is especially important for readers unfamiliar with the rationale or elements of the NPT. Thereafter, the chapter addresses the three motivating questions in turn.

11.2 Conceiving international security

The Latin *securus* is the root of the English "security," which in mainstream international security studies (ISS) refers to the freedom of any state from the harms of military aggression (Morgan 2006: 6–13). Whereas many of the authors of this volume have the security of individuals or communities in the back of their minds, for mainstream ISS state security is *ceteris paribus* a necessary condition of individual and community security.[1] With respect to this volume's themes, therefore, the ultimate concern of mainstream ISS has been with the potential for nuclear weapons proliferation as more states seek nuclear energy capabilities.

Mainstream ISS distinguishes between three kinds of international order of import for states as security seekers. Under the starkest mode of Hobbesian anarchy, every state is compelled to provide for its own survival and safety (Wendt 1999; Booth and Wheeler 2008: 21–61). In this condition, no state can trust any other state to refrain from aggression in the pursuit of their vital interests, or even reciprocate acts of good will. Such deficits of trust and reciprocity anchor the "Realist" claim that ethics or morality is irrelevant in international politics (Beitz 1999: 15–49). And since the term *international security* must be restricted to the tenuous freedom from warfare produced by military defense and deterrence capabilities, the risks or harms of nuclear energy programs ought not to be classified as matters of international security. Thus, Hobbesian-influenced scholars or policymakers are not likely to rank the risks of nuclear energy programs as an existential priority, unless the programs' environmental or economic damages had significant impact on a state's defense or deterrence capabilities.

A second kind of international order is called, following Alexander Wendt's classification, Lockean anarchy (Wendt 1999: 279–97). This order is anarchic insofar as sovereign states are not supplanted by a world government. However, the Hobbesian deficits of trust and reciprocity are mitigated under Lockean anarchy by the processes of recognition and cultivation of common interests among states. Such processes include the building of international institutions, which results in an increase in confidence and security among

---

[1] State security is not, however, a sufficient condition of individual or community security. A secure state is quite capable of inflicting harm on one or more of its citizens, in which case state security causes individual or communal insecurity (e.g. Nazi Germany prior to WWII). The debate over the proper referents of security is summarized in Buzan and Hansen (2009: ch. 2).

states and a corresponding disincentive to engage in warfare. The intended result is to transform Hobbesian enemies into Lockean cohabiters which abide by a "live and let live" motto. Moreover, this Lockean mode introduces the possibility that morality can be relevant for state interactions insofar as some conception of natural law can be codified in international positive law (Beitz 1999: 63–91).

In this Lockean mode, international security is produced by the joint efforts of states to mitigate or resolve conflicts within a collective security "regime" (Booth and Wheeler 2008: 104–37). Collective security regimes are composed of states that attempt to abide by the maxim "one-for-all-and-all-for-one." The United Nations was established as a collective security regime, although in practice it has not succeeded in genuine collective security and has relied on the great powers to function as a "sheriff's posse" (Weiss et al. 2010: 17). As such, we find that the application of "international security" is broader, and it is more likely that concerns over nuclear energy's environmental and economic impacts will attract the attention of security experts and policymakers (Buzan and Hansen 2009: 183, 232). This is due to the recognition that environmental and economic harm can lead to military confrontation and that some peaceful nuclear energy programs can be weaponized.[2] Indeed, one reason to think the contemporary world is organized around Lockean and not Hobbesian anarchy is the existence of collective security regimes, the NPT regime being the largest one to date (Booth and Wheeler 2008: 123–31). It is not accidental that the NPT, as I will show in more detail below, addresses both the issues of nuclear weaponization and appropriate procedures in the pursuit of nuclear energy.

The third kind of international order has been called Kantian anarchy (Wendt 1999: 297–308). Like the previously mentioned orders, a Kantian order comprises sovereign states without a world government, but it cultivates trust and reciprocity beyond the wariness of Lockean self-interested cooperation. Among what I call "Kantian state partners," the dominant practices of peaceful conflict resolution enhance the confidence that war is not a thinkable foreign policy option. And, as the name of Kant signals, the role of morality becomes indispensable in such international orders. Thus, on questions of nuclear policy, Kantian state partners are likely to take seriously the human and environmental aspects of civil nuclear energy programs. If trust among states dissolves concerns over aggression, the only "international security" concerns that will arise among Kantian state partners will be matters like the environmental, economic, or health risks of nuclear energy. Accordingly, the debates would shift to embrace notions like "environmental security" or "human security"

---

[2] Some "gold standard" nuclear energy programs are proliferation resistant insofar as they lack the technology that could be weaponized, such as uranium enrichment or plutonium processing technologies. Many thanks to Behnam Taebi for pointing this out to me.

(Buzan and Hansen 2009: 128–29, 187–88, 202–05), largely under the rubric of "global distributive justice." (Beitz 1999: 143–53; Jones 2000).

The foregoing theoretical survey has presented us with three distinct models of international order. Today's world appears to include features of all three models. This is to say, some international dynamics reflect Hobbesian enmity (e.g. the USA – North Korea; Israel – Iran; India – Pakistan), while others reflect Lockean cooperation (e.g. the United Nations, the North Atlantic Treaty Organization, the NPT) and yet others reflect a Kantian peace (e.g. the European Union).[3] A world of mixed international orders suggests that state A (assuming state A is a liberal democracy) might be simultaneously a Hobbesian enemy toward state B, a Lockean cohabiter with state C, and a Kantian state partner with state D. Accordingly, it is not surprising to find liberal democracies constructing smaller collective security arrangements (e.g. NATO) to defend against or deter aggression from illiberal states, the latter of whom are Hobbesian enemies and who might also be members of the UN or NPT. It is expected that liberal security collectives are especially intent on preventing the spread of nuclear weapons to illiberal states, and so the justification of collective controls on all aspects of the nuclear energy trade and nuclear weapons non-proliferation policy generally will likely include an ethical dimension beyond the traditional strategic dimension.

The rest of the chapter will proceed on the premise that the actual international order is a mixture of Hobbesian, Lockean, and Kantian modes. Section 11.3 introduces the Nuclear Non-Proliferation Treaty, and it will largely describe interactions among states whose macro-structures are Lockean and yet whose dynamics are tied to Kantian state-parties worried about Hobbesian "rogue" states.

11.3 A brief history of the NPT

The 1968 Nuclear Non-Proliferation Treaty (NPT) constitutes the largest international security regime in today's world (Booth and Wheeler 2008: 124). Originally comprising 55 states, the NPT now includes every state in the world except India, Israel, North Korea, and Pakistan.[4] Moreover, the NPT is the only international security regime in which membership is two-tiered: Five states retain the legal right to maintain nuclear arsenals (i.e. the *de jure*

---

[3] I acknowledge the degree to which this characterization is sketchy. However, I believe it gestures in the right direction. For readers interested in a more comprehensive account of these three international orders, and the corresponding dynamics and agencies which inhabit them, refer to Booth and Wheeler (2008). Following their account, I have classified institutions such as the UN and NATO within the Lockean framework, and the EU within a nascent Kantian framework.
[4] Moreover, these four non-NPT states are also nuclear-weapon states.

nuclear weapon states[5]), and all other states are proscribed from acquiring or developing them. The NPT's two-tiered nature is the product of two grand bargains, the outcomes of which involve considerable political, legal, and moral concerns for member states.

One grand bargain involves the *de jure* nuclear weapon states' (or *de jure* NWS) commitment to nuclear disarmament in exchange for the non-nuclear weapon states' (or NNWS) commitment to forgo nuclear weapons. Articles I, II, and VI of the treaty codifies this bargain. Article I proscribes the transfer of nuclear weapons programs to the NNWS, Article II proscribes their acquisition by the same, and Article VI commits the *de jure* NWS to their eventual abolition. With this first grand bargain, the majority of the state-parties developed an expectation that the *de jure* NWS's arsenals were not meant to endure indefinitely. Rather, this majority would temporarily tolerate the maintenance of these weapons as good faith negotiations among the *de jure* NWS progressed toward, first of all, an end to the nuclear arms race and, eventually, the abolition of their arsenals.

The second grand bargain concerned the peaceful expansion of nuclear energy programs. Immediately after World War II, the United States and its closest allies believed that the economic promise of nuclear energy could not be bypassed. Nonetheless, they feared the potential of nuclear weapons proliferation unless nuclear energy research, development, and management could be placed under United Nations' supervision. The United States proposed to the UN this very idea in the 1946 Baruch Plan (Smoke 1993: 127–30). For better or worse, Soviet opposition guaranteed the Baruch Plan's failure and the freedom of every capable state to pursue their own nuclear energy and weapons program. By 1949, the USSR had tested a nuclear weapon. Great Britain followed in 1952, France in 1960, and China in 1964 (Smoke 1993: chs. 4–7). Such a rapid series of nuclear tests induced a grave fear of rampant nuclear proliferation. The Chinese nuclear test triggered a particular urgency (especially in the United States and the USSR) to contain further nuclear spread. The NPT was signed four years later, and Article IV codified the terms of the second grand bargain: All state-parties retain an inalienable right to peaceful nuclear energy programs only if they permit international inspections by the International Atomic Energy Agency (IAEA). If evidence of weaponization in a given state's nuclear energy complex emerged, the IAEA would report to the United Nations Security Council which had authority to impose economic or other political sanctions.

By design, the NPT needed to be renewed every five years as of the ratification year of 1970. This mandate gave each state-party the opportunity of holding all others accountable to the terms of both grand bargains on pain of treaty dissolution. In short, the NPT renewal process tested intermittently the

---

[5] The *de jure* nuclear-weapon states are the United States, the Russian Federation, the United Kingdom, the French Republic, and the People's Republic of China.

degree to which a Lockean cooperation or confidence had emerged among member states. During the Cold War, for instance, the NNWS's expectations on Article VI issues were confined to successful arms control treaties, given that total nuclear disarmament seemed quite unlikely. With the signing and ratification of the Strategic Arms Limitation Talks (SALT) treaties, and the discussion over a comprehensive test ban treaty, some minimum level of confidence was sufficiently sustained that encouraged more NNWS to join the NPT. Their hope of nuclear abolition resurfaced with the end of the Cold War, and it was in this climate that state-parties looked forward to the twenty-fifth anniversary of the NPT's ratification in 1995 (Bunn 2006).

In the preparations for the 1995 NPT Review Conference, the United States was reticent to surrender nuclear deterrence "prematurely," even though the prospect of superpower nuclear conflict no longer haunted the world. The United States and its allies remained concerned about the prospect of new nuclear proliferation to "rogue" states such as Iraq, North Korea, Syria, and Iran, and they believed their collective security depended upon the maintenance of nuclear deterrence. This posture reflected a basic mistrust by the United States and its allies for the so-called "rogue" states. Other NNWS in the NPT regime still maintained the belief that compliance with all NPT articles was mandatory. So, when the United States pressed other state-parties to renew the NPT indefinitely, the NNWS's longstanding worries over the *de jure* NWS's Article VI compliance once again took center stage (Wittner 2009: 205–06). Many NNWS worried about a perpetual nuclear apartheid and a corresponding abandonment of nuclear abolition (MacFhionnbhairr 2004). In response to these worries and to secure the NPT's indefinite renewal, the *de jure* NWS reaffirmed the first grand bargain. After the NPT was renewed indefinitely, the following NPT Review Conferences were marked by disappointment and declining trust of the *de jure* NWS insofar as the latter remain committed to an indefinite possession of their arsenals.

Overall, the NPT's 45-year record of success is mixed (Dunn 2009). To its credit, the NPT has limited the number of *de jure* NWS to five. It has contributed to the emergence of the nuclear taboo: the international norm that proscribes the first-use of nuclear weapons in warfare (Tannenwald 2007). Ultimately, the NPT's main success is that nuclear war has been avoided since 1945. It has also encouraged the creation of parallel non-proliferation organizations, such as the 46-member Nuclear Suppliers Group which coordinates nuclear trade with non-nuclear countries.[6] To its discredit, it has failed so far to facilitate the nuclear abolition that many NNWS expected. It has failed to attract India, Pakistan, and Israel into the regime, and each of these countries is a *de facto* nuclear weapon state. It also failed to retain North Korea, which

---

[6] www.armscontrol.org/factsheets/NSG.

conducted nuclear tests in 2006, 2009, and early 2013 and in late 2012 successfully tested a long-range ballistic missile. If Iran successfully tests a nuclear device in the next few months or years, some experts are likely to conclude that the NPT has been undermined (Bunn 2006: 92–113). It is not therefore surprising that much international political and policy effort has concentrated on preventing Iran from advancing their uranium enrichment program.

In short, the history of the NPT reflects the management of insecurities through mitigation strategies commensurate with a Lockean mode of interaction. As such, it is possible to undertake an ethical analysis of the non-proliferation pressures exerted by some NPT member states on others, and then draw inferences on the relationship between justice and international security.

11.4 The morality of nuclear non-proliferation

The issue of the moral legitimacy of preventing nuclear proliferation does not arise in Hobbesian settings, where efforts to gain security are strictly matters of necessity and prudence. However, in a Lockean anarchy the morality of non-proliferation rests on two planks. One is international legal ethics, which holds that every state bears a presumptive and voluntaristic moral obligation to honor its treaty commitments. The other is collective security, in which each member of a security collective is obliged to defend all other members alike from external threats. Let us examine these two planks in some detail.

11.4.1 Plank 1: International legal ethics

The moral legitimacy of non-proliferation is based on the treaty commitments that states voluntarily assumed upon joining the NPT. The customary international legal norm of *pacta sunt servanda* (hereinafter, "*pacta*") indicates that states should honor their treaty commitments (Bederman 2006: 15). In terms of legal reasoning, it is important to note that *pacta* is not a part of positive international law. For, as a positive legal principle it could not validly prescribe that states honor their positive international legal obligations without succumbing to the circular fallacy or inviting an infinite regress of reasons. *Pacta* thus counts as a justificatory ground on which international legal obligation rests, and its informality suggests the moral content of this norm.

One might wonder, however, if *pacta* is anything more than a promise to honor treaty commitments and, if so, how such promises can generate inescapable obligations on their own merit. Would not *pacta* itself need to be grounded on a moral principle, such as the natural law obligation to do well to all others within one's reach or on the Kantian categorical imperative? Would not political custom or convention alone be insufficient to ground legal obligation of states? Such questions resurrect the numerous debates about philosophical foundations and their self-referential in/coherence, which is not something this chapter can adequately settle.[7] Accordingly, it is stipulated only that *pacta* is a part of international legal morality and it is a necessary justificatory anchor to fix state-parties' treaty obligations.

On the foregoing, states' duties to observe the NPT Article I and II prohibitions on nuclear weapons transfers to NNWS and Article IV limitations on nuclear energy development are grounded in the moral content of *pacta*. It follows that the enforcement of these articles in situations of noncompliance is also morally and legally legitimate. Thus, the NPT member states have presumptive moral legitimacy in pressuring noncompliant states like Iran to make their nuclear programs more transparent to IAEA inspectors or face stiff penalties.

The moral legitimacy of non-proliferation policies might, however, be suspended or overturned if another customary international legal norm is validly applied – i.e. *rebus sic stantibus* (Bederman 2006: 39) *Rebus* permits a state's withdrawal from treaty obligations if conditions have fundamentally changed such that the treaty's continued enforcement threatens a state-party's vital interests. The fundamental change in treaty conditions might be purely accidental or the result of a purposeful departure from the treaty regime by one or more parties. *Rebus* thus invites consideration of the various kinds of noncompliance in the (de)stabilizing of treaty conditions. For the *de jure* NWS, Iranian noncompliance might unwind the treaty if it unleashes a proliferation cascade in the Middle East or beyond, making non-proliferation policy thereafter ineffective or irrelevant (Reiss 2004). For states like Iran, the *de jure* NWS's avoidance of Article VI obligations might count as a fundamental change in treaty conditions given the NPT grand bargains related above. And even if Iranian charges of Article VI noncompliance prove unwarranted, it could nonetheless provide its officials with justificatory cover for withdrawal from the NPT on Article X grounds (Bunn 2006: 114).

Two inferences are important to draw at this point. One is that *rebus* can be understood as a moral side constraint on *pacta*. This is to say, international legal ethics (or, what Charles Beitz calls "the morality of states") privileges state survival and vital security interests over treaty obligations (Beitz 1999: 63–66, 83–91). The morality of states is incapable of granting to some members of a security collective a greater moral regard than any other set of state-parties. This is due to the formal sovereign equality of all members (UN Charter, Chapter 1, Article 2, Section 1). For these reasons, non-proliferation pressures

---

[7] See e.g. Monteiro and Ruby (2009) and Chernoff (2009).

can become morally illegitimate if they cause or constitute an existential threat against the targeted state-party.

A second and corollary inference is that *pacta* is not subject to further side constraints. On the morality of states, state-parties must accept that their obligations to treaty members outside any smaller security community to which they belong are as fundamental as to those within the security collective. As indicated already, such states have a *prima facie* moral right to pressure states to honor non-proliferation agreements, but they must do so without threatening the existential interests of the targeted state. Alternately, so-called "rogue" states remain obliged under *pacta* to their NPT obligations, and cannot validly use *rebus* as rhetorical cover for undertaking nuclearization if their existence is not genuinely or objectively threatened.

A second and corollary inference is that *pacta* is not subject to further side constraints for international legal ethics. Thus, NPT NNWS which do not face an imminent existential threat are ethically and legally bound to forgo nuclear weapons proliferation on pain of sanctions short of war. Moreover, any appeal to *rebus* must be examined carefully and rejected if specious. Finally, any and every NPT state-party thus bears a *prima facie* moral right to pressure nuclear aspirant states to honor their non-proliferation agreements. It is this right that suggests the second plank of the ethics of collective security.

11.4.2 *Plank 2: the ethics of collective security*

Collective security theory maintains that the security of each state-party is dependent upon the security of all others. (Weiss et al. 2010: 4–5) Collective security thus amounts to reconceiving and restructuring security such that each state is secure "with" their fellow state partners instead of maintaining security "against" them.[8] As David Hendrickson puts it, an "essential feature of a collective security system is the conviction that peace is indivisible" (1999: 224) If the number of states in a security collective is relatively small – i.e. if a few states form a security community – the ethical maxim of one-for-all-and-all-for-one is more likely to endure since the requisite conditions of consensus, commitment, and organization are easier to sustain (Weiss et al. 2010: 7). However, this indivisibility of peace is more likely to erode or dissolve if the security collective comprises many states (Weiss et al. 2010: 5–6). In large security collectives, states are more likely to defect from treaty commitments if national interest exerts a strong pull. Treaty defection dissolves the indivisibility of peace, and insofar as such acts are "illegal" they count as "a crime against not only the immediate victim but also the entire foundation of

---

[8] I borrow the terms "security against" and "security with" from Booth and Wheeler (2008).

international society," which presumably calls for a collective security response (Hendrickson 1999: 224).

A fundamental ethical paradox is produced in this latter case: namely, that the treaty infractions of some states are met with economic or military sanctions by other states in the name of the indivisibility of peace. However, such responses are no longer "collective" in the term's strict sense, and in many instances the handful of states responding in the name of collective security are better understood as members of a "sheriff's posse" which are more intent on guarding narrow national interests instead of the collective interest (Weiss et al. 2010: 17). A foremost case of this has been the US-led sanctions against Iran. The "security with" conception correlated to the one-for-all-and-all-for-one maxim is voided, and a preponderance of power is amassed against the so-called "rogue" state-party. This enforcement effort thus opens up the possibility that the security collective cannot be repaired. Nonetheless, in the case of Iranian NPT noncompliance, the preponderantly powerful NPT state-parties (e.g. the USA, UK, France, etc.) are not interested in formally expelling Iran from the regime. Paradoxically, the ethical justification of treaty enforcement is anchored on the indivisibility of peace while at the same time they regard Iran as a *de facto* Hobbesian adversary against whom they must seek security. This makes it to where Iran is justified and simultaneously unjustified in invoking *rebus* as a side constraint on their legal non-proliferation commitments.

11.5 Justice, international security, and global nuclear energy

What does the foregoing suggest about the relationship between justice, international security, and global nuclear energy? First, on the basis of *pacta*, "justice" with respect to international security arrangements is satisfied when state-parties honor their treaty obligations. More precisely, if each NPT state-party honors its Article I–IV commitments, the issues of corrective, compensatory, or punitive justice in relation to global nuclear energy and nuclear proliferation would never arise. Such issues arise only in relation to treaty noncompliance by one or more NPT state-parties.

Second, Section 11.4 points toward the social contractarian literature and John Rawls's work in particular, given the modern fact of interstate relations under international law and Rawls's prominent place in this literature. In his earlier work, Rawls concentrated on explicating a concept of political liberalism in which "justice as fairness" is a central defining element. In some of his later work, Rawls turned to apply this conception to international society (Rawls 1999). He imagines representatives of the world's peoples meeting in a second "original position" and constructing principles from which global relations might proceed. He distinguishes between peoples and states on the grounds that the concept of peoples is more coherent when analyzing social collectivities and their moral properties and given that state formation often has been indifferent to the social boundaries between peoples (Rawls 1999: 23–30). He thus argues that representatives in this second original position would choose a set of eight "Principles of the Law of Peoples" (Rawls 1999: 37). These principles are:

1. Peoples are free and independent, and their freedom and independence are to be respected by other peoples.
2. Peoples are to observe treaties and undertakings.
3. Peoples are equal and are parties to the agreements that bind them.
4. Peoples are to observe a duty of non-intervention.
5. Peoples have a right of self-defense but no right to instigate war for reasons other than self-defense.
6. Peoples are to honor human rights.
7. Peoples are to observe certain specified restrictions in the conduct of war.
8. Peoples have a duty to assist other peoples that live in unfavorable conditions that prevent them from having a just or decent political or social regime.

Rawls does not claim that this list is complete, and he stresses that each of the rights claims is subject to qualification. It is important to dwell on two of his qualifications, neither of which directly addresses the issue of global nuclear energy; however, both seem anchored on one or more moral intuitions that define the content of "justice" as it relates generally to international security. By identifying these intuitions, we can determine their appropriate application to the matters of global nuclear energy and nuclear weapons proliferation.

One qualification is that any people's right to freedom and independence cannot come at the expense of another people's subjugation (Rawls 1999: 38). This qualification implicitly evokes J.S. Mill's Harm Principle: "the sole end for which mankind are warranted, individually or collectively, in interfering with the liberty of action of any of their number, is self-protection." (Mill 1999: 51) This is to say, the liberty and independence of any people within a scheme of cooperation among peoples is rightful only if it does not negate the freedom and independence of other peoples. Notwithstanding Rawls's insistence on maintaining the analysis on peoples and not states, the same line of reasoning on this qualification presumably applies to states as well. Thus, any state may freely pursue their interests unless other states are threatened with or suffer harms against which they deserve protection. It follows on this first qualification that the security of individual states is a necessary condition of justice among states.

As applied, it can be claimed that any state's pursuit of global nuclear energy under the NPT is permissible if it does not harm or pose a serious and immediate threat of harm to another state. The NPT itself counts as evidence that nuclear weapons proliferation is considered a global security threat. If the proliferation pessimists are right and nuclear weapons programs will tend to follow nuclear energy programs (Fuhrmann 2009), it would follow that advocates of nuclear energy programs will carry a greater burden of proof to demonstrate that their efforts do not constitute an existential threat to members of the NPT regime.

Another qualification is that any people's right of independence or non-interference is conditional upon its respect for human rights (Rawls 1999: 38). Again, the Harm Principle is the operative moral intuition. It should be noted here again that Rawls's reference to "peoples" seems to apply to states as well, since the problem of human rights abuses by states was a primary international concern after the end of the Cold War. Rawls's line of thought is consistent with the emerging norm of "responsibility to protect" (R2P) among UN member states, which anchored the policy of humanitarian intervention (Weiss et al. 2010: 81–84). In particular, this emerging norm dictates that any state's right to non-intervention is suspended or revoked if it perpetrates human rights abuses that rise to the level of ethnic cleansing or genocide (e.g. Rwanda or Darfur). It follows that the security of individuals against their government, as well as state security against external enemies, is a necessary condition of justice among states or peoples.

On this second Rawlsian qualification, we can infer that any state's pursuit of nuclear energy is permissible in part if it does not constitute an abuse of human rights. With respect to nuclear weapons proliferation, the qualification's application seems more contestable. It was noted that some states believe that nuclear weapons are effective instruments of deterrence. Rawls himself defends nuclear deterrence against rogue states as important for preserving liberal democracy (Rawls 1999: 8–9). In contrast, I have argued elsewhere that nuclear deterrence is unjust if it infuses despotic governance practices into democratic institutions, which in turn pose a direct threat to citizens' civil and human rights (Doyle 2010, 2013). Moreover, nuclear deterrence is unjust on deontological grounds if it cannot avoid holding hostage peoples of other countries (Lee 1985). If these last two claims are valid, they mark a possible point of incoherence in the Rawlsian view, one to which I will return shortly.

The Rawlsian view examined so far suggests a mutually constitutive relation between justice as fairness *and* security among states over the pursuit of nuclear energy or nuclear weapons. On the one hand, a state victimized by aggression is altogether insecure, and in international legal terms aggression counts as a supreme injustice (Walzer 2000: ch. 2). States construct security regimes to prevent such aggression, and to mitigate or alleviate the insecurities that accompany a world politics driven by narrow national interest. Their agreements specify an understanding on what constitutes just and fair interactions under a specification of members' concrete rights and duties. Noncompliance necessitates the exercise of self-protective measures by one or more state-parties, and possibly even external interventions, in order to secure rights and restore a semblance of fairness in interaction. On the other hand, the injustice of treaty noncompliance constitutes a form of insecurity precisely because benefits, burdens, dangers, and harms are redistributed unfairly among peoples or states within a security regime. Restoring justice as fairness will often require corrective measures and subsequently measures to maintain the correction until it is solidified. Once solidified, it can be asserted that justice as fairness is a necessary condition of security.

This account of the mutual constitution of security and justice as fairness explains the complex and contradictory condition of the moral legitimacy of non-proliferation pressures under *pacta sunt servanda* and the moral legitimacy of the seemingly contradictory resistance to non-proliferation pressures under *rebus sic stantibus*. On the one hand, it explains how Iranian noncompliance over their Article II and IV obligations constitutes a *prima facie* injustice *qua* insecurity that must be corrected. On the other hand, it explains how Iran's noncompliance might be taken as their effort to address a perceived change in the fundamental conditions of the NPT regime. As of now, Iran has yet to officially invoke *rebus* by announcing its intention to withdraw from the NPT or to confirm beyond a shadow of a doubt to the IAEA that its uranium enrichment program is altogether restricted to nuclear energy production. In this sense, Iran's posture is ambiguous, and it thereby continues to sustain the insecurities of states like Israel, Saudi Arabia, and the United States.[9]

Turning now to the objection mentioned above that Rawls's view suffers from incoherence, we recall that he affirms that states are to honor human rights but also that liberal democracies ought to retain nuclear weapons to deter rogue states. It seems to me that liberal nuclear deterrence falls short of satisfying the duty to honor human rights because the liberal nuclear state cannot avoid sweeping innocent civilians into the set of anticipated nuclear targets within the so-called rogue state. If deterrence failed, any subsequent nuclear reprisal strikes against these targets would clearly violate *jus in bello* constraints (Rawls 1999: 94–97). And one might also argue that if it is wrong to conduct nuclear reprisal strikes, it is also wrong to intend to do so (Walzer 2000: 269–73). In short, a liberal democracy cannot both observe human rights and employ nuclear deterrence policies. From the viewpoint of *rebus*, it makes sense to think that a state so targeted – e.g. Iran – is morally justified in doing what is necessary to offset this existential threat, even if it means resisting non-proliferation pressures which are ordinarily justified by international legal ethics and even if that resistance is simultaneously unjustified by the norms of liberal democratic collective security.

---

[9] For a more comprehensive view on the motives and strategies of nuclear ambiguity, see Levite (2002/03).

One response to this objection is that Rawls's view expresses an unavoidable inconsistency related to international norm evolution, as when a new international human rights norm is emerging but has not yet won a sufficient degree of respect among the world's states.[10] Accordingly, we might acknowledge the difficulties Rawls faces in applying particular ideal notions of justice as fairness to non-ideal contexts insofar as any such applications will not be perfect (Rawls 1999: 89–120). Such contexts of norm evolution can correspond to the dynamics of mixed Hobbesian–Lockean–Kantian international orders. If, then, the duty to observe human rights sits alongside the right of states to enjoy non-interference in a Law of Peoples, the risk which nuclear deterrence poses to human rights must be balanced against the actuality of human rights violations by outlaw state regimes against their own people and against liberal peoples at the point (nuclear) aggression occurs. As Walzer argues:

Deterrence is a way of coping . . ., and though it is a bad way, there may well be no other that is practical in a world of sovereign and suspicious states. We threaten evil in order not to do it, and the doing of it would be so terrible that the threat seems in comparison to be morally defensible. (Walzer 2000: 274)

Of course, global nuclear energy and nuclear weapons proliferation are not implicated in the kinds of human rights violations as are genocide and ethnic cleansing. Given the risks of exposure to harmful ionizing radiation arising from nuclear plant meltdowns or an attack on a nuclear facility, though, the Rawlsian concern for human rights might justify an international legal mandate against further nuclear energy production. However, Rawls does not address the issues of nuclear energy. Instead, he is concerned that a rogue NWS might use nuclear weapons against liberal or decent peoples (Rawls 1999: 9). Unfortunately, Rawls doesn't consider that "rogue" states might merely want to deter nuclear-armed liberal democracies. Indeed, it is a mistake to claim *a priori* that any new NWS would necessarily have an offensive nuclear orientation as opposed to a preference for a stable balance of nuclear energy or threat. So, while nuclear aggression would most certainly count as a crime against humanity, it is far from clear that nuclear deterrence by "rogue" states against liberal democracies counts as a crime against humanity given Rawls's favorable position on nuclear deterrence for liberal democracies.

11.6 Implications for nuclear aspirant states

The Rawlsian view developed above suggests that the state pursuit of nuclear energy after Fukushima Daiichi is just (or not unjust) if it is consistent with the

---

[10] For the literature on the evolution of international norms, see Finnemore and Sikkink (1998) for the seminal account.

Principles of the Law of Peoples, the NPT non-proliferation of nuclear weapons requirement, and if harmful impacts on the environment and human society are avoided. In contrast, the Law of Peoples' requirement on peoples/states to honor treaty commitments entails that nuclear weapons proliferation is unjust given the NPT Article I and II requirements. For the same reasons, the pursuit of nuclear energy that promotes nuclear weapons proliferation is *prima facie* morally illegitimate even if it successfully avoids causing environmental, economic, or sociopolitical harms on citizens or entire peoples. The Rawlsian view does not appear to admit of exceptions where a valid *rebus* claim could be exercised, especially if it is by a so-called outlaw or rogue state.

Arguments against the Rawlsian view might point to instances of morally and legally justifiable suspensions of nuclear aspirant states' NPT treaty commitments. Such arguments might begin with the claim that, in a world ordered by Lockean anarchy, security cooperation is important but compliance with international legal commitments is not absolute. On this view, the security of each state within a security collective is a necessary condition of international justice, and likewise the justice of the cooperative arrangements is a necessary condition of each member's security. One implication of this view for nuclear aspirant states is the reaffirmation of the argument that NPT obligations on peaceful nuclear energy development and nuclear weapons avoidance are binding on legal and moral grounds (i.e. the *pacta* norm) unless some material or political element of the relevant collective security arrangements alters the fundamental conditions of treaty relations such that the aspirant state's vital national interests are existentially threatened. In this latter condition, the exercise of the right of withdrawal from treaty obligations (i.e. the *rebus* norm) also rests on legal and moral grounds which are not easily dismissed.

It is expected that this anti-Rawlsian position on NPT commitments will not be politically palatable among states that have the most to gain by maintaining the status quo. The Rawlsian position appears committed to eventually conditioning *rebus* on *pacta* and institutionalizing the logic and ethics of collective security *qua* interstate policing. In the case where all the world's states become members of a Kantian pacific federation, the logic and ethics of collective security would not involve contradictions. The indivisibility of peace condition would actually obtain, and the exercise of the "sheriff's posse" in the name of collective security would be avoided. However, the anti-Rawlsian position would insist that, as long as the world order is composed of mixed anarchic dynamics, genuine collective security is likely to devolve into Hobbesian security competition among rival security communities. In this instance, nuclear aspirant states are likely to find collective *Realpolitik* in the form of a sheriff's posse hiding behind a mask of international law and collective security ethics. It is this context where the anti-Rawlsian view argues that the *rebus* principle justifies noncompliance with or eventual withdrawal from the discriminatory and existentially harmful applications of NPT treaty provisions.

In short, the ethics of nuclear energy generation is not (yet) altogether independent of the ethics of nuclear weapons proliferation and non-proliferation policy. The central political fear is that if Iran or other "rogue" states were to mask nuclear weapons proliferation behind nuclear energy programs, then non-nuclear-armed liberal democratic states like Japan and Germany, which belong to the same security community as the United States, might be allowed to weaponize their nuclear programs on collective security grounds. Such outcomes would most likely mark the NPT's end. This outcome, while not absolutely certain, is suggested by the current US preferential treatment of the liberal nuclear democracies of India and Israel over the illiberal nuclear state of Pakistan (Dunn 2009). From the Rawlsian viewpoint, this double standard is ethically justifiable. From the contrary viewpoint where liberal democracy is but one of many domestic political orders in a world of mixed anarchies, this double standard smacks of moral hypocrisy.

Acknowledgments

The author thanks Behnam Taebi and Sabine Roeser for the invitation to write this chapter. Thanks also to the participants in the March 2014 Nuclear Knowledge Summit at TU Delft, the Netherlands, for their insightful remarks on rough drafts of this chapter. Thanks also to Paul DeHart for his comments on an earlier draft of this chapter.

12 Nuclear energy, the capability approach, and the developing world

Paolo Gardoni and Colleen Murphy

12.1 Introduction

Sustainable development is fundamentally about improving the well-being of individuals in current and future generations by expanding their valuable choices and opportunities. This chapter evaluates nuclear energy as a potential engine of sustainable development from the perspective of its impact on the well-being of members of current and future generations of a society. The literature on nuclear energy implicitly assumes the context of a developed community. However, the moral and factual questions to consider when evaluating nuclear energy shift when the context becomes that of a developing community. We present in this chapter a theoretical framework for evaluating the promise and peril of nuclear energy for developing countries and for assessing different nuclear technologies that might be available now or in the future. The proposed framework has at its core a concern for individual capabilities. Capabilities refer to the genuine opportunities individuals are free to achieve, such as an opportunity to be educated or adequately nourished. In evaluating the role of nuclear energy in sustainable development, it is critical to consider the risks that nuclear energy poses; sustainable development promotes opportunities in a secure manner, and risks threaten that security. Our framework considers the costs, benefits, and risks associated with the use of nuclear energy to enhance development.

There are four sections in this chapter. Section 12.2 provides an overview on the general issues influencing the moral justifiability of nuclear energy. Section 12.3 then discusses why these issues take a different form in developing contexts. Section 12.4 outlines a capability approach to sustainable development. Finally, Section 12.5 illustrates how the justifiability of nuclear energy in a given developing society would be approached using that framework.

12.2 Background

There are a number of subjects of debate in relation to nuclear energy (United Nations Development Program 2007). Three main themes in the literature are sustainability, safety, and security (including weapon proliferation and malicious activity that could impose radiation exposure, such as sabotage and dirty bombs.) Below we summarize how these three subjects are discussed. We then argue in Section 12.3 that debates typically assume the context of a developed community. The question of sustainability, safety and weapon proliferation take a different form when the context becomes a developing country.

12.2.1 Sustainability

Since in the 1980s more attention has been paid to the concept of sustainability. The World Commission on Environment and Development (WCED 1987) made a special contribution to this increased awareness. Sustainability requires attention to inter- and intragenerational equity, adequate standards of living for all individuals, and concern for the environment (Mileti 1999: 232). In particular, increasing concern is placed on ensuring that ecosystems are able to renew themselves, replacing a general disregard toward ecosystems. Concerns toward the ecosystems stem both from a care for the ecosystems themselves and the belief that well-being can be more prosperous when natural ecosystems also are so.

One subject of ongoing dispute is whether nuclear energy is a sustainable alternative energy source (e.g. Hubbert 1956, 36; Newton-Small 2005; WNA 2010; Patterson 2013). Proponents of nuclear energy argue that nuclear energy is sustainable for the following reasons. Using nuclear energy rather than more conventional sources that rely on fossil fuels reduces carbon emissions. Moreover, nuclear energy is not itself a finite resource. Finally, the availability of nuclear energy is more reliable and less sporadic than other forms of alternative energy (like wind and solar). Opponents of nuclear energy challenge these claims, noting that when one considers the total life cycle emission intensity, greenhouse gas emissions per unit of electricity generated is comparable to other sources (Shrader-Frechette 2011a). Nor is nuclear energy cheap as an electricity source from this perspective (Diesendorf 2007a, 2007b; Kleiner 2008: 130–31).

12.2.2 Safety

A second important source of debate is the degree to which nuclear energy is a safe energy source. Here the central focus is on risks nuclear energy poses to individuals, communities, and the environment. One set of risks surrounds the storage of nuclear waste. Opponents argue that the risks associated with processing, transporting, and storing nuclear waste are significantly underestimated (Sturgis 2009). Radioactive waste is harmful to living organisms for an extremely long time period (Vandenbosch and Vandenbosch 2007), from 10,000 to literally millions of years. Extremely advanced techniques are needed to successfully isolate nuclear waste permanently and/or transform it into a non-toxic form. Production of nuclear energy also generates a conspicuous amount of waste with low level of radioactivity including cloth, tools, and general construction material used to build reactors. While the US Nuclear Regulatory Commission has pushed for such waste to be considered as normal waste, a debate remains about whether that would be appropriate.

Proponents of nuclear energy argue that the risks from such storage are sufficiently small to justify nuclear energy's use. They point to technological advances in nuclear reactors and the safety record of nuclear plants in the developed world to support this point (Cohen 1990). Nuclear waste, they argue, comprises less than 1 percent of total industrial toxic waste. Hvistendahl (2007) points out that other forms of energy produce radioactive waste. Specifically, burning coal produces toxic and low-radioactive ash. Similarly, Gabbard (1993) in a report from the Oak Ridge National Laboratory stated that coal plants release more radioactive material into the environment per unit energy generated than nuclear energy reactors in their regular operations. To clarify, fly ash is significantly less radioactive than spent nuclear fuel per unit weight. However, fly ash is released in large amounts into the environment while spent nuclear fuel is stored (during ideal operations) in, for example, dry cask storage vessels (Montgomery 2010: 137).

Consideration of the risks associated with the ideal operation of nuclear plants is not sufficient because this overlooks possible accidents. There have been a number of notorious nuclear accidents including the Three Mile Island accident (1979), the Chernobyl disaster (1986), and the more recent Fukushima Daiichi nuclear disaster (2011), in addition to some, less publicized submarine accidents (Johnston 2007). The most recent, Japan's 2011 Fukushima Daiichi nuclear accident, pushed some countries to reconsider their position toward nuclear energy. Germany, where nuclear energy accounted for 22.4 percent of the national electricity in 2010, announced plans to phase out nuclear energy by 2022. Similarly Switzerland (where nuclear energy accounts for 39.9 percent of the country's total production of electricity) decided not to build any more nuclear reactors and not to replace the five reactors at the end of their service life (with plans to decommission the last reactor in 2034.)

There are a number of debates surrounding how best to calculate the costs of such accidents and the seriousness of nuclear accidents relative to those stemming from other energy sources. Proponents of nuclear energy point to the fact that there are fewer fatalities per unit of energy generated than the other more popular sources of energy. Some proponents claim that coal, petroleum, natural gas, and hydropower produce a higher number of fatalities per unit of energy generated (Markandya and Wilkinson 2007; Burgherr and Hirschberg 2008; MacKay 2008), when deaths from air pollution and energy accidents are calculated. Nuclear energy accidents impose not just costs in terms of lives, but economic and social costs as well, in terms of damaged property, cleanup costs, human and economic costs associated with evacuating populations and lost livelihoods. On this point, US scientist Frank N. von Hippel noted following the 2011 Fukushima nuclear disaster that "fear of ionizing radiation could have long-term psychological effects on a large portion of the population in the contaminated areas" (von Hippel 2011). An accurate assessment of the costs of nuclear accidents relative to the accidents related to other energy sources must consider this broader set of consequences.

12.2.3 Security

Nuclear security refers to the "prevention and detection of, and response to, theft, *sabotage*, unauthorized access, illegal transfer or other *malicious* acts involving *nuclear material*, other *radioactive substances* or their associated facilities" (IAEA 2007: 133). Technologies, knowledge, and materials used in nuclear energy programs in many cases have a dual use capability. Enriched uranium on the one hand and separated plutonium during reprocessing on the other can be used to produce nuclear weapons (Taebi and Kloosterman 2008). Further risks include those posed by the possibility of nuclear weapons proliferation and terrorism.

Scholars engage in the above debates about nuclear energy by subjecting two kinds of claims to critical scrutiny. The first kind of claim is factual. For example, with respect to safety, scholars concentrate on issues that include determining what the actual benefits and risks from nuclear energy are and whether it is empirically accurate to characterize nuclear energy as a sustainable energy source. The second kind of claim is moral. Here conversation will focus, for example, on justifying a particular way of comparing or balancing different kinds of risks and benefits. To illustrate, critics do not believe that new technologies can sufficiently reduce the risks of nuclear energy to justify their imposition on a community.

Resolving these factual and moral disputes is a complex undertaking. In part this is because the factual and moral issues are difficult to resolve in isolation. Moreover, factual and moral questions are interconnected in many cases. For example, determining the factual issue of whether nuclear energy is sustainable depends on first determining how sustainability is best understood. This in turn will be informed by value judgments regarding what about our natural world is fundamentally worth preserving. Many of the chapters in this volume focus on these questions.

12.3 Contemporary debates in developing contexts

The literature on nuclear energy for the most part implicitly assumes the context of a developed community. However, the moral and factual questions to consider when debating nuclear energy shift when the context becomes that of a developing community. We discuss in this section how the considerations to take into account when evaluating nuclear energy vary when the focus becomes a developing community.

Consider first the issue of *sustainability*. Developing countries are often not the main users of scarce, non-renewable resources, significantly contributing to their depletion and in the process contributing significantly to the concentration of greenhouse gases, which accounts for part of the appeal of nuclear energy. The contribution of most developing countries, with the exception of China, to the depletion of non-renewable resources is minimal. Therefore developing countries are less responsible for threats to sustainability.

Nor is the issue how best to use scarce resources to guarantee to future generations the conditions for a standard of living that is at least as good and prosperous as the present is for us. The core challenge for many developing communities is expanding opportunities and the standard of living for present, as well as future, generations. The *de facto* present standard of living is not taken as a benchmark for what it is reasonable for all people, present as well as future, to accept. Rather, in many contexts the *de facto* standard of living is in need of dire improvement. Not simply maintaining, but rather striving to improve, the standard of living highlights two further complications when it comes to sustainability. Developing countries have many more competing demands on resources, demands which in many cases are for the basic conditions taken for granted as existing in developed contexts (e.g. access to safe drinking water). Not only are demands greater, the available pool of resources with which to try to meet basic demands is typically smaller.

Given the above, the issue of sustainability for developing countries is broader in scope and at its core asks: Is nuclear energy the most sensible path to take to achieve sustainable development? Answering this question requires a comprehensive picture of what development is fundamentally about, that is, what the goals of development and practices should be. We turn to this point in greater detail in the Section 12.4. It also requires appreciating the significantly greater competing demands which must be met with a more limited pool of resources relative to developed countries.

Similarly, *safety* considerations are different. For one thing, the statistics of the occurrence of accidents are not necessarily a relevant guide for what to expect in developing contexts. Developing nations are often less equipped to deal with accidents and lack the number of experts required to operate reactors. If you do not have the same context for ensuring safety, you cannot use rates from a different context as a guide for what to expect. Moreover, there is a question about the appropriateness of ensuring the same level of safety in a developing as in a developed context. Guaranteeing the same level of safety may effectively price nuclear energy out of the ability of developing countries. In other industries and contexts, different levels of safety are used. Finally, guarding against possible nuclear accidents in the future may seem less pressing relative to other present needs. Why should a developing country be concerned about long-term radiation when children die of hunger each day? Why should a developing country prioritize the storage of radioactive waste when its citizens do not have access to clean water?

In addition, there is a clear issue about who takes the risk and who would pay the associated consequences. While one developing country might be willing to use nuclear energy because the benefits clearly offset the risks for the specific country, this might not be the case of neighboring (or not too distant) countries. For example, if a developing country decides to generate nuclear energy, the possible effects of radiation, in particular in the case of an accident, would often be felt well beyond the boundaries of that country, possibly affecting countries who might have decided that nuclear energy is not worth the risks. Whether this counts as a permissible risk imposition is even more vivid in contexts where communities do not have the resources needed to respond satisfactorily to the consequences of a nuclear accident with the resources at their disposal.

Finally, *security* may become even more concerning when such proliferation occurs in countries with unstable and repressive forms of government. In this case, concerns about nuclear weapon proliferation seem to be more acute.

In light of the questions that nuclear energy raises for developing countries, a framework is needed that provides resources for assessing: (1) the relative contribution of nuclear energy to sustainable development; (2) the risks associated with nuclear energy in developing contexts; and (3) the appropriate way to balance the assessments from (1) and (2). We argue in the next two sections that these questions are best considered from a capability perspective. A capability approach evaluates policies and technologies based on how the opportunities of individuals will be impacted. Capability approaches to development and to risk already exist. Such approaches can be combined and used to evaluate nuclear energy in developing contexts, where development and risk are intimately connected. In Section 12.4 we outline the capability approaches to development and to risk. Finally, Section 12.5 looks at nuclear energy for developing countries from a capability perspective.

12.4 A capability approach to sustainable development and risks

A capability refers to a genuine opportunity to achieve a particular valuable doing or being, such as being educated or being adequately nourished (Sen 1999; Nussbaum 2001). A genuine opportunity to achieve a given doing or being is a function of *what an individual has* and *what she can do with what she has*. "What an individual has" is understood broadly, to include financial resources and other sources of wealth, as well as talents, skills, and a support network from family and friends. "What an individual can do with what she has" is conditioned by institutional and environmental factors of different kinds. Legal rules, political processes, and the engineered built environment all influence what we are able to achieve with a given set of resources.

To illustrate, consider mobility and the conditions that must be in place for an individual to have a genuine opportunity to be mobile. A personal resource like a car can contribute to mobility, but possession of a car is not sufficient for mobility. An individual must know how to drive a car. She must be legally permitted to drive, in virtue of satisfying conditions laid out in law (e.g. being of a certain minimum age, possessing car insurance, not having received a certain number of tickets in the previous years). In addition, an individual must usually have extra financial resources to pay for gas and repairs to a car when needed. Finally, the built infrastructure must be present, in terms of roads and bridges, to enable an individual who knows how to drive a car, has the financial wherewithal to support a car, and the legal permission to use a car to be effectively free to drive.

In a capability approach, the standard of living or quality of life of individuals is defined in terms of the genuine opportunities individuals have to do and become things of value. Measuring the standard of living of individuals requires making a set of choices. The first choice concerns which opportunities are sufficiently important and definitive of the standard of living to consider in an analysis. The second choice surrounds how those capabilities or opportunities will be measured. Capabilities are not themselves directly measurable. Indicators are needed that provide proxy information about the kind of opportunities individuals enjoy. For example, one indicator of the ability to live a long and healthy life is life expectancy at birth.

Complicating the question of measurement further is the issue of opportunity versus achievements. Capabilities capture the *opportunity* an individual has to do or become something of value. Underpinning many analyses of capabilities is a general commitment to liberalism, according to which the purpose of government and public policy is not to require or force individuals to live a certain kind of life, but rather to provide a framework within which individuals are free to pursue a life they have reason to value. One challenge in implementing the capability approach is determining which range of opportunities should be left open to individuals to pursue.

Another challenge for any implementation of the capability framework then becomes determining which indicators or use of indicators tell you the opportunities available to individuals, which can be broader than the doings and beings he or she in fact chooses to achieve. Opportunities do not track achievements because there can be opportunities an individual enjoys that he/she does not choose to take. An individual may have the talents and skills, grades, family support, and financial wherewithal to attend college, but lack the desire to do so. Moreover opportunities are interdependent. In the abstract and absent any choice, an individual may be genuinely free to be educated, have a demanding career, and become a parent. However, in practice certain choices may foreclose others and/or make choices available. Choosing to raise a family may limit certain especially demanding careers or the possibility of demanding careers for both parents (on this point, see Robeyns 2005). In contexts of poverty, a set amount of resources may be sufficient for buying enough food to satisfy nutritional needs or for paying rent, but not both.[1]

Tabandeh et al. (2014) developed a reliability-based capability approach (RCA) using a system reliability formulation. A system reliability formulation establishes the probability of not meeting a desirable level of well-being, not by considering the threshold for each single capability, but rather by considering a system of capabilities interacting simultaneously. The RCA has several benefits both conceptual and toward the implementation of a capability approach. It uses a system reliability method to compute the probability that the levels of achievement in a specified subset of capabilities are not adequate. The RCA also explicitly models the interactions between indicators when computing the probability of a change in the level of the indicators. Instead of considering an aggregate measure, it translates in a transparent way the performance in individual indicators into a system performance

12.4.1 Sustainable development from a capability approach

In a capability approach, development is defined as a process for enhancing the quality of life of individuals. The goal of development is more specifically to work toward ensuring a decent "standard of living" for individuals, which puts them in a position to pursue a life they have reason to value. Development policies aim not simply to provide individuals with a genuine opportunity to achieve a decent standard of living at a discrete moment, but rather in a durable, sustainable manner. Development is sustainable when emphasis is placed on maintaining a certain level of opportunities in a secure manner. When secure,

---

[1] For a detailed description on how to measure capabilities, see Murphy and Gardoni (2010) and Tabandeh et al. (2014).

achievements in doings and beings like being nourished or sheltered are not temporary or require the undue assumption of risks to other important doings and beings in order to be maintained.

Sustainable development from a capability perspective has three key features. (1) Emphasis is placed on *social equity* or *intragenerational justice* such that the key opportunities defining the standard of living are available to individuals in a given generation in the present and future in a secure manner (WCED 1987: 188). (2) *Intergenerational justice* is also important. The promotion of opportunities of the current generations should not compromise the possibilities of future generations to have a quality of life that is at least as good as the one of the current generations. (3) Sustainability requires attention to the *environmental impacts* of development's pursuit.

There are two important sources of uncertainties that make it hard to determine whether a development plan achieves intra- and intergenerational justice. The first source of uncertainty is in the impact that a development plan will actually have (which is not necessarily the same as the desired or foreseen impact). The second source of uncertainty is related to the actual conditions that are needed for maintaining the current level of well-being in the future. There is uncertainty in what future generations will need to fulfill their needs. In Robert Goodin's words, "Allowing for substitutability, future generations might be as well off as present ones in terms of all the functional tasks performed, albeit using a different array of material items to perform those functions" (Goodin 1999: 250).

Because we cannot assume that future generations will simply continue to need the same resources that are available now, it is difficult to determine which resources, and how much of such resources, must be left to future generations. Future generations will inevitably develop new engineering solutions and make new scientific discoveries that might create new opportunities, making conserving current resources unnecessary. If, for example, in the future a new non-fossil fuel based source of energy becomes the foundation for most economies, there would not be the same pressing need to be concerned about the relative scarcity of fossil fuel. In addition, future generations might discover that some technologies, materials, and general engineering solutions are worse than other alternatives. For example, at the time of the Roman Empire lead was ubiquitous. It was used as a component in a number of cosmetics including face powders and mascaras, as a pigment in paints, a spermicide, a condiment for food, a wine preservative, an easy to work with and inexpensive metal for kitchen utensils and tableware, as a key metal in coins, and a piping material for water supply. Lead was later found to be highly poisonous.

12.4.2 Risk from a capability approach

Whether and to what extent nuclear energy promotes sustainable development is only one factor to consider in its adoption. Nuclear energy poses risks, which must also be taken into account. In this section we describe a capability approach to risk analysis. We then use this framework to evaluate nuclear energy in developing contexts in Section 12.5.

Murphy and Gardoni (2006, 2007, 2008, 2010, 2011a, 2012), and Gardoni and Murphy (2008, 2009, 2010, 2013, 2014) proposed a Capability-based Risk Analysis (CRA) for risk determination, risk evaluation, and risk management for natural and artificial hazards, and disaster response and recovery. The CRA uses changes in capabilities to quantify the impact of hazards and past disasters. More specifically, in CRA the possible consequences of hazardous scenarios are defined in terms of capabilities. Risk analysis considers the change in capabilities that result from such a scenario. Risk is the probability that capabilities are reduced.

Which capabilities should be considered is hazard-dependent. That is, the relevant capabilities to consider depend on which doings and beings are characteristically affected by a given hazard. As with development policies, CRA uses indicators to track changes in capabilities. The prediction of the impact of a hazard on capabilities requires a method of prediction for this purpose. The CRA proposed by Tabandeh et al. (2014) is ideally suited for this. In the context of risk analysis specifically, the RCA translates the performance in individual indicators into a system performance so that the system performance can be evaluated for its acceptability or tolerability based on the definitions in Murphy and Gardoni (2007). Evaluation of the impact of a given disaster can be based on the same basic framework. The impact of a nuclear accident, for example, would be the function of the reduction of selected capabilities, as measured by changes in certain indicators of the requisite capabilities.

This way of analyzing the consequences of a given hazardous scenario is different from common methods in risk analysis. Often engineers and social scientists consider specific resource losses when determining the risk from a given hazard (Rowe 1980; Vose 2000; Bedford and Cooke 2001). Consequences analyzed include market resources lost (e.g. time through construction delays, money, structures). As the capability approach recognizes, such resource losses do not translate automatically or uniformly into impacts on individual lives. A lost structure may have little impact if abandoned or underutilized, or if it is one of many buildings a given individual owns. In such cases, the opportunities open to an individual who owns the building may not be constricted in any meaningful sense. Conversely, the loss of a home can be devastating for individuals who lack resources to rebuild what was lost or to relocate to another home. When many individuals or a community are vulnerable to a hazard, CRA assesses the overall impact as a function of a sum of the impacts on individual.

The evaluation of risks from a capability perspective involves asking two kinds of questions. One is evaluative in an absolute sense and queries: "are risks associated to, for example, nuclear energy the kind of risks individuals and/or communities should at all permit?" The second kind of evaluation is comparative, answering the question "are those risks preferable compared with the risks associated to alternative options, including the option of not doing anything?"

To address the first question, Murphy and Gardoni (2008) argue that risks should be compared against two basic thresholds. The starting point for risk evaluation from a capability approach is the idea that there is a certain threshold minimum level of capabilities that individuals should enjoy and should be in a position to continue to enjoy with a specified degree of confidence. The inclusion of a "threshold degree of confidence" reflects the fact that principles of justice should be understood probabilistically. It is impossible to guarantee with certainty that capabilities will be maintained by any given policy or action; for instance, we do not know with absolute certainty if efforts to mitigate risks will be successful should a particular hazardous scenario be realized. So any requirement concerning the protection of capabilities must demand that it is sufficiently likely that capabilities will be maintained at or above a required level. A necessary condition for a risk to be acceptable is that the probability that such risk threatens the ability of individuals to maintain a threshold level of capabilities is sufficiently small. Murphy and Gardoni (2008) recognize that it could be tolerable that the level of capabilities falls below the acceptable level under temporary and reversible conditions. To deal with such situations they introduce the concept of tolerable risk. The tolerable threshold is lower than the acceptable threshold and specifies the absolute minimum below which nobody should go irrespective of whether the situation is temporary and reversible. A risk is tolerable, though not acceptable, when the probability that capabilities will fall below the less demanding tolerable threshold is sufficiently small.

The comparative judgment evaluates potential risk policy alternatives in the following manner. Combining a concern for the promotion of development with a concern for risk yields the overall objective of maximizing capability expansion while minimizing the impact of risks. Any given policy should satisfy a target risk, which the acceptable risk threshold provides.

12.5 Nuclear energy in the developing world

How should we think about nuclear energy in developing contexts using a capability approach? In this section we outline the considerations that should inform such an analysis. The overall judgment about the use of nuclear energy in any particular context would of course need to be based on the specific empirical facts pertaining to that context.

The first step in evaluating the possible adoption and use of nuclear energy in any particular context is to determine whether the risks associated with nuclear energy satisfy the threshold of acceptability. This follows from the overarching objective of CRA, protecting and furthering individuals' capabilities (Murphy and Gardoni 2007). Because the tolerability threshold requires the consequences to be temporary and reversible, they might not apply to risks associated to nuclear energy, which tend to be extremely long-term. To some degree, the specification of the standards for acceptable risk might be society-specific. As with human rights, the international community may come to identify broad principles that a threshold for acceptable risk must satisfy in terms of the probability and magnitude of impact on capabilities for a given hazard. However, there are reasons to support a role for democratic decision-making in terms of how those broad principles will be satisfied in a given context. There can be variation among communities in the precise specification for the threshold for acceptable risk. Communities may vary in the particular impact on general capabilities, such as an opportunity for education or mobility, which they are concerned to guard against. There may be a range of values for the target probability that a set of thresholds for acceptable risk could permit. As mentioned earlier, the target probability would also require a comparative risk analysis where there is a direct comparison with the risk associated to nuclear energy with the risks already faced by a community (Gardoni and Murphy 2014).

In developing contexts there is one additional challenge to specifying the threshold of acceptable risk. Within many developing communities capability levels may be below an acceptable, and even tolerable, level initially. For the billions of individuals subsisting on less than $2/day this will almost certainly be the case. Thus, the introduction of risks associated with a technology like nuclear energy may not always threaten to bring capability levels to an unacceptable level; they are already there. In these contexts, the question then becomes when, and under what conditions, it is permissible to potentially worsen the already unjustified level of capabilities individuals enjoy for the sake of a possible increase in the present level of capabilities. Ruling out the introduction of any further risk to capabilities levels is not necessarily justified; this could foreclose important avenues for enhancing the capabilities of individuals. At the same time, caution must be taken so as to not exploit or unnecessarily harm an already vulnerable population. There may be reason to pursue a policy that economizes threats to the further erosion of the capabilities of individuals, identifying the pathways for a given source of development that pose the minimum risk to the possibilities that individuals fall further below the acceptable threshold. In the case of nuclear energy, a number of different kinds of risks must be considered when making this judgment, importantly security and short- and long-term safety risks for both current and future generations (Taebi 2011). This tension is best dealt with through dialogue among the various actors working for sustainable societies in different ways. Such dialogue would serve as a corrective to the relatively little interaction and communication between advocates of sustainable development and risk analysts.

If nuclear energy passes the acceptable threshold, the second step is to assess the contribution of nuclear energy to the goals of development relative to the costs that the pursuit of nuclear energy entails and sustainability considerations, and then compare that contribution against alternative energy paths that a developing country might pursue. For the second comparative evaluation, we ask of nuclear energy: "are the risks associated with it preferable compared to other risks associated to alternative options, including the option of not doing anything?"

Benefits include the provision of electricity for a given population; in many cases in developing contexts this may be available for the first time. In 2011, 59.6 percent of the population of Bangladesh 26 percent and of the Democratic Republic of Korea had access to electricity.[2] Electricity contributes in fundamental ways to education, allowing individuals to study longer and learn more each day. It can be crucial for the functioning of businesses, whose flourishing in turn increases the economic resources generated by a community. It allows for food refrigeration, which is essential for a healthy diet. Precisely what gains in capabilities result from the introduction or increase in nuclear energy in any given society will depend on how many individuals are effectively able to access nuclear energy, given, for example, the extent to which it is produced, the reliability of its supply, and the costs for consumers of using it relative to their income level and their other competing expenses.

Consideration of the costs of nuclear energy in developing contexts must begin with the recognition that nuclear energy currently plays a much smaller role in developing countries than in developed ones. Though comprising 17 percent of the global electricity generation, 346 reactors in OCED contain 80 percent of this capacity (UNDP 2007). For example, while the EU derives 30 percent of its electricity from nuclear energy, in many developing countries nuclear energy is not used at all.

Given the relatively low reliance on nuclear energy in developing contexts, for the vast majority of developing countries the question is not: What are the costs associated with continuing to use or expand reliance on nuclear energy?

---

[2] World Bank database, http://data.worldbank.org/indicator/EG.ELC.ACCS.ZS/countries/1W?display=default.

Rather, the question is: What are the entry costs associated with nuclear energy, to determine whether they are worthwhile to incur. The entry costs for nuclear energy are significant. Nuclear energy requires a substantial upfront and ongoing investment in engineering knowhow and nuclear structures and infrastructure. The infrastructure and expertise required for nuclear energy production is characteristically not present in many developing contexts. The infrastructure needed to produce and sustain nuclear energy must be created, including an electricity grid size and structure. "In many developing countries, this is an important factor limiting the introduction of nuclear energy: the grid is often too small and fragmented to permit introduction of the fairly large nuclear energy reactors which are available" (Laue et al. 1977: 8). Other components of the requisite infrastructure include qualified manpower to absorb the technology transfer from a developed country (the typical case), as well as the resources and knowledge needed to construct and to run facilities needed for nuclear energy production. These conditions are also frequently absent. Facilities once constructed must also be maintained, with the requisite support and surveillance structures in place. Developing countries are among the most vulnerable to rising sea levels and increased flooding due to climate change, which increases safety risks. In this context, developing countries might or might not have the relevant resources to invest in nuclear energy as a long-term solution to the provision for and satisfaction of energy needs, either as a matter of upfront investment in preparing the infrastructure and possessing the expertise needed for the construction and maintenance of nuclear facilities or as a matter of ongoing maintenance.

Even if the resources are available, developing countries must consider whether it is worth devoting a significant amount of the scarce resources available to this purpose, relative to the other pressing needs that might be served with the same set of resources and the costs associated with other alternative forms of energy. Other forms of energy might increase capabilities more quickly because they do not require the same significant upfront investment. They may also pose fewer risks. However, alternative energy sources may also prove less reliable. Developing countries must then decide how to best try to maximize capabilities now and for future generations given the realistic options available.

Going beyond the individual country considering nuclear energy, one final consideration for the international community is related to the distinction between *voluntary* and *involuntary* risk (Murphy and Gardoni 2011b; Gardoni and Murphy 2014). Because the consequences of a nuclear accident, for example, would typically cross state boundaries, while a single country might decide to pursue nuclear energy, we believe that the international community should have a clear role in determining whether safety conditions are met or not.

12.6 Conclusions

This chapter takes up the question: "Should developing countries produce nuclear energy?" The chapter proposes a framework for conceptualizing and evaluating the risks and opportunities that nuclear energy might bring to developing countries. Opportunities and risks, we argue, should be assessed using a capability approach to development and to risk. A capability approach to development can be used to quantify the opportunities brought by the production of nuclear energy and gauge the possible impact of hazards in term of changes in capabilities. Our chapter highlights the ways in which consideration of the risks and opportunities created by nuclear energy must be different when looking at developing, as opposed to developed, countries. In particular, in developing contexts the entry costs and pressing other basic needs to which a country may devote its resources must be taken into account.

Acknowledgments

This chapter was made possible by the NPRP Grant 4-1195-6-032 from the Qatar National Research Fund (a member of Qatar Foundation). The statements made herein are solely the responsibility of the authors.

13 The role of nuclear energy in the future energy landscape: energy scenarios, nuclear energy, and sustainability

Rafaela Hillerbrand

13.1 Introduction

When contemplating the ethics of energy supply it is always slightly incongruent to assess individual energy technologies in total isolation. If one withdraws from nuclear energy today there is the inevitable risk of having to depend on alternative energy technologies in the future, all of which have their own specific drawbacks. It is therefore better to consider whole energy mixes rather than single energy technologies. Furthermore, the risks and benefits of nuclear energy need to be compared with the risks attached to renewables or fossil fuels. Assessing energy mixes thus warrants a long-term perspective and the developing of scenario analyses. The risks of specific energy mixes are not only linked to the different energy technologies themselves but also to energy demand, in other words, to the intensity of industrial and household energy consumption, the energy efficiency of various technologies, and, from a global perspective, population growth.

It is often the negative impact of increasing energy consumption that prompts authors of global energy studies to call for countermeasures that can considerably impede individual autonomy. Not only people's second car might come into the firing line but there might also be pressure to generally reduce consumer goods expenditure or even the birth rate. For instance, a recent Club of Rome report based China's ability to achieve sustainable production and consumption on its ability to address the population challenge (Randers 2012). This theory was linked to China's Confucian tradition as evidenced in meritocracy and centralized government and often contrasted with the alleged inability of democratic societies to react adequately to environmental problems. Still, it does not seem easy to square the overall perspective on environmental problems with the worries about single individuals, their autonomy, and their well-being: Does sustainable energy supply really necessitate intervention into otherwise very private decisions such as choosing the number of children one has – decisions that may be considered sacrosanct when juxtaposed to government intervention? If so, a serious conflict between sustainability and other values in the social realm, such as democratic participation, is likely to arise.

These tensions between a general view on sustainability involving environmentally friendly energy sources on the one hand and the individual's perspective on the other provide the starting point for this chapter's analyses. It is not so much the political or institutional aspects of sustainable energy supply and demand as the underlying values that will be discussed. Section 13.2 stresses the necessity to view nuclear energy as part of a broader energy landscape and expands on the implications of such a broad decision horizon. The German withdrawal from nuclear energy in reaction to the Fukushima Daiichi nuclear accidents aptly illustrates how various value conflicts can arise. The main question to be addressed in this chapter is that of how to ethically evaluate the energy supply and demand; specific attention will be given to energy mixes that incorporate nuclear power.

Most of the philosophical discussions on energy supply and demand do not discuss the broad energy landscape but tend rather to zoom in on a certain aspect. For example, obligations to future generations (e.g. Gardiner et al. 2010) or to a certain type of energy technology, such as any emitting greenhouse gases or nuclear energy (e.g. Taebi 2012a), are discussed in isolation. By contrast, the more commonly adopted analysis of energy supply takes the broader picture into consideration. This frequently falls within the realm of "sustainability" where it is particularly in the context of nuclear energy sustainability analysis that risk assessment may be included. In Section 13.3, an influential indicator set for the analysis of energy supply is introduced in the form of the *Energy Indicators for Sustainable Development* (EISD), as proposed by the International Atomic Energy Agency (IAEA) in 2005. Like most sustainability indicator sets, the EISD are viewed as specifications of Brundlandt's original definition of sustainability as applied to energy supply. In this chapter, I do not challenge Brundlandt's definition but remain within the anthropocentric framework it provides. It is argued that the EISD, just like other similar indicators, does not provide an ethical analysis because in Brundlandt's original definition a framework that details the term "needs" is lacking. In Section 13.4 the capability approach is introduced as a possible ethical framework for the addressing of issues of sustainable energy supply and demand.[1] It is shown how taking the capability approach helps to resolve the

---

[1] As noted in the literature, the capability approach does not provide a full theory of justice. However for the purposes of providing a framework for sustainability analysis, this is not necessary, see Section 13.4.2.

aforementioned tension between the aggregated good and an individual's perspective in favor of the latter.

Just like any sustainability analysis, an ethical evaluation of energy mixes is predominantly concerned with the long-term impacts of the present energy landscape. Scenarios and mathematical models of various sorts are implemented to estimate these energy mixes. These prognoses present high uncertainties that are crucial to ethical assessment. The models and their uncertainties are briefly discussed in Section 13.5. It is my contention that the uncertainty associated with the long-term impacts of energy supply and demand makes it only more urgent to focus more on social values such as intergenerational equity than has been customary in current sustainability discussions.

13.2   Framing the decision to withdraw from nuclear energy

The German Energy Transition, the *Energiewende*, is seen as an ambitious plan to remodel the entire energy landscape of a whole country – from power stations to the accompanying infrastructures like electric grids – merely on the basis of ethical considerations. The relevance therefore extends beyond national boundaries. Originally the term *energy transition* indicated a transition from a high-carbon energy supply to a system involving low carbon emissions and a high rate of renewable energy sources (Nitsch et al. 2012). The German *Energiewende* proposes that 80 percent of all electricity and 60 percent of the overall energy should come from renewable resources by 2050 while there should be a 70 percent cut in greenhouse gas emissions by 2040. Furthermore, the German *Energiewende* is embedded in various EU policies on energy, the most noteworthy of which are the EU "20-20-20" targets, which demand that within the EU an increase in efficiency of 20 percent in all energy consumption should be seen by 2020, a reduction in greenhouse gases of 20 percent, a 20 percent energy level derived from renewable resources, and a bio fuel use rate of 10 percent. Since the German withdrawal from nuclear energy in 2011, the term *Energiewende* has sometimes been adopted to refer to this phasing-out though, given the generic meaning of the term, it is not at all clear what role a withdrawal from nuclear energy might play in an energy transition. Many facets still need to be considered. I will elucidate some of these in this section.

13.2.1   Various energy technologies and their uses

In the short term we cannot expect to see a significant increase in the energy efficiency of household appliances or such efficiency with energy in industry; neither can we expect to see a drastic decline in energy consumption. Withdrawing from one energy technology, such as nuclear energy, thus implies that more extensive use will need to be made of others. Nuclear energy does, beyond any shadow of a doubt, raise serious ethical questions related to safety (the risk of accidents), security (protection against the threat of sabotage), and proliferation (the spread of fissile material and weapon-applicable nuclear technology). These issues not only emerge during the lifespan of any given energy plant but they are also of relevance to the nuclear repository or the reprocessing plant. But ultimately no form of power generation comes without its risks.[2] The potential negative impact of nuclear energy may arguably be much greater than the negative impacts presented by climate change that are attributable to the burning of fossil fuels. As the Chernobyl accident of 1986 demonstrated, major radiation release can directly yield to loss of human life and can make vast tracts of land uninhabitable for decades. Contamination can derive from plants from repositories, nuclear weapons, or what has come to be known as "dirty bombs" (speculated weapons combining conventional explosives with radioactive material). This illustrates how the negative impacts of energy technologies may well extend far beyond the realm of power generation. However, climate change caused by the combustion of fossil fuels also has the potential to set in motion a catastrophic impact.

At the end of the day, risk is not all about the magnitude of potential negative impacts, it also considers the likelihood of such scenarios. While the vast majority of scientists see anthropogenic climate change as a fact and while the ballpark figures of the estimated change have not diminished in the last decades, an accident in a nuclear energy plant may or may not happen. Even the widely praised renewables are not without their risks. Accidents in hydroelectric facilities, for example, can cause fatalities, and the use of hydropower reshapes and destroys nature in a way that usually tends to be irreversible.

13.2.2 *Various values*

Without necessarily having to buy into a consequentialist viewpoint, the pros and cons of various energy technologies must be compared in one way or another. The German Energy Transition provides an excellent case study if we want to show how such a comparison was made in practice. In top-down fashion, the German energy system was remodeled, also on the basis of ethical considerations.[3] In reaction to the Fukushima Daiichi accidents, eight

---

[2] This chapter adopts the colloquial use of the term "risk" as commonly used in philosophical discussions, namely: that of referring to possible yet uncertain negative impacts.

[3] Despite the fact that the government looked to an ethics committee that had been set up after the accident to evaluate the future of nuclear energy in Germany, the precise role actually played by ethical arguments in this decision has been debated. This is not, however, the topic of discussion in this chapter, cf. note 4.

nuclear plants were shut down in 2011, the remaining nine will be gradually phased out in the 2015–22 period.

The impacts of an accident like the one in Fukushima were thought to counter all possible positive effects of the civil use of nuclear energy, and so the German government opted for a complete withdrawal from nuclear energy. This decision was primarily based on safety considerations.[4] While today the opposition to nuclear energy is still very high in Germany – according to a survey by EMNID (.ausgestrahlt 2013) slightly more than half of those polled would even like to speed up the German phasing-out of nuclear energy. Indeed, the focus of the public debate on energy policy has shifted significantly over the last few years. Whereas for a long time it was environmental and economic aspects that dominated the discussions on suitable future energy sources, today's German discussions place rather different aspects at the center of the energy debate, aspects that directly affect those alive today. One example is the *reliability of energy supplies*. As renewables only provide intermittent energy, they threaten the stability of the electricity grid. This, in turn, increases the likelihood of blackouts. Developing countries or even the United States have considerable experience of power failure. Though not usually caused by intermittent electricity supply attributable to renewables, the impacts have shown how damaging large energy failures can be both to industry and households. The risks attached to various energy conversion methods also need to be compared with the risk of losing stable and reliable energy supplies.

Another aspect that took center stage in the public debate in the wake of the *Energiewende* was what became known as *Energiearmut*: energy poverty or lack of access to modern energy services. In the German context, this mainly relates to affordability as certain societal groups, such as pensioners, are to an increasing extent unable to afford the high electricity costs in the wake of the energy transition. Cost-efficiency has certainly always been a central part of the discussion on energy supply, but energy poverty is not a mere consequence of economic considerations. It shifts the emphasis from the national or regional economy to the individual – to the end-consumer – and raises issues like justice (intragenerational or otherwise) and fairness, which have far wider implications than matters such as energy supply or demand on their own.

---

[4] Whether the decision to withdraw from nuclear energy was actually based on a rational decision-making process or whether it was more of a populist decision by a government seeking to be re-elected in several federal states in the approaching election remains a point of debate. Unlike in many other countries, public opinion in Germany has produced an anti-nuclear majority ever since the Chernobyl disaster of 1986. The forthcoming elections may well have been the decisive factor in the German government's decision to withdraw from nuclear energy. This is not, however, of further relevance to the present discussion since our aim is to provide a normative framework for a rational decision-making process.

13.2.3 The broad spatial and temporal decision horizon

Many of the potential value conflicts mentioned above emanate from the broad decision horizon that spreads before one when reasoning on energy technologies such as nuclear energy. Not only must alternative energy technologies also be taken into consideration but the risks of energy technologies also transcend national borders and affect future generations. This is why reasoning in principle on energy technologies from an ethical point of view needs to be done from a global and intergenerational perspective. The possible negative impacts of nuclear energy as well as the risk posed by global warming illustrate this very clearly.

Since the middle of the last century, the well-being of future generations has received increasing attention in decision-making, particularly when reasoning about energy supply. Within the public and political debating arena, this is often termed "sustainability" (WCED 1987). While it is important to consider intergenerational justice, this opens up the debate to the matter of the inevitable conflict between the interests of those living now and future generations. The above-mentioned problems that Germany is facing in the wake of the *Energiewende* do not seem to be peculiar to the German Energy Transition. In fact such conflict seems to be inevitable when the broad temporal decision horizon enters into the picture: The legitimate claims of those alive today concerning, for instance, for safe and reliable provision of energy clash with those of future generations, for example when seeking to keep the environment intact and avoid major climatic change.

If one takes the long-term perspective into account, this implies that the risks of specific energy combinations are not only linked to the energy technologies themselves but also to the energy demand. The energy intensity of industry and domestic use and the energy efficiency of various technologies is what influences energy demand and all of this depends on consumer choice and on the progress of future technologies, two factors that are generically hard to assess and which invite ethical assessment to call for certain consumer behavior that is less energy-intensive. A further decisive factor when contemplating future energy demand is population growth. Particularly from a global perspective, the latter is an important aspect. When assessing energy supply and energy demand this broad perspective leaves the door wide open to yet another reaction to the risk of power generation technologies, namely the notion that drastic cutbacks in birth rates would lead to lower energy demands.

The idea of limiting consumer choice and reducing the birth rate gave rise to even more conflict between various values when deliberating about the energy future as both these factors impede people's autonomy. Modern democracies value the autonomy of the individual and will thus, many fear, have problems finding solutions to all the threats energy technologies may pose. This has prompted some global energy experts to take China as a sustainability role model because of its proven ability to deal with its major population challenges (e.g. Randers 2012). The conflict between sustainability and social values already mentioned within the context of the German *Energiewende* thus seems to become even more acute when a global decision horizon is introduced and future energy demand hinges very much on future population growth.

13.3 Energy and sustainability

Energy technologies may negatively impact on future generations on a global scale. An ethical assessment therefore needs to consider both the actual and the possible current impact upon the present generation while still accounting for future generations (in the form of long-term environmental concerns) and global issues. Furthermore, whole energy mixes (as opposed to single technologies) and energy demand have to be considered as well in any ethical assessment. Reasoning on energy policies then starts to resemble the opening up of a Pandora's box: The practical complexity of keeping track of and actually discussing so many possible energy futures seems to become unmanageable and unresolved conceptual issues come to the fore, the most urgent possibly being those related to value incommensurability. It may well prove impossible to compare the negative impacts of global warming to the risk of an accident occurring in a nuclear energy plant. Various energy futures seem *incomparable* since the underlying abstract values such as reliability and safety may be incommensurable. Incommensurability means that not even an ordinal ranking of the values is possible; no positive comparative judgment (e.g. no "better than") of these values can be made (cf. Chang 1997 on the philosophical discussions surrounding the notion of incommensurability). In this chapter, I do not want to dwell on the general philosophical debate on value incommensurability, but I do want to look at how it is dealt with in concrete decision-making in relation to various energy futures. As reference is frequently made to the concept of sustainability, that is what provides the starting point for the analysis in this section. I shall review an influential indicator set to simultaneously assess isolated energy technologies and the mixes of different energy technologies, namely, the EISD as proposed by the IAEA, and argue how this fails to provide a good guideline for an ethical assessment of energy mixes.

13.3.1 Indicators for sustainable energy supply

In the public debate as well as within industry, the broad perspective on the future of our energy sources is often couched in terms of sustainability. Although sustainability may at first glance seem to be a descriptive concept, it is often used to make normative claims. We can therefore analyze sustainability as a thick concept, in other words, as one that does contain evaluative as well as descriptive elements (cf. Möller 2012, 70ff.; Kirchin 2013). Generally, people seem to agree that power production *must* be sustainable. The Brundtland report, which is often cited as the origin of the modern debate on sustainability, defines sustainability as a state of affairs "that meets the needs of the present without compromising the ability of future generations to meet their own needs" (WCED 1987).

When people merely examine climate change, nuclear power production is sometimes claimed to be sustainable because there is no emission of greenhouse gases. The problem is that it is not only climate-related sustainable energy supply issues that are involved. As soon as the focus shifts to the depletion of natural resources, nuclear energy no longer presents such a clear-cut case in support of sustainability. The fissile resources that can be used in reactors are uranium and thorium, though the latter has hardly yet been used. The reserves of both will last much longer than the current coal, oil, and gas supplies. Furthermore, aided by reprocessing, fissile sources like uranium and thorium can be quite significantly extended (e.g. Cohen 1983; Taebi and Kadak 2010). However, when nuclear reactors are compared to genuine renewable energy sources such as solar or wind energy, or even to the use of nuclear fusion, fission cannot be called sustainable in terms of natural resource depletion: On the basis of the current open fuel cycle system and the current number of working reactors (OECD 2012) it is estimated that uranium reserves will last at least 100 years. Thorium is more difficult to estimate, but is expected to last longer in terms of orders of magnitude.

Just as climate change is not the only environmental issue to be considered, so sustainability cannot be subsumed in environmental issues alone. The IAEA report builds on what might be termed the three-pillar concept of sustainability that distinguishes economic, environmental, and societal "pillars" of sustainability. Within these three columns, the IAEA identified various themes within the economic, ecological, and social domain, such as "equity" in the last one. Under the theme of equity, various subthemes like "accessibility" and the "affordability" of electricity and other energy sources are identified. These subthemes are then translated into measurable indicators. For example "share of household income spent on fuel and electricity" is used to measure affordability, which in philosophical jargon may pertain to an instrumental value.

Though the EISD provides an excellent proxy for the sustainability of energy conversions, it gives rise to criticism. For example, the report itself suggests that most of the social and environmental indicators are "unequivocal measures of progress" (IAEA 2005: 15), while most of the economic indicators "are not designed to distinguish between 'good' and 'bad' but rather describe and give an indication of an aspect of energy use" (IAEA 2005: 15). As a basis for normative assessment this requires further refinement. Furthermore, within the social pillar of sustainability procedural values such as procedural justice are not taken into consideration.[5]

13.3.2 Whose needs? In need of a theory for well-being

The IAEA (2005: 1) lists "good health, high living standards, a sustainable economy and a clean environment" as intrinsically valuable matters. It is likely that many people will agree with these four valuable entities. But are they intrinsically valuable? The IAEA gives no further justification. Moreover, it seems that defining sustainability by alluding to a sustainable economy is in danger of becoming a circular definition. Within the realm of anthropocentric ethics to which Brundtland's definition of sustainability subscribes, the environment is no end in itself, merely a means to an end in conjunction with the survival and well-being of present and future generations. The same may be said of the sustainable economy. Brundtland's definition of sustainability, in terms of *needs*, first requires further specification of the needs that are of importance. It clearly asserts that it is the needs of present and future generations that have to be given equal consideration; however, it seems evident that not all needs can be taken into account in the same way. There seems to be an ethically relevant discrepancy between the need for more energy to buy a car and the need for reliable electricity supplies to run a hospital. The needs that are to be considered cannot be satisfactorily established until the question regarding what is intrinsically valuable to human beings has been addressed. Following Shue (1993), the "needs" that correspond to what is intrinsically valuable form the minimum requirements for a sustainability analysis.

The matter of what constitutes intrinsic value has been discussed within Western philosophy ever since Antiquity. It is a discussion that is even older than the addressing of the more fundamental question that seeks to define intrinsic value. Unfolding the various theories of intrinsic value goes beyond the remit of the present discourse. What I want to do is choose two strategies commonly pursued in sustainability assessments to determine what is of intrinsic value. The first strategy asserts that it is possible to formulate in a general way a concept of what constitutes a worthy and well-lived life, a concept that sometimes harks back to John Rawls's theory on basic goods; the second strategy assumes that what is important in human life can only be determined by each individual himself. The latter approach to sustainability

---

[5] The importance of procedural values has been stressed in various energy technologies and citing issues, e.g. for offshore wind, shale gas, CCS technologies and others (Basta 2012; Künneke et al. forthcoming).

analysis relies heavily on empirical surveys for an indication of people's preferences. The resultant sustainability analysis can thus be seen as a certain interpretation of utilitarian calculus.

If taken as a basis for sustainability analysis, the first strategy has clear advantages. It facilitates inter-individual comparison and the creation of general strategies for the measurement of intrinsic values. One such approach widely reflected in the literature on sustainability assessment in relation to energy technologies is the one that is based on John Rawls's list of basic goods (Rawls 1971). Rawls assumes that a decent human life consists in developing a reasonable life plan and adhering to it. He argues that every such reasonable plan requires certain specifiable resources if it is to be realized: this is what he terms "primary goods." These include civil and political rights, income and wealth or certain liberties. Since these goods are, he supposes, things that everyone needs and since they are taken to be measurable, Rawls recommends them as a basis for interpersonal comparisons. Though Rawls develops his notion within the context of political theory, it lends itself to being expanded to extend to environmental problems.[6] For example, Schlör et al. (2012) use Rawls's idea to justify their analysis of the German energy system. Similarly, Naqvi (1998) uses Rawls's theory to derive policy advice for the energy supply in Pakistan.

According to this concept, a certain distribution of energy or natural resources is justified if it contributes to a just distribution of primary goods. Even if it were in principle possible to determine the distribution of primary goods, there would still be a gap between the possession of goods and the actual benefit a person stands to gain from such goods. So it is possible for two persons to be relatively equal in terms of their primary goods but to differ considerably in terms of what they can make and achieve with these goods. The second strategy of determining what is of intrinsic value takes up these concerns. Essentially it is assumed that what is of intrinsic value in a human life can only be determined by each individual. This means to say that there would be no substitute for asking each individual what life holds for him or her. The most common theoretical basis for this view is the preference-based version of utilitarianism that is commonly implemented in economic cost–benefit analyses. What is valuable is each individual's utility. The versions of utilitarianism used in the sustainability analyses commonly made by economists usually take utility to be the fulfillment of subjective preferences. Consequently, the measurement and inter-individual comparison possibilities, not to mention the possibility to inquire about the satisfaction of future generations, remain severely impeded, which could be devastating when it

---

[6] Manning (1981), Bell (2004), and others take a Rawlsian approach to environmental ethics. There are also critical voices though, see e.g. Langhelle (2000) and Schramme (2006).

comes to assessing justice. One common strategy that is taken when dealing with these problems is the "revealed preference approach." Closely connected are the willingness-to-pay (WTP) or the willingness-to-accept (WTA) approaches. These, as well as the concept of Quality Adjusted life Years (QALY) are commonly used in sustainability analysis.

What all these approaches have in common is the fact that they propose that an individual's utility should be measured with the help of empirical surveys. When dealing with future generations, which is one of the core foci of sustainability analysis, this is only of limited value as no survey participation is obviously possible and, at least in part, the preferences of future generations remain unknown. It might well prove impossible to establish anything substantial about what people hold to be intrinsically valuable without asking them directly. Consequently, we may not be able to determine what is of intrinsic value to future generations. If this is true, there is no sensible and reasonable basis for sustainability. However, we should not be too quick to be dismissive. Moreover, it should be noted that the empirical surveys commonly do not determine what is necessarily of value, they provide instead a monetary equivalent for things that are of value, intrinsically or otherwise.

13.4   A capability perspective on energy supply and demand

13.4.1   Energy and freedom

From the viewpoint of technology acceptance, we may consider the contest between the two opposing strategies when determining what is of intrinsic value to human beings as sketched in Section 13.3.2 in a slightly different way. Any sustainability assessment needs to take into consideration two conflicting priorities. On the one hand, it has to be somewhat paternalistic because an ethically sustainable energy supply situation can only be achieved by assuming that the "needs" to be addressed in sustainability analysis are somewhat universal, as reflected in the first strategy. On the other hand, we live in a modern value-pluralistic society, and individuals differ in the respective goals that they have in life. The second strategy takes this value pluralism seriously and is extremely important to sustainability analysis. This applies even more so to decisions on certain energy mixes in which the resulting risks are born by many who are not actually given the power to decide about the respective technologies.

The capability approach proposed by Sen (1992) and Nussbaum (2001) can be seen as the middle ground between the objective paternalism notions of human well-being on the one hand and the too liberal and too unrestrictive stance of subjective views on the other hand. As such, it can provide a conceptual framework for the assessment of sustainable energy (Hillerbrand

and Peterson 2014). Instead of addressing the question of what, for example, constitutes a good life, the capability approach can be reconstructed to step back and address the question of what needs to be fulfilled so that people can develop their own individual definition of a good life. According to the capability approach, it is the freedom to choose and to actively realize the things one has reason to value. A person's *functioning* has to do with facts about what one is and what one is able to do; *capability* is defined as a set of alternative functioning combinations that can feasibly be achieved by the person in question.

Comparisons across alternative energy scenarios are therefore made on the basis of people's freedom to choose and actively realize the things they have reason to value. One does not focus on the impact that an energy scenario has on human well-being as such but rather on the freedom of action it affords constituting, for instance, the prerequisites for well-being. By assessing quality of life in terms of freedom of action, the capability theorist is then able to account for the fact that human beings differ in their capacity to utilize goods and resources. In this respect, this may be distinguished from the first strategy identified in the last section on the determining of intrinsic values. Moreover, the levels of freedom and functioning identified in the capability approach constitute what is intrinsically valuable; they are not mere prerequisites in the way that for instance primary goods are in Rawls's theory. Adopting the capability approach does not amount to just another form of subjectivism about value. Advocates of the capability approach believe that what holds as a morally valuable capability can, at least in principle, be determined in a non-subjective way and can also be measured across different individuals.

Capability theorists agree that what is valuable in itself is each person's freedom to choose and act, but the way in which this idea is played out can vary significantly. Irrespective of which particular version of the capability approach one adopts, there is a strong and clear connection between technology and capabilities. The former is often used to enhance the latter, as pointed out by Robeyns (2005: 98): "[w]e are not interested in the bicycle because it is an object made from certain materials with a specific shape and colour, but because it can take us to places where we want to go, and in a faster way than if we were walking." With energy technologies and electricity generating technologies in particular this connection between technology and the freedom to choose and act is especially striking. Electricity can be used in very versatile ways – for storing ice cream, driving a car, or powering life-sustaining technology in an intensive care unit. It can significantly enhance our capabilities. By contrast, irreversible resource depletion caused by the burning of fossil fuels, for example, or environmental changes resulting from the construction of hydro facilities significantly reduce our capabilities.

Despite the fact that technologies impact on our freedom to act and choose in significant positive and negative ways, the capability approach has so far received little attention in ethical discussions on technology, let alone in energy discussions.[7] Here the focus is still often on the role of energy in developing economies. However, the capability approach can be broadened. Having a capability perspective on the energy landscape implies that in the evaluation of an energy mix it is not only its actual implications that are taken into consideration but also the alternative course of action it enables, for instance through the reversibility of an action (Hillerbrand and Peterson 2014). If future generations were to discover at some point in time that, for one reason or another, wind energy brings with it unacceptable risks, it would be relatively straightforward to dismantle all the wind turbines. The same does not hold true for, for example, hydroelectric energy. In the event of future generations discovering that such huge hydroelectric facilities impose unacceptable risks, large hydroelectric facilities cannot simply be dismantled and the landscape restored. In this connection, it should be noted that the burning of fossil fuels also has an irreversible impact on the environment. Even with geoengineering, the impact made on climate systems is irreversible.[8] The irreversible effects of some technologies are accompanied by a reduction in the capabilities (or freedom) of future generations; this is indeed one of the issues that need to be taken into consideration from a capability perspective.

In the case of nuclear energy, the high levels of radioactive waste pose severe problems. Even when we take into account reprocessing or the future possibility of transmutation, the high volume of radioactive waste is something that present and future generations need to deal with in one way or another. The risks of nuclear energy cannot be eliminated by simply withdrawing from that technology. This also needs to be reflected in the political decisions taken on that technology. In the ongoing German debate this is reflected in the fact that despite the vast majority of the people disapproving of nuclear energy, the notion that there is a need for further research into the nuclear waste disposal options is acknowledged by 85 percent (Forsa 2013).

The potential loss of freedom for future generations is not sufficiently acknowledged by current sustainability indicators. What the capability approach highlights is that this loss should be taken into account in an ethical evaluation of alternative energy scenarios. Let us therefore for a moment look at nuclear energy as a single energy technology. In this simplified view, there are not just drawbacks from a capability perspective. Technologies generally,

---

[7] Some exceptions are Reitinger et al. (2011), Rauschmayer and Lessmann (2011), and Gardoni and Murphy (Chapter 12 in this volume).
[8] For example, McCusker et al. (2014) showed how certain geoengineering measures are irreversible.

especially energy technologies, enhance our freedom to act in unique ways. This is something to be valued from a capability perspective. Higher energy density opens up more opportunities for future action. With respect to this aspect, it might thus be claimed that nuclear energy has clear advantages over very low energy density renewables. The latter require much more space to generate the same amount of electricity.

13.4.2 The under-determination of the morally correct energy landscape

From a capability perspective, nuclear energy has positive and negative impacts on the freedom of individuals living now and in the future. In other words, one cannot jump to conclusions on energy supply too quickly when taking this capability perspective on whether an energy mix with or one without nuclear power is to be favored. As discussed in Section 13.2, nuclear power cannot be discussed in isolation and the answer to this question depends on energy demand as well as on many other context-dependent features, such as the available alternative energy technologies, the existing energy grid, or the concrete nuclear technology.

When comparing different nuclear technologies from a capability perspective, those that reduce resource depletion by means of reprocessing may be favored over the direct disposal of spent fuel but only if effective measures are in place to ensure the minimization of the risk of proliferation. If such precautions do not exist, then reprocessing may not be a favorable option. The existence of such bodies depends on the national state in question, its international integration, and so on. Another aspect that may change the evaluation of nuclear power from a capability perspective and which depends very much on the existing national energy supply is the energy infrastructure. This is an essential part of the energy landscape and one that needs to differ depending on the energy mix. In the German case, for example, *withdrawing* from nuclear energy threatens the stability of the existing electricity grid since base-load nuclear provision is a big base-load factor that, with the energy transition, will be replaced by intermittent forms of electricity provision from renewables. By contrast, for developing countries, *going* nuclear may threaten the net stability: As pointed out by Gardoni and Murphy (Chapter 12 in this volume), installing nuclear technologies in developing countries is not yet feasible because at first nuclear power generation requires expansions in the electricity grid to keep it stable. Any changes made to the grid by introducing new overhead or underground cables tend not only to be cost-intensive but also directly impact on the environment. This all affects individual capabilities. The same may, however, also be said of net instability. Particularly in the face of unpredictable energy failure this reduces the freedom to act. So, while in one case this may represent a yielding to the temptation to maintain a nuclear energy program, in yet other countries it may mean not starting a nuclear energy program.

A capability perspective on energy mixes does not, by definition, make the inclusion of nuclear energy immoral. While the circumstances in some countries may make nuclear energy unfavorable, it may be a legitimate if not even ethically desirable aspect of electricity production in other countries. It is acknowledged that such flexibility toward context-dependent features is an essential feature of sustainability indicator sets (e.g. IAEA 2005). From a bird's eye perspective, like that taken in this chapter, the moral status of nuclear energy cannot, however, be analyzed any further. As just explained, many context-dependent features, ranging from the specifics of the nuclear technologies to the political and institutional setting of the respective national states, need to be considered. Such considerations are beyond the scope of this chapter since we merely seek to provide the normative framework for such an assessment.

There are two further reasons why the capability approach provides no simple answer to the question of which energy mix, either with or without nuclear energy, is preferable. The capability approach neither provides a full theory of justice nor demonstrates how to operationalize the capabilities, that is to say, shows how to convert the general freedom to act into measurable quantities that can serve as sustainability indicators. I would like to see these features as the under-determination of the capability approach: The capability approach alone cannot provide us with an action guiding principle. I would like to elucidate on how these two types of under-determination are actually advantageous when it is the capability approach that forms the basis for sustainability assessment in the energy context.

The first kind of under-determination, the failure to account for a full theory of justice, is often criticized in the literature. The capabilities provide a "metric of justice," they tell us what needs to be taken into consideration when we reason about a fair, sustainable form of energy supply. Most capability approach theorists reject a simple calculus on the balancing and trading off of various fundamental human freedoms. So normative analysis as far as the capability approach is concerned leaves us with a multidimensional space spanned by various capabilities; concrete recommendations on which energy scenario is good or bad would, however, require a reduction of this multi-dimensional space to one cardinal value. It was argued in Hillerbrand and Peterson (2014) that this under-determination actually pleads in favor of at least certain versions of the capability approach.

When applying the capability approach to concrete choices between alternative energy scenarios, the relevant capabilities have to be operationalized (cp. Comim et al. 2008). This is highly likely to be context-dependent: people living today may, for instance, have reason to strive for other functions than people living in the future, since the actions that constitute a valuable life (the agent's functioning) may change over the course of time. Thus, while the capability approach provides a form of value universalism at a fundamental level, the proxies of the relevant capabilities may have plural, context-dependent instantiations. This would be a great advantage for anyone seeking to assess energy technologies from a moral point of view, since sustainability indicators have to be flexible enough to be adaptable (within reasonable limits) to the specific situation in a given country or region (IAEA 2005). Moreover, the enterprise of operationalizing the capability approach is an interdisciplinary enterprise (e.g. Robeyns 2005). It is notably the assessment of technologies that requires input from the social, engineering, and natural sciences (e.g. Reitinger et al. 2011). Few negative impacts of energy technologies are directly caused by a given energy technology itself (fatalities due to a nuclear accident being in this case the exception) but indirectly there is an impact on human health and well-being through the changes created in the environment. It is the use and abuse of any technology, including its public perception and acceptance, that is of importance here. Estimating and addressing the multifaceted impacts that technology can have on human beings requires an interdisciplinary approach that draws on the humanities as well as the social and natural sciences. Only with combined effort from various disciplines can suitable proxies for the capabilities be given.

13.5   The open energy future: energy demand and uncertain scenarios

Given the focus on capabilities as potential functioning aspects, would it not be advisable from a capability perspective to then go all the way in finding a fully renewable energy supply? Several recent studies have suggested that by the middle of this century or even earlier large parts of the world's energy could be generated from renewables, while Greenpeace (Greenpeace and European Renewable Energy Council 2012) predicts that 97 percent of the energy for the EU27 could come from renewable sources by 2050, WWF (2011) even sees 100 percent renewable energy supply for the whole world possible within the same time frame. Jacobson and Delucchi (2009) present a scenario in which the latter could already be achieved by 2030.

As noted above, such an "all-renewable" scenario does not exclusively have advantages. The negative impacts of renewables (like the relatively high demand for space) are mainly related to their low energy density. Given the possibly catastrophic impacts of other energy technologies like fossil fuel or nuclear sources, opting for an "all-renewable" scenario may still be the best option. Before jumping to conclusions one does, however, need to take a closer look at these predictions and at the underlying assumptions. All of the all-renewable or almost-all-renewable scenarios are based on very low total energy consumption rates, sometimes as low as half of that given in the common *Business as Usual* (BAU) scenario.[9] This may or may not make the renewable energy scenarios less attractive from an ethical point of view; but it is particularly from a capability perspective that this reduction in energy demand needs to be carefully considered.

Current trends indicate the opposite to a future increase in global energy demand: The latest World Energy Outlook predicts a growth of one-third between 2011 and 2035 (IEA 2013b). The *New Lens Scenarios* of Royal Dutch Shell, which is both a pioneer in scenario development for use in strategic decisions and internal communication and, more generally, a pioneer of the methodology for energy scenarios, even assumes that we shall see an energy demand increase of 80 percent by 2050. Moreover, at least for developing countries, increases in material well-being and energy demand are correlated. According to IEA (2013b) it is the emerging economies such as China, India, South East Asia, and the Middle East that account for more than 90 percent of the net energy demand growth. Beyond that, from a capability perspective, the freedom that abundant availability of energy provides is – notwithstanding its negative side effects – something to be valued.

Quite generally, the capability approach places more emphasis on the individual's perspective than does common sustainability analysis. Cutbacks in energy demand that are not merely achieved by increasing energy efficiency but which require rigorous changes in individual lifestyles are harder to justify. This holds for the wider implications that reduced economic growth in developing countries or reduced birth rates have for the freedom of choice of the individual; simultaneously, it is not straightforward to argue that running a second or even a third car is immoral. People might need several cars in a family to operate effectively in society or simply get so much out of this that cutbacks are hard to justify. Following the analysis given in Section 13.4, there is certainly no quick answer to the question of what cutbacks in energy demand are morally allowed or even required in order to go "all renewable." Instead various energy futures have to be carefully evaluated to ascertain how they impact on various functioning and capabilities.

When comparing the different energy futures (Grunwald 2011), it is very important to consider all the underlying assumptions, which are often not very clearly communicated. The above-mentioned fully renewable scenarios provide examples as they do not openly communicate the assumptions concerning the level of the energy demand. These and similar assumptions frequently emerge in

---

[9] Cf. http://thebreakthrough.org/images/pdfs/DecarbonizationWord_BTI.pdf. BAU assumes that there will be increases in the energy efficiency of industrial and household appliances but no policies to restrict energy consumption.

energy futures from scenario analyses. Scenarios provide "alternative images of how the future might unfold" (Nakicenovic et al. 2000, Section 12). A scenario contains assumptions on the future development of energy demand and supply over the course of the twenty-first century. Such scenarios not only give estimates for the birth rates and productivity but also make assumptions regarding energy efficiency, various energy policies (e.g. the restricting of carbon dioxide emissions), and so forth. Scenarios thus also provide input for, for example, global climate models for which they provide information on matters such as the rise in greenhouse gas concentrations as well as other relevant climate factors like aerosol concentrations and changes in the albedo during the course of the twenty--first century (van Vuuren et al. 2011).

Due to the long-term impacts of energy technologies, such scenarios are essential in any energy model. They may be quantitative, such as the SERES or RCP scenarios underlying the IPCC reports on climate change, or of a more qualitative nature. Qualitative scenarios may be directly used as energy futures, while quantitative scenarios most often provide the input for mathematical energy models. These models may be very sophisticated from a modeler's perspective, an example being global climate models or the rather simple extrapolations of current trends as given in some economic models (cf. EWI 2012) In order to evaluate whole energy mixes, the output of climate models must, for example, be combined with nuclear energy risk analysis, predictions on renewables, and so forth. For this reason world models that evaluate whole energy mixes may provide the best solution (e.g. IEA 2013b).

All models pertaining to energy are associated with high degrees of uncertainty. For risk analysis, particularly in relation to nuclear energy, there has been broad debate on methodological issues, both within and outside the modeling community; the same may be said of the methodology underlying global climate models. Methodological discussions on energy models and economic impact models are much more recent though (e.g. Frisch 2013) and the same applies to the systematic study of scenario analysis (e.g. Grunwald 2014). Generally, the more complex the model output is (e.g. regional temperature distribution instead of global averaged temperature), the higher the associated uncertainty will be. The uncertainty of the negative impact of human actions on the environment generally leads to the formulation and implementation of what is known as the precautionary principle. Though various formulations and interpretations of this principle exist, all of them embody "the *in dubio pro natura* idea: if in doubt, decide in favor of the environment" (Atheensuu and Sandin 2012: 962). If the capability perspective is taken, thus again placing the individual in the center of the ethical analysis, the case is no longer so clear-cut, particularly when we consider that there could also be uncertain yet potentially serious impacts on the social as well as the ecological realm. One conclusion that can be drawn from both the high uncertainties of predicting energy futures and the capability perspective is that possible impacts should not be mistaken for certain ones.

To summarize, using the capability approach to play out the concept of need featuring in Brundtland's original definition of sustainability introduces a more individual perspective than the perspectives presented in most current sustainability analyses in the energy field. With respect to the three-pillar view, this would involve a shift from the present often dominating focus on the economic and ecologic pillar to the social pillar. Such an individual-based approach brings its own challenges. This chapter did not set out to argue that the capability approach is the desired one or that it provides the best normative framework for sustainability analysis in relation to energy supply and demand; it aimed instead to point out certain of the structural advantages of adopting a capability approach to energy futures.

Considering the full spectrum of problems related to energy supply and demand is a multifaceted matter and one that presents many intricate problems. The way in which the capability approach was reconstructed in this chapter helps it to provide a magic bullet to solving all these problems by singling out a certain energy mix and taking it to be the morally good or bad one. And rightly so. The capability approach facilitates the addressing of the problem of how to shape our energy futures in its own complexity way instead of praising oversimplified solutions. The crux lies in the under-determination of the capability approach as a normative framework.

Bibliography

Adams, J.S. 1965. "Inequity in Social Exchange." In *Advances in Experimental Social Psychology*, edited by L. Berkowitz, 267–99. New York: Academic Press.
Ailworth, E. 2013. "Changing Energy Landscape May Save Plymouth Nuclear Plant." *Boston Globe*, December 22. www.bostonglobe.com/business/2013/12/22/changing-energy-landscape-may-save-aging-plymouth-nuclear-plant/rGxD6hQwkxlu0xfsmwqshM/story.html?s_campaign=8315.
AkEnd. 2002. "Site Selection Procedure for Repository Sites." *Recommendations of the AkEnd – Committee on a Site Selection Procedure for Repository Sites*. Köln: W & S Druck GmbH.
Albert, H. 2013. "Fukushima Report Sheds Light on Future Health Risks." *News Medical*, March 6. http://news-medical.net/news/20130306/Fukushima-report-sheds-light-on-future-health-risks.aspx.
Allers, U.S. and W.V. O'Brien, eds. 1961. *Christian Ethics and Nuclear Warfare*. Washington, DC: Georgetown University.
Allison, W. 2011. "We Should Stop Running Away from Radiation." *Philosophy and Technology* 24: 193–95.
ANS (American Nuclear Society). 2012. *Fukushima Daiichi: ANS Committee Report*. http://fukushima.ans.org/report/Fukushima_report.pdf.
Anspaugh, L.R. 2007. "Doses to Members of the General Public and Observed Effects on Biota: Chernobyl." *Journal of Environmental Radioactivity* 96: 13–19.
Anspaugh, L., R. Catlin, and M. Goldman. 1988. "The Global Impact of the Chernobyl Reactor Accident." *Science* 242: 1513–19.
Ardagh, D. 1990. "The Immorality of Nuclear Deterrence." *International Philosophical Quarterly* 30 (3): 343–58.
Aristotle. 2012. *The Nicomachean Ethics: Aristotle in Twenty-Three Volumes*, Vol. 19, edited by H. Rackham. Cambridge, MA: Harvard University Press.
Arthur, B.W. 2009. *The Nature of Technology: What It Is and How It Evolves*. New York: Free Press.
Ashford, N.A. and C.C. Caldart. 1996. *Technology, Law and the Working Environment*. Washington, DC: Island Press.
Ashford, N.A. and C.C. Caldart. 2008. *Environmental Law, Policy, and Economics: Reclaiming the Environmental Agenda*. Cambridge, MA: MIT Press.
Associated Press. 2012. "Protests in Japan as Nuclear Power Plant Reopens." *The Guardian*, July 1. www.guardian.co.uk/world/2012/jul/01/japan-protest-nuclear-plant-reopens.
Asveld, L. and S. Roeser. 2009. *The Ethics of Technological Risk*. London: Earthscan.

Atheensuu, M. and P. Sandin. 2012. "The Precautionary Principle." In *Handbook of Risk Theory*, edited by S. Roeser, R. Hillerbrand, P. Sandin, and M. Peterson, 961–78. Dordrecht: Springer.

Attfield, R. 1991. *The Ethics of Environmental Concern*, 2nd ed. Athens, GA: University of Georgia Press.

.ausgestrahlt. 2013. "56 Prozent der Bevölkerung wollen schnelleren Atomausstieg." Umfrage von EMNID im Auftrag von.ausgestrahlt. www.ausgestrahlt.de/hinter grundinfos/umfragen/umfrage-schneller-atomausstieg.html

Backhaus, K., B. Erichson, W. Plinke, and R. Weiber. 2006. *Multivariate Analysemethoden: Eine anwendungsorientierte Einführung*. 11th ed. Berlin: Springer.

Baggini, J. 2002. *Making Sense: Philosophy Behind the Headlines*. Oxford: Oxford University Press.

Baker, P.J. and D.G. Hoel. 2007. "Meta-analysis of Standardized Incidence and Mortality Rates of Childhood Leukemia in Proximity to Nuclear Facilities." *European Journal of Cancer Care* 16 (4): 355–63.

Barber, R.C., P. Hickenbotham, T. Hatch, D. Kelly, N. Topchiy, G. Almeida, G.G. Jones, G.E. Johnson, J.M. Parry, K. Tothkamm, and Y.E. Dubrova. 2006. "Radiation-Induced Transgenerational Alterations in Genome Stability and DNA Damage." *Oncogene* 25 (56): 7336–42.

Barkenbus, J.N. 1992. "The Ethics of Nuclear Deterrence: An Introduction." In *Ethics, Nuclear Deterrence and War*, edited by J.N. Barkenbus, 1–18. Saint Paul, MN: Paragon House.

Barnosky, A. et al. 2011. "Has the Earth's Sixth Mass Extinction Already Arrived?" *Nature* 471: 51–57.

Basta, C. 2012. "Risk and Spatial Planning." In *Handbook of Risk Theory*, edited by S. Roeser, R. Hillerbrand, P. Sandin, and M. Peterson, 265–94. Dordrecht: Springer.

Bauer, M.W., ed. 1995. *Resistance to new technology: Nuclear power, information technology and biotechnology*. Cambridge, UK: Cambridge University Press.

BBC News Asia. 2013. *Fukushima*. www.bbc.co.uk/news/world-asia-21867705.

Beauchamp, T.L. and J.F. Childress. 2001. *Principles of Biomedical Ethics*, 5th ed. Oxford: Oxford University Press.

Beauchamp, T.L. 2003. "The Nature of Applied Ethics." In *A Companion to Applied Ethics*, edited by R.G. Frey and C.H. Wellman, 1–16. Malden, MA: Blackwell Publishing.

Beck, U. 1992. *Risk Society: Towards a New Modernity*. Newbury Park, London: Sage Publications.

Bederman, D.J. 2006. *International Law Frameworks*, 2nd ed. New York: Foundation Press.

Bedford, T. and R. Cooke. 2001. *Probabilistic Risk Analysis: Foundations and Methods*. Cambridge, UK: Cambridge University Press.

Beitz, C.R. 1999. *Political Theory and International Relations, with a New Afterword by the Author*. Princeton, NJ: Princeton University Press.

Bell, D. 2004. "Environmental Justice and Rawls' Difference Principle." *Environmental Ethics* 26 (3): 287–306.

Benjamin, J.1988. *The Bonds of Love: Psychoanalysis, Feminism and the Problem of Domination*. London: Virago.

Benschop, Y., J. Helms-Mills, B. Mills, and J. Tienari. 2012. "Editorial: Gendering Change: The Next Step." *Gender, Work and Organisation* 19 (1): 1–8.

Beresford, N.A., C.I. Barnett, S.M. Wright, and N.M. Crout. 2008. "Post-Chernobyl Restrictions Still Affecting UK Sheep." *Agra Europe* 2203: 2.

Bertell, R. 1991. "Ethics of Nuclear Option in the 1990s." In *Nuclear Energy and Ethics*, edited by K.S. Shrader-Frechette, 161–81. Geneva: World Council of Churches Publications.

BFE (Bundesamt für Energie). 2008. "Sectoral Plan Deep Geological Repositories." *Conceptual part*. Bern: Swiss Federal Office of Energy.

BFE. 2013. *Radioactive waste: Nuclear Installations and Areas for Deep Geological Repositories*. Bern: Swiss Federal Office of Energy.

Bickerstaff, K., I. Lorenzoni, N. Pidgeon, W. Poortinga, and P. Simmons. 2008. "Re-framing Nuclear Power in the UK Energy Debate: Nuclear Power, Climate Change Mitigation and Radioactive Waste." *Public Understanding of Science* 17: 145–69.

Blau, P.M. 1964. *Exchange and Power in Social Life*. New York: Wiley.

Bloor, D. 1976. *Knowledge and Social Imagery*. London/Henley/Boston: Routledge & Kegan Paul.

Bluth, C., M. Kroenig, R. Lee, W.C. Sailor, and M. Fuhrmann. 2010. "Correspondence: Civilian Nuclear Cooperation and the Proliferation of Nuclear Weapons." *International Security* 35 (1): 184–200.

Booth, K., and N.J. Wheeler. 2008. *The Security Dilemma: Fear, Cooperation, and Trust in World Politics*. New York: Palgrave MacMillan.

Borchardt, R.W. 2011. "Prioritization of Recommended Actions to be Taken in Response to Fukushima Lessons Learned." *USNRC*, October 3.

Bostek, C. *vs*. Entergy Nuclear Generation Co. 2014. "Plaintiffs' Memorandum in Opposition to Defendant Entergy's Motion to Dismiss Plaintiffs' Amended Complaint for Lack of Standing," *Land Court Department of Trial Court, March 7*. www.capecodbaywatch.org/wp-content/uploads/2014/07/06.09.14-Pl aintiffs-Memorandum-in-Opposition-to-Entergy-Motion-to-Dismiss-on-Standi ng.pdf.

Boyle, P. 1997. "Cancer, Cigarette Smoking and Premature Death in Europe: a Review Including the Recommendations of European Cancer Experts Consensus Meeting, Helsinki, October 1996." *Lung Cancer* 17 (1):1–60.

Broad, W.J. and D.E. Sanger. 2014. "U.S. Ramping Up Major Renewal in Nuclear Arms." *The New York Times*, September 21. www.nytimes.com/2014/09/22/us-ramping-up-major-renewal-in-nuclear-arms.html.

Brockner, J. and B.M. Wiesenfeld. 1996. "An Integrative Framework for Explaining Reactions to Decisions: Interactive Effects of Outcomes and Procedures." *Psychological Bulletin* 120 (2):189–208.

Buck, H.J., A.R. Gammon, and C.J. Preston. 2014. "Gender and Geoengineering." *Hypatia* 29 (3): 651–69.

Bunn, G. 2006. "The Nuclear Nonproliferation Regime and its History." In *U.S. Nuclear Weapons Policy: Confronting Today's Threats*, edited by G. Bunn and C.F. Chyba, 75–125. Washington DC: Brookings Institution Press.

Bupp, I.C. and J.C. Derian. 1978. *Light Water: How the Nuclear Dream Dissolved*. New York: Basic Books.

Burgherr, P. and S. Hirschberg. 2008. "A Comparative Analysis of Accident Risks in Fossil, Hydro, and Nuclear Energy Chains." *Human and Ecological Risk Assessment: an International Journal* 14 (5): 947–73.

Burgos, R. and O. Defeo. 2004. "Long-Term Population Structure, Mortality and Modeling of a Tropical Multi-Fleet Fishery: the Red Grouper Epinephelus Morio of the Campeche Bank, Gulf of Mexico." *Fisheries Research* 66: 325–35.

Burn, D.L. 1978. *Nuclear Power and the Energy Crisis: Politics and the Atomic Industry*. London: Macmillan.

Burrell, C. 2013. "Pentagon Says Pilgrim Among Most Vulnerable Nuke Plants." Patriot Ledger. Last modified August 17. www.patriotledger.com/article/20130817/News/308179690.

Burrell, C. 2014a. "Pilgrim On List of Degraded Nuclear Power Plants." *Wicked Local Plymouth*. Last modified February 4. http://plymouth.wickedlocal.com/article/20140204/NEWS/140208545/0/SEARCH.

Burrell. C. 2014b. "Pilgrim Neighbors in Plymouth Argue Nuclear Plant Depresses Property Values." *The Patriot Ledger*. Last modified August 27. www.enterprisenews.com/article/20140827/NEWS/140827360/12153/NEWS.

Butler, C., K.A. Parkhill, and N. Pidgeon. 2013. "Nuclear Power After 3/11: Looking Back and Thinking Ahead." In *Nuclear Disaster at Fukushima Daiichi: Social, Political and Environmental Issues*, edited by Richard Hindmarsh, 135–53. London: Routledge.

Brumfiel, G. 2011. "Fukushima Reaches Cold Shutdown." *Nature*. Last modified December 16. www.nature.com/news/fukushima-reaches-cold-shutdown-1.9674.

Busby, C. and M. Scott-Cato. 1997. "Death Rates from Leukemia are Higher than Expected in Areas Around Nuclear Sites in Berkshire and Oxfordshire." *British Medical Journal* 315: 309.

Buzan, B., and L. Hansen. 2009. *The Evolution of International Security Studies*. Cambridge: Cambridge University Press.

Caldeira, K., K. Emanuel, J. Hansen, and T. Wigley. 2013. "Top Climate Scientists Letter to Policy Influencers." CNN, November 3. Available at: http://edition.cnn.com/2013/11/03/world/nuclear-energy-climate-change-scientists-letter/.

Campbell, D.T. and J.C. Stanley. 1966. *Experimental and Quasi-Experimental Designs for Research*. Chicago: R. McNally.

Campbell, P. 1996. "Chernobyl's Legacy to Science." *Nature* 380 (5676): 653.

Caney, S. 2005. "Cosmopolitan Justice, Responsibility, and Global Climate Change." *Leiden Journal of International Law* 18 (04):747–75.

Cardis, E. et al. 2003. *Reconstruction of Doses for Chernobyl Liquidators*. Atlanta, GA: US Centers for Disease Control and Lyon: International Agency for Research on Cancer (IARC).

Casal, P. 2007. "Why Sufficiency Is Not Enough." *Ethics* 117 (2): 296–326.

Chang, R., ed. 1997. *Incommensurability, Incomparability, and Practical Reason*. Cambridge, MA: Harvard University Press.

Chernoff, F. 2009. "Defending Foundations for International Relations Theory." *International Theory* 1 (3): 466–77.

Chistiakov, D.A., N.V. Voronova, and P.A. Chistiakov. 2008. "Genetic Variations in DNA Repair Genes, Radiosensitivity to Cancer and Susceptibility to Acute Tissue Reactions in Radiotherapy-Treated Cancer Patients." *Acta Oncologica* 47 (5): 809–24.

Clapp, R.W., S. Cobb, C.K. Chan, and B. Walker. 1987. "Leukaemia Near Massachusetts Nuclear Power Plant." *The Lancet* 336: 1324–25.
Clapp, R. 2014. *"Testimony Presented at the Plymouth District Court."* Boston School of Public Health, March 19.
Clarke, L. 2005. *Worst Cases: Terror and Catastrophe in the Popular Imagination.* Chicago: University of Chicago Press.
Clarke, L. and C. Perrow.1996. "Prosaic Organizational Failure." *American Behavioral Scientist* 39 (8): 1040–56.
Clarke, R.H. 2003. "Changing Philosophy in ICRP: The Evolution of Protection Ethics and Principles." *International Journal of Low Radiation* 1 (1): 39. doi:10.1504/IJLR.2003.003490. www.inderscience.com/link.php?id=3490.
Clarke, R.H. and J. Valentin. 2009. "The History of ICRP and the Evolution of Its Policies." *Annals of the ICRP* 39 (1): 75–110.
Cohen, B.L. 1983. "Breeder Reactors: A Renewable Energy Source." *American Journal of Physics* 51 (1): 75–76.
Cohen, B. 1990. *The Nuclear Energy Option.* New York: Plenum Press.
Cohen, G.A. 1989. "On the Currency of Egalitarian Justice." *Ethics* 99 (4): 906–44.
Collins, H. 1985. *Changing Order.* London: SAGE.
Coltart, C. and K.L. Henwood. 2012. "On Paternal Subjectivity: A Qualitative and Psychosocial Case Analysis of Men's Classed Positions and Transitions to First Time Fatherhood." *Qualitative Research* 12 (1): 435–52.
Comim, F., M. Qizilbash, and S. Alkire, eds. 2008. *The Capability Approach: Concepts, Measures, and Applications.* Cambridge: Cambridge University Press.
Compton, T. and T. Kasser. 2009. *Meeting Environmental Challenges: The Role of Human Identity.* Godalming, Surrey: WWF-UK.
Commonwealth of Massachusetts Senate. 1987. "Senate Report No. 2023 of the Joint Special Committee Established for the Purpose of Making an Investigation and Study Relative to The Pilgrim Nuclear Generating Facility at Plymouth." July. www.nesl.edu/research/Legislative_Council/S2023_pilgrim_nuclear.pdf.
Constant, E. 1999. "Reliable Knowledge and Unreliable Stuff: On the Practical Role of Unreliable Beliefs." *Technology and Culture* 40 (2): 324–57
Cooper, M. 2013. "Renaissance in Reverse: Competition Pushes Aging U.S. Nuclear Reactors to the Brink of Economic Abandonment Institute for Energy and the Environment." *Vermont School of Law*. Last modified July 18. http://216.30.191.148/071713%20VLS%20Cooper%20at%20risk%20reactor%20report%20FINAL1.pdf.
Corcoran, S. 2011. "Power Struggle: Relicensing Pilgrim Nuclear." *WGBH*. Last modified November 21. www.wgbh.org/articles/Power-Struggle-Part-1-Relicensing-Pilgrim-Nuclear-4855.
CoRWM (Committee on Radioactive Waste Management). 2006. "Managing Our Radioactive Waste Safely." *CoRWM's recommendations to Government.* London: Committee on Radioactive Waste Management.
COWAM-2 (Community Waste Management-2). 2007. *Quality of Decision-Making Processes WP3: Decision-Making Processes in Radioactive Waste Governance – Insights and Recommendations.* Paris: COWAM.
Dancy, J. 2004. *Ethics Without Principles.* Oxford: Oxford University Press.

DARA. 2012. *Climate Vulnerability Monitor* 2nd ed. Development Assistance Research Associates. Accessed November 1, 2013. http://daraint.org/climate-vulnerability-monitor/climate-vulnerability-monitor-2012/report/.
Darst, G. 1988. "Pilgrim Rated Second Worst Nuclear Plant in the Country." *The Telegraph*, April 27.
Davidson, D. and W.R. Freudenberg. 1996. "Gender and Environmental Concerns: A Review and Analysis of Available Research." *Environment and Behaviour* 28 (3): 302–39.
DBER. 2008. *A White Paper on Nuclear Power*. London: Department for Business Enterprise and Regulatory Reform, HMSO.
Dean, M. 1999. *Governmentality: Power and Rule in Modern Society*. London: Sage.
DECC. 2011. *The Carbon Plan*. London: Department of Energy and Climate Change HMSO.
Denzin, N. 1997. *Interpretive Ethnography: Ethnographic Practices for the C21*. London: Sage.
DTI. 2003. *Energy White Paper: Our Energy Future: Creating a Low Carbon Economy*. London: Department of Trade and Industry HMSO.
de-Shalit, A. 1995. *Why Posterity Matters: Environmental Policies and Future Generations*. London: Routledge.
Deutch, J. and Lester R. 2004. *Making Technology Work: Applications in Energy and the Environment*. Cambridge, UK: Cambridge University Press.
Deutsch, M. 1975. "Equity, Equality, and Need: What Determines Which Value Will Be Used as the Basis of Distributive Justice?" *Journal of Social Issues* 31 (3): 137–49.
Dewey, J. (1957 [1920]). *Reconstruction in Philosophy*. Boston: Beacon Press.
Diesendorf, M. 2007a. *Greenhouse Solutions with Sustainable Energy*. Sydney, Australia: University of New South Wales Press.
Diesendorf, M. 2007b. "Is Nuclear Energy a Possible Solution to Global Warming?" www.ceem.unsw.edu.au/sites/default/files/uploads/publications/NukesSocialAlternativesMD.pdf.
Dobson A., ed. 1999. *Fairness and Futurity: Essays on Environmental Sustainability and Social Justice*. Oxford: Oxford University Press.
Dolley, S. 2014. "US NRC expects application to extend nuclear licenses beyond 60 years, DOE official." Platts, February 26. www.platts.com/latest-news/electric-power/washington/us-nrc-expects-application-to-extend-nuclear-21273628.
Douglas, M. and A. Wildavsky. 1982. *Risk and Culture: An Essay in the Selection of Technological and Environmental Dangers*. Berkeley, CA: University of California Press.
Downer, J. 2007. "When the Chick Hits the Fan: Representativeness and Reproducibility in Technological Testing." *Social Studies of Science* 37 (1): 7–26.
Downer, J. 2011a. "'737-Cabriolet': The Limits of Knowledge and the Sociology of Inevitable Failure." *American Journal of Sociology* 117 (3): 725–62.
Downer, J. 2011b. "On Audits and Airplanes: Redundancy and Reliability-Assessment in High Technologies." *Accounting, Organizations and Society* 36 (4): 269–83.
Downer, J. 2013. ""Disowning Fukushima: Managing the Credibility of Nuclear Reliability Assessment in the Wake Of Disaster." *Regulation and Governance*. http://onlinelibrary.wiley.com/doi/10.1111/rego.12029/pdf.

Doyle II, T.E. 2010. "Reviving Nuclear Ethics: A Renewed Research Agenda for the Twenty-first Century." *Ethics and International Affairs* 24 (3): 287–308.

Doyle II, T.E. 2013. "Liberal Democracy and Nuclear Despotism: Two Ethical Foreign Policy Dilemmas." *Ethics and Global Politics* 6 (3): 155–74.

Dutzik, T. and T. Madsen. 2012. "Fukushima." *Environmental California*. Accessed April 20 2012. www.environmentcalifornia.org/reports/cae/fukushima-one-year-later.

Dubrova, Y.E. 2003. "Radiation-Induced Transgenerational Instability." *Oncogene* 22: 7087–93.

Dubrova, Y.E., V.N. Nesterov, N.G. Krouchinsky, V.A. Ostapenko, R. Neumann, D.L. Neil, and A. Jeffreys. 1996. "Human Minisatellite Mutation Rate after the Chernobyl Accident." *Nature* 380 (6576): 683–86.

Dubrova, Y.E., O.G. Polshchanskaya, O.S. Kozionova, and A.V. Akieyev. 2006. "Minisatellite Germline Mutation Rate in the Techna River Population." *Mutation Research* 602: 74–82.

Dubrova, Y.E., P. Hickenbotham, C.D. Glen, K. Monger, H-P. Wong, and R.C. Barber. 2008. "Paternal Exposure to Ethylnitrosourea Results in Transgenerational Genomic Instability in Mice." *Environ. Mol. Mutagen* 49: 308–11.

Dunn, L.A. 2009. "The NPT: Assessing the Past, Building the Future." *The Nonproliferation Review* 16 (2): 143–72.

Dvorak, P. 2012. "Fukushima Daiichi's Unit 4 Spent-Fuel Pool: Safe or Not?" *Wall Street Journal Japan*. Last modified April 17. http://blogs.wsj.com/japanrealtime/2012/05/21/fukushima-daiichis-unit-4-spent-fuel-pool-safe-or-not/.

Dworkin, R. 2000. *Sovereign Virtue: the Theory and Practice of Equality*. Cambridge, MA: Harvard University Press.

EcoLaw. 2012a. "Clean Water Act, § 505 Notice of Intent to Initiate Citizen Suit for Violations at Pilgrim Nuclear Power Station, Plymouth, Massachusetts." *NPDES Permit* No. MA 0000355. Last modified October 5. http://jonesriver.org/legal/entergy-water-pollution-at-pilgrim-nuclear-is-subject-of-federal-notice-of-intent-to-sue-for-831-million-in-penalties/.

EcoLaw. 2012b. "Request to the National Marine Fisheries Service: ESA § 7: Nuclear Regulatory Commission Biological Assessment on Entergy's Pilgrim Nuclear Power Station, Plymouth, Massachusetts." Last modified April 24. www.capecodbaywatch.org/library/.

EcoLaw. 2013. "Zoning Board Appeal under M.G.L. 40A, §§ 7,8,15 and 17 Plymouth Zoning By-Law 205–15." Last modified April 25. www.capecodbaywatch.org/wp-content/uploads/2012/10/04.25.13-appeal-letter-final-filed_signed.pdf.

EcoLaw *vs*. Entergy Nuclear Generation Company. 2013. "Board of Appeals Decision," Case No. 3712, July 10. www.capecodbaywatch.org/wp-content/uploads/2012/10/zba-decision-of-july-24-2013.pdf.

EIA. 2012. "Massachusetts Nuclear Profile 2010." US Energy Information Administration, April 26. www.eia.gov/nuclear/state/massachusetts/.

Emerson, R.W. 1904. *The Works of Ralph Waldo Emerson*, edited by G. Sampson. London: George Bell.

English, R., ed. 1985. *Ethics and Nuclear Arms: European and American Perspectives*. Washington, DC: Ethics and Public Policy Center.

EPA (Environmental Protection Agency). 2013. *Learn About Your Right to Know*. Washington, DC: US Environmental Protection Agency. Accessed 14 November. www.epa.gov/epahome/r2k.htm

EPA. 2014. "*Environmental Justice.*" United States Environmental Protection Agency Website. www.epa.gov/environmentaljustice/.

Erikson, K. 1991. "Radiation's Lingering Dread." *Bulletin of the Atomic Scientists* 47 (2): 34–39.

EWI (Institute for Energy Economics). 2011. Roadmap 2050 – a Closer Look. www.ewi.uni-koeln.de/publikationen/studien.

Fackler, M. 2011. "Nuclear Crisis Set Off Fears Over Tokyo, Report Says." *New York Times*. Last modified February 27, 2012. www.nytimes.com/2012/02/28/world/asia/japan-considered-tokyo-evacuation-during-the-nuclear-crisis-report-says.html?_r=1.

Faulkner, W. 2000a. "The Power and the Pleasure? A Research Agenda for 'Making Gender Stick' to Engineers." *Science, Technology and Human Values* 25: 87–119.

Faulkner, W. 2000b. "Dualisms, Hierarchies and Gender in Engineering." *Social Studies of Science* 30: 759–92.

Filippi, A.R., P. Franco, and U. Ricardi. 2006. "Is Clinical Radiosensitivity a Complex Genetically Controlled Event?" *Tumori* 92 (2): 87–91.

Finn, M. and K.L. Henwood. 2009. "Exploring Masculinities within Men's Identificatory Imaginings of First-time Fatherhood." *British Journal of Social Psychology* 48(3): 547–62.

Finnemore, M. and K. Sikkink. 1998. "International Norm Dynamics and Political Change." *International Organization* 52 (4): 887–917.

Fischer, S. and K. Davis. 1993. *Negotiating at the Margins: The Gendered Discourse of Power and Resistance*. New Brunswick, NJ: Rutgers University Press.

Flüeler, T. 2006. *Decision Making for Complex Socio-Technical Systems: Robustness from Lessons Learned in Long-term Radioactive Waste Governance*. Environment & Policy Vol. 42. Dordrecht: Springer.

Flynn, J., P. Slovic, and C.K. Mertz. 1994. "Gender, Race and Perception of Environmental Health Risks." *Risk Analysis* 14: 1101–08.

Folger, R., D. Rosenfield, J. Grove, and L. Cornkran. 1979. "Effects of 'Voice' and Peer Opinions on Responses to Inequity." *Journal of Personality and Social Psychology* 37: 2253–61.

Ford, H.P. and F.X. Winters, eds. 1977. *Ethics and Nuclear Strategy?*. Maryknoll, NY: Orbis Books.

Forman, D., P. Cook-Mozaffari, S. Darby, G. Davey, I. Stratton, R. Doll, and M. Pike. 1987. "Cancer Near Nuclear Installations." *Nature* 329: 499–505.

Forsa Gesellschaft für Sozialforschung und statistischen Analysen mbh. 2013. www.kernenergie.de/kernenergie-wAssets/docs/themen/2013-05-forsa-umfrage-kernkraft.pdf.

Foster, M. 2013. "Stress a Major Health Issue." *Japan Today*, March 10. www.japantoday.com/category/national/view/stress-a-major-health-issue-for-dsplaced-fukushima-residents.

Freudenberg, W.R. and S.K. Pastor. 1992. "Public Responses to Technological Risks: Toward a Sociological Perspective." *The Sociological Quarterly* 33: 389–412.

Frickel, S. and K. Moore. 2006. *The New Political Sociology of Science: Institutions, Networks, and Power*. Madison, WI: University of Wisconsin Press.

Frisch, M. 2013. "Modeling Climate Policies: A Critical Look at Integrated Assessment Models." *Philosophy & Technology* 26: 117–37.
Frosh, S. 2002. *Afterwords: The Personal in Gender, Culture and Psychotherapy*. Basingstoke: Palgrave-Macmillan.
Fuhrmann, M. 2009. "Spreading Temptation: Proliferation and Peaceful Nuclear Cooperation Agreements." *International Security* 34 (1): 7–41.
Fuller, J. 1976. *We Almost Lost Detroit*. NewYork: Ballantine Books.
Funabashi, Y. and K. Kitazawa. 2012. "Fukushima in Review." *Bulletin of the Atomic Scientists* 68 (2): 9–21.
FuseNet, the European Fusion Education Network. 2013. www.fusenet.eu/node/38.
Gabbard, A. 1993. "Coal Combustion: Nuclear Resource or Danger." *Oak Ridge National Laboratory Review* 26 (3–4).
GAO. 2013. *Nuclear Reactor License Renewal*. Government Accountability Office 13–493. May. http://gao.gov/assets/660/654949.pdf.
Gardiner, S.M. 2003. "The Pure Intergenerational Problem." *Monist* 86: 481–500.
Gardiner, S.M. 2004. "Ethics and Global Climate Change." *Ethics* no. 114: 555–600.
Gardiner, S.M. 2005. "Ethics and the Principles of Radiological Protection: An Outsider's View." Conference Presentation: Universite Catholique de Louvain, Louvain-la-Neuve, Belgium: Ethics and Radiological Protection: Critical Perspectives on Justification, Liability and Intergenerational Justice.
Gardiner, S.M. 2006a. "Why Do Future Generations Need Protection?" *Chaire Développement Durable:* 1–16.
Gardiner, S.M. 2006b. "A Core Precautionary Principle." *Journal of Political Philosophy* 14 (1): 33–60.
Gardiner, S.M. 2008. "Why We Need More than Justification in the Ethics of Nuclear Protection." In *Ethics and Radiological Protection*, edited by G. Eggermont and B. Feltz, 97–111. Louvain-Le-Neuve: Academia.
Gardiner, S.M. 2009. "A Contract on Future Generations?" In *Intergenerational Justice*, edited by Axel Gosseries and Lukas Meyer, 77–118. Oxford: Oxford University Press. doi:10.1093/acprof.
Gardiner, S.M. 2011. *A Perfect Moral Storm*. New York: Oxford University Press.
Gardiner, S.M., S. Caney, D. Jamieson, and H. Shue, eds. 2010. *Climate Ethics: Essential Readings*. Oxford: Oxford University Press.
Gardner, M.J., M.P. Snee, A.J. Hall, C.A. Powell, S. Downes, and J.D. Terrell. 1990. "Results of Case Control Study of Leukemia and Lymphoma among Young People near Sellafield Nuclear Plant in West Cumbria." *British Medical Journal* 300: 423–34.
Gardoni, P. and C. Murphy. 2008. "Recovery from Natural and Man-Made Disasters as Capabilities Restoration and Enhancement." *International Journal of Sustainable Development and Planning* 3 (4): 1–17.
Gardoni, P. and C. Murphy. 2009. "A Capabilities-Based Approach to Measuring the Societal Impacts of Natural and Man-Made Hazards in Risk Analysis." *ASCE Natural Hazards Review* 10 (2): 29–37.
Gardoni, P. and C. Murphy. 2010. "Gauging the Societal Impacts of Natural Disasters Using a Capabilities-Based Approach." *Disasters* 34 (3): 619–36.
Gardoni, P. and C. Murphy. 2013. "A Capability Approach for Seismic Risk Analysis and Management." In *Seismic Risk Analysis and Management of Civil*

Infrastructure Systems, edited by S. Tesfamariam and K. Goda, 255–67. Cambridge, UK: Woodhead Publishing Ltd.

Gardoni, P. and C. Murphy. 2014. "A Scale of Risk." *Risk Analysis* 34 (7): 1208–27.

Gibson, B.E., O.B. Eden, A. Barrett, C.A. Stiller, and G.J. Draper. 1988. "Leukemia in Young Children in Scotland." *Lancet* 2: 630.

Giel, R. 1991. "Hoe Erg Was Chernobyl? De Psychosociale Gevolgen van Het Reactorongeluk." *Nederlands Tijdschrift voor Geneeskunde* 135 (25): 1137–41.

Gieryn, T. F. 1999. *Cultural Boundaries of Science: Credibility on the Line*. Chicago: University of Chicago Press.

Gofman, J. 1995. "Foreword." In A. Yaroshinska. *Chernobyl*, 1–2. Lincoln, NE: University of Nebraska Press.

Gilligan, C. 1982. *In a Different Voice*. Cambridge, MA: Harvard University Press.

Goldberg, S. M. and R. Rosner. 2011. *Nuclear Reactors: Generation to Generation*. Cambridge, MA: American Academy of Arts & Sciences.

Gonzales, W.J. 2010. "Recent Approaches on Observation and Experimentation: A Philosophical-Methodological Viewpoint." In *New Methodological Perspectives on Observation and Experimentation in Science* edited by W.J. Gonzales, 9–48. La Coruna: Netbiblo.

González, A.J., M. Akashi, J.D Boice, M. Chino, T. Homma, N. Ishigure, M. Kai, et al. 2013. "Radiological Protection Issues Arising during and after the Fukushima Nuclear Reactor Accident." *Journal of Radiological Protection: Official Journal of the Society for Radiological Protection* 33 (3): 497–571 doi:10.1088/0952-4746/33/3/497. www.ncbi.nlm.nih.gov/pubmed/23803462.

Goodin, R. 1999. "The Sustainability Ethic: Political, Not Just Moral." *Journal of Applied Philosophy* 16(3): 247–54.

Goodwin, G.L., ed. 1982. *Ethics and Nuclear Deterrence*. New York: St. Martin's Press.

Gosseries, A. 2008. "Radiological Protection and Intergenerational Justice." In *Ethics and Radiological Protection*, edited by G. Eggermont and B. Feltz, 167–95. Louvain-la-Neuve: Academia-Bruylant.

Gosseries, A. and L. Meyer eds. 2009. *Intergenerational Justice*. Oxford: Oxford University Press.

Gottweis, H. 1998. *Governing Molecules: The Discursive Politics of Genetic Engineering in Europe and in the United States*. Cambridge, MA: MIT Press.

Greenpeace and European Renewable Energy Council. 2012. *Energy [R]evolution: Towards a Fully Renewable Energy Supply in the EU 27*. www.erec.org/fileadmin/erec_docs/Documents/Publications/EU%20Energy%20[R]evolution%20Scenario%202050.pdf.

Grunwald, A. 2011. "Energy Futures: Diversity and the Need for Assessment." *Futures* 8 (43): 820–30.

Grunwald, A. 2014. "Modes of Orientation Provided by Futures Studies: Making Sense of Diversity and Divergence." *European Journal of Futures Research* 2 (1): 2–30.

Guidi, M.E.L. 2008. "Everybody to Count for One, Nobody for More than One." *Revue d'études benthamiennes* 4. http://etudes-benthamiennes.revues.org/182.

Guizard, A.V., O. Boutou, D. Pottier, X. Troussard, D. Pheby, G. Launoy, R. Slama, and A. Spira. 2001. "The Incidence of Childhood Leukaemia around the La Hague Nuclear Waste Reprocessing Plant (France): A Survey for the Years 1978–1998." *Journal of Epidemiology and Community Health* 55: 469–74.

Gunderson, A. 2012. "Tokyo Soil Samples Would Be Considered Nuclear Waste In The US." *Fairewinds Energy Education*, March 25. www.fairewinds.org/node/223.

Gustafson, P. 1998. "Gender Differences in Risk Perception: Theoretical and Methodological Perspectives." *Risk Analysis* 18: 805–11.

Gustafsson, A., A. Hermann, and F. Huber. 2007. *Conjoint Measurement: Methods and Applications* 4th ed. Berlin: Springer.

Hagendijk, R. and A. Irwin. 2006. "Public Deliberation and Governance: Engaging with Science and Technology in Europe." *Minerva* 44: 167–84.

Hamada, K. and O. Tsukimori. 2014. "Japan's Regulator OKs Nuclear Plant Return While Pushing to Close Old Reactors." *The Japan Times Online*, September 10. www.japantimes.co.jp/news/2014/09/10/national/japan-ok-nuclear-plant-return-pushing-close-old-reactors/.

Hanauer, S.H. 1972. "U.S. Atomic Energy Commission, memo on Pressure-Suppression Containment to J.F. O'Leary, F.E. Kruesi, and L. Rogers." September 20.

Hansson, S.O. 2003a. "Are Natural Risks Less Dangerous Than Technological Risks?" *Philosophia Naturalis* 40: 43–54.

Hansson, S.O. 2003b. "Editorial: Applying Philosophy." *Theoria* 69 (1–2): 1–3.

Hansson, S.O. 2003c. "Ethical Criteria of Risk Acceptance." *Erkenntnis* 59: 291–309.

Hansson, S.O. 2007. "Ethics and Radiation Protection." *Journal of Radiological Protection* 27: 147–56.

Hansson, S.O. 2009a. "Ethics Beyond Application." In *Cutting Through the Surface: Philosophical Approaches to Bioethics*, edited by T. Takala, P. Herissone-Kelly, and S. Holm, 19–28. Amsterdam and New York: Rodopi.

Hansson, S.O. 2009b. "Risk and Safety in Technology." In *Handbook of the Philosophy of Science Volume 9: Philosophy of Technology and Engineering Sciences*, edited by A. Meijers, 1069–1102. Oxford: Elsevier.

Hansson, S.O. 2009c. "Should We Protect the Most Sensitive People?" *Journal of Radiological Protection* 29: 211–18.

Hansson, S.O. 2011a. "Radiation Protection: Sorting Out the Arguments." *Philosophy and Technology* 24: 363–68.

Hansson, S.O. 2011b. "Risk." *Stanford Encyclopedia of Philosophy.* Last modified August 11, 2011. Accessed 23 March 2010. http://plato.stanford.edu/entries/risk/.

Hansson, S.O. 2012. "A Panorama of the Philosophy of Risk." In *Handbook of Risk Theory*, edited by S. Roeser, R. Hillerbrand,P. Sandin, and M. Peterson, 27–54. London: Springer.

Hansson, S.O. 2013a. *The Ethics of Risk: Ethical Analysis in an Uncertain World.* Basingstoke, UK: Palgrave Macmillan.

Hansson, S.O. 2013b. "Moral Thinking and Radiation Protection." In *Social and Ethical Aspects of Radiation Risk Management*, edited by D. Oughton and S.O. Hansson, 33–52. Oxford: Elsevier.

Hansson, S.O. 2013c. "ALARA: What Is Reasonably Achievable?" In *Social and Ethical Aspects of Radiation Risk Management*, edited by D. Oughton and S.O. Hansson, 143–58. Oxford: Elsevier.

Hare-Mustin, R. and J. Maracek. 1990. *Making a Difference: Psychology and the Construction of Gender.* New Haven, CT: Yale University Press.

Harwell, M. A. and T. C. Hutchinson. 1985. *Environmental Consequences of Nuclear War, Volume II: Ecological and Agricultural Effects*. Chichester, UK: John Wiley & Sons.

Hashmi, Sohail H. and Steven P. Lee. 2004. *Ethics and Weapons of Mass Destruction: Religious and Secular Perspectives*. Cambridge, UK: Cambridge University Press.

Hatch, M.C., J. Beyea, J.W. Nieves, and M. Susser. 1990. "Cancer Near the Three Mile Island Nuclear Plant." *American Journal of Epidemiology* 132 (3): 397–412.

Hatch, M.C., S. Wallenstein, J. Beyea, J.W. Nieves, and M. Susser. 1991. "Cancer Rates After the Three Mile Island Nuclear Accident." *American Journal of Public Health* 81 (6): 719–24.

Hatch, T., A.A. Derijck, P.D. Black, G.W. Van Der Heiden, P. DeBoer, and Y.E. Dubrova. 2007. "Maternal Effects of the Scid Mutation on Radiation-Induced Transgenerational Instability in Mice." *Oncogene* 26: 4720–24.

Hausman, D.S. and M.S. McPherson. 2009. "Preference Satisfaction and Welfare Economics." *Economics and Philosophy* 25: 1–25.

Health and Safety Executive. 2001. *Reducing Risks, Protecting People: HSE's Decision-Making Process*. Norwich: Her Majesty's Stationery Office. www.hse.gov.uk/risk/theory/r2p2.pdf.

Heasman, M.A., I.W. Kemp, J.D. Urquhart, and R. Black.1986. "Childhood Leukaemia in Northern Scotland." *Lancet* 1: 266.

Hendee, W. R. and F. M. Edwards. 1986. "ALARA and an Integrated Approach to Radiation Protection." *Seminars in Nuclear Medicine* 16:142–50.

Hendrickson, D.C. 1999. "The Ethics of Collective Security." In *Ethics and International Affairs*, edited by J.H. Rosenthal, 221–41. Washington, DC: Georgetown University Press.

Henshaw, D.L. 1996. "Chernobyl 10 Years On." *British Medical Journal* 312 (7038): 1052–53.

Henwood, K.L. 2008. "Qualitative Research, Reflexivity and Living with Risk: Valuing and Practicing Epistemic Reflexivity and Centring Marginality." *Qualitative Research in Psychology* 5 (1): 45–55.

Henwood, K.L. and N. Pidgeon. 2013. "What is the Relationship Between Identity and Technological, Economic, Demographic, Environmental and Political Change as Viewed through a Risk Lens?" *UK Foresight Future Identities Project*. Report DR18, Department of Business, Innovation and Skills. www.gov.uk/government/uploads/system/uploads/attachment_data/file/275780/13-519-identity-and-change-through-a_risk-lens.pdf.

Henwood, K.L., C. Griffin, and A. Phoenix. 1998. *Standpoints and Differences: Essays in the Practice of Feminist Psychology*. London: Sage.

Henwood, K.L., R. Gill, and C. Mclean. 2002. "The Changing Man." *Psychologist* 15 (4): 182–86.

Henwood, K.L., K.A. Parkhill, and N. Pidgeon. 2008a. "Science, Technology and Risk Perception: From Gender Differences to the Effects Made by Gender." *Equal Opportunities International* 27 (8): 662–76.

Henwood, K.L., N. Pidgeon, S. Sarre, P. Simmons, and N. Smith. 2008b. "Risk, Framing and Everyday Life: Methodological and Ethical Reflections from Three Socio-cultural Projects." *Health, Risk and Society* 10: 421–38.

Henwood, K.L., N. Pidgeon, K.A. Parkhill, and P. Simmons. 2010. "Researching Risk: Narrative, Biography, Subjectivity [43 paragraphs]." Forum: Qualitative Social Research 11 (1):Art. 20. Reprinted in *Historical Social Research* 2011 36 (4).

Henwood, K.A., N. Pidgeon, and K.A. Parkhill. 2015 "Explaining the 'gender-risk effect' in risk perception research: A qualitative secondary analysis study. Special edition of *Psyecology: Bilingual Journal of Environmental Psychology*. DOI:10.1080/21711976.2014.977532.

Herbst, A.M. and G.W. Hopley. 2007. *Nuclear Energy Now*. Hoboken, NJ: John Wiley: 138.

Herman, B. 1993. *The Practice of Moral Judgement*. Cambridge, MA: Harvard University Press.

Hillerbrand, R. and M. Peterson. 2014. "Nuclear Power is Neither Right nor Wrong: the Case for a Tertium Datur in the Ethics of Technology." *Science and Engineering Ethics* 20 (2): 583–95.

Hitchcock, J.L. 2001. "Gender Differences in Risk Perceptions: Broadening the Contexts." *Risk: Health, Safety and Environment* 12: 179–204.

Hohenemser, C., M. Deicher, H. Hofsäss, G. Lindner, E. Recknagel, and J.I. Budnick. 1986. "Agricultural Impact of Chernobyl." *Nature* 321: 817.

Hollyday, J. 1991. "In The Valley of the Shadow of Three Miles Island." In *Nuclear Energy and Ethics*, edited by K.S. Shrader-Frechette, 136–60. Geneva: World Council of Churches Publications.

Homans, G.C. 1961. *Social Behavior: Its Elementary Forms*. New York: Harcourt, Brace.

Hsieh, N. 2007. "Is Incomparability a Problem for Anyone?" *Economics and Philosophy* 23: 65–80.

Hubbert, M.K. 1956. "Nuclear Energy and the Fossil Fuels' Drilling and Production Practice." www.hubbertpeak.com/hubbert/1956/1956.pdf.

Hume, D. 2000. *A Treatise of Human Nature*, Oxford Philosophical Texts, edited by D.F. Norton. Oxford: Oxford University Press.

Hunt, P. 2012. *The Future of Nuclear Energy in the UK: Report of the Birmingham Policy Commission*. Birmingham: University of Birmingham.

Hvistendahl, M. 2007. "Coal Ash Is More Radioactive than Nuclear Waste." *Scientific American*. www.scientificamerican.com/article/coal-ash-is-more-radioactive-than-nuclear-waste/.

IAEA (International Atomic Energy Agency). 1991. *International Chernobyl Project: Technical Report*. Vienna: International Atomic Energy Agency.

IAEA. 1995. *The Principles of Radioactive Waste Management*. Vienna: International Atomic Energy Agency.

IAEA. 1997. *Joint Convention on the Safety of Spent Fuel Management and on the Safety of Radioactive Waste Management (Information Circular)*. Vienna: International Atomic Energy Agency.

IAEA. 2001. *Safety Assessment and Verification for Nuclear Power Plants Safety Guide*. IAEA Safety Standards Series. Vienna: International Atomic Energy Agency.

IAEA. 2002. *Dosimetry for Food Irradiation*. Vienna: International Atomic Energy Agency 3.

IAEA. 2003. *The Long Term Storage of Radioactive Waste: Safety and Sustainability: A Position Paper of International Experts*. Vienna: International Atomic Energy Agency.

IAEA. 2005. *Energy Indicators for Sustainable Development: Guidelines and Methodologies*. Vienna: International Atomic Energy Agency.

IAEA. 2007. *IAEA Safety Glossary: Terminology Used in Nuclear Safety and Radiation Protection*. Vienna: International Atomic Energy Agency. www-pub.iaea.org/MTCD/publications/PDF/Pub1290_web.pdf.

IAEA. 2010. *Development and Application of Level 1 Probabilistic Safety Assessment for Nuclear Power Plants*. Specific Safety Guide No. SSG-3. Vienna: International Atomic Energy Agency.

IAEA. 2012. *Communication with the Public in a Nuclear or Radiological Emergency*. Vienna: International Atomic Energy Agency. 16.

IAEA, Euratom, FAO, ILO, IMO, OECD-NEA, PAHO, UNEP, and WHO. 2006. *Fundamental Safety Principles*. IAEA Safety Standards Series No. SF1. Vienna: A joint publication of Euratom, FAO, IAEA, ILO, IMO, OECD-NEA, PAHO, UNEP, WHO.

ICRP (International Commission on Radiological Protection). 1977. "Recommendations of the ICRP: ICRP Publication 26." *Annals of the International Commission on Radiological Protection* 1 (3).

ICRP. 1998. "Radiation Protection Recommendations as Applied to the Disposal of Long-Lived Solid Radioactive Waste: ICRP Publication 81." *Annals of the International Commission on Radiological Protection* 28 (14).

ICRP. 2007. "The 2007 Recommendations of the International Commission on Radiological Protection: ICRP Publication No. 103." *Annals of the International Commission on Radiological Protection* 37 (2–4): 1–332.

ICRP. 2012. "Report of ICRP Task Group 84 on Initial Lessons Learned from the Nuclear Power Plant Accident in Japan vis-à-vis the ICRP System of Radiological Protection." International Commission on Radiological Protection. www.icrp.org/docs/ICRP%20TG84%20Summary%20Report.pdf.

ICRP. 2013. "Radiological Protection in Geological Disposal of Long-Lived Solid Radioactive Waste: ICRP Publication 122." *Annals of the International Commission on Radiological Protection* 42 (3): 1–58.

IEA (International Energy Agency). 2013a. *Key World Energy Statistics 2012*. Paris: International Energy Agency.

IEA. 2013b. *World Energy Outlook 2013*. Paris: International Energy Agency.

Inaiima, T. and Y. Okada. 2012. "Japan May Be Atomic-Power Free Next Month After Shutdown." *Bloomberg Businessweek*, April 17. www.businessweek.com/news/2012-04-16/japan-may-beatomic-power-free-next-month-after-shutdown.

IPCC (Intergovernmental Panel on Climate Change). 2007. *Climate Change 2007: Synthesis Report*. Cambridge, UK: Cambridge University Press.

Irwin, A., and B. Wynne. 1996. *Misunderstanding Science*. Cambridge, UK: Cambridge University Press.

Jacobs, J.F., I. van de Poel, and P. Osseweijer. 2010. "Sunscreens with Titanium Dioxide (TiO2) Nano-Particles: A Societal Experiment." *Nanoethics* 4: 103–13.

Jacobson, M.Z. and M.A. Delucchi. 2009. "A Path to Sustainable Energy by 2030." *Scientific American*, November 2009, 58–65.

Jasanoff, S. 2005. *Designs on Nature: Science and Democracy in Europe and the United States*. Princeton, NJ: Princeton University Press.

Jasper, J.M. 1990. *Nuclear Politics: Energy and the State in the United States, Sweden, and France.* Princeton, NJ: Princeton University Press.

Jeanes, E.L. 2007. "The Doing and Undoing of Gender: The Importance of Being a Credible Female Victim." *Gender, Work and Organisation* 14 (6): 552–71.

Joffe, H. 1999. *Risk and the Other.* Cambridge, UK: Cambridge University Press.

Johnston, E. 2012. "Nation Marks First Anniversary of Disasters." *The Japan Times*, March 12. www.japantimes.co.jp/news/2012/03/12/national/nation-marks-first-anniversary-of-disasters/#.VOvfGPnF__M.

Johnston, R. 2007. *Database of Radiological Incidents and Related Events.* www.johnstonsarchive.net/nuclear/radevents/radevents1.html.

Jones, P. 2000. "Global Distributive Justice." In *Ethics in International Affairs*, edited by A. Valls, 169–83. Lanham, MD: Rowman & Littlefield Publishers, Inc.

Jones-Lee, M. and T. Aven. 2011. "ALARP – What Does It Really Mean?" *Reliability Engineering and System Safety* 96: 877–82.

Joskow, P.L., J.E. Parsons, and G. Harrison. 2012. *The Future of Nuclear Power after Fukushima.* Boston: MIT Press.

Jungk, R. 1977. *Der Atom-Staat: vom Fortschritt in d. Unmenschlichkeit.* 2nd ed. München: Kindler.

Kaatsch, P., C. Spix, R. Schulze-Rath, S. Schmiedel, and M. Blettner. 2008. "Leukemia in Young Children Living in the Vicinity of German Nuclear Power Plants." *International Journal of Cancer* 1220: 721–26.

Kahn, L. 2011. "Is the United States Prepared for a Nuclear Reactor Accident?" *Bulletin of the Atomic Scientists*, April 2011. http://thebulletin.org/node/8705.

KASAM. 1988. *Ethical Aspects on Nuclear Waste.* Report No. 29. Stockholm: National Council for Nuclear Waste.

KASAM. 2005. *Nuclear Waste State-of-the-Art Reports 2004.* SOU 2004:67. Stockholm: National Council for Nuclear Waste.

KASAM. 2007. *Nuclear Waste State-of-the-Art Report 2007 – Responsibility of Current Generation, Freedom of Future Generations.* SOU 2004:67. Stockholm: National Council for Nuclear Waste..

Kasperson, R.E. 1983. *Equity Issues in Radioactive Waste Management.* Cambridge, MA: Oelgeschlager, Gunn & Hain.

Kasperson, R.E., D. Golding, and S. Tuler. 1992. "Social Distrust as a Factor in Siting Hazardous Facilities and Communicating Risks." *Journal of Social Issues* 48 (4):161–87.

Kathren, R.L. and P.L. Ziemer. 1980. "The First Fifty Years of Radiation Protection – A Brief Sketch." In *Health Physics: A Backward Glance*, edited by R.L. Kathren and P.L. Ziemer, 1–9. Elmsford, NY: Pergamon Press.

Kathren, R.L., L.H. Munson, and D.P. Higby. 1984. "Application of Risk-Cost Benefit Techniques to ALARA and De-Minimis." *Health Physics* 47: 195.

Kennedy, H. 2012. "Japan Quake & Tsunami: 1 Man Stays Behind." *NY Daily News*, March 12. www.nydailynews.com/news/world/japan-earthquake-tsunami-man-stays-tend-animals-left-radioactive-zone-article-1.1036148.

Kirchin, S. ed. 2013. *Thick Concepts.* Oxford: Oxford University Press.

Kleiner, K. 2008. "Nuclear Energy: Assessing the Emissions." *Nature Reports* 2 www.nature.com/climate/2008/0810/pdf/climate.2008.99.pdf.

Kneese, A.V. 1973. "The Faustian Bargain." *Resources* 44: 1–5.

Koike, R., N. Tsuzaka, and K. Uechi. 2013. "Oi Nuke Reactors to Stay Online." *The Asahi Shimbun*, March 20. http://ajw.asahi.com/article/0311disaster/fukushima/AJ201303200067.
Kraft, M.E. and B.B. Clary. 1991. "Citizen Participation and the Nimby Syndrome: Public Response to Radioactive Waste Disposal." *The Western Political Quarterly* 44 (2): 299–328.
Krimsky, S. 2003. *Science in the Private Interest: Has the Lure of Profits Corrupted Biomedical Research?* Lanham, MD: Rowman & Littlefield.
Krimsky, S. 2010. "Combating the Funding Effect in Science: What's Beyond Transparency?" *Stanford Law & Policy Review* 21: 101–23.
Kritidis, P. and H. Florou. 2001. "Radiological Impact in Greece of the Chernobyl Accident." *Health Physics* 80 (5): 440–46.
Krohn, W. and P. Weingart. 1987. "Commentary: Nuclear Power as a Social Experiment-European Political "Fall Out" from the Chernobyl Meltdown." *Science, Technology, & Human Values* 12: 52–58.
Krohn, W. and J. Weyer. 1994. "Society as a Laboratory: The Social Risks of Experimental Research." *Science and Public Policy* 21: 173–83.
Krütli, P. 2007. "Lagerung radioaktiver Abfälle – wie eine einst betroffene Bevölkerung die Dinge sieht." In *Entscheidungsprozesse Wellenberg – Lagerung radioaktiver Abfälle in der Schweiz. ETH-UNS Fallstudie 2006*, edited by R.W. Scholz, M. Stauffacher, S. Bösch and P. Krütli, 51–83. Zurich: Rüegger.
Krütli, P. 2010. *Radioactive Waste Management: Justice and Decision-Making Processes in Repository Siting*. DISS. ETH NO. 19016, Environmental Sciences, ETH, Zurich.
Krütli, P., T. Flüeler, M. Stauffacher, A. Wiek, and R.W. Scholz. 2010. "Technical Safety vs. Public Involvement? A Case Study on the Unrealized Project for the Disposal of Nuclear Waste at Wellenberg (Switzerland)." *Journal of Integrative Environmental Sciences* 7 (3): 229–44.
Krütli, P., M. Stauffacher, D. Pedolin, C. Moser, and R.W. Scholz. 2012. "The Process Matters: Fairness in Repository Siting For Nuclear Waste." *Social Justice Research* 25 (1): 79–101.
Kuhn, T. 1962. *The Structure of Scientific Revolutions*. Chicago: The University of Chicago Press.
Künneke, R., D. Mehos, R. Hillerbrand, and K. Hemmes. Forthcoming. "Understanding Values Embedded in Offshore Wind Energy Systems: Towards a Purposeful Institutional and Technological Design." *Environmental Science & Policy*.
Kyodo. 2014. "Fault beneath Tsuruga Nuclear Reactor Is Active, Watchdog Panel Reaffirms." *The Japan Times Online*, November 20. http://www.japantimes.co.jp/news/2014/11/20/national/fault-beneath-tsuruga-nuclear-reactor-is-active-watchdog-panel-reaffirms/#.VOttxi5GR8E.
Landrigan, P. 2001. *Testimony before the Committee on Environment and Public Works, US Senate*. Garden City, NY: Adelphi University.
Langhelle, O. 2000. "Sustainable Development and Social Justice: Expanding the Rawlsian Framework of Global Justice." *Environmental Values* 9 (3): 295–323.
Lash, S. 2000. "Risk Culture." In *The Risk Society and Beyond Critical Issues for Social Theory*, edited by B. Adam, U. Beck, and J. Van Loon, 47–62. London: Sage.

Lash, S. and B. Wynne. 1992. "Introduction." In *Risk Society: Towards a New Modernity*, U. Beck, 1–8. London: Sage.
Laue, H.J., L.L. Bennett, and R. Skjoeldebrand. 1977. "Nuclear Power in Developing Countries." *IAEA Bulletin* 26 (1): 3–8.
Lean, G. 2012. "Why Nuclear is in Meltdown." *The Telegraph*, March 2. www.telegraph.co.uk/comment/9118831/Why-nuclear-is-in-meltdown.html
Lee, C.J. and C.D. Schunn. 2011. "Social Biases and Solutions for Procedural Objectivity." *Hypatia* 26 (2): 352–73.
Lee, S.P. 1985. "The Morality of Nuclear Deterrence: Hostage Holding and Consequences." *Ethics* 95: 549–66.
Legere, C. 2013. "Plymouth Nuclear Plant Receives Lower Performance Rating." *Cape Cod Times*, November 7. www.capecodtimes.com/article/20131107/NEWS11/13 1109748?template=printart.
Leventhal, G.S. 1976. "Fairness in Social Relationships." In *Contemporary Topics in Social Psychology*, edited by J.W Thibaut, J.T. Spence and R.C. Carson, 211–39. Morristown, NJ: General Learning Press.
Leventhal, G.S. 1980. "What Should Be Done with Equity Theory? New Approaches in the Study of Fairness in Social Relationships." In *Social exchange. Advances in Research and Theory*, edited by K.J. Gergen, M.S. Greenberg and R.S. Willis, 27–55. New York: Plenum Press
Levin, R.J. 2009. "Incidence of Thyroid Cancer in Residents Surrounding the Three Mile Island Nuclear Facility." *Laryngoscope* 118 (4): 618–28.
Levite, A.E. 2002/03. "Never Say Never Again: Nuclear Reversal Revisited." *International Security* 27 (3): 59–88.
Lewis, H.W., R.J. Budnitz, H.J.C. Kouts, W.B. Loewenstein, W.D. Rowe, F. von Hippel, and F. Zachariasen. 1978. *Risk Assessment Review Group Report to the US Nuclear Regulatory Commission*.
Lind, E.A. and T.R. Tyler. 1988. *The Social Psychology of Procedural Justice*. New York: Plenum Press.
Lindell, B. 1996 "The History of Radiation Protection." *Radiation Protection Dosimetry* 68: 83–95.
Lindell, B. and D.J. Beninson. 1981. "ALARA Defines its Own Limit." *Health Physics* 41: 684–85.
Lipscy, P.Y., K.E. Kushida, and T. Incerti. 2013. "The Fukushima Disaster and Japan's Nuclear Plant Vulnerability in Comparative Perspective." *Environmental Science & Technology* 47: 6082–88.
Lochbaum, D. 2012. "To Filter Or Not To Filter That Is The Question With Only One Sane Answer." *Union Of Concerned Scientist*. http://allthingsnuclear.org/to-filter-or-not-to-filter-that-is-the-question-with-only-one-sane-answer/.
Löfquist, L. 2008. "Ethics Beyond Finitude, Responsibilities Towards Future Generations and Nuclear Waste Management (PhD Dissertation)." Uppsala: Uppsala University.
Lohan, M. 2000. "Constructive Tensions in Feminist Studies." *Social Studies of Science* 30 (6): 895–916.
Longino, H. 1990. *Science as Social Knowledge*. Princeton, NJ: Princeton University Press.
Longino, H. 2002. *The Fate of Knowledge*. Princeton, NJ: Princeton University Press.

MacCormick, C. and M. Strathern. 1992. *Nature, Culture, Gender*. Cambridge, UK: Cambridge University Press.
Macfarlane, A. and R.C. Ewing. 2006. *Uncertainty Underground: Yucca Mountain and the Nation's High-Level Nuclear Waste*. Cambridge, MA: MIT Press.
MacFhionnbhairr, D. 2004. "The New Agenda Coalition." In *Nuclear Disarmament in the Twenty-First Century*, edited by W.L. Huntley, K. Mizumoto, and M. Kurosawa, 275–88. Hiroshima: Hiroshima Peace Institute.
MacKay, D. 2008. *Sustainable Energy without the Hot Air*. Cambridge: UIT.
MacKenzie, D. 1990. *Inventing Accuracy: A Historical Sociology of Nuclear Weapon Guidance*. Cambridge, MA: MIT Press.
Mackenzie, D. 1996. "How Do We Know the Properties of Artifacts? Applying the Sociology of Knowledge to Technology." In *Technological Change*, edited by R. Fox, 249–51. Amsterdam: Harwood Academic.
Maier, D.S. 2012. *What's So Good about Biodiversity? A Call for Better Reasoning about Nature's Value*. Dordrecht: Springer.
Mand, F. 2013. "Performance Issues Plague Plant." *Wicked Local Plymouth*, December 31. www.wickedlocal.com/plymouth/news/x800891513/PILGRIM-STATION-Performance-issues-plague-plant#ixzz2pIIvCgKx.
Mand, F. 2014. "Plymouth Town Election: Dry Cask on Ballot." *Wicked Local Plymouth*, April 5. http://plymouth.wickedlocal.com/article/20140405/NEWS/140407690/0/SEARCH.
Mangano, J.J. 2000. "Improvements in Local Infant Health after Nuclear Power Reactor Closing." *Environmental Epidemiology and Toxicology* 2: 32–36.
Mangano, J.J. 2002. "Infant Death and Childhood Cancer Reductions after Nuclear Plant Closings in the United States." *Archives of Environmental Health* 57: 23–31.
Mangano, J.J. 2006. "A Short Latency Between Radiation Exposure From Nuclear Plants and Cancer In Young Children." *International Journal of Health Services* 36 (1): 113–35.
Mangano, J.J. 2008. "Excess Infant Mortality after Nuclear Plant Startup in Rural Mississippi." *International Journal of Health Services* 38: 277–29.
Mangano, J.J. and J.D. Sherman. 2008. "Childhood Leukemia Near Nuclear Installations." *European Journal of Cancer Care* 17 (4): 416–18.
Manning, R. 1981. "Environmental Ethics and Rawls' Theory of Justice." *Environmental Ethics* 3 (2): 155–65.
Markandya, A. and P. Wilkinson. 2007. "Electricity Generation and Health." *The Lancet* 370 (9591): 979–90.
Markey, E. 2013. "New NRC Policy Restricts Congressional Oversight, Undermines Transparency." November 21. www.markey.senate.gov/news/press-releases/markey-new-nrc-policy-restricts-congressional-oversight-undermines-transparency.
Martin, M.W. and R. Schinzinger. 1989. *Ethics in Engineering*. New York: McGraw-Hill.
Masco, J. 2006. *The Nuclear Borderlands*. Princeton, NJ: Princeton University Press.
Massachusetts Department of Public Health. 2013. *Pilgrim Nuclear Power Station: Tritium in Groundwater Monitoring Wells*. November 22. www.mass.gov/eohhs/docs/dph/environmental/radiationcontrol/tritium/2013-updates/pnps-update-11-22-2013.pdf.
Matsumura, A. 2012. "Fukushima Daiichi Site: Cesium-137 is 85 Times Greater than at Chernobyl Accident." *Finding the Missing Link*, April 3. http://akiomatsumura.com/2012/04/682.html.

Mazrani, W., K. McHugh, and P.J. Marsden. 2007. "The Radiation Burden of Radiological Investigations." *Archives of Disease in Childhood* 92: 1127–31.

McCusker, K.E., K.C. Armour, C.M. Bitz, and D.S. Battisti. 2014. "Rapid and Extensive Warming Following Cessation of Solar Radiation Management." *Environmental Research Letters* 9 (2) 024005 doi:10.1088/1748-9326/9/2/024005.

Mc Mahon, J. 2013. "Six Nuclear Plants That Could Be Next to Shut Down." *Forbes*, November 11. www.forbes.com/sites/jeffmcmahon/2013/11/07/6-nuclear-plants-that-may-be-next-to-shut-down/#comments_header.

McShane, K. 2004. "Ecosystem Health." *Environmental Ethics* 26: 227–45.

Merlo, D.F., L.E. Knudsen, K. Matusiewicz, L. Niebrój, and K.H. Vähäkangas. 2007. "Ethics in Studies on Children and Environmental Health." *Journal of Medical Ethics* 33 (7): 408–13.

Metzger, A. 2014 "Gov. Patrick Calls for shutting down Plymouth Nuclear Plant." *Wicked Local Plymouth*, March 19. http://plymouth.wickedlocal.com/article/201 40319/NEWS/140315712/0/SEARCH.

MEXT (Japanese Ministry of Education, Culture, Sports, Science, and Technology). 2011. *To Educators, For Correctly Understanding Radioactivity*. Translated by Setsuko Shiqa, University of Notre Dame. Tokyo: MEXT.

Miano, S. 2014. "Pilgrim's Spent Nuclear Fuel Needs to be Moved as Soon as Possible." *Manomet Current*, April 10. http://manometcurrent.com/opinion-pilgrims-spent-nuclear-fuel-needs-moved-soon-possible/.

Michaelis, J., B. Keller, G. Haaf, and P. Kaatsch. 1992. "Incidence of Childhood Malignancies in the Vicinity of West German Nuclear Power Plants." *Cancer Causes and Control* 3: 255–63.

Michaels, D.M. and C. Monforton. 2005. "Manufacturing Uncertainty: Contested Science and the Protection of the Public's Health and Environment." *American Journal of Public Health* 95: S39–S48.

Middleton, N. "Environment." *Geographical* 72 (12): 24–28.

Mikula, G. 1980. "On the Role of Justice in Allocation Decisions." In *Justice and Social Interaction: Experimental and Theoretical Contributions from Psychological Research*, edited by G. Mikula, 127–66. New York: Springer-Verlag.

Mileti, D.S. 1999. *Disasters by Design: A Reassessment of Natural Hazards in the United States*. Washington, DC: Joseph Henry Press.

Mill, John Stuart. 1999. *On Liberty*. Peterborough: Broadview Press.

Miller, D. 1999. *Principles of Social Justice*. Cambridge, MA: Harvard University Press.

Millo, Y., and J. Lezaun. 2006. "Regulatory Experiments: Genetically Modified Crops and Financial Derivatives on Trial." *Science and Public Policy* 33: 179–90.

Moller, E.G.A.P. and T.A. Mousseau. 2009. "Reduced Abundance of Insects and Spiders Linked to Radiation at Chernobyl 20 Years after the Accident." *Biology Letters* doi:10.1098/rsbl.2008.0778.

Möller, N. 2012. "The Concepts of Risk and Safety." In *Handbook of Risk Theory*, edited by S. Roeser, R. Hillerbrand, P. Sandin and M. Peterson, 55–85. Dordrecht: Springer.

Monteiro, N.P. and K.G. Ruby. 2009. "IR and the False Promise of Philosophical Foundations." *International Theory* 1 (1): 15–48.

Montgomery, S.L. 2010. *The Powers That Be*. Chicago: University of Chicago Press.

Morgan, P.M. 2006. *International Security: Problems and Solutions*. Washington DC: CQ Press.
Morris, M. and R. Knorr. 1990. "The Southeastern Massachusetts Health Study 1978–1986." *Massachusetts Department of Public Health*, October.
Morris, M. and R. Knorr. 1994. *The Southeastern Massachusetts Health Study 1978–1986*. Boston: Massachusetts Department of Public Health.
Mosk, M. 2011. "Fukushima: Mark 1 Nuclear Reactor Design Caused GE Scientist to Quit in Protest." ABC News, March 15.
Mulgan T. 2006. *Future People: A Moderate Consequentialist Account of our Obligations to Future Generations*. Oxford: Clarendon Press.
Murphy, C. and P. Gardoni. 2006. "The Role of Society in Engineering Risk Analysis: a Capabilities-Based Approach." *Risk Analysis* 26 (4): 1073–83.
Murphy, C. and P. Gardoni. 2007. "Determining Public Policy and Resource Allocation Priorities for Mitigating Natural Hazards: a Capabilities-Based Approach." *Science and Engineering Ethics* 13 (4): 489–504.
Murphy, C. and P. Gardoni. 2008. "The Acceptability and the Tolerability of Societal Risks: a Capabilities-Based Approach." *Science and Engineering Ethics* 14 (1): 77–92.
Murphy, C. and P. Gardoni. 2010. "Assessing Capability Instead of Achieved Functionings in Risk Analysis." *Journal of Risk Research* 13 (2): 137–47.
Murphy, C. and P. Gardoni. 2011a. "Design, Risk and Capabilities" in *Human Capabilities, Technology, and Design*, edited by J. van den Hoven and I. Oosterlaken, 173–88. Heidelberg: Springer.
Murphy, C. and P. Gardoni. 2011b. "Evaluating the Source of the Risks Associated with Natural Events." *Res Publica* 17: 125–40.
Murphy, C., and P. Gardoni. 2012. "The Capability Approach in Risk Analysis." In *Handbook of Risk Theory*, edited by S. Roeser, 979–97. Heidelberg: Springer.
NAIIC (Nuclear Accident Independent Investigation Commission). 2012. "The Official Report of The Fukushima Nuclear Accident Independent Investigation Commission: Executive summary." Tokyo: National Diet of Japan.. http://reliefweb.int/node/508828
Nakicenovic, N., O. Davidson, G. Davis, A. Grübler, T. Kram, E. Lebre La Rovere, B. Metz, T. Morita, W. Pepper, H. Pitcher, A. Sankovski, P. Shukla, R. Swart, R. Watson, and Z. Dadi. 2000. *IPCC Special Report: Emission Scenarios*. http://se-server.ethz.ch/staff/af/fi159/N/Na020.pdf
Naqvi, F. 1998. "A Computable General Equilibrium Model of Energy, Economy and Equity Interactions in Pakistan." *Energy Economics* 20 (4): 347–73.
National Research Council. 2001. *Disposition of High-Level Waste and Spent Nuclear Fuel: The Continuing Societal and Technical Challenges*. Washington, DC: National Academy Press.
National Research Council. 2003. *One Step at a Time: The Staged Development of Geologic Repositories for High-Level Radioactive Waste*. Washington, DC: National Academy Press.
National Research Council/National Academy of Sciences. 2006. *Health Risks from Exposure to Low Levels of Ionizing Radiation: BEIR VII, Phase 2*. Washington, DC: National Academy Press.
NEA-OECD (Nuclear Energy Agency-Organisation for Economic Co-operation and Development). 2002. *Chernobyl: Assessment of Radiological and Health Impact*

2002. Paris: Nuclear Energy Agency, Organisation for Economic Co-operation and Development. http://www.oecd-nea.org/rp/reports/2003/nea3508-chernobyl.pdf.

NEA-OECD. 1995. *The Environmental and Ethical Basis of Geological Disposal of Long-Lived Radioactive Wastes: A Collective Opinion of the Radioactive Waste Management Committee of the Nuclear Energy Agency.* Paris: Nuclear Energy Agency, Organisation for Economic Co-operation and Development.

NEA-OECD. 2004. *Learning and Adapting to Societal Requirements for Radioactive Waste Management.* Paris: Nuclear Energy Agency, Organisation for Economic Co-operation and Development.

Newton-Small, J. 2005. "U.S. Energy Legislation May Be 'Renaissance' for Nuclear Power." *Bloomberg.* www.bloomberg.com/apps/news?pid=newsarchive&sid=aXb5iuqdZoD4&refer=us.

Nisbet, A. and R. Woodman. 2000. "Options for the Management of Chernobyl-Restricted Areas in England and Wales." *Journal of Environmental Radioactivity* 51 (2): 239–54.

Nishikawa, J. 2012. "Some Progress, But Radiation Remains High at Fukushima Nuclear Plant." *The Asahi Shimbum*, October 13. http://ajw.asahi.com/article/0311disaster/fukushima/AJ201210130030

Nitsch, J., T. Pregger, T. Naegler, D. Heide, D.L. de Tena, F. Trieb, and Y. Scholz. 2012. "Langfristszenarien und Strategien für den Ausbau der erneuerbaren Energien in Deutschland bei Berücksichtigung der Entwicklung in Europa und global." *Schlussbericht* BMU – FKZ 03MAP146. www.energiesystemtechnik.iwes.fraunhofer.de/de/presse-infothek/publikationen/uebersicht/2012/-_leitstudie-2011—langfristszenarien-und-strategien-fuer-den-a.html.

Nolt, J. 2009. "The Move from Is to Good in Environmental Ethics." *Environmental Ethics* 31 (2): 135–54.

Nolt, J. 2010. "Hope, Self-Transcendence and Environmental Ethics." *Inquiry* 53 (2): 162–82.

Nolt, J. 2013a. "Comparing Suffering Across Species." *Between the Species* 16 (1): 86–104.

Nolt, J. 2013b. "Anthropocentrism and Egoism." *Environmental Values* 22 (4): 441–59.

Nolt, J. 2015. *Environmental Ethics for the Long Term.* London: Routledge.

Normile, D. 2012. "Commission Spreads Blame for 'Manmade' Disaster." *Science* 337 (6091): 143.

Nozick, R. 1974. *Anarchy, State, and Utopia.* New York: Basic Books.

NRC (US Nuclear Regulatory Commission). 1975. *Reactor Safety Study: An Assessment of Accident Risks in US Commercial Nuclear Power Plants* (WASH-1400). US Nuclear Regulatory Commission.

NRC. 1989. "Letter submitted by James G. Partlow, Associate Director of Projects, NRC to All Holders of Operating Licenses for Nuclear Power Reactors with Mark 1 Containments on Installation of a Hardened Wetwell Vent." (generic letter 89–16). US Nuclear Regulatory Commission. September 1. http://i2.cdn.turner.com/cnn/2012/images/02/16/nrc.gl.89.16.pdf.

NRC. 2001. "Review of Findings for Human Error Contribution to Risk in Operating Events." NUREG INEEL/EXT-01–01166. Nuclear Regulatory Commission Office of Nuclear Reactor Regulation, August 2001. Washington, DC.

NRC. 2007. "Generic Environmental Impact Statement for License Renewal of Nuclear Plants: Regarding Pilgrim Nuclear Power Station -Final Report." US Nuclear Regulatory Commission. (NUREG-1437, 29).

NRC. 2011a. "Pilgrim Watch Request for Hearing on a New Contention Regarding Inadequacy of Environmental Report, Post Fukushima." *Nuclear Regulatory Commission*, June 1. (ADAMS Accession No. ML111320647).

NRC. 2011b. "Ruling on Energy's Motion for Summary Disposition of Pilgrim Watch Contention 1, Regarding Adequacy of Aging Management Program for Buried Pipes and Tanks and Potential Need for Monitoring Wells to Supplement Program." *Nuclear Regulatory Commission*, May 12. (Accession # ML061630125).

NRC. 2014a. "1Q/2014 Plant Inspection Findings 2013–2014." US Nuclear Regulatory Commission. www.nrc.gov/NRR/OVERSIGHT/ASSESS/PILG/pilg_pim.html.

NRC. 2014b. "Pilgrim Nuclear Power Station." US Nuclear Regulatory Commission. Last modified April 23. www.nrc.gov/info-finder/reactor/pilg.html.

NRC and DOE (Department of Energy). 2008. "Life Beyond 60 Workshop Summary Report, NRC/DOE Workshop on U.S. Nuclear Power Plant Life Extension Research and Development." US Nuclear Regulatory Commission. February 19–21.

Nussbaum, M.C. 2001. *Women and Human Development: The Capabilities Approach*. Cambridge, UK: Cambridge University Press.

NWMO (Nuclear Waste Management Organization). 2005. *Choosing a Way Forward; The Future Management of Canada's Used Nuclear Fuel (Final Study)*. Ottawa (Ontario), Canada: Nuclear Waste Management Organization. www.nwmo.ca/studyreport.

Nye, J.S. 1986. *Nuclear Ethics*. New York: Free Press.

Obama, B. 2009. "Obama Prague Speech On Nuclear Weapons." *Huffington Post*, May 6.

OECD (Organisation for Economic Co-operation and Development). 2010. "Comparing Nuclear Accident Risks with Those from Other Energy Sources." *Nuclear Energy Agency Report* 6861. Paris: OECD Publications. www.oecd-nea.org/ndd/reports/2010/nea6862-comparing-risks.pdf

OECD. 2012. *Uranium 2011: Resources, Production and Demand: A Joint Report by the OECD Nuclear Energy Agency and the International Atomic Energy Agency 2012*. Paris: OECD Publications. https://www.oecd-nea.org/ndd/pubs/2012/7059-uranium-2011.pdf.

Oels, A. 2005. "Rendering Climate Change Governable: From Biopower to Advanced Liberal Government." *Journal of Environmental Policy and Planning* 7 (3): 198–207.

Ohmae, K. 2012. "Fukushima." *Japan Times*, 18 April. www.kohmae.com/en/.

Okasha, S. 2007. "Rational Choice, Risk Aversion, and Evolution." *Journal of Philosophy* 104: 217–35.

Okasha, S. 2011. "Optimal Choice in the Face of Risk: Decision Theory Meets Evolution." *Philosophy of Science* 78: 83–104.

Okrent, D. 1978. *On the History of the Evolution of Light Water Reactor Safety in the United States*. http://fissilematerials.org/library/1978/06/on_the_history_of_the_evolutio.html

Okrent, D. and N. Pidgeon. 2000. "Special Collection on Intergenerational Versus Intragenerational Equity and Risk Policy." *Risk Analysis* 20 (6): 759–929.

Orcutt, M. 2014. "Why Japan's Government Is Bringing Nuclear Back." *MIT Technology Review*. www.technologyreview.com/news/525421/the-numbers-behind-japans-renewed-embrace-of-nuclear/.
O'Riordan, T. and J. Cameron, eds. 1994. *Interpreting the Precautionary Principle*. London: Earthscan.
O'Riordan, T., J. Cameron, and A. Jordan, eds. 2001. *Reinterpreting the Precautionary Principle*. London: Cameron May.
Osnos, E. 2011. "The Fallout. Seven Months Later: Japan's Nuclear Predicament." *The New Yorker*, October 17: 26–61.
Oughton, D. and S.O. Hansson. 2013. *Social and Ethical Aspects of Radiation Risk Management*, Radioactivity in the Environment 19. 1st ed. Amsterdam: Elsevier.
Page, E. 2008. "Distributing the Burdens of Climate Change." *Environmental Politics* 17 (4): 556–75.
Parfit, D. 1984. *Reasons and Persons*. Oxford: Clarendon Press.
Parisi, A.J. 1977. "'Soft Energy,' Hard Choices." *The New York Times*, October 16.
Parkhill, K.A., N. Pidgeon, K.L. Henwood, P. Simmons, and D. Venables. 2010. "From the Familiar to the Extraordinary: Local Residents' Perceptions of Risk when Living with Nuclear Power in the UK." *Transactions of the Institute of British Geographers* 35: 39–58.
Parkhill, K.A., K.L. Henwood, N. Pidgeon, and P. Simmons. 2011. "Laughing It Off: Humour, Affect and Emotion Work in Communities Living with Nuclear Risk." *British Journal of Sociology* 62 (2): 324–46.
Partridge, E. ed. 1980. *Responsibilities to Future Generations*. Buffalo, NY: Prometheus.
Paté-Cornell, M.E. 1996. "Uncertainties in Risk Analysis: Six Levels of Treatment." *Reliability Engineering & System Safety* 54: 95–111.
Patterson, T. 2013. "Climate change warriors: It's time to go nuclear." *CNN*, April 14. www.cnn.com/2013/11/03/world/nuclear-energy-climate-change-scientists/index.html
Perin, C. 2005. *Shouldering Risks: The Culture of Control in the Nuclear Power Industry*. Princeton, NJ: Princeton University Press.
Perrow, C. 1984. *Normal Accidents: Living with High-Risk Technologies*. Princeton, NJ: Princeton University Press.
Perrow, C. 1999. *Normal Accidents: Living with High-Risk Technologies*, 2nd ed. Princeton, NJ: Princeton University Press.
Perrow, C. 2007. *The Next Catastrophe: Reducing Our Vulnerabilities to Natural, Industrial, and Terrorist Disasters*. Princeton, NJ: Princeton University Press.
Perrow, C. 2011. "Fukushima and the Inevitability of Accidents." *Bulletin of the Atomic Scientists* 67 (6): 44–52.
Persson, A.J. 2008. "Occupational and Non-Occupational Health Risks: Can Double Standards Be Justified?" *International Journal of Risk Assessment and Management* 10: 160–71.
Peterson, M.B. 2013. "New Technologies Should Not Be Treated as Social Experiments." *Ethics, Policy & Environment* 16: 349–51.
Petroski, H. 1992. *To Engineer is Human: The Role of Failure in Successful Design*. New York: Vintage Books.

Pidgeon, N. 1998. "Risk Assessment, Risk Values and the Social Science Programme: Why We Do Need Risk Perception Research." *Reliability Engineering and System Safety* 59: 5–15.

Pidgeon, N. and C. Butler. 2009. "Risk Analysis and Climate Change." *Environmental Politics* 18 (5): 670–88.

Pidgeon, N. and C.C. Demski. 2012. "From Nuclear to Renewable: Energy System Transformation and Public Attitudes." *Bulletin of the Atomic Scientists* 68 (4): 41–51.

Pidgeon, N., C. Hood, D. Jones, B.A. Turner, and R. Gibson. 1992. "Risk Perception." In *Risk – Analysis, Perception and Management: Report of a Royal Society Study Group*, edited by E. Warner, 89–34. London: The Royal Society.

Pidgeon, N., K.L. Henwood, A. Irwin, K.A. Parkhill, and D. Venables. 2007. "Gender and Risk Perception: A Secondary Analysis." *End of Award Report* RES 160-25-0046. Swindon: Economic and Social Research Council.

Pidgeon, N., I. Lorenzoni, and W. Poortinga. 2008. "Climate Change or Nuclear Power – No Thanks! A Quantitative Study of Public Perceptions and Risk Framing in Britain." *Global Environmental Change* 18: 69–85.

Pinch, T. 1993. "'Testing – One, Two, Three … Testing!': Toward a Sociology of Testing." *Science, Technology, & Human Values* 18 (1): 25–41.

Pinch, T and W. Bijker. 1984. "The Social Construction of Facts and Artifacts: or How the Sociology of Science and the Sociology of Technology Might Benefit Each Other." *Social Studies of Science* 14: 339–441.

Pittock, A.B., T.P. Ackerman, P.J. Crutzen, M.C. MacCracken, C.S. Shapiro, and R.P. Turco. 1986. *Environmental Consequences of Nuclear War, Volume I: Physical and Atmospheric Effects*. Chichester, UK: John Wiley & Sons.

Poortinga, W., N. Pidgeon, S. Capstick, and M. Aoyagi. 2013. *Public Attitudes to Nuclear Power and Climate Change Two Years after the Fukushima Disaster.* London: UK Energy Research Centre.

Potter, V.R. 1970. "Bioethics: The Science of Survival." *Perspectives in Biology and Medicine* 14: 127–53.

Quintana, M. 2012. "Fukushima Crisis Concealed: Japanese Government Kept Worst-Case Scenario Under Wraps." *The Asia Pacific Journal*, January 31. http://japanfocus.org///events/view/129.

Ramana, M.V. 2011. "Beyond Our Imagination: Fukushima and the Problem of Assessing Risk." *Bulletin of the Atomic Scientists*, April 19. http://thebulletin.org/beyond-our-imagination-fukushima-and-problem-assessing-risk-0.

Randers, J. 2012. *2052: A Global Forecast for the Next Forty Years. A Report to the Club of Rome Commemorating the 40th Anniversary of The Limits of Growth.* Chelsea: Chelsea Green Publishing.

Rasmussen, J., K. Duncan, and J. Leplat, 1987. *New Technology and Human Error.* New York: John Wiley and Sons.

Rauschmayer, F. and O. Lessmann. 2011. "Assets and Drawbacks of the CA as a Foundation for Sustainability Economics." *Ecological Economics* 70: 1835–36.

Rawls, J. 1971. *A Theory of Justice*. Cambridge, MA: Harvard University Press.

Rawls, J. 1999. *The Law of Peoples*. Cambridge, MA: Harvard University Press.

Rawls, J. 2005. *A Theory of Justice*. Original ed. Cambridge, MA: Belknap Press.

Rayner, S. 2004. "The Novelty Trap: Why does Institutional Learning about New Technologies Seem So Difficult." *Industry and Higher Education* 18 (5): 340–55.

Reich, W.T. 1994. "The Word 'Bioethics': Its Birth and the Legacies of Those Who Shaped It." *Kennedy Institute of Ethics Journal* 4: 319–35.

Reich, W.T. 1995. "The Word 'Bioethics': the Struggle Over Its Earliest Meanings." *Kennedy Institute of Ethics Journal* 5: 19–34.

Reiss, M.B. 2004. "The Nuclear Tipping Point: Prospects for a World of Many Nuclear Weapons States." In *The Nuclear Tipping Point: Why States Reconsider Their Nuclear Choices*, edited by K.M. Campbell, R.J. Einhorn, and M.B. Reiss, 3–17. Washington, DC: Brookings Institution Press.

Reitinger, C., M. Dumke, M. Barosevcic, and R. Hillerbrand. 2011. "A Conceptual Framework for Impact Assessment Within SLCA." *The International Journal of Life Cycle Assessment* 16 (4): 380–88.

Renn, O. 1998. "Three Decades of Risk Research: Accomplishments and New Challenges." *Journal of Risk Research*. 1: 49–71.

Renn, O. and B. Rohrmann. 2000. *Cross-Cultural Risk Perception: A Survey of Empirical Studies*. Netherlands: Kluwer Academic Publishers.

Rich, V. 1991. "USSR: Chernobyl's Psychological Legacy." *Lancet* 337 (8749): 1086.

Richardson, B. 2004. "The Public's Right to Know: A Dangerous Notion." *Journal of Mass Media Ethics* 19 (1): 46–55.

Rip, A. 1986. "The Mutual Dependence of Risk Research and Political Context." *Science & Technology Studies* 4 (3/4): 3–15

Roberts, A. 2011. "The WikiLeaks Illusion." *The Wilson Quarterly* 35 (3): 16–21.

Robeyns, I. 2005. "The Capability Approach: A Theoretical Survey." *Journal of Human Development* 6 (1): 94–114.

Robinson, J.P. 1979. *The Effects of Weapons on Ecosystems*. United Nations Environment Programme, Oxford: Pergamon Press.

Roeser, S. 2009. "The Relation Between Cognition and Affect in Moral Judgments About Risk." In *The Ethics of Technological Risk*, edited by L. Asveld and S. Roeser, 182–201. London: Earthscan.

Roeser, S. 2011. "Nuclear Energy, Risk, and Emotions." *Philosophy & Technology* 24: 197–201.

Roeser, S., R. Hillerbrand, P. Sandin, and M. Peterson. 2013. *Essentials of Risk Theory*. London: Springer.

Rolston III, H. 1988. *Environmental Ethics: Duties to and Values in the Natural World*. Philadephia: Temple University Press.

Rosa, E.A. and D.L. Clark. 1999. "Historical Routes to Technological Gridlock: Nuclear Technology As Prototypical Vehicle." In *Research in Social Problems and Public Policy, Vol 7*, edited by W.R. Freudenberg and T.I.K. Youn, 21–57. Stamford, CT: JAI Press.

Rosa, E.A. and W.R. Freudenberg. 1993. "The Historical Development of Public Reactions to Nuclear Power: Implications for Nuclear Waste Policy." In *Public Reactions to Nuclear Waste: Citizens' Views of Repository Siting*, edited by R.E. Dunlap, M.E. Kraft and E.A. Rosa, 32–63. Durham, NC: Duke University Press.

Routley, R. and V. Routley. 1981. "Nuclear Energy and Obligations to the Future." In *Responsibilities to Future Generations*, edited by E. Partridge, 277–301. Buffalo, NY: Prometheus Books.

Rowe, W.D. 1980. "Risk Assessment: Theoretical Approaches and Methodological Problems." In *Society, Technology, and Risk Assessment*, edited by J. Conrad, 3–29. New York: Academic Press.
Royal Commission on Environmental Pollution. 2000. *Energy: The Changing Climate*. London: HMSO.
Rytömaa, T. 1996. "Ten Years After Chernobyl." *Annals of Medicine* 28 (2): 83–87.
Sagoff, M. 1988. *The Economy of the Earth: Philosophy, Law and the Environment*. Cambridge, UK: Cambridge University Press.
Salpukas, A. 1998. "Entergy Bid of $80 Million Wins Massachusetts Nuclear Plant." *New York Times*, November 20.
Sandler, R., and P. Pezzullo, eds. 2007. *Environmental Justice and Environmentalism: The Social Justice Challenge to the Environmental Movement*. Cambridge, MA: MIT Press.
Saoshiro, S. and N. Layne. 2011. "Pockets of High Radiation Remind of Fukushima Plant Danger." *Reuters News Service*, August 2. www.reuters.com/article/2011/08/02/japan-nuclear-radiation-idUSL3E7J203D20110802.
Satterfield, T. 2003. *The Anatomy of a Conflict*. Vancouver: UBC Press.
Satterfield, T., C.K. Mertz, and P. Slovic. 2004. "Discrimination, Vulnerability and Justice in the Face of Risk." *Risk Analysis* 24: 115–29.
Savchenko, V.K. 1995. *The Ecology of the Chernobyl Catastrophe: Scientific Outlines of an International Programme of Collaborative Research*. London/New York: UNESCO and The Parthenon Publishing Group Ltd.
Sayers, A. 2011. *Why Things Matter to People: Social Science, Values and the Ethical Life*. Cambridge, UK: Cambridge University Press
Scheffler, S. 2015. "The Practice of Equality." In *Social Equality: Essays on What it Means to be Equals*, edited by C. Fourie, F. Schuppert, and I. Wallimann-Helmer, 21–44. Oxford: Oxford University Press.
Scheman, N. 1993. "Introduction: The Unavoidability of Gender." In *Engenderings: Constructions of Knowledge, Authority and Privilege*, edited by N. Scheman, 1–8. London: Routledge.
Schlör, H., W. Fischer, and J.-F. Hake. 2012. "Measuring Social Welfare, Energy and Inequality in Germany." *Applied Energy* 97: 135–42.
Schlosberg, D. 2007. *Defining Environmental Justice: Theories, Movements, and Nature*. Oxford: Oxford University Press.
Schlosberg, D. 2009. *Defining Environmental Justice: Theories, Movements, and Nature*. Oxford: Oxford University Press.
Schmid, S. 2011. "When Safe Enough is Not Good Enough: Organizing Safety at Chernobyl." *Bulletin of the Atomic Scientists* 67 (2): 19–29.
Scholz, R.W., M. Stauffacher, S. Bösch, P. Krütli, and A. Wiek. 2007. *Entscheidungsprozesse Wellenberg – Lagerung radioaktiver Abfälle in der Schweiz. ETH-UNS Fallstudie 2006*. Zurich, Chur: Rüegger.
Schramme, T. 2006. "Is Rawlsian Justice Bad for the Environment?" *Analyse & Kritik* 28: 146–57.
Schuppert, F., and I. Wallimann-Helmer. 2014. "Environmental Inequalities and Democratic Citizenship: Linking Normative Theory with Empirical Research." *Analyse & Kritik* 36 (2): 345–66.

Schwartz, K. 2012. *Public Meeting at Barnstable County Regional Emergency Planning Committee Harwich Community Center.* October 3.
Segal, L. 1997. *Slow Motion: Changing Masculinities, Changing Men.* London: Virago
Sen, A. 1992. *Inequality Reexamined.* Oxford: Clarendon Press.
Sen, A. 1999. *Development as Freedom.* New York: Knopf.
Senate Bill H.1906 188th – An Act increasing nuclear power plant protections to a twenty mile radius. https://malegislature.gov/Bills/188/House/H1906.
Senate Bill H.1907. 188th – An Act to amend Section 5K(E). https://malegislature.gov/Bills/188/House/H1907.
Senate Bill H.2045 188th – An Act increasing nuclear power plant protections to a twenty mile radius. https://malegislature.gov/Bills/188/House/H2045.
Senate Bill H.2046 188th – An Act relative to radiological air monitoring. https://malegislature.gov/Bills/188/House/H2046.
Sevenhuijsen, S. 1998. *Citizenship and the Ethics of Care: Feminist Considerations on Justice, Morality and Politics.* London: Routledge.
Shrader-Frechette, K.S. 1980. *Nuclear Power and Public Policy. The Social and Ethical Problems of Fission Technology.* Dordrecht: D. Reidel Publishing Company.
Shrader-Frechette, K.S., ed. 1991a. *Nuclear Energy and Ethics.* Geneva: World Council of Churches Publications.
Shrader-Frechette, K.S. 1991b. "Nuclear Waste and Ethics." In *Nuclear Energy and Ethics*, edited by K.S. Shrader-Frechette, 182–202. Geneva: World Council of Churches Publications.
Shrader-Frechette, K.S. 1991c. *Risk and Rationality.* Berkeley, CA: University of California Press.
Shrader-Frechette, K.S. 1993. *Burying Uncertainty: Risk and the Case against Geological Disposal of Nuclear Waste.* Berkeley, CA: University of California Press.
Shrader-Frechette, K.S. 1994. "Equity and Nuclear Waste Disposal." *Journal of Agricultural and Environmental Ethics* 7 (2): 133–56.
Shrader-Frechette, K.S. 2000. "Duties to Future Generations, Proxy Consent, Intra- and Intergenerational Equity: The Case of Nuclear Waste." *Risk Analysis* 20: 771–78.
Shrader-Frechette, K.S. 2002. *Environmental Justice: Creating Equality, Reclaiming Democracy.* Oxford: Oxford University Press.
Shrader-Frechette, K.S. 2005. *Environmental Justice: Creating Equality, Reclaiming Democracy.* Oxford: Oxford University Press.
Shrader-Frechette, K.S. 2007. *Taking Action, Saving Lives: Our Duties to Protect Environmental and Public Health.* Oxford: Oxford University Press.
Shrader-Frechette, K.S. 2011a. *What Will Work: Fighting Climate Change with Renewable Energy, Not Nuclear Power.* New York: Oxford University Press.
Shrader-Frechette, K.S. 2011b. "Fukushima, Flawed Epistemology, and Black-Swan Events." *Ethics, Policy & Environment* 14: 267–72.
Shrader-Frechette, K.S. 2012. "Nuclear Catastrophe, Disaster-Related Environmental Injustice, and Fukushima." *Environmental Justice* 5 (3): 133–39.
Shrader-Frechette, K.S. 2013. "Environmental Injustice Inherent in Radiation Dose Standards." *Social and Ethical Aspects of Radiation Risk Management* 19: 197–213.
Shrader-Frechette, K.S. and L. Persson. 2001. "Ethical Problems in Radiation Protection." doi: ISSN0282-4434. www.stralsakerhetsmyndigheten.se/Global/Publikationer/Rapport/Stralskydd/2001/ssi-rapp-2001-11.pdf.

Shue, H. 1993. "Subsistence Emissions and Luxury Emissions." *Law & Policy* 15: 39–60.
Siegrist, M. and V. Visschers. 2013. "Acceptance of Nuclear Power: The Fukushima Effect." *Energy Policy* 59: 112–19.
Silbey, S. 2009. "Taming Prometheus: Talk About Safety and Culture." *Annual Review of Sociology* 35: 341–69.
Singer, P. 2002. *Animal Liberation*. Revised ed. New York: HarperCollins.
Sjöberg, L. and B.-M. Drottz-Sjöberg. 2001. "Fairness, Risk and Risk Tolerance in the Siting of a Nuclear Waste Repository." *Journal of Risk Research* 4 (1): 75–101.
Slovic, P. 1987. "Perception of Risk." *Science* 236 (4799): 280–85.
Slovic, P. 1999. "Trust, Emotion, Sex, Politics, and Science: Surveying the Risk-Assessment Battlefield." *Risk Analysis* 19: 689–701.
Slovic, P., B. Fischhoff, and S. Lichtenstein. 1982. "Why Study Risk Perception?" *Risk Analysis* 2(2): 83–93.
Small, A.W. 1921. "The Future of Sociology." *Publications of the American Sociological Society* 15: 174–93.
Smith, B. 2007. *Insurmountable Risks: The Dangers of Using Nuclear Power to Combat Global Climate Change*. Bandon, OR: RDR Books.
Smoke, R. 1993. *National Security and the Nuclear Dilemma: An Introduction to the American Experience in the Cold War*, 3rd ed. New York: McGraw-Hill.
Snook, S. 2000. *Friendly Fire*. Princeton, NJ: Princeton University Press.
Sollie, P. and M. Düwell, eds. 2009. "Evaluating New Technologies: An Introduction." In *Methodological Problems for the Ethical Assessment of Technology Developments*, edited by P. Sollie and M. Düwell, 1–8. Dordrecht: Springer.
Spix, C. 2008. "Do Nuclear Plants Boost Leukemia Risk?" *New Scientist* 2642: 6.
Starr, C. 1969. "Social Benefits Versus Technological Risks." *Science* 165 (3899): 1232–38.
Stauffacher, M., P. Krütli, and R.W. Scholz. 2008. *Gesellschaft und radioaktive Abfälle: Ergebnisse einer schweizweiten Befragung*. Zürich, Chur: Rüegger.
Stocker, T.F. 2013. "The Closing Door of Climate Targets." *Science* 339: 280–82.
Strickland, E. 2011. "24 Hours at Fukushima: A Blow-by-Blow Account of the Worst Nuclear Accident Since Chernobyl." *IEEE Spectrum special report: Fukushima and the Future of Nuclear Power*. November. http://spectrum.ieee.org/energy/nuclear/24-hours-at-fukushima/0.
Sturgis, P. and N. Allum. 2004. "Science in Society: Re-evaluating the Deficit Model of Public Attitudes." *Public Understanding of Science* 13: 55–74.
Sturgis, S. 2009. "Investigation: Revelations about Three Mile Island disaster raise doubts over nuclear plant safety." www.southernstudies.org/2009/04/post-4.html.
Sunder Rajan, K. 2005. *Biocapital: The Constitution of Postgenomic Life*. Durham, NC: Duke University Press.
Susser, M. 1997. "Consequences of the 1979 Three Mile Island Accident Continued." *Environmental Health Perspectives* 105 (6): 566–67.
Sweeney, P.D., and D.B. McFarlin. 1993. "Workers' Evaluations of the 'Ends' and the 'Means': An Examination of Four Models of Distributive and Procedural Justice." *Organizational Behavior and Human Decision Processes* 55 (1): 23–40.
Tabandeh, A., P. Gardoni, and C. Murphy. 2014. "Reliability-Based Capability Approach: A System Reliability Formulation for the Capability Approach." *Journal of Human Development and Capabilities*, Under Review.

Tabuchi, H. 2014. "Reversing Course, Japan Makes Push to Restart Dormant Nuclear Plants." *The New York Times*, February 25. www.nytimes.com/2014/02/26/world/asia/japan-pushes-to-revive-moribund-nuclear-energy-sector.html.

Taebi, B. 2011. "The Morally Desirable Option for Nuclear Power Production." *Philosophy and Technology* 24: 169–92.

Taebi, B. 2012a. "Intergenerational Risks of Nuclear Energy." In *Handbook of Risk Theory: Epistemology, Decision Theory, Ethics and Social Implications of Risk*, edited by S. Roeser, R. Hillerbrand, P. Sandin and M. Peterson, 295–318. Dordrecht: Springer.

Taebi, B. 2012b. "Multinational Nuclear Waste Repositories and Their Complex Issues of Justice." *Ethics, Policy & Environment* 15 (1): 57–62.

Taebi, B. and A.C. Kadak. 2010. "Intergenerational Considerations Affecting the Future of Nuclear Power: Equity as a Framework for Assessing Fuel Cycles." *Risk Analysis* 30 (9):1341–62.

Taebi, B. and J.L. Kloosterman. 2008. "To Recycle or Not to Recycle? An Intergenerational Approach to Nuclear Fuel Cycles." *Science and Engineering Ethics* 14: 177–200.

Taebi, B., and J.L. Kloosterman. 2014. "Design for Values in Nuclear Technology." In *Handbook of Ethics, Values and Technological Design: Sources, Theory, Values and Application Domains*, edited by J. van den Hoven, P.E. Vermaas, and I. Van de Poel Springer.

Taebi, B., and I.R. van de Poel, eds. 2015. *Socio-Technical Challenges of Nuclear Power Production and Waste Disposal in the Post-Fukushima Era*. Special Issue of Journal of Risk Research.

Taebi, B., S. Roeser, and I. van de Poel. 2012. "The Ethics of Nuclear Power: Social Experiments, Intergenerational Justice, and Emotions." *Energy Policy* 51: 202–06.

Taira, T. and Y. Hatoyama. 2011. "Nuclear Energy." *Nature* 480 (7377): 313–14.

Talbott, E.O., A.O. Youk, K.P. McHugh-Pemu, and J.V. Zborowski. 2000. "Mortality Among the Residents of the Three Mile Island Accident Area: 1979–1992." *Environmental Health Perspectives* 108 (6): 545–52.

Talbott, E.O., A.O. Youk, K.P. McHugh-Pemu, and J.V. Zborowski. 2003. "Long Term Follow-Up of the Residents of the Three Mile Island Accident Area." *Environmental Health Perspectives* 111 (3): 341–48.

Tannenwald, N. 2007. *The Nuclear Taboo: the United States and the Non-Use of Nuclear Weapons Since 1945*. New York: Cambridge University Press.

Taylor, P.W. 1986. *Respect for Nature: A Theory of Environmental Ethics*. Princeton, NJ: Princeton University Press.

Tengs T., M. Adams, J. Pliskin, et al. 1995. "Five Hundred Life-Saving Interventions and Their Cost Effectiveness." *Risk Analysis* 15 (3): 369–90.

Teravainen, T., M. Lehtonen, and M. Martiskainen. 2011. "Climate Change, Energy Security and Risk: Debating Nuclear New Build in Finland, France and the UK." *Energy Policy* 39: 3434–42.

Thibaut, J. and H. Kelley. 1959. *The Social Psychology of Groups*. New York: Wiley & Sons.

Thibaut, J., and L. Walker. 1975. *Procedural Justice: A Psychological Analysis*. Hillsdale, NJ: Earlbaum.

Törnblom, K.Y. and D.R. Jonsson. 1985. "Subrules of the Equality and Contribution Principles: Their Perceived Fairness in Distribution and Retribution." *Social Psychology Quarterly* 48: 249–61.

Törnblom, K.Y. and R. Vermunt. 1999. "An Integrative Perspective on Social Justice: Distributive and Procedural Fairness Evaluations of Positive and Negative Outcome Allocations." *Social Justice Research* 12 (1): 39–64.

Tugendhat, E. 1993. *Vorlesungen über Ethik*. Frankfurt am Main: Suhrkamp.

Tulloch, J. and D. Lupton. 2003. *Risk and Everyday Life*. London: Sage.

Turner, B.A. 1976. "The Organizational and Interorganizational Development of Disasters." *Administrative Science Quarterly* 21 (3): 378–97.

Turner, B.A. and N.F. Pidgeon. 1997. *Man-Made Disasters*, 2nd ed. Oxford: Butterworth-Heinemann.

UCS (Union of Concerned Scientists). 2006a. "Pilgrim Planned Outage Dec 1983 – Dec 1984." September 18. www.ucsusa.org/assets/documents/nuclear_power/pilgrim-i.pdf.

UCS. 2006b. "Pilgrim Planned Outage Dates April 1986 – June 1989." September 18. www.ucsusa.org/assets/documents/nuclear_power/pilgrim-ii.pdf.

UNDP (United Nations Development Programme). 2007. *Human Development Report 2007/2008*. New York: Palgrave Macmillan.

UNDP. 2013. *2013 Human Development Report*. Human development index. http://hdr.undp.org/en/statistics/hdi/.

Vaughan, D. 1996. *The Challenger Launch Decision*. Chicago: University of Chicago Press.

Vandenbosch, R. and S.E. Vandenbosch. 2007. *Nuclear Waste Stalemate: Political and Scientific Controversies*. Salt Lake City, UT: University of Utah Press.

Vandenbosch, R. and S.E. Vandenbosch. 2015. "Nuclear Waste Confidence: Is Indefinite Storage Safe?" *Physics and Society* 44 (1): 5–7.

van de Poel, I. 1998. *Changing Technologies: A Comparative Study of Eight Processes of Transformation Of Technological Regimes*. Enschede: University of Twente.

van de Poel, I. 2009. "The Introduction of Nanotechnology as a Societal Experiment." In *Technoscience in Progress: Managing the Uncertainty of Nanotechnology*, edited by S. Arnaldi, A. Lorenzet and F. Russo, 129–42. Amsterdam: IOS Press.

van de Poel, I. 2011. "Nuclear Energy as a Social Experiment." *Ethics, Policy & Environment* 14 (3): 285–90.

van de Poel, I. Forthcoming. "Society as a laboratory to experiment with new technologies." In *Embedding and Governing New Technologies*, edited by E. Stokes, D. Bowman and A. Rip. Singapore: Pan Stanford Publishing.

van Vuuren D.P., J. Edmonds, M. Kainuma, K. Riahi, A. Thomson, K. Hibbard, G.C. Hurtt, T. Kram, V. Krey, J.-F. Lamarque, T. Masui, M. Meinshausen, N. Nakicenovic, S.J. Smith, and S.K. Rose. 2011. "The Representative Concentration Pathways: An Overview." *Climatic Change* 109 (1–2): 5–31.

Varner, G.E. 2012. *Personhood, Ethics and Animal Cognition: Situating Animals in Hare's Two-Level Utilitarianism*. Oxford: Oxford University Press.

Victorin, K. 1991. *Gränsvärden – vad de innebär och hur myndigheterna använder dem. [Exposure Limits – What They Mean and How the Authorities Use Them.]* Rapport från Kemikalieinspektionen 13/91. Stockholm: Kemikalieinspektionen.

Viel, J.F. and D. Pobel. 1997. "Case-Control Study of Leukaemia Among Young People Near La Hague Nuclear Reprocessing Plant: The Environmental Hypothesis Revisited." *British Medical Journal* 314 (7074): 101–06.

Viel, J.F., D. Pobel, and A. Carre. 1995. "Incidence of Leukemia in Young People around the La Hague Nuclear Waste Reprocessing Plant." *Statistics in Medicine* 14: 2459–72.

von Hippel, F.N. 2011. The Radiological and Psychological Consequences of the Fukushima Daiichi Accident. *Bulletin of the Atomic Scientists* 67 (5): 27–36.

Vose, D. 2000. *Risk Analysis: A Quantitative Guide*. New York: Wiley.

Wald, M. 1998. "Management Cited at 16 'Problem' Nuclear Plants." *New York Times*, July 16.

Walker, H.A., and D. Willer. 2007. "Experiments and the Science of Sociology." In *Laboratory Experiments in the Social Sciences*, edited by M. Webster and J. Sell, 25–55. Amsterdam: Elsevier.

Walker, S. 2004. *Three Mile Island*. Berkeley, CA: University of California Press.

Walker, W.E., P. Harremoes, J. Rotmans, J.P. van der Sluijs, M.B.A. van Asselt, P. Janssen, and M.P. Krayer von Krauss. 2003. "Defining Uncertainty: A Conceptual Basis for Uncertainty Management in Model-Based Decision Support." *Integrated Assessment* 4: 5–17.

Walters, J.W., ed. 1989. *War No More? Options in Nuclear Ethics*. Minneapolis, MN: Fortress Press.

Walzer, M. 1977. *Just and Unjust Wars*. New York: Basic Books.

Walzer, M. 2000. *Just and Unjust Wars: A Moral Argument with Historical Illustrations*, 3rd ed. New York: Basic Books.

Wang, Q. and X. Chen. 2012. "Regulatory Failures for Nuclear Safety – the Bad Example of Japan." *Renewable and Sustainable Energy Review* 16 (5): 2610–17.

Watson, W. and D. Sumner. 1996. "Measurement of Radioactivity in People Living Near the Dounreay Nuclear Establishment, Caithness, Scotland." *International Journal of Radiation Biology* 70 (2): 117–30.

WCED (World Commission on Environment and Development). 1987. *Our Common Future*. Oxford: Oxford University Press.

Weart, S. 1988. *Nuclear Fear: A History of Images*. Cambridge, MA: Harvard University Press.

Webster, M., and J. Sell. 2007. "Why Do Experiments?" In *Laboratory Experiments in the Social Sciences*, edited by M. Webster and J. Sell, 5–23. Amsterdam: Elsevier.

Webster, R. 2008. "Testimony Submitted by Richard Webster, Legal Director, Eastern Environmental Law Center to the Subcommittee on Clean Air and Nuclear Safety, Committee on Environment and Public Works, United States Senate." July 16. www.nirs.org/reactorwatch/licensing/20080710testimonyrenrcreform.pdf.

Weingart, P., A. Engels, and P. Pansegrau. 2000. "Risks of Communication: Discourses of Climate Change in Science, Politics and the Mass Media." *Public Understanding of Science* 9: 261–83.

Weiss, T.G., D.P. Forsythe, R.A. Coate, and K.K. Pease. 2010. *The United Nations and Changing World Politics*. 6th ed. Philadelphia: Westview Press.

Welsh, I. 2000. *Mobilising Modernity: The Nuclear Moment*. London: Routledge.

Wendt, A. 1999. *Social Theory of International Politics*. Cambridge, UK: Cambridge University Press.

Werlin, K. 2008. "Department Approves Divestiture of Pilgrim Nuclear Power Station." *Find Law*, March 26. http://corporate.findlaw.com/law-library/department-approves-divestiture-of-pilgrim-nuclear-power-station.html.

Wester, M. 2012. "Risk and Gender: Daredevils and Ecoangels." In *Handbook of Risk Theory*, edited by S. Roeser, R. Hillerbrand, P. Sandin, and M. Peterson, 1030–48. London: Springer.

Westing, A.H. 2013. *Arthur H. Westing: Pioneer on the Environmental Impact of War*. Dordrecht: Springer.

Westra, L. and B. Lawson, eds. 2001. *Faces of Environmental Racism: Confronting Issues of Global Justice*. Lanham, MD: Rowman and Littlefield.

Wetherell, M. 1986. "Interpretive Repertoires and Literary Criticism: New Directions in the Social Psychology of Gender." In *Feminist Social Psychology*, edited by S. Wilkinson, 77–95. London: Sage.

Wetherell, M. 1996. "Life Histories, Social Histories." *Identities, Groups and Social Issues*, 299–361. London: Sage (in association with the Open University).

Whitney, M. 2012. "Is Fukushima's Doomsday Machine About To Blow?" *Eurasia Review*, April20. www.eurasiareview.com/20042012-is-fukushimas-doomsday-machine-about-to-blow-oped/.

Whitmore, T., ed. 1989. *Ethics in the Nuclear Age: Strategy, Religious Studies, and the Churches*. 1st ed. Dallas, TX: Southern Methodist University Press.

WHO (World Health Organization). 1995. *Fact Sheet*. Geneva: WHO.

WHO. 2006a. *Health Effects of the Chernobyl Accident and Special Health Care Programmes*. Geneva: WHO.

WHO. 2006b. *Health Effects of the Chernobyl Accident: An Overview*. Geneva: WHO.

WHO. 2013. *WHO Global Status Report on Road Safety 2013: Supporting a Decade of Action*. Geneva: WHO.

Wigley, D. and K.S. Shrader-Frechette. 1996. "Environmental Justice: A Louisiana Case Study." *Journal of Agricultural and Environmental Ethics* 9 (1): 61–82.

Wikman, P. 2004. "Trivial Risks and the New Radiation Protection System." *Journal of Radiological Protection* 24: 3–11.

Wikman-Svahn, P. 2012. "Radiation Protection Issues Related to the Use of Nuclear Power." *Wiley Interdisciplinary Reviews: Energy and Environment* 1 (3): 256–69. doi:10.1002/wene.22. http://doi.wiley.com/10.1002/wene.22.

Wikman-Svahn, P., M. Peterson and S.O. Hansson. 2006. "Principles of Protection: A Formal Approach for Evaluating Dose Distributions." *Journal of Radiological Protection* 26: 69–84.

Williams, D. and K. Baverstock. 2006. "Too Soon For A Final Diagnosis." *Nature* 440: 993–94.

Williford, M. 1975. "Bentham on the Rights of Women." *Journal of the History of Ideas* 36: 167–76.

Wilson, L. 2000. *Nuclear Waste: Exploring the Ethical Dilemmas*. Toronto: United Church Publishing House.

Wing, S. 1995. "Affidavit in TMI Litigation Cases Consolidated II, Civil Action No 1: CV-88–1452." Harrisburg, PA: US District Court for the Middle District of Pennsylvania.

Wing, S. 2003. "Objectivity and Ethics and Environmental Health Science." *Environmental Health Perspectives* 111 (14): 1809–18.

Wing, S., D. Richardson, and D. Armstrong. 1997. "A Re-Evaluation of Cancer Incidence Near the Three Mile Island Nuclear Plant." *Environmental Health Perspectives* 105 (1): 52–57.
Winner, L. 1980. "Do Artifacts have Politics?" *Daedalus* 109 (1): 121–36.
Wittner, L.S. 2009. *Confronting the Bomb: A Short History of the World Nuclear Disarmament Movement*. Stanford, CA: Stanford University Press.
WNA (World Nuclear Association). 2008a. *Chernobyl Accident*. http://world-nuclear.org/info/chernobyl/inf07.html.
WNA. 2008b. *The Economics of Nuclear Power*. www.world-nuclear.org/info/inf02.html.
WNA. 2009. *Health Impacts, Chernobyl Accident*. London: WNA. www.world-nuclear.org/info/Safety-and-Security/Safety-of-Plants/Appendices/Chernobyl-Accident—Appendix-2–Health-Impacts/.
WNA. 2010. *Renewable Energy and Electricity*. www.world-nuclear.org/info/Energy-and-Environment/Renewable-Energy-and-Electricity/.
WNA. 2014. *Chernobyl Accident, 1986*. www.world-nuclear.org/info/Safety-and-Security/Safety-of-Plants/Chernobyl-Accident/.
Wolf, D. 2014. "Senator Wolf Wants Pilgrim Nuclear Plant Shuttered." Plymouth Wicked Local, February 28. http://plymouth.wickedlocal.com/article/20140228/NEWS/140226014/0/SEARCH.
Woodward, J. 2003. "Experimentation, Causal Inference and Instrumental Realism." In *The Philosophy of Scientific Experimentation*, edited by H. Radder, 87–118. Pittsburgh: University of Pittsburgh Press.
World Nuclear News. 2012. *The Health Effects of Fukushima*. www.world-nuclear-news.org/RS_The_health_effects_of_Fukushima_2808121.html.
Wright, S., J. Smith, N. Beresford, and W. Scott. 2003. "Monte-Carlo Prediction of Changes in Areas of West Cumbria Requiring Restrictions on Sheep Following the Chernobyl Accident." *Radiation and Environmental Biophysics* 42 (1): 41–47.
Wrixon, A.D. 2008. "New ICRP Recommendations." *Journal of Radiological Protection: Official Journal of the Society for Radiological Protection* 28 (2): 161–68. doi:10.1088/0952–4746/28/2/R02.
WWF (World Wide Fund for Nature). 2011. *The Energy Report, 100% Renewable Energy by 2050*. http://wwf.panda.org/what_we_do/footprint/climate_carbon_energy/energy_solutions22/renewable_energy/sustainable_energy_report/.
Wynne, B. 1983. "Redefining the Issues of Risk and Public Acceptance: The Social Viability of Technology." *Futures* 15 (1): 13–32.
Wynne, B. 1992. "Uncertainty and Environmental Learning: Reconceiving Science and Policy in the Preventive Paradigm." *Global Environmental Change* 2 (2): 111–27.
Yablokov, A.V., V.B. Nesterenko, A.V. Nesterenko, and J.D. Sherman-Nevinger. 2009. *Chernobyl: Consequences of the Catastrophe for People and the Environment: Annals of the New York Academy of Sciences*. Malden, MA: John Wiley.
Yang, J.L. 2011. "Nuclear Experts Weigh in on GE Containment System." *Washington Post*, March 14. www.washingtonpost.com/business/economy/nuclear-experts-weigh-in-on-ge-containment-system/2011/03/14/ABspN1V_story.html.
Zakharov, V.M. 1988. *Consequences of the Chernobyl Catastrophe*. Detroit: International Scholars.

Zeebe, R.E. 2013. "Time-Dependent Climate Sensitivity and the Legacy of Anthropogenic Greenhouse Gas Emissions." *Proceedings of the National Academy of Sciences* 110 (34): 13739–44.

Zeebe, R.E. and J.C. Zachos. 2013. "Long-Term Legacy of Massive Carbon Input to the Earth System: Anthropocene Versus Eocene." *Philosophical Transactions of the Royal Society A* 371: 20120006. doi: 10.1098/rsta.2012.0006.

Zellor Jr., T. 2011. "Experts Had Long Criticized Potential Weakness in Design of Stricken Reactor." *New York Times*, March 15.

Index

accountability, 9, 54, 72, 94–95, 118, 144
   corporate, 154
ALARA, 7, 20, 28–30, 111
ALARP, 28, 29
anarchy
   Hobbesian, 201, 202
   Kantian, 202
   Lockean, 201–2, 206, 214
anthropocentrism, 157–58, 160, 162–63, 165, 173–75, 232, 239
argumentum ad naturam, 30–31
attribute
   importance, 129–36
   level, 129–36
autonomy, 6, 8, 54–55, 231, 236
   moral, 195

background radiation, 56, 60, 63
biocentrism, 11, 14, 157, 158, 160–61, 162–64, 165, 166, 167, 173–75
biodiversity loss, 164, 167, 171–72
blaming the victim, 62, 65

capability approach, 7, 13–14, 162, 216, 222–30, 232, 241–49
care, 9, 67, 71, 76, 77, 79–82, 217
casualty rates, 163
CBA, *See* cost-benefit analysis
Chernobyl, 3, 8, 36, 38, 41, 53, 57–60, 62–66, 68, 80, 168, 169, 170, 194, 218, 234
climate change, 3, 6, 33, 66, 68, 71, 77, 87, 96, 101, 115, 117, 151, 153, 155, 165, 170–71, 229, 234, 238, 248
collective dose, 21–22, 29, 33, 98, 105
collective security, 12, 202–3, 205, 212, 214
   ethics of, 208–9
community contentions, 142, 144–56
conjoint analysis, 129
consent, 54, 154, 193
consequentialism, 11, 157, 159–61, 162–65, 167, 174, 234

cost–benefit analysis (CBA), 7, 20, 27, 30, 32, 98, 99, 101, 142, 164
credible risk, 37, 38, 52
culture, 73, 75–76, 79, 81

deontology, 11, 18, 21–22, 109, 159–61, 211
discount rate, 32–33, 99, 101
discounting, 31–34, 101, 166
discourse, 9, 17–18, 37, 42, 68–69, 71–72, 74–84, 89, 143, 152
DLP, *See* Dose Limit Principle
Dose Limit Principle (DLP), 92, 100, 108–9
dry cask storage, 149, 150, 151, 152, 153, 218

electricity, 2, 56, 66, 68, 119, 124, 125, 131, 144, 157, 167, 170, 171–72, 173, 175, 217, 218, 228–29, 233, 235, 238, 239, 242, 244–45
Energiewende, 233–37
energy
   poverty, 235
   scenarios, 13, 242, 243, 245, 247
   transition, 83, 233–37
epistemic
   accident, 50
   limitations, 8, 39, 45–50
   subject, 67, 76, 77–79
epistemology, 12, 39, 48–50, 180, 185–92, 198
ethics
   environmental, 17, 18, 165, 240
   intergenerational, 115, 165–67
   international, 200
   legal, 206–8, 212
   nuclear, 3–6, 12, 67–68, 71–72, 81–84, 88, 89–91, 107, 200
   research, 17, 195, 198
expectation value, 26–27
experiment
   real-world, 12, 180–81, 183, 185–99
   social, 7, 14, 46, 189–90, 194, 197–98
   with human subjects, 194

Index

experimenting
  ethics of, 11, 179–99
exposure limits, 7, 19, 22–25
extinction, 165, 169, 171–72, 175

fairness
  distributive, 10, 99, 122–23, 125–39
  procedural, 10, 122–23, 125–39
fission reactor, 167
fossil fuels, 69, 87, 102, 170–73, 175, 217, 231, 234, 242–43
framing limitations, 8, 39–42, 51
Fukushima-Daiichi, 1–3, 8, 35–38, 40–41, 47, 53, 56–58, 60, 62–64, 65–66, 69, 87, 93, 145, 147–49, 168, 170, 179, 183–91, 200–1, 213, 218–19, 232, 234
fusion reactor, 167, 174
future generations, 3, 7, 20, 32, 60, 79, 82, 87, 113–15, 117, 123, 138, 143, 153, 155, 165, 185, 188, 193, 194, 197, 216, 220, 224, 228, 229, 232, 236–37, 239, 240, 243–44
future risks, 32

gender, 6, 8–9, 14, 67–84
gender-risk
  effect, 76–81
  relationship, 82
geological disposal, 180
governance, 8, 142, 154, 187, 211

hazard, 13, 32, 67, 76, 142, 189, 193, 225–26
  nuclear, 38, 39, 40, 51–52, 61, 64, 83, 181, 193–94, 196, 227
HDI, *See* Human Development Index
Hinkley Point, 37
history of
  ICRP principles, 97–100
  nuclear energy, 181–85
  nuclear ethics, 3–6
  nuclear risk assessment, 7, 36–37
  the NPT, 203–6
holism, 167
Human Development Index (HDI), 162, 164
hypothetical hazards, 39

IAEA, *See* International Atomic Energy Agency
ICRP, *See* International Commission on Radiological Protection
identity
  positions, 74, 78, 81
  work, 68, 77, 80
ignorance, 158, 179, 181, 184, 186, 188, 193, 198
incommensurability, 237

individual dose, 7, 20–22, 29, 33, 92, 98, 103, 105, 108–11
inherent safety, 180, 187
institutions, 61, 81, 94–95, 119, 129, 154, 180, 187, 190, 201, 203, 211
international
  order, 201–3, 213
  relations, 3–5, 14
International Atomic Energy Agency (IAEA), 2, 6, 32, 51, 53, 55, 58–60, 62–63, 64, 66, 91, 95, 103, 105, 106, 109, 113–18, 129, 181, 204, 207, 212, 219, 232, 237–39, 245, 246
International Commission on Radiological Protection (ICRP), 18, 24, 87–118
interpretive social science, 74
Iran, 2, 4–5, 12, 169, 200, 203, 205, 206, 207, 209, 212, 215
Israel, 4, 12, 203, 205, 212, 215

just war theory, 4
justice
  distributive, 7, 11, 119–24, 127–39, 141, 143, 152, 155, 203
  intergenerational, 14, 143, 194, 224, 236
  intragenerational, 224, 235
  procedural, 7, 10–11, 88, 92–99, 119–38, 141, 143, 152–53, 155, 239
  social psychological, 120–23, 139
justification principle, 92, 97–104

learning, 12, 180, 186–87, 190, 192, 195, 199
license renewal, 10, 141–56
limitations
  epistemic, 8, 39, 45–50
  framing, 8, 39–42, 51

meltdown, 8, 27, 35, 36–38, 42, 44, 52, 56–58, 60, 62, 181–82, 183, 200, 213
moral
  acceptability, 5, 10, 11, 23, 138, 193–94, 197–99
  framework, 192, 194–95, 199
mortality rate, 163–64
Murphy's law, 42

NAT, *See* Normal Accident Theory
NNWS, *See* non-nuclear weapon states
non-anthropocentrism, 11, 154, 157–75
non-nuclear weapon states (NNWS), 204–5, 207, 208
non-proliferation
  morality of, 206–9
Non-Proliferation Treaty (NPT), 4, 12, 201, 202–15

286   Index

Normal Accident Theory (NAT), 42, 45
Normal Accidents, 42, 44, *See also* NAT
normative theory, 120–23, 137–39
North Korea, 4, 12, 200, 203, 205
NPT, *See* Non-Proliferation Treaty
NRC, *See* Nuclear Regulatory Commission
nuclear
　risk, 3, 6–7, 8–9, 39, 51–52, 67, 83–84, 181
　war, 4, 169–71, 173, 205
　waste, 3, 5–6, 8–9, 10, 12, 31–34, 87, 89, 100, 113, 116, 119–39, 151–53, 155, 165, 169, 174, 179–80, 184–85, 187, 192, 193, 218, 243
Nuclear Regulatory Commission (NRC), 7, 36, 40, 45, 57, 63, 141–42, 144, 147–49, 150–55, 218
nuclear weapons
proliferation of, 169
nuclear weapon states (NWS), 204–7, 213
NWS, *See* nuclear-weapon states

occupational exposure, 22
operator error, 41
optimization principle, 92, 104, 106, 107, 111, 115
outcome valence, 123, 129–35, 139

pacta sunt servanda, 206–8, 209, 212, 214
Pakistan, 4, 12, 203, 205, 215, 240
part-worth utility, 131–35
Pilgrim Nuclear Power Station, 10–11, 141–56
policy
　nuclear, 88–89, 100, 108, 111, 113, 202
population growth, 174, 231, 236–37
poverty, 13, 107, 173, 175, 223
PRA, *See* probabilistic risk assessment
probabilistic risk assessment (PRA), 181–82, 187, 191
public concern, 71–72, 96
publicity, 9, 62, 88, 95–97, 99, 102, 105, 107, 110, 116–18

radiation
　protection, 7, 17–34, 97
　sensitivity, 7, 20, 24–25, 33
radionuclides, 58–60, 64, 168–69, 171
ranking problem, 11, 161–63
reactor design, 144, 180, 181, 191
rebus sic stantibus, 207–9, 212–15

renewable, 6, 69, 131, 172, 220, 233, 238, 246–47
repository site selection process, 120–39
resource depletion, 72, 238, 242, 244
respect, 9, 11, 34, 108, 118, 123, 153, 157, 159–61, 194–95, 210, 211, 213
right to know, 8, 53–56, 64, 66
risk
　assessment, 6–7, 10, 20, 27–28, 35–52, 72, 81, 141–42, 155, 181–82, 184, 188, 192, 193, 232
　governance, 71–72, 187
　perception, 8, 38, 51, 67–71, 72–76, 83, 142

security
　collective, 12, 202–3, 205, 212, 214
　international, 4, 5, 12, 200–15
　nuclear, 3, 12, 219
sentientism, 159–60, 175
structural deepening, 44
sustainability, 13–14, 217, 219–20, 224, 228, 231–49
systemic limitations, 8, 39, 42–45

technocentrism, 9, 78–80
technology transfer, 229
Three Mile Island (TMI), 8, 41, 43, 51, 60–62, 63–66, 68, 183, 218
TMI, *See* Three Mile Island
Tomioka, 35–36
total fairness model, 123, 129–35

ultima facie rights, 8, 55
uncertainty, 8, 11, 27, 33, 47–52, 77, 83, 142, 179–81, 184–86, 188, 192–93, 195, 198–99, 224, 233, 246–49
utilitarianism, 7, 19, 20–22, 99, 102, 104, 240

victims, 5, 56, 57, 62, 65–66
vignette studies, 129, 134

WASH-1400, 8, 26, 36, 45
waste
　hazardous, 132–35
welfare, 9, 18, 29, 97–104, 107, 118, 157, 159–60, 161–67, 172–75
WHO, *See* World Health Organization
World Health Organization (WHO), 17, 58, 59, 62, 63–64

Lightning Source UK Ltd.
Milton Keynes UK
UKHW02f1354110318
319235UK00009B/130/P